DATE DUE

MR 27 02			

DEMCO 38-296

THE ECONOMICS OF TRANSNATIONAL COMMONS

THE ECONOMICS OF TRANSNATIONAL COMMONS

Edited by

PARTHA DASGUPTA
KARL-GÖRAN MÄLER
and
ALESSANDRO VERCELLI

*A study prepared for the World Institute for Development
Economics Research of the United Nations University
(UNU/WIDER)*

CLARENDON PRESS · OXFORD

1997

_arendon Street, Oxford OX2 6DP

_ew York

_kok Bogota Bombay

_own Dar es Salaam Delhi

Florence Hong Kong Istanbul Karachi
Kuala Lumpur Madras Madrid Melbourne
Mexico City Nairobi Paris Singapore
Taipei Tokyo Toronto Warsaw
and associated companies in
Berlin Ibadan

Oxford is a trade mark of Oxford University Press

Published in the United States
by Oxford University Press Inc., New York

Copyright © The United Nations University 1997

UNU/WIDER:World Institute for Development Economics
Research of the United Nations University, Katajanokanlaituri 6B
FIN-00160 Helsinki, Finland

British Library Cataloguing in Publication Data
Data available

Library of Congress Cataloging in Publication Data
The economics of transnational commons / edited by Partha Dasgupta,
Karl-Göran Mäler, and Alessandro Vercelli.
"A study prepared for the World Institute for Development
Economics Research of the United Nations University (UNU/WIDER)."
Includes bibliographical references.
1. Natural resources—Management. 2. Natural resources, Communal—
Management. 3. Commons. I. Dasgupta, Partha. II. Mäler, Karl-Göran.
III. Vercelli, Alessandro. IV. World Institute for
Development Economics Research.
HC21.E26 1997 333.7—dc21 96-52403

ISBN 0-19-829220-1

1 3 5 7 9 10 8 6 4 2

Typeset by Alliance Phototypesetters
Printed in Great Britain by
Bookcraft (Bath) Ltd, Midsomer Norton, Somerset

Preface

People in poor countries are for the most part agrarian and pastoral folk. In 1988 rural people accounted for about 65 per cent of the population of what the World Bank classifies as low-income countries. The proportion of the total labour force in agriculture was a bit in excess of this. The share of agriculture in gross domestic product in these countries was 30 per cent. These figures should be contrasted with those from industrial market economies, which are 6 per cent and 2 per cent for the latter two indices, respectively.

Rural communities in poor countries are biomass-based subsistence economies, in that their rural folk eke out a living from products obtained directly from plants and animals. For example, studies in the Indian sub-continent have shown that in a number of regions as much as 40–50 per cent of the working hours of villagers are devoted to fodder and fuel collection, animal care, and grazing. Moreover, inquiries in Central and West Africa have revealed the importance of forest products in the lives of rural folk. Poor countries, especially those in the Indian sub-continent and Sub-Saharan Africa, can be expected to remain largely rural economies for some while yet.

The dependence of poor countries on their natural resources, such as soil and its cover, water, forests and their products, animals, and fisheries should be self-evident: ignore the environmental resource-base, and we are bound to obtain a misleading picture of production and consumption activities there. Nevertheless, if there has been a single thread running through forty years of investigation into the poverty of poor countries, it has been a neglect of this base. Until very recently, environmental resources made but perfunctory appearances in government planning models, and were cheerfully ignored in most of what goes by the name of development economics. This was harmful not only for public economics and the economics of development, but also for environmental economics. Specialized fields are often driven by internal logic, and the gap between topics that are most intensively discussed and those that are most urgent and tractable can become large. In fact, there was an additional loss associated with the unwillingness of development and environmental economists to talk to one another. Environmental economics, heavily involved as it is with the science of ecology, is an intellectually exciting subject. There is much in it to enthuse the young.

There have been exceptions to all this, of course. Independently of what could be called official development economics, a number of economists developed environmental economics within the context of rural communities in poor countries with a view to studying the interconnections between rural poverty, population growth, and the environmental resource-base. We have now in hand a body of work that amounts to a new perspective on matters.[1] It has involved a fusion of theoretical modelling to empirical findings drawn from a number of disciplines; most notably anthropology, demography, ecology, and economics. In short, environmental economics has now reached a stage where it can be taught to university students in poor countries in a form that can motivate them.

Thus far we have stressed developments in the supply of ideas. There have been changes in demand as well. As regards timing, the shift in attitude can probably be identified with the publication in 1987 of the Report of the Brundtland Commission, and today no account of economic development would be regarded as adequate, even by economists in poor countries, if the environmental resource-base were absent from it. Indeed, today people throughout the world are expressing concerns about environmental matters. On occasion their concerns are of a global kind, but most often they address matters of local origin and impact. Unhappily though, they often do not possess a reliable language in which to articulate their concerns. Environmental economics offers the necessary language.

The subject has found a niche in both undergraduate and graduate curricula in universities of the West. But it remains conspicuously absent from universities in poor countries, for reasons we have suggested above. This is unfortunate. Until the environmental resource-base becomes a commonplace piece of furniture within economic thinking and modelling in poor countries, it will continue to be neglected in the design and implementation of public policies there.

It has seemed to us for some time that, in the first instance, environmental matters need to be introduced into the teaching of economics in poor countries. Otherwise, the next generation of teachers, researchers, and policymakers would be oblivious of the available tools of social and economic analysis pertinent to their purposes. But in order that teachers in poor countries are able to develop courses for their students, they need suitable teaching material. This volume is part of a programme that was designed to produce such material.

The programme in question was initiated at the United Nations University's World Institute for Development Economics Research (UNU/WIDER), Helsinki, in 1989, by its then Director, Lal Jaywardena. Dr Jaywardena invited two of the present editors (Partha Dasgupta and Karl-Göran Mäler) to devise and direct a programme on environment and development, and agreed that it should be aimed at the teaching of the subject to

---

[1] Accounts of varying lengths of this new perspective can be found in P. Dasgupta and K.-G. Mäler, 'The Environment and Emerging Development Issues', *Proceedings of the World Bank Annual Conference on Development Economics, 1990*; P. Dasgupta, *An Inquiry into Well-Being and Destitution* (Oxford: Clarendon Press, 1993); P. Dasgupta and K.-G. Mäler, 'Poverty, Institutions, and the Environmental Resource-Base', in J. Behrman and T. N. Srinivasan (eds.), *Handbook of Development Economics*, iii (Amsterdam: North Holland, 1995); and P. Dasgupta, 'The Population Problem: Theory and Evidence', *Journal of Economic Literature*, 1995.

university teachers of economics in poor countries. This meant that, as a first step, an attempt ought to be made to codify central aspects of the subject. It was felt also that the codification ought to be attempted from the perspective of modern resource allocation theory, which in turn meant that attention needed to be given on occasion to matters of analysis that, on the face of it, have little to do with either poverty or the environment. Otherwise, it was felt, the subject could easily appear to be divorced from economics.

Two companion volumes contain twenty-four essays on themes that are likely to prove enduring in the field of environmental economics.[2] In choosing the topics an attempt was also made to identify those that lend themselves to treatments that possess wide validity. The volumes also emphasize economic analysis. In short, the essays in those volumes are on themes that would be covered in any reasonable course on the economics of the environment. However, the collection docs not discuss global environmental issues in any detail. Transnational environmental problems are the subject of this volume of essays.

The present volume is based on a conference held in April 1991 at the Certosa de Pontignano of the University of Siena as part of the University's celebration of its 700th anniversary. It was held under the joint auspices of the University of Siena, UNU/WIDER, the International Economic Association, and the Fondazione Eni Enrico Mattei, to whom we are most grateful. The subject of transnational commons is interdisciplinary, and the papers at the conference reflected this fact. We were at pains to ensure that 'transboundary externalities' are perceived with greater generality than they typically have been. Thus, the collection contains essays not only on global warming and biodiversity, but also on cultural externalities and fertility behaviour

Publication of these volumes will mark the completion of the first part of the intended programme. A second component consists of teaching workshops for young university teachers of economics from poor countries. The present volume and its companion volumes form the basis of the course material for such workshops.[3] In order to reduce costs, these workshops are organized on a regional basis. The idea has been to invite some twenty to twenty-five participants on each occasion and some half-dozen environmental economists and ecologists, who lecture on the subject over a period of ten to twelve days. To date, four such workshops have been conducted (in Sri Lanka, Malta, Jamaica, and Malaysia), involving in the main participants from the Indian sub-continent and Sri Lanka, Sub-Saharan Africa, the Caribbean, and South-East Asia, respectively. Further teaching workshops will be held in Latin America, East Asia, Sub-Saharan Africa, and the Indian

---

[2] P. Dasgupta and K.-G. Mäler (eds.), *The Environment and Emerging Development Issues* (Oxford: Clarendon Press, 1995).

[3] Friends at the World Bank have also contributed greatly to the reading materials that are made available to participants at these workshops.

sub-continent. Our hope is that, through these teaching workshops, over the next five years or so some 150 to 175 university teachers of economics in poor countries will be able to join the international network of people who teach environmental economics in universities. If, as we economists tend to believe, there are multiplier effects in the dissemination of knowledge, the eventual size of the network could be expected to be a good deal larger.

Teaching workshops on their own would not be enough. They would need to be supplemented by research aid. To be sure, international aid agencies and private foundations have always supported research in poor countries. However, we believe that what has been relatively neglected is the creation of opportunities for indigenous scholars engaged in small, independent research projects to discuss their work with their international peer-group from the earliest stages of formulation and design. Peer-group review, through even informal discussions, is essential if it is to prove successful. We take it for granted in the West; its paucity in the poorest regions of the world is an often unnoted phenomenon. With this in mind, we have begun the process of initiating a regular series of research workshops (each about half the size of the typical teaching workshop), at which researchers from poor countries working in environmental economics are able to present research-in-progress not only to one another, but also to specialists working in the West. In April 1994 the first such research workshop was organized in Arusha, Tanzania. Participants were drawn from those who had attended the teaching workshops in Colombo and Gozo. Since then, we have conducted such research workshops in Malta, Malaysia, and Venezuela.

If capability in environmental economics is to be developed in poor countries, teaching and research workshops need to be supplemented by the creation of opportunities for indigenous scholars to publish their work in reputable journals. Towards this end, a number of us interested in environmental economics and the economics of development have recently launched a new international journal, *Environment and Development Economics* (Cambridge University Press). It is the stated aim of the Board of Editors that submissions from environmental economists in poor countries will be treated with the same care, sympathy, and critical standard that we who work in the West take for granted. Intellectual infrastructure varies greatly among poor countries. Libraries in the leading universities in, for example, India subscribe to prominent journals, whereas those in the poorest of Sub-Saharan African countries are starved of them. If this network of environmental economists we are trying to help create in poor countries is to be productive, it will need to have access to a certain minimum amount of publications.

All this has required financial support, and it will continue to need such aid. Our greatest debt in this is to Lal Jaywardena, who asked us to initiate UNU/WIDER's project on environment and development. He gave us a free hand in developing our ideas and sought and obtained additional support from the United Nations Development Programme, the Arab Fund, the World Bank, and the Swedish International Development Authority. Mihaly Simai, Dr Jaywardena's successor at UNU/WIDER, has been an enthusiastic supporter of our programme, and we are grateful to him as well. Carol Dasgupta undertook the arduous task of editing these volumes, and her patience with us and the diverse cast of authors is most gratefully acknowledged. Ann Halme and Virpi Niemenen of UNU/WIDER, and Christina Leijonhufvud and Astrid Auraldsson of the Beijer Institute have provided us with invaluable administrative support. To them we are very grateful.

As with any other endeavour, academic programmes evolve, even as we learn from experience and as new ideas suggest themselves. We are indebted to Dr Dan Martin of the MacArthur Foundation, who has taken particular interest in the teaching and research workshops of the programme. He has encouraged us to extend their reach and purpose. The Foundation's commitment to this aspect of the endeavour will enable the workshops to be conducted on a long-term basis. It will also enable those who submit the most promising papers to the research workshops to visit our own institutions at the stage of completion of their work. These are all long-term investments with uncertain social returns. Despite this, people of widely different backgrounds and involvements are contributing to the programme most willingly and generously. For this we are most grateful.

Partha Dasgupta, Cambridge
Karl-Göran Mäler, Stockholm
Alessandro Vercelli, University of Siena

April 1996

Contents

List of Figures

List of Tables

Abbreviations

Bcm	Billion cubic metres
BOD	Biochemical Oxygen Demand
COD	Chemical Oxygen Demand
COPUOS	Committee on the Peaceful Uses of Outer Space
CRAMRA	Convention on the Regulation of Antarctic Mineral Resource Activity
EPM	Environment Programme for the Mediterranean
FAO	Food and Agriculture Organization
IMO	Intergovernmental Maritime Organization
ITU	International Telegraphic Union
LDC	Less-Developed Country
NGO	Nongovernmental Organization
NIC	Newly Industrializing Country
OSPD	One-sided Prisoners' Dilemma
SAP	Structural Adjustment Programme
SGPE	Sub-game Perfect Equilibrium
UNCLOS	United Nations Conference on the Law of the Sea
UNEP	United Nations Environment Programme

Notes on Contributors

Partha Dasgupta, Faculty of Economics and Politics, University of Cambridge, UK

Karl-Göran Mäler, The Beijer International Institute of Ecological Economics, Stockholm, Sweden

Alessandro Vercelli, Department of Economics, University of Siena, Italy

Roger B. Myerson, Kellog School of Management, Northwestern University, USA

Ignazio Musu, Department of Economics, University of Venice, Italy

Paul R. Ehrlich, Department of Biological Sciences, Stanford University, USA

Anne H. Ehrlich, Department of Biological Sciences, Stanford University, USA

John C. Caldwell, Centre for Epidemiology and Population Health, Australian National University, Canberra, Australia

Pat Caldwell, Centre for Epidemiology and Population Health, Australian National University, Canberra, Australia

A. L. Hollick, Woods Hole Oceanographic Institution, Woods Hole, USA

Richard N. Cooper, Kennedy School of Government, Harvard University, USA

Michael Hoel, Department of Economics, University of Oslo, Norway

Cario Carraro, Department of Economics, University of Venice, Italy

Domenico Siniscalco, Fondazione Eni Enrico Mattei, Italy

Robert Dorfman, Department of Economics, Harvard University, USA

Lynton Keith Caldwell, School of Public and Environmental Affairs, Indiana University, USA

Avner Greif, Department of Economics, Stanford University, USA

Ulf Hannerz, Department of Social Anthropology, Stockholm University, Sweden

1

Introduction

Partha Dasgupta, Karl-Göran Mäler, and
Alessandro Vercelli

RESOURCE ALLOCATION FAILURE AND
ENVIRONMENTAL PROBLEMS

Environmental economics is generally regarded as a branch of the economics
of externalities (Pigou, 1920; Lindahl, 1958; Meade, 1973; Baumol and
Oates, 1975). More particularly, environmental problems are commonly
associated with the failure of market institutions. The starting-point of this
literature is the observation that in many cases the malfunctioning of market
forces can be ascribed to the fact that for certain commodities and services
competitive prices simply do not exist. Sometimes they happen not to exist
for historical or accidental reasons; sometimes there are logical reasons why
they cannot exist (e.g. the putative markets may be too 'thin' to permit price-
taking behaviour on the part of agents; Arrow, 1971); sometimes the nature
of the physical or political situation keeps markets from existing, or makes
them function wrongly if they do exist (e.g. if property rights are ill-defined
or are hard to enforce). A garden variety of environmental resources, ranging
from the earth's atmosphere and the oceans to forests in mountainous
regions, are known to be vulnerable to such problems. This is attested by the
fact that the market price of the services these resources offer *in situ* is often
nil, even though they are clearly of value.

There is, however, a tradition in the economics literature that defines
markets in more general terms (Coase, 1960; Meade, 1973). The assumption
of price-taking behaviour is eschewed in this strand of thinking. Markets are
taken to be institutions that make available to interested parties the
opportunity to negotiate courses of actions. To be sure, there can be market
failure even under this wide definition. Thus, a market would malfunction if
negotiations were not possible, that is, if the market were missing because of,
say, vague property rights or large set-up costs; or if negotiations could at best
be carried out only partially because, say, the parties do not know one another
well and conclude their negotiation before exploiting all possible gains from
trade (Farrell, 1987); or if the negotiations were overly one-sided because of
large differences in the bargaining powers of the respective parties (this latter
allows us to capture the distributional aspects of rights and resource allocations in bargains and transactions).

So wide a definition of markets could appear at first blush to be of limited use. In fact, there is much to be said in favour of adopting it. If we were to do so, we could interpret a number of activities within what are traditionally called 'non-market' institutions (such as the extended family and international bodies) and a variety of social norms in what are called traditional societies (such as 'reciprocity' or 'gift-exchanges') as transactions in goods and services (Dasgupta, 1993). We will find this a useful point of view in what follows.

The literature we have just alluded to associates environmental problems with market failure. Recently, however, a new strand has developed within it. The new strand acknowledges that market failure is the proximate cause of many environmental problems, but it identifies inappropriate government policies (more generally, government failure) as the cause of many others (Feder, 1977; Durham, 1979; Binswanger, 1991), and poverty and population growth as both a cause and effect of many others still (Ehrlich and Ehrlich, 1990; Dasgupta and Mäler, 1991; 1993; Wilson, 1992; Dasgupta, 1993; 1995). Taken together, the new literature suggests that a large class of environmental problems can be traced to certain patterns of resource allocation failure, brought about by inappropriate property rights, information asymmetries, paucity of infrastructure, and general transaction costs. The present volume and the two accompanying volumes of essays (Dasgupta and Mäler, 1993) address a number of environmental problems from this more general perspective.

TWO TYPES OF EXTERNALITIES

Resource allocation failures that lead to environmental problems typically involve externalities in production, exchange, and consumption activities. Two broad categories of environmental externalities suggest themselves: 'unidirectional' and 'reciprocal'. Prominent examples of the former are those unnegotiated effects on the lowlands of watersheds that result from deforestation in the uplands (but see Rogers's essay in this volume on the Ganges–Brahmaputra basin), and the infliction of acid rain by people in one region on those in another (Mäler, 1993).

The issues are somewhat different for those unnegotiated economic and ecological interactions that are reciprocal. Here, each party's actions affect all. Reciprocal externalities are the hallmark of common property resources, such as grazing lands, forests, fisheries, the atmosphere, aquifers, village tanks, ponds, lakes, and the open seas. They are sometimes referred to simply as the 'commons'. They are often common property because private property rights to them are for a number of reasons difficult to define (e.g. in the case of mobile resources, such as air). Even when definable, they are on occasion difficult to enforce (e.g. in the case of forest products in mountainous terrains). However, unlike public goods, consumption of common property resources is rivalrous: it is possible for at least one party to increase its consumption at the expense of others' consumption of them.

Resources such as local forests, grazing lands, village ponds, and rivulets, are often common property because that is how they have been since time immemorial. Moreover, in poor countries they have remained common property for long because they are basic needs. For example, rivers may be long, but they are narrow, and do not run through everyone's land. Upstream farmers would have untold advantages over downstream farmers if they were in a position to turn off the 'tap'. Exclusive private territoriality over them would leave non-owners at the mercy of the owners at the 'bargaining table', most especially in communities where markets are thin. Societies typically do not risk the institution of private-property rights over such resources.[1] Grazing lands in semi-arid regions are often common property because productivity risks are not perfectly correlated across space. Communal ownership therefore enables herders to share their risks, thereby affording each a form of insurance.

However, unless there is collective action at some level, a common property is over-exploited: the private cost of using the resource falls short of its shadow price. Free-riding is the problem. This was the point of Scott Gordon's classic article (Gordon, 1954; see also Scott, 1955; Milliman, 1956). It was popularized subsequently by Hardin (1968), who coined the phrase 'the tragedy of the commons'.[2]

In some parts of the world, community leaders, non-government organizations, and a free press (where they exist) have been known to galvanize activity on behalf of those who are relatively powerless to defend themselves against unidirectional harm sustained by weak property rights. In recent years this has happened on a number of occasions in different contexts. One of the most widely publicized has been the Chipko Movement in India, which involved the threatened disenfranchisement of historical users of forest products. This was occasioned by the state's claiming its rights over what was stated to be 'public property' and then embarking on a logging operation. The connection between environmental protection and civil and political rights is a close one. As a general rule, political and civil liberties are instrumentally powerful in protecting the environmental resource-base, at least when compared with the absence of such liberties in countries run by authoritarian regimes (Dasgupta, 1993). The environmental havoc that was caused by the communist regimes of eastern Europe is a case in point.

[1] Rulers had control over such resources in many early societies. But that was not the same as private property rights. Rulers were obliged to make them available to the ruled. Indeed, one of the assumed duties of rulers was to expand such resource-bases.
[2] It should be noted that a resource being common property does not mean that people have free access to it. Often, only those households with a historical right of access are permitted by the community to avail themselves of local common-property resources (Dasgupta and Heal, 1979: ch. 3).

Economic analysis is thought by some to have implied that common-property resources can be managed only through centralized co-ordination and control, where by a 'centralized agency' is meant the government (in the case of problems confined within a nation), or more generally, to some agency external to the community of users. Referring to solutions to the problem of the commons in the theoretical literature, Wade (1987: 220) writes: 'The prevailing answer runs as follows: when people are in a situation where they could mutually benefit if all of them restrained their use of a common-pool resource, they will not do so unless an external agency enforces a suitable rule'. And he proceeds to describe enforcement mechanisms in a sample of villages in South India that do not rely on external agencies.

Wade's is a bad reading of modern economic analysis. The theory of games has unravelled a number of institutional mechanisms (ranging from taxes to quantity controls) that can in principle support effective allocations of common-property resources. The theory makes clear, and has made clear for some time, that enforcement of the controlled allocation can in a variety of circumstances be undertaken by the users themselves (Dasgupta and Heal, 1979: ch. 3). In many cases, such participatory arrangements of control may well be the most desirable option.[3]

As always, monitoring, enforcement, and information costs play a critical role in the relative efficacy of the mechanisms that can be used for controlling common-property resources. It matters whether the common property is geographically contained (contrast a village pond with the open seas); it matters whether the users know one another and whether they are large in number (contrast a village grazing-ground with a tuna fishery); and it matters whether individual use can easily be monitored, so as to prevent 'free-riding' (contrast the use of a village tube-well with littering the streets of a metropolis; or the grazing of cattle in the village commons with firewood collection from forests in mountainous terrain). The confirmation of theory by current evidence on the fate of different categories of common-property resources has been one of the pleasing features of modern economic analysis.

Public concerns about environmental degradation are often prompted by disasters, such as nuclear leakage or floods.[4] The environmental impact of large undertakings (e.g. dams and irrigation systems, such as the Narmada Project in India) also catch the public eye. This is not surprising. Large-scale effects caused by single happenings are easy to detect. They thereby invite debate. In contrast, the examples of environmental externalities offered for study in this volume are not so easy to detect. They often involve large

---

[3] Not everyone writing on the subject has misread the literature. For illuminating accounts of the way communities have jointly controlled common-property resources, see Feeny et al. (1990), Ostrom (1990), and Stevenson (1991). Seabright (1993) contains a good theoretical discussion of the problems.

[4] Kreimer and Munasinghe (1991) is an excellent collection of studies on the management of natural disasters.

numbers of resource users, each inflicting only a tiny damage on each of the others, which, however, sum to a substantial amount; usually, over an extended period of time (Dasgupta and Heal, 1979). It would seem that much of the environmental degradation we are witnessing (or not witnessing, as the case may be) in the world today is due to this kind of subtle interaction that creeps up over time, and not due to large projects (Repetto, 1988).

INTERNATIONAL EXTERNALITIES, NEGOTIATIONS, AND POLICY DESIGN

Two companion volumes of essays (Dasgupta and Mäler, 1997) contain a variety of studies on local environmental problems. By 'local' we mean problems that are confined to geographical areas covered by an established structure of power and political authority. The present volume addresses externalities across national borders. Of particular interest are problems of transnational commons. The essays included here contain discussions of biodiversity (Ehrlich and Ehrlich), population growth (John Caldwell and Ann Caldwell), global climate (Hollick and Cooper; Dorfman; Carraro and Siniscalco), international watersheds (Rogers), international agreements, the open seas (Musu; Hollick and Cooper; Lynton Caldwell), and cultural externalities (Greif; Hannerz). Their importance cannot be overstated; indeed, much has already been written on them. But to the best of our knowledge, there has been no attempt so far to bring together leading experts on such diverse transnational externalities as the ones covered in this volume, and to encourage them to write professional articles on their subjects in a relatively non-technical style. Our reason for attempting this inter-disciplinary study was that while seemingly different, these problems have structural commonalities. Insights gained from a study of one can, therefore, help in our understanding of another. For this reason, the authors have stressed the overarching features of the various transnational problems that are discussed here.

Discussions on such matters as the international waters and cultural externalities can rapidly become a litany of case-studies. But case-studies without the backing of theory can at best inform, they cannot illuminate. Moreover, the structural similarities among problems that are posed by transnational commons suggest that we should pay close attention to analysis. But no analysis of international problems can be undertaken without an explicit recognition of the possibilities of negotiation and of the link that exists between the agreements themselves and the ability of parties to enforce them. In the opening contribution, Myerson provides an account of the one theoretical framework on these matters that we currently possess, namely, the one on offer by game theory. The power of game-theoretic analyses has been increasingly recognized. In this volume game-theoretic models of bargaining are also used for the study of specific problems by Rogers, Greif, and Carraro and Siniscalco.

The idea of a game is intended here to capture the basic structure of social systems. A game is specified by the participants' characteristics. Of course, in speaking of a person's characteristics we mean not only his motivation (i.e. his values and preferences; which are often called his pay-off function), but also what he is able to do (his feasible set of strategies) and what he knows and can observe (his information set). The well-known Prisoners' Dilemma provides a game-theoretic formulation of certain environmental problems, most perspicuously those involving the use of common property resources. The dilemma in question arises because, in the absence of enforceable agreements, the parties have an incentive to break agreements unilaterally: they 'free-ride'. We may now interpret 'institutional failure' as an instance of a game whose equilibrium outcome is collectively sub-optimal (i.e. there is a set of strategies, one for each party, which if chosen, would yield higher pay-offs to all parties), where, by an equilibrium outcome, we mean a Nash equilibrium. And by a Nash equilibrium we mean a set of strategies, one for each party, possessing the property that no party, by making a unilateral deviation, could attain a higher pay-off for himself. From this definition it follows that a Nash equilibrium is self-enforcing. The problem is that such equilibria are typically sub-optimal (see Binmore and Dasgupta, 1986).

One would imagine that, faced with the possibility of institutional failure, participants in a game would wish to negotiate a co-ordinated set of strategies so as to bring about a better outcome. The question arises as to how one should model this sort of co-operative enterprise. In the opening essay, Myerson shows that it is fruitful to study the possible outcomes of negotiation by analysing the negotiation process explicitly. The outcome can then be interpreted as a Nash equilibrium of the larger, negotiation game. In a negotiation game a strategy is a statement of how to conduct the negotiations under all possible eventualities, and how finally to choose a strategy (e.g. proposing national targets for carbon emissions) on the course the negotiations took. Since the co-operative infrastructure (e.g. the powers of the central authority, if any) is specified in the negotiation model, Nash equilibria of the negotiation game are 'co-operative' outcomes of the bargaining problem. In his analysis of the idea of cultural beliefs, Greif pursues this route to an understanding of repeated interactions among members of a community.

The problem with this approach is that, in having always to specify the negotiation game before thinking of solutions to bargaining problems, one is embarking on a formidable taxonomy. As it also happens, except in the simplest of negotiation games, computing Nash equilibria is very hard. A parallel research tactic is therefore to avoid modelling the negotiation process, and to consign the details of the process to intelligent speculation and informed guesswork. In practical terms this means choosing an appropriate 'solution concept', such as the core, or the Nash bargaining solution, or the Shapley value, and to see them as outcomes of non-cooperative negotiation games whose negotiation procedures have not been formalized. This is the route followed in the papers by Rogers and by Carraro and Siniscalco.

We noted earlier that bargaining under incomplete information can lead to inefficient outcomes (Farrell, 1987). The literature on mechanism design has shown why a central agency is needed for co-ordination and control when the members of a social organization who intend to co-operate possess different information structures. The literature in particular has demonstrated why decentralization under the guidance of a central authority is the right framework for the allocation of resources (Dasgupta, 1980). In their contributions, Dorfman and Hoel address problems associated with the design of international environmental policies for the management of global commons.

One broad category of policies well worth exploring in the international context involves making the global commons quasi-private. The basic idea, which originated in Dales (1968), would have the community of nations set bounds on the total annual use of the global commons, such as the atmosphere, have it allocate an initial distribution of transferable national rights that add up to the aggregate bound, and allow the final allocation among different users to be determined by competitive markets.[5]

To give an example, consider the emission of greenhouse gases. Suppose that it is desired by the community of nations that emissions should be reduced to a prescribed global level. Units of the various gases would then be so chosen that all gases have the same (expected) effect on global climate. Thus, the emission of one unit of any one gas at the margin would have the same (expected) climatic effect as the emission of one unit of any other gas. The scheme would allow countries to exchange permits for one gas for permits for any other. Countries would receive an initial assignment of marketable permits. (This is where the distributional implications on international incomes raise their heads.) As is well known, this scheme has informational advantages over both taxes and quantity controls on individual emissions. Furthermore, if the permits were to refer to net emissions (i.e. net of absorption of carbon dioxide by green plants), the scheme would provide an incentive for countries with fast-growing tropical rain forests to earn export revenue by encouraging forest growth and then selling permits to other countries. The scheme also has the advantage that the necessary side-payments required to induce all (or most) countries to participate in the agreement can be made through the initial distribution of emission permits. Countries which do not expect severe damages from global warming would also wish to participate if they were to be provided initially with a sufficient number of permits (or rights).

---

[5] See Dasgupta (1982) and Tietenberg (1990), respectively, for reviews of the analytical and institutional features underlying such schemes.

The sticking-point will clearly be over reaching an agreement on the initial distribution of permits among nations.[6] But if the bound that is set on annual aggregate greenhouse emissions is approximately optimal, it is possible to distribute the initial set of rights and a set of monetary transfers in such a way that all countries have an incentive to join the scheme. For this reason one cannot emphasize strongly enough that there are large potential gains to be enjoyed from international co-operation: a scheme involving the issue of marketable permits in principle offers a way in which all nations can enjoy these gains. The argument that 'national sovereignty' would be endangered is in fact no argument, for the point about global commons is precisely that they are beyond the realm of national sovereignty.

Admittedly, if there are insufficient inducements, not all nations would wish to agree to be party to an international agreement. In their contribution, Carraro and Siniscalco provide an illuminating analysis of incomplete co-operation among nations.[7]

INTERNATIONAL FISHERIES: AN EXAMPLE OF A GLOBAL COMMONS

If biodiversity and the emission of greenhouse gases dominate the literature on the global commons today, it is not because international fisheries pose no problems; rather, it is because global food production has not been on the agenda of international concerns in recent years. But disputes in the Atlantic, the South China Sea, and the Pacific reflect unresolved conflicts of interest among contending parties. At the widest international level, the United Nations Law of the Sea Conferences were initiated several decades ago because of a clear recognition that the open seas pose a serious resource-allocation problem. However, the move on the part of nations to extend their 'exclusive economic zones' to 200 nautical miles off the coast-line has had a marked effect on the potentials for an international sharing of oceanic resources.

There is irony in this. Eckert (1979: 47), for example, argued that it was the United Nations Law of the Sea Conferences themselves that stimulated an increase in the rate of oceanic enclosures; and he observed that, 'many who believed (and still may believe) that international procedures are the most effective mechanism for halting enclosures may be somewhat galled to learn that this mechanism actually promotes enclosures.' He may be right, but there is something unseemly about the sight of mature nations making a

---

[6] How a national government allocates the nation's rights among agencies within the country is a different matter.

[7] The Declaration on the Human Environment signed at the United Nations Stockholm Conference in June 1972 states that nations have an obligation to 'ensure that activities within their jurisdiction or control do not cause damage to the environment of other states or of areas beyond the limits of national jurisdiction'.

scramble for oceanic resources, taking actions that would stimulate the transfer of fisheries from international to national control.

The enclosure movement has shifted the balance of management problems associated with ocean fisheries from the international to the national sphere; so it is tempting to think that there would be less overfishing. But we would be wrong in thinking so: the record of purely national regulations of limited resources does not make for pleasant reading either.[8]

The maximum potential harvest of ocean fisheries is estimated to be in the range 60 to 90 million metric tons.[9] There is evidence that, globally, stocks have declined in recent years through over-fishing: worldwide, the extraction rate of wild fish reached a peak of 82 million metric tons in 1989. It is not only increases in world population and incomes that have caused this: fishing technology has become awesome, having both lowered the unit cost of large-scale fishing considerably and increased the rate of what is euphemistically called 'by-catch'.[10] Allied to this is the enormous subsidy a number of the most prominent national fishing industries receive from their governments. Recently, the cost of catching US$70 billion worth of fish amounted to US$124 billion. The deficit was largely covered by subsidies (Safina, 1995).

Cooper (1977) estimated that the annual revenue that could be generated from international marine fisheries by a Pigovian tax on harvests is of the order of US $2.5 billion. He suggested that the tax could be administered by the United Nations, possibly as a contribution to its Development Fund. Thus, there is the possibility of a 'double dividend'. But we are nowhere near such a form of international co-operation.

CONTRACT AGREEMENTS AND THE STRUCTURE OF AUTHORITY

The enforcement of agreements on the use of local commons (e.g. a village pond) is often easier than it is in the case of agreements on the use of transnational commons. This is not only because of differences in the ease with which actions can be monitored (a matter we discussed earlier), but also because of differences in the reach of the corresponding 'enforcement agencies'. To be sure, in times of civil unrest or general political instability, the

---

[8] In this volume Lynton Caldwell expresses disquiet at the international community's performance over the management of a number of global commons. Unless an agreement is so designed that the parties have an incentive to comply, it amounts to little. French (1994) argues that such incentives are lacking in most of the 170 or so environmental treaties that have been drafted in recent years.

[9] Maximal potential harvest is not the same as maximum sustainable yield. This is because a good fraction of a fishery's production has to be left unharvested on ecological grounds. World Resources Institute (1994) and Safina (1995) offer succinct accounts of the problem of marine fisheries.

[10] By-catch refers to inadvertent harvest. Roughly one of every four animals harvested from the open seas is unwanted.

reach of national governments can be a good deal weaker than that of, say, the United Nations Security Council. Nevertheless, international agencies typically do not possess the coercive powers that national governments are ideally taken to possess. The essay by Lynton Caldwell addresses such problems as have now arisen in the international sphere because of this.

Insights into the range of options open in the international sphere can be obtained by asking a prior question: how are agreements implemented in the case of local environmental problems? Notice that, while related, this is different from asking what agreement would be expected to be reached if the parties were to bargain. Myerson's essay gives us an idea of what game theory has to say on the latter question. In what follows, we will discuss the former.

Broadly speaking, there would appear to be three mechanisms by which an agreement can be implemented. (Of course, none may work in a particular context, in which case people will find themselves in a hole they can't easily get out of, and what could have been mutually beneficial agreements won't take place.)

In the first mechanism the agreement is translated into a contract, and is enforced by an established structure of power and authority. This may be the national government, but it need not be. In rural communities, for example, the structures of power and authority are in some cases vested in tribal elders (as within nomadic tribes in Sub-Saharan Africa), in others in dominant landowners (such as the zamindars of eastern India), feudal lords (as in the state of Rajasthan in India), chieftains, and priests. On occasion there are even attempts at making rural communities mini-republics: village Panchayats in India try to assume such a form. The idea there is to elect officers, the officials being entrusted with the power to settle disputes, enforce contracts (whether explicit or only tacit), communicate with higher levels of state authority, and so forth. Wade's account (Wade, 1987) of the collective management of common-property resources in South India describes such a mechanism of enforcement in detail.[11]

The question why such a structure of authority as may exist is accepted by people is a higher-order one, akin to the question why people accept the authority of government. The answer is that general acceptance itself is a self-enforcing behaviour: when all others accept the structure of authority, each has an incentive to accept it (or, in short, general acceptance is a Nash equilibrium). Contrariwise, when a sufficiently large number don't accept it, individual incentives to accept it weaken, and the system unravels rapidly. General acceptance of the structure of authority is held together by its own bootstraps, so to speak.

The second mechanism consists in the development of a disposition to abide by agreements, a disposition formed through the process of communal living, role-modelling, education, and the experiencing of rewards and

[11] See also Gadgil and Guha (1992) for a narrative on India's ecological history as seen from this perspective.

punishments. This process begins at the earliest stages of our lives. We internalize social norms, such as that of paying our dues, keeping agreements, returning a favour; and higher-order norms, as for example frowning on people who break social norms (even shunning them), and so forth. By internalizing such norms as keeping agreements, a person makes the springs of his actions contain the norm. The person therefore feels shame or guilt in violating a norm, and this prevents him from doing so, or, at the very least, it puts a brake on his violating it unless other considerations are found by him to be overriding. In short, his upbringing ensures that he has a disposition to obey the norm. When he does violate it, neither guilt nor shame is typically absent, but the act will have been rationalized by him. A general disposition to abide by agreements, to be truthful, to trust one another, and to act with justice is an essential lubricant of societies. Communities where the disposition is pervasive save enormously on transaction costs. There lies its instrumental virtue.[12] In the world as we know it, such a disposition is present in varying degrees. When we refrain from breaking the law, it isn't always because of a fear of being caught. On the other hand, if relative to the gravity of the misdemeanour the private benefit from malfeasance were high, some transgressions could be expected to take place. Punishment assumes its role as a deterrent because of the latter fact.

However, where people repeatedly encounter one another in similar situations, agreements could be reached and kept even if people were not trustworthy; and even if a higher authority were not there to enforce the agreements. This is a third kind of mechanism.

How does it work? A simple set of contexts in which it works is one where far-sighted people know both one another and the environment, where they expect to interact repeatedly under the same circumstances, and where all this is commonly known.[13] By a far-sighted person I mean someone who applies a low discount rate to the future costs and benefits associated with alternative courses of action. This means in particular that people in the community are not separately mobile; otherwise the chance of future encounters with others in the community would be low, and people would discount heavily the future benefits of co-operation.

The basic idea is this: if people are far-sighted, a *credible* threat by others that they would impose sanctions on anyone who broke the agreement would deter everyone from breaking it. Let us see how this works.

For expositional ease, consider those circumstances where actions are publicly observable, and where everyone has perfect memory of how all others have behaved in the past.[14] Imagine, then, a group of people who have agreed

[12] See Dasgupta (1988) for further discussion of the value of trust in a community.

[13] These are not necessary conditions, they are sufficient. For a good account of what is known in this line of inquiry, see Fudenberg and Tirole (1991).

[14] Each of these qualifications can be relaxed. See Radner (1981) for weakening the first qualification, and Sabourian (1988) for relaxing the second.

upon a joint course of action. The agreement could, for example, be over the sharing of the benefits and burdens associated with the construction and maintenance of an irrigation system. We may suppose that the co-operative arrangement that has been agreed upon assigns various responsibilities to the parties on a period-by-period basis (e.g. maintaining a canal system annually, diverting to one's own fields only the quantity of water that is one's due, and so forth). How is this agreement to be kept in the absence of an external enforcement authority?

One might think that a social norm, requiring people to keep their agreements, has a role here. But this merely begs the question: we would want to know *why* the norm is accepted by all; that is, what incentives people have for not violating the norm. Since by a social norm we mean a rule of behaviour that is commonly obeyed by all, we would need to show that it is in the interest of each party to obey the norm if all others were to obey it.[15] For simplicity of exposition, consider the case where the private gain to someone from breaking the agreement unilaterally for a period is less than the discounted value of the loss he would suffer if all others were to refrain from co-operating with him in the following period. Call a person 'deserving' if and only if he co-operates with all who are deserving. This sounds circular, but isn't; because we now assume that the norm requires all parties to start the process of repeated interactions by keeping their agreement (viz. maintaining the canal system, diverting to one's own fields only the quantity of water that is one's due, and so forth). It is then easy to confirm that, by recursion, it is possible for any party in any period to determine who is deserving and who is not. If someone's actions in any period made him non-deserving, the norm would enjoin each of the other parties to impose a sanction on him (i.e. not co-operate with him) in the following period (e.g. deny him the water he needs). In longhand, the norm requires that sanctions be imposed upon those in violation of an agreement; upon those who fail to impose sanctions upon those in violation of the agreement; upon those who fail to impose sanctions upon those who fail to impose sanctions upon those in violation of the agreement; . . . and so on, indefinitely. This indefinite chain of what amounts to higher- and higher-order norms makes the threat of sanctions against deviant behaviour credible; because, if all others were to obey the norm, it would not be worth anyone's while to disobey the norm. In short, keeping one's agreement would be self-enforcing.[16]

This argument generalizes to other situations. Provided people are sufficiently far-sighted, a social norm which instructs one to co-operate with, and only with, deserving parties, can lift communities out of a number of potentially troublesome social situations, including the repeated Prisoners'

[15] In technical parlance, for a rule of behaviour to be a social norm, it must be a subgame-perfect Nash equilibrium. Fudenberg and Tirole (1991) offer an account of this.

[16] Notice though that, as co-operation is self-enforcing, there would be no deviance along the path of co-operation; so, no sanctions would be observed. The higher-order norms pertain to behaviour off the path of co-operation.

Dilemma game. The reason each party conforms to the norm when a sufficient number of others conform is pure and simple self-interest: if someone were not to conform (i.e. were not to abide by the norm), he would suffer from sanctions from others for a period of time long enough to make non-conformism 'unprofitable'.[17]

This sort of argument, which has been established in a general setting only recently, has been put to effective use in explaining the emergence of a number of institutions which facilitated the growth of trade in medieval Europe. Greif (1993), for example, has shown how the Maghribi traders during the eleventh century in Fustat and across the Mediterranean acted as a collective to impose sanctions on agents who violated their commercial codes. Greif, Milgrom, and Weingast (1994) have offered an account of the rise of merchant guilds in late medieval Europe. These guilds afforded protection to members against unjustified seizure of their property by city-states. Guilds decided if and when a trade embargo was warranted against the city. In a related work, Milgrom, North, and Weingast (1990) have analysed the role of merchant courts in the Champagne fairs. These courts facilitated members in imposing sanctions on transgressors of agreements.

Something approximating to the opposite of this occurred in medieval Europe, where transgressions by a party were sometimes met by the rest of society imposing sanctions on the entire kinship of the party, or on the guild to which the transgressor belonged. The norm provided collectives with a natural incentive to monitor their own members' behaviour. (For a different instance of this, the context being the use of local common-property resources, see Howe, 1986.)

As things stand, international agreements on environmental matters could be expected to be sustained by the latter two mechanisms in the list we have just discussed, not by the first. Ultimately, however, it is the second route that offers the strongest hopes for the emergence of collective responsibility over transnational commons. The problem is that institutional changes are easier to bring about than changes in personal and collective attitudes; or so it would seem. Economists generally take 'preferences' and 'demands' as given and try to devise policies that would be expected to improve matters collectively. This is the spirit in which ecological economics has developed, and there is an enormous amount to be said for it. But in the process of following this research strategy, we shouldn't play down the strictures of those social thinkers who have urged the rich to curb their material demands, to alter their preferences in such ways as to better husband the earth's limited resources. If such strictures seem quaint in today's world, it may be because we are psychologically uncomfortable with this kind of vocabulary. But that isn't an argument for not taking them seriously.

---

[17] Of course, the non-cooperative outcome is also self-enforcing; that is, it is also a subgame-perfect Nash equilibrium. Repeated games, such as the one I am studying here, have many equilibria.

REFERENCES

Abreu, D. (1988), 'On the Theory of Infinitely Repeated Games with Discounting', *Econometrica*, 56.

Arrow, K. J. (1971), 'Political and Economic Evaluation of Social Effects of Externalities', in M. Intriligator (ed.), *Frontiers of Quantitative Economics*, i (Amsterdam: North Holland).

Baumol, W. M. and Oates, W. (1975), *The Theory of Environmental Policy* (Englewood Cliffs, NJ: Prentice-Hall).

Binmore, K. and Dasgupta P. (eds.) (1986), *Economic Organizations as Games* (Oxford: Basil Blackwell).

Binswanger, H. (1991), 'Brazilian Policies that Encourage Deforestation in the Amazon', *World Development*, 19.

Chopra, K., Kadekodi, G. K., and Murty, M. N. (1990), *Participatory Development: People and Common Property Resources* (New Delhi: Sage).

Coase, R. (1960), 'The Problem of Social Cost', *Journal of Law and Economics*, 3.

Cooper, R. (1975), 'An Economist's View of the Oceans', *Journal of World Trade Law*, 9.

—— (1977), 'The Oceans as a Source of Revenue', in J. Bhagwati (ed.), *The New International Economic Order* (Cambridge, Mass.: MIT Press).

Dales, J. H. (1968), *Pollution, Property and Prices* (Toronto: University of Toronto Press).

Dasgupta, P. (1980), 'Decentralization and Rights', *Economica*, 47.

—— (1982), *The Control of Resources* (Oxford: Basil Blackwell).

—— (1988), 'Trust as a Commodity', in D. Gambetta (ed.), *Trust: Making and Breaking of Cooperative Agreements* (Oxford: Basil Blackwell).

—— (1993), *An Inquiry into Well-Being and Destitution* (Oxford: Clarendon Press).

—— (1995), 'The Population Problem: Theory and Evidence', *Journal of Economic Literature*, 33.

—— and Heal, G. M. (1974), 'The Optimal Depletion of Exhaustible Resources', *Review of Economic Studies* 41 (Symposium on the Economics of Exhaustible Resources).

—— and Mäler, K.-G. (1991), 'The Environment and Emerging Development Issues', *Proceedings of the Annual World Bank Conference on Development Economics* (Supplement to the *World Bank Economic Review* and the *World Bank Research Observer*); reprinted in R. Layard and S. Glaister (eds.), *Cost-Benefit Analysis* (Cambridge: Cambridge University Press, 1994).

—— —— (1993), 'Poverty, Institutions and the Environmental Resource-Base', in J. Behrman and T. N. Srinivasan (eds.), *Handbook of Development Economics* (Amsterdam: North Holland, 1995).

—— —— (eds.) (1997), *The Environment and Emerging Development Issues*, i and ii (Oxford: Oxford University Press).

Durham, W. H. (1979), *Scarcity and Survival in Central America: Ecological Origins of the Soccer War* (Stanford, Calif.: Stanford University Press).

Ehrlich, P. and Ehrlich, A. (1990), *The Population Explosion* (New York: Simon & Schuster).

Farrell, J. (1987), 'Information and the Coase Theorem', *Journal of Economic Perspectives*, 1.

Feder, E. (1977), 'Agribusiness and the Elimination of Latin America's Rural Proletariat', *World Development*, 5.

Feeny, D. *et al.* (1990), 'The Tragedy of the Commons: Twenty-two Years Later', *Human Ecology*, 18.

French, H. F. (1994), 'Making Environmental Treaties Work', *Scientific American*, 272/6.

Fudenberg, D. and Maskin, E. (1986), 'The Folk Theorem in Repeated Games with Discounting and Incomplete Information', *Econometrica*, 54.

—— and Tirole, J. (1991), *Game Theory* (Cambridge, Mass.: MIT Press).

Gadgil, M. and Guha, R. (1992), *This Fissured Land: An Ecological History of India* (Delhi: Oxford University Press).

Gordon, H. Scott (1954), 'The Economic Theory of Common-Property Resources', *Journal of Political Economy*, 62.

Greif, A. (1993), 'Contract Enforceability and Economic Institutions in Early Trade: The Maghribi Traders' Coalition', *American Economic Review*, 83.

——, Milgrom, P., and Weingast, B. (1994), 'Coordination, Commitment, and Enforcement: The Case of the Merchant Guild', *Journal of Political Economy*, 102.

Hardin, G. (1968), 'The Tragedy of the Commons', *Science*, 162.

Howe, J. (1986), *The Kuna Gathering* (Austin, Tex.: University of Texas Press).

Kreimer, A. and Munasinghe, M. (eds.) (1991), *Managing Natural Disasters and the Environment* (Washington DC: World Bank).

Lindahl, E. R. (1958), 'Some Controversial Questions in the Theory of Taxation', in R. A. Musgrave and A. T. Peacock (eds.), *Classics in the Theory of Public Finance* (London: Macmillan); originally published in Swedish, in 1928.

Mäler, K.-G. (1993), 'The Acid Rain Game II', Discussion Paper Series No. 32, Beijer International Institute of Ecological Economics, Stockholm.

Meade, J. E. (1973), *The Theory of Externalities* (Geneva: Institut Universitaire de Hautes Etudes Internationales).

Milgrom, P., North, D., and Weingast, B. (1990), 'The Role of Institutions in the Revival of Trade: The Law Merchant, Private Judges, and the Champagne Fairs', *Economics and Politics*, 2.

Milliman, J. W. (1956), 'Commodities and Price Systems and Use of Water Supplies', *Southern Economic Journal*, 22.

Ostrom, E. (1990), *Governing the Commons: The Evolution of Institutions for Collective Action* (Cambridge: Cambridge University Press).

Pigou, A. C. (1920), *The Economics of Welfare* (London: Macmillan).

Radner, R. (1981), 'Monitoring Cooperative Agreements in a Repeated Principal-Agent Relationship', *Econometrica*, 49.

Repetto, R. (1988), 'Economic Policy Reform for Natural Resource Conservation', World Bank Environment Department Working Paper No. 4.

Sabourian, H. (1988), 'Repeated Games: A Survey', in F. H. Hahn (ed.), *The Economic Theory of Missing Markets, Information, and Games* (Oxford: Basil Blackwell).

Safina, C. (1995), 'The World's Imperiled Fish', *Scientific American*, 273/5.

Scott, A. D. (1955), 'The Fishery: The Objectives of Sole Ownership', *Journal of Political Economy*, 63.

Seabright, P. (1993), 'Managing Local Commons: Theoretical Issues in Incentive Design', *Journal of Economic Perspectives*, 7.

Stevenson, G. G. (1991), *Common Property Resources: A General Theory and Land Use Applications* (Cambridge: Cambridge University Press).

Tietenberg, T. H. (1990), 'Economic Instruments for Environmental Regulation', *Oxford Review of Economic Policy*, 6.

Wade, R. (1987), 'The Management of Common Property Resources: Finding a Cooperative Solution', *World Bank Research Observer*, 2.

Wilson, E. O. (1992), *The Diversity of Life* (New York: W. W. Norton).

World Resources Institute (1994), *World Resources 1994–1995* (New York: Oxford University Press).

2

Game-Theoretic Models of Bargaining: An Introduction for Economists Studying the Transnational Commons

Roger B. Myerson

THE IMPORTANCE OF BARGAINING

The transnational commons are the resources of the world, from the ozone layer to the deep ocean floor, that do not belong to any individual, organization, or nation. These resources are understood to be in danger of over-exploitation and neglect, because of the lack of any owner who would have a strong interest in protecting them. However, Coase (1960) argued that efficient use of resources would be expected independently of ownership structures, if we could assume that contracts and treaties are enforceable and bargaining costs are negligible. Thus, an understanding of bargaining costs may be fundamental to understanding the problems of the transnational commons.

To apply Coase's argument to the transnational commons, let us suppose that the international community can mobilize sanctions to punish violators of international treaties, so that treaties are enforceable. Then, in the absence of bargaining costs, we might well expect the nations of the world to sign treaties to guarantee efficient usage of all common resources. If everyone can be made better off when common resources are efficiently managed than when they are neglected or over-exploited, then everyone should be willing to sign a treaty that prevents such over-exploitation. The difficulty is that a treaty to restrict abuse of common resources must necessarily specify how to allocate the benefits from using these resources and the costs of maintaining them. When a resource has an identified owner, the allocation of these benefits and costs is clear; the owner is both entitled to all the benefits and responsible for all the costs of maintaining the resource. Without an owner, international bargaining is needed to allocate these benefits and costs, before an efficient pattern of use can be agreed on.

Thus, the costs of bargaining over the allocation of benefits from common resources must be seen as an essential contributing factor to the waste and mismanagement of the transnational commons, and economists who seek ways to mitigate the problems of the transnational commons should try to understand the sources of bargaining costs. To establish a basic conceptual framework for understanding the sources of bargaining costs, we turn to game theory. In this essay, we survey some of the most important game-theoretic models of bargaining, to see what they may tell us about the problems of the transnational commons.

To describe these general game-theoretic models in the context of transnational commons, let us think about a simple situation in which a lake lies on the border between two nations. Suppose that the fish population in the lake is in danger of being destroyed, unless there is some international agreement to control water pollution and restrict catches on both sides of the lake. Let us suppose for now that, if fishing and pollution are regulated optimally, then the lake could provide a harvest worth $1 million per year, but unregulated pollution or over-fishing would destroy the resources of the lake.

NASH'S DEMAND GAME

Any survey of game-theoretic models of bargaining must begin with the simple demand game that was discussed first by Nash (1953) and subsequently by Schelling (1960). In Nash's demand game, each player simultaneously and independently demands some level of pay-off. If their pay-off demands are jointly feasible then they get their demands, but otherwise they both get the disagreement outcome that would occur without bargaining. In our fishing example, this game would be played as follows. The negotiator for each of the two nations brings to the bargaining session a written demand for some value of the harvest that his nation's fishing fleets should be allowed to take from the lake per year. If these two demands sum to $1 million or less, then they will optimally regulate the lake and each will take exactly the amount that it demanded. If their demands sum to more than $1 million, then the bargaining ends in disagreement, and unregulated pollution or over-fishing will rapidly destroy the value of the lake's resources. Nash's demand game may seem unrealistically simple, but it is worthy of careful consideration, because many of the insights from more sophisticated game-theoretic models can be understood as extensions of the insights that we derive from the Nash demand game.

The first thing to say about Nash's demand game is that it has multiple equilibria. For any number X between 0 and 1 million, there is an equilibrium of this game in which nation 1 (say, the nation on the north side of the lake) demands to take a harvest worth X dollars per year from the lake, and nation 2 (the nation on the south side of the lake) demands to take a harvest worth 1,000,000 − X dollars per year from the lake. For example, if nation 1 is expected to demand $123,456, then nation 2's optimal demand is $1,000,000 − $123,456 = $876,544; and if nation 2 is expected to demand $876,544, then nation 1's optimal demand is $1,000,000 − $876,544 = $123,456. Thus, the demand pair ($123,456, $876,544) forms an equilibrium (or self-fulfilling expectation) of Nash's demand game for this example. Obviously the number 123,456 was completely arbitrary, and any number X between 0 and 1,000,000 would have made an equilibrium just as well.

The equilibria discussed in the preceding paragraph are all Pareto-efficient. If these were the only equilibria, then we would infer that bargaining may be unpredictable but not necessarily costly. However, there are inefficient equilibria as well. There is an equilibrium in which each nation demands to take an annual harvest worth $1,000,000, and so bargaining ends in disagreement and both nations get $0 (which we assume for now is the value of the fisheries in the case of disagreement). When each nation expects the other nation to demand everything, neither nation can do better by unilaterally lowering its demand.

There are also randomized equilibria that can be very inefficient. For example, there is an equilibrium in which each nation independently demands either $1000 with probability 1/999, or $999,000 with probability 998/999. In this equilibrium, the probability of agreement is only

$$1/999 + 1/999 - (1/999)^2 = 0.002003,$$

and each nation would get an expected profit of only $1000 from either of its positive-probability demands. In this equilibrium, a demand of $999,000 has a probability 1/999 of being successful, as would any demand between $999,000 and $1000. (Notice that $999,000 × 1/999 = $1000.) A demand of $1000 or less would be successful with probability 1, but a demand of more than $999,000 would have no chance of success, given the other nation's equilibrium strategy. In this equilibrium, the two sides use un-coordinated bargaining strategies that generate a high probability of disagreement when both sides are more aggressive in their demands. Such un-coordinated and inefficient equilibria of Nash's demand game give us our first model of the potential costs of bargaining. Thus, we see that a key to efficient bargaining may be to co-ordinate the players' expectations and focus them on one feasible and efficient allocation.

Schelling (1960) argued that, in games with multiple equilibria, anything in the environment that focuses players' attentions on any one equilibrium may make them expect it and hence fulfil it. To understand this 'focal-point effect', consider the basic game-theoretic definition of equilibrium (due to Nash (1951)). An 'equilibrium' is defined to be any scenario for the players' behaviour in the game (that is, any possible prediction of strategic behaviour for all the players in all possible events in the game) such that, if each player believed that all other players would behave according to this scenario then no player could expect to do better by using a strategy other than the one described for himself in the scenario. Thus, an equilibrium is by definition a possible self-fulfilling prophecy. If we could, by psychological manipulation, persuade all the players to expect each other to behave according to some particular equilibrium, then each player would perceive it to be in his best interests to behave according to our prediction, and so the players' faith in our prediction would be justified. Conversely, any scenario that is not an equilibrium could not be a self-fulfilling prophecy. If we tried to persuade the players to expect each other to behave according to some scenario that is not an equilibrium, then at least one player must either want to violate our prediction for him or disbelieve our prediction for other players.

From a game-theoretic perspective, 'cultural norms' can be defined to be the rules that a society uses to determine focal equilibria in game situations. Similarly, we may here define an 'arbitrator' to be any individual who attempts to determine a focal equilibrium by advocating it to the players. In the Nash demand game for our example, the equilibrium in which each nation demands $500,000 has an obvious symmetry which might attract the players' attention, and so we might expect it to be the focal equilibrium that the players implement. However, if 63 per cent of the lake is in the territory of nation 1 (when national boundaries are extended straight across the lake), then the nations might naturally focus on an equilibrium in which nation 1 demands $630,000 and nation 2 demands $370,000. On the other hand, if the fishing fleets of nation 2 have traditionally brought in 75 per cent of the annual harvest, then this proportion might make focal the equilibrium in which nation 1 demands $250,000 and nation 2 demands $750,000. Finally, if a fact-finding team sent by the United Nations has publicly recommended that the harvest should be shared according to the average of the above three allocations, $460,000 for nation 1 and $540,000 for nation 2, then this non-binding recommendation could make the two nations focus on the equilibrium in which each demands its recommended share. In general, the focal equilibrium that the players expect and hence fulfil may be determined by any salient factor, in the mathematical structure of the game, or in the physical environment, or in the shared traditions of the players, or in the statement of an arbitrator.

Essentially, the focal-point effect tells us that cultural norms, arbitration, and other psychological factors may be very important in such bargaining games with multiple equilibria, even if both players are rational utility-maximizers. This conclusion might be disappointing to economists who expected to predict or explain everything purely from the structure of economic incentives. However, a more realistic view of the scope of economics should allow us to admit a role for social psychology or cultural anthropology.

The focal-point effect creates a link between normative theories of impartial arbitration and positive theories of bargaining. To see why, suppose that a game theorist has derived some formula or criterion that characterizes a unique allocation as the most equitable among all Pareto-efficient allocations. Then an impartial arbitrator who was recommending an agreement to the bargainers might be expected to recommend the allocation that is identified by this formula. But if this formula has been published and is known to the players in the bargaining game, then they will know what allocation would have been recommended by an impartial arbitrator even when they

are bargaining without any arbitrator present. Then the fact that this allocation would have been recommended, if there had been an arbitrator present,
may lead the players to focus on the equilibrium in which each player demands and gets his 'fair share' as defined by our formula, even in the absence
of any arbitrator.

The Nash (1950, 1953) bargaining solution may be interpreted as just
such a formula for determining an equitable and efficient allocation, which
an impartial arbitrator might prescribe, or on which a pair of bargainers
might focus in unarbitrated bargaining. Nash (1950, 1953) derived his solution from a set of axioms which may be interpreted in terms of impartial arbitration. These axioms assert that a symmetric allocation should be selected
in bargaining problems that can be represented symmetrically, and certain
'irrelevant' transformations of the problem should not affect the selected
allocation. The Nash bargaining solution selects the allocation that maximizes
the multiplicative product of the player's utility gains over the disagreement
outcome. In our simple example, if pay-offs would be $0 for both countries
in the absence of any bargained agreement (because the resources in the lake
would be rapidly destroyed) then the Nash bargaining solution is simply to
divide the available wealth equally, $500,000 per year for each nation. We
have already remarked that it is an equilibrium for both nations to demand
such an equal division, in Nash's demand game.

So we may summarize at least three basic lessons from Nash's demand
game. First, equilibrium outcomes of bargaining (in which each player is
rationally responding to the expected behaviour of the other player) may be
very diverse and Pareto-inefficient. In particular, inefficient outcomes (or
high costs of bargaining) may result when each player has wide uncertainty
about the other player's behaviour and expects a high probability of very
aggressive behaviour and a low but positive probability of submissive accom-
modating behaviour. Second, the outcome of bargaining can depend on cultural and psychological factors that transcend the economic parameters of
the situation. In particular, non-binding recommendations of an arbitrator
can determine the outcome of the bargaining game, if the arbitrator has
sufficient prestige to get the attention of the bargainers and if his recommendation is to implement some equilibrium of the game. Third, criteria of
equity and efficiency may have some significance in determining the outcome
in unarbitrated bargaining, if the players are predisposed to focus on the
allocations that satisfy these criteria and if these criteria can be clearly applied
to the existing situation.

MULTIPLE EQUILIBRIA IN DYNAMIC BARGAINING

The above conclusions may be exposed to doubt by the highly unrealistic
nature of Nash's demand game. Most prominently, the assumption that

bargaining must terminate in disagreement if the players' initial demands are jointly infeasible seems particularly unrealistic. One might wonder whether this assumption is responsible for our conclusion that bargaining outcomes may be inefficient. In fact, dropping this assumption does not substantially change our conclusions. This result was argued informally by Schelling (1960) and later formalized in extensive game models (for example, see Van Damme, Selten, and Winter (1990) and chapter 8 of Myerson (1991)).

Dropping the single-demand assumption means going to a sequential-demand model. So let us assume that there is an infinite sequence of points in time at which the bargainers can submit demands, until they submit a pair of jointly feasible demands, at which point bargaining stops and they both get their demands. To be specific, let us suppose that the bargainers submit their new demands at 9.00 a.m. each day, until a feasible agreement is reached.

When we allow bargainers to make a sequence of offers over time, we must take account of the cost of waiting for an agreement. So let us suppose that each player evaluates income streams at a 10 per cent annual interest rate. That is, suppose that an investment giving \$1,000,000 per year (= \$2739.73 per day) would have a present discounted value of \$10,000,000. Then any arbitrary stream of profits $(\pi_0, \pi_1, \pi_2, \ldots)$, where π_k is the profits earned on day k and today is day 1, has present discounted value

$$\sum_{k=1}^{\infty} \delta^k \pi_{k'}$$

where the daily discount factor is

$$\delta = 0.9997261.$$

We suppose that the players' daily incomes in the bargaining game are equal to some given disagreement level until they make jointly feasible demands, and thereafter each gets the income streams that he or she demanded. Each player's objective is to maximize the expected present discounted value of his income stream. In our simple example, where the players are nations 1 and 2, demands are feasible if they sum to at most \$1,000,000 per year or \$2739.73 per day. For now, let us suppose that the disagreement incomes are \$0. (The reader might imagine that the lake's resources have already been destroyed, and the bargaining question is how to allocate the harvest which will begin immediately on the day that pollution stops and the lake is restocked with fish.)

This game has an enormous range of equilibria, which may be efficient or inefficient, just like Nash's simple one-period demand game. As before, for any number X between 0 and 1,000,000, there is an equilibrium in which nation 1 plans always to demand income from the lake at an annual rate of \$X, and nation 2 plans always to demand income at an annual rate of \$1,000,000 − X, and so an agreement at $(X, 1,000,000 - X)$ is reached on the first day of bargaining. To see why any such scenario is an equilibrium, consider an extreme case where X is 900,000, and so nation 1 is demanding 90 per cent of the income from the lake. If nation 1 would always demand 90 per cent of the income, then nation 2 could never hope to get more than 10 per cent of the income. It would be better for nation 2 to start getting this 10 per cent sooner rather than later, and so demanding only 10 per cent is the optimal response for nation 2. Conversely, if nation 1 always expects nation 2 to demand only 10 per cent at the next bargaining session, then nation 1 should always bring a demand for 90 per cent of the income. Such an equilibrium, in which nation 1 demands most of the income and nation 2 demands only a small fraction, may be called a '2-submissive equilibrium'. Similarly, there are '1-submissive equilibria' in which nation 1 demands only a small share of the income and nation 2 would always demand all the rest. Of course, there is also an equilibrium in which the two nations expect to share the income equally (in the case where $X = 500,000$).

All of the equilibria described in the preceding paragraph are efficient, although some may seem quite unequitable. It is also easy to construct inefficient randomized equilibria for this sequential-demand bargaining game. In particular, we can construct a 'stand-off equilibrium' as follows. Suppose that, every day, each player randomizes between two options: either demand 10 per cent of the income ($100,000 per year = $274 per day) with probability Q, or demand 90 per cent of the income ($900,000 per year = $2466 per day) with probability $1 - Q$. If this scenario is to be an equilibrium, then each player must get the same expected present-discounted value from each of the following two strategies (both of which he uses with positive probability, when $0 < Q < 1$): demand only 10 per cent of the profits today (and so immediately reach agreement), or demand 90 per cent today and then demand 10 per cent tomorrow if a feasible agreement is not reached today. The first strategy is sure to give nation 1 a present discounted value of $1,000,000 (= 10 per cent of an income stream worth $10,000,000 in present discounted value). The second strategy gives nation 1 a present discounted value of either $9,000,000 (= 90 per cent of an income stream worth $10,000,000) with probability Q, or $1,000,000\delta = $999,726 (where the daily discount factor δ appears because of the cost of waiting one day to get 10 per cent of an income stream worth $10,000,000) with probability $1 - Q$. To make nation 1 willing to randomize between these two strategies, we must have

$$1,000,000 = (1 - Q) \times 999,726 + Q \times 9,000,000$$

and so

$$Q = 0.0000342, \quad 1 - Q = 0.9999658.$$

This number Q, the probability of any one side conceding on any given day, is remarkably low. For each nation, the time until it will lower its demand from 90 per cent to 10 per cent (if the other nation does not concede first) has a geometric distribution with an expected value of approximately 29,000 days or 80 years! Both nations get an expected present discounted value of only $1,000,000 in this equilibrium; that is, both sides expect only 10 per cent of the potential profits of the lake. The other 80 per cent is lost to the costs of delay in a long bargaining process.

To understand this stand-off equilibrium, notice that the cost of waiting another day to accept 10 per cent of the profits is quite small, only about $274, and so a very small probability of getting 90 per cent of the profits (and thus increasing present discounted value of income by $8,000,000 = $9,000,000 − $1,000,000) may be sufficient to make each player willing to wait another day, in hopes of a possible concession from the other side. On any given day, one side would not want to concede at all if the probability of the other nation conceding were larger than 274/8,000,000 = 0.0000342. The essential problem is that both sides are making such extreme demands that neither side has much incentive to concede.

It might seem that a bargainer could get out of such a standoff equilibrium by making a more moderate demand, to give his opponent more incentive to reach an agreement quickly. It is easy to see that a more moderate demand from nation 1 would not necessarily elicit a matching concession from nation 2, if nation 2 expected nation 1 to go back to withdraw the moderate demand before nation 2 could accept it. So let us now suppose that offers cannot be withdrawn. That is, let us modify the rules of the sequential-demand bargaining game by supposing that a player is not allowed to increase his demands over time. Even with this modification, there still exists a standoff equilibrium in which both sides get expected present discounted values of only 10 per cent of the efficient total. To sustain this standoff equilibrium, it is only necessary to modify our above construction of the standoff equilibrium in one way: if either nation j ever lowers its demand below 90 per cent of the profits, then both sides will expect future behaviour to be as in a j-submissive equilibrium. Thus, for example, if nation 1 ever reduced its demand to some amount between 90 per cent and 10 per cent, then nation 2 thereafter would always expect nation 1's next demand to be only 10 per cent, and so nation 2 would never want to reduce its own demand below 90 per cent. Thus nation 1 is inhibited from making moderate demands by the anticipation that such moderation would merely cause nation 2 to expect more submissive concessions from nation 1.

This same kind of logic can support almost any pattern of demands and concessions that eventually lead to an agreement that gives some positive gains to both sides. There is, for example, an equilibrium in which both sides make extreme demands for exactly seven years and then agree to split the profits equally, after seven wasted years of bargaining. To support this outcome in equilibrium, we may suppose that each side believes that, if it ever lowered its demand below 100 per cent of the profits during the first seven years of stand-off, then it would always be expected thereafter to submit and accept a mere 10 per cent of the profits. After the seven years of stand-off have passed, then each side will confidently expect the other side to demand 50 per cent at all bargaining sessions thereafter, and so each side will then find it optimal to demand 50 per cent, and thus an agreement will be reached. In general, almost any cultural definition of what is the 'right offer at the right time' can be sustained in such a rational equilibrium of our sequential-demand bargaining game. Examples of such equilibria have been discussed by Schelling (1960).

Thus, the general lessons from the simple one-stage demand game can be extended to a sequential-demand bargaining game. There are multiple equilibria that essentially cover the set of all feasible pay-off allocations that are (at least slightly) better than perpetual disagreement for both players. Environmental factors, cultural traditions, arbitration, standards of equity and efficiency, and psychological manipulation can all play a role in deter-mining which equilibrium may be focal and thus implemented by the players. From this perspective, the ideal bargaining strategy is to identify the best possible outcome about which you can convincingly say: 'It is obviously fair for me to demand this much. I could not offer any concessions below this point without giving you the impression that I would submit to anything. I am sure that you understand this and I look forward to your acceptance of this demand.'

Game theorists have sought escape from this enormous multiplicity of equilibria by considering refinements of equilibria and other rules for the bargaining game. Two notable examples are the smoothed demand games of Nash (1953) and the alternating-offer bargaining games of Rubinstein (1982). These games generate unique (subgame-perfect) equilibria that can be very useful for making theoretical predictions about the impact of chang-ing various economic parameters, when all else is held fixed. However, the uniqueness of subgame-perfect equilibria in the models of Rubinstein (1982) is a very delicate technical result, easily lost when incomplete informa-tion or simultaneous offers or indivisible monetary units are introduced into the model (see Myerson, 1991: ch. 8). Furthermore, the models with unique equilibria have very large sets of approximate equilibria (that is, ε-equilibria) that cannot be ruled out if players are only slightly less than rational. Thus, it is hard to escape the logical conclusion that the economic parameters alone do not determine the outcomes of bargaining. Culture and psychology have a role in determining the outcome, and the role of these factors can be recognized within economic analysis itself through the focal-point effect.

PROBLEMS OF ARBITRATION

The multiplicity of bargaining equilibria lead us to understand the potential importance of arbitration as a way systematically to focus bargainers on efficient equilibria in bargaining games. Indeed, the scarcity of reputable arbitrators who can facilitate international bargaining may be a fundamental problem in our contemporary world system. Of course, it is not a trivial matter to find someone who can arbitrate between great powers. Arbitration gives power, and power to judge nations is an enormous and potentially corrupting power. An international arbitrator must be an individual of great prestige (so that his or her recommendations will be respected) and must be disciplined so as not to abuse his or her power. For any given international dispute, an arbitrator might be a leader of a neutral nation, a retired president, a religious leader, an international judicial panel, or a commission sponsored by a multinational organization. An arbitrative authority that could exercise focal leadership systematically in all international disputes with minimal danger of abuse would probably have to derive both its prestige and its discipline from some kind of world political system. We may speculate that, if there were a global president who was elected by the population of the world at large but had no formal governmental powers, he or she would act as an arbitrator (or a certifier of arbitrators) and thus could help to get international bargaining processes away from inefficient stand-off equilibria.

At least three cautions about arbitration are in order here. First, we must recognize the 'chilling effect': that players who anticipate a future arbitration process, which will use the current status quo as a bench-mark to determine equitable recommendations, may find that they now have a positive incentive to harm one another to get a relative advantage in the status quo. That is, the anticipation of arbitration tomorrow may make parties more belligerent today. Nash's (1953) theory of rational threats is a formal model of this chilling effect. For example, suppose that there would be W dollars available to divide in an agreement, but each player i would get v_i by himself in the status quo, without any agreement. (Here $W > v_1 + v_2$.) Suppose that an arbitrator would be expected to lead the players to divide W in such a way as to equalize their gains over disagreement. Then player 1 expects to get

$$(W + v_1 - v_2)/2$$

after arbitration. But then, before arbitration, player 1 would be willing to invest resources in lowering player 2's disagreement payoff v_2, even if the cost included some smaller decrease in W or v_1.

Second, we should note that finding the Pareto-efficient frontier is not a trivial problem in most real-life situations. Much of the applied bargaining literature (see Fisher and Ury, 1981, for example) is concerned mainly with the problem of identifying opportunities for mutually beneficial exchanges in the various terms of a complex bargaining agreement. Finding such Pareto-improving opportunities involves assessing each bargainer's preferences and trade-offs over the set of possible collective decisions, rather than simply exchanging demands.

Third, we should note that an arbitrator can do damage if he misunderstands the bargainers' preferences or serves contrary preferences of his own.

Crawford's (1979, 1981) analysis of final-offer arbitration gives very nice insights into this problem. To illustrate Crawford's results, consider a simple example as follows. There are two players, 1 and 2. The set of feasible utility allocations for the two players is

$$F = [(x_1, x_w) \mid x_1 \geq 0, x_2 \geq 0, 2x_1 + 2x_2 \leq 150, x_1 + 2x_2 \leq 150].$$

This feasible region has corners at (0,0), (75,0), (50,50), and (75,0). Each player i wants to maximize his expected utility payoff x_i. Suppose, however, that the arbitrator will use the following rather perverse criterion to select his recommendation: he will recommend the feasible allocation that minimizes the quantity $(x_1)^2 + (x_2)^2$.

To prevent such a perverse arbitrator from doing too much damage to the players' interests, a number of procedures have been proposed for restricting an arbitrator's range of choice. One of the best-known of these procedures is 'final-offer arbitration'. Under final-offer arbitration, each player must submit a proposed allocation to the arbitrator, and the arbitrator must select one of the two proposals that are submitted to him. Crawford showed that this procedure creates a game in which the unique equilibrium is for both players to submit the proposal that is best according to the arbitrator's criterion, that is (0,0) for this example! If player 1 were proposing any feasible allocation (x_1, x_2) such that $x_1 > 0$, then there would exist a feasible proposal (y_1, y_2) such that $y_2 > x_2$ and $(y_1)^2 + (y_2)^2 < (x_1)^2 + (x_2)^2$. So, in a non-randomized equilibrium, player 1 cannot be submitting the proposal that the arbitrator selects unless player 1 is giving himself 0. A similar argument holds for player 2. So we cannot rely on final-offer arbitration to mitigate the effects of a perverse arbitrator. The failure of final-offer arbitration to help the players in this example is particularly striking because final-offer arbitration does succeed in leading them to an 'agreement' before the action of the arbitrator, in that both players are offering (0,0). Thus, when arbitration is anticipated, a seemingly voluntary agreement may actually be quite inefficient.

Consider now the following modification of final-offer arbitration. As before, each player submits a primary offer (which must be a feasible utility allocation) to the arbitrator, who then selects the offer that is better by his (perverse) criterion. Then, the player who has proposed the selected offer (call him the 'primary winner') is allowed to propose another feasible allocation as a secondary (or 'post-final') offer. Then, under the rules of this procedure, the arbitrator must let the other player (the primary loser) choose between the primary winner's primary offer and secondary offer. The arbitrator's ultimate recommendation is required to be the allocation chosen by the primary loser at this second stage.

Under this procedure, the primary winner's best secondary offer will be the best feasible allocation for himself subject to the constraint that the primary loser should not be worse off than in the primary offer selected by the arbitrator. Thus, the ultimate recommendation under this procedure will be Pareto-efficient (at least in a complete-information example such as this). However, this procedure still gives the players a strong incentive to please the (perverse) arbitrator in their primary offers. Thus, there is still an equilibrium in which both players make the same primary offer (0,0). Let us suppose that, in the case of a primary-offer tie, the arbitrator will randomly select one of the two players to be the 'primary winner' who makes the secondary offer. Then the outcome will be (75,0) if player 1 is selected to make the secondary offer, and the outcome will be (0,75) if player 2 is selected. So the expected utility outcome in equilibrium will be (37.5, 37.5). This expected utility allocation is better than (0,0), but it is still not Pareto-efficient.

Now consider another modification of final-offer arbitration that differs from the above procedure only in that the primary loser (that is, the player whose primary offer is not selected by the arbitrator) is now the player who gets to make the secondary offer. Under this procedure, the ultimate outcome is chosen by the primary winner from among his own primary offer and the primary loser's secondary offer.

Under this procedure, the primary loser's right to make the secondary offer reduces the incentive to become the primary winner. There is an equilibrium in which player 1's primary offer is (50,0) and player 2's primary offer is (0,50). Then, no matter which player wins the primary arbitration stage, the primary loser's secondary offer and the ultimate outcome of the game will be (50,50), which is Pareto-efficient (and is Pareto-superior to the expected equilibrium outcomes from the procedures discussed previously). To verify that this scenario is an equilibrium, notice that player 1 would not change the outcome if he asked for more in his primary offer (because player 2 would just be the primary winner), and player 1 could only reduce his ultimate pay-off below 50 if he asked for less than 50 in his primary offer. Notice that this procedure succeeds in guaranteeing a risk-free Pareto-efficient outcome in equilibrium even though, unlike the two procedures discussed above, this procedure does not drive the players to a 'voluntary' pre-arbitration consensus in their primary offers.

Rubinstein's (1982) analysis of alternating-offer games suggests that unarbitrated alternating-offer games can also guarantee Pareto-efficient outcomes in bargaining problems with complete information. However, neither the alternating-offer game nor the two-stage arbitration procedure discussed above can guarantee Pareto-efficient outcomes when we drop the assumption that players know everything about each other's preferences.

MEDIATION

Once we admit that the various players in a bargaining game have incomplete information about each others' preferences, the question of substantive communication comes into the analysis of bargaining. The need for communication introduces a second role for outside interveners in the bargaining process: mediation.

From a theoretical perspective, arbitration and mediation can be distinguished as logically different roles, although any one individual may fill both of them to varying degrees. From the perspective of game theory, (nonbinding) arbitration is any act of judging to determine a focal equilibrium of a bargaining process. Mediation may be defined to be any act that communicates and filters information between the various players in the bargaining process.

To appreciate the need for mediation, let us reconsider our example of bargaining over the lake, but now suppose that the value to each nation of allowing unrestricted pollution of the lake is unknown to the other side. To be specific, let us suppose that each nation (or its prime minister) has an independent probability ½ of being indifferent between the disagreement outcome (in which the lake is freely polluted) and getting 60 per cent of the harvest from the unpolluted lake, in which case we may say that the nation's type is 'strong'. If a nation's type is not strong then it would evaluate the disagreement outcome as worth $0, and so any positive fraction of the harvest from the unpolluted lake would be preferred to disagreement; in this case we may say that the nation's type is 'weak'. We assume that, when the two sides begin to bargain over the allocation of profits from the lake, each side knows its own type, but thinks that the other's type is equally likely to be weak or strong.

In this case, it is clear that no mutually beneficial agreement is possible if both sides are strong, which happens with probability ¼. When one side is weak and the other side is strong, then a mutually beneficial agreement is possible, provided that the strong side gets more than 60 per cent of the profits. So we might suppose that, when one nation is strong and the other is weak, the outcome should be that the profits from the unpolluted lake should be divided in some asymmetric fashion, for example 70 per cent for the strong nation and 30 per cent for the weak nation. When both nations are weak, we might expect them to keep the lake unpolluted and share the profits equally, 50 per cent for each.

The problem with this plan is that it requires the two nations to reveal their types, and neither nation should want to admit weakness first. After one side has announced weakness, the other side knows that it can get a larger share by claiming to be strong, even if it is weak. So we have a dilemma: no nonpolluting agreement is possible unless at least one side admits to being weak, but neither side wants to be the first to admit that it is weak.

A mediator can help the bargainers to solve this first-announcement problem, by taking confidential reports from the two sides before the recommended outcome is announced to both. That is, a mediator can meet separately with the representative of each nation and ask him confidentially to report his nation's type. Then it is an equilibrium for both sides to report honestly to a mediator if the mediator is expected to follow these meetings with an arbitrative recommendation that depends on the reports as follows:

| | | Nation 2's report | |
		'Strong'	'Weak'
Nation 1's report	'Strong'	no agreement	70%, 30%
	'Weak'	30%, 70%	50%, 50%

(The percentages shown are the shares, for nations 1 and 2 respectively, of the harvest after a non-pollution agreement.)

The key to this mediation plan is that each side reports to the mediator without knowing the report of the other side, so a weak nation would get higher expected profits by admitting weakness [$(\frac{1}{2}) \times 0.30 + (\frac{1}{2}) \times 0.50$] than by claiming to be strong [$(\frac{1}{2}) \times 0 + (\frac{1}{2}) \times 0.70$], when the other nation is expected to report honestly. Adding a mediator (who acts as an information-holder) enables each side to reveal information without reducing the other side's incentive to reveal information. We may say that this mediation plan is 'incentive-compatible', which means that honest participation by all players is an equilibrium of the mediated bargaining game when the outcome will depend on the players' reports according to this plan.

Some mediation plans may be infeasible, because even with a confidential mediator they would generate incentives for someone to lie or withhold information. For example, it would not be an equilibrium for both sides to communicate honestly with the mediator if he were expected to implement the following plan:

| | | Nation 2's report | |
		'Strong'	'Weak'
Nation 1's report	'Strong'	no agreement	80%, 20%
	'Weak'	20%, 80%	50%, 50%

If nation 2 were expected to report honestly, then a weak nation 1 would get a higher expected share by lying and claiming to be strong [$(\frac{1}{2}) \times 0 + (\frac{1}{2}) \times 0.80$] than by honestly reporting its weakness [$(\frac{1}{2}) \times 0.20 + (\frac{1}{2}) \times 0.50$]. So this mediation plan is not incentive compatible.

The 'revelation principle' (see Myerson, 1985, for example) asserts that any equilibrium of any communication game can be simulated by a mediator who meets separately and confidentially with each player, and who uses the players' statements according to an incentive-compatible mediation plan. The set of all incentive-compatible mediation plans, which make honest reporting an equilibrium, is straightforward to characterize mathematically. This mathematical simplicity makes it possible to characterize optimal mediation plans (given any social objective function) for many bargaining problems with incomplete information.

For example, suppose we change the above example by saying that each player thinks that the other player has a probability 0.9 of being weak (instead of probability ½). Then there is no incentive-compatible mediation plan that can guarantee prompt agreement whenever gains from agreement exist (whenever at least one player is weak). For example, consider a mediation plan that allocates only 60 per cent of the profits to a nation that claims to be a strong nation when the other reports that it is weak, and divides the profits equally when both nations report that they are weak. That is, consider the plan:

| | | Nation 2's report | |
		'Strong'	'Weak'
Nation 1's report	'Strong'	no agreement	60%, 40%
	'Weak'	40%, 60%	50%, 50%

This plan would not be incentive-compatible because a weak nation would get a higher expected share of the potential profits by claiming to be strong if the other nation was expected to be honest ($0.1 \times 0 + 0.9 \times 60 > 0.1 \times 40 + 0.9 \times 50$). By the revelation principle, if there is no incentive-compatible mechanism that guarantees an efficient agreement, then there is no equilibrium of any bargaining game that can guarantee an efficient agreement in this example. That is, when bargainers are uncertain about each others' preferences, informational incentive constraints (that is, the need to give people an incentive to reveal their relevant private information) may make it impossible for any equilibrium of any bargaining game to guarantee that all possible gains from agreement will be realized (with probability 1).

To design a good mediation plan for this example, we may ask what is the lowest probability of inefficient disagreement that we must tolerate, when one nation is strong and the other is weak, to make an incentive-compatible mediation plan. The answer for this example is 1/10. To see why, consider a mediation plan in which, if both nations claim to be strong then there will be no agreement, if only one nation reports that it is strong then with probability P there will be an agreement to given the strong nation 60 per cent of the profits (and with probability $1 - P$ there will be no agreement), and if both nations report that they are weak then there will be an agreement to each take 50 per cent of the profits. Then incentive compatibility requires that P must satisfy

$$0.1 \times P \times 40 + 0.9 \times 50 \geq 0.1 \times 0 + 0.9 \times P \times 60,$$

so that a weak nation's expected share is greater from honesty than from claiming to be strong, when the other nation is expected to be honest. (Recall that each nation is now supposed to think that the probability of the other nation being weak is 0.9). This informational incentive constraint algebraically implies that $9/10 \geq P$, and so $1 - P \leq 1/10$.

Thus, bargaining outcomes can be improved by mediation (that is, confidential communication channels), as well as by improved international understanding (which would eliminate the uncertainty about each other's type that created the need for mediation in this example). For more on incentive compatibility and the design of efficient mediation plans, see Myerson (1991: chs. 6 and 10; 1992).

The above mediation plan involves a 1/10 probability of permanent disagreement when one nation is strong and the other is weak. But if disagreement is recommended when one nation is weak, why should the weak nation not follow the recommendation by a subsequent offer to settle for 40 per cent (or perhaps 39 per cent) of the profits? It is important to the incentive-compatibility of our plan that a recommendation to disagree would be obeyed and would not be followed by subsequent offers that lead to an agreement. If nation 1 anticipated that nation 2 would, if weak, make such an offer after a recommendation to disagree, then a weak nation 1 would get a higher expected share by claiming to be strong than by honestly admitting weakness ($0.1 \times 0 + 0.9 \times 60 > 0.1 \times 40 + 0.9 \times 50$). However, such subsequent offers can be inhibited if the parties anticipate behaviour as in a stand-off equilibrium after disagreement has been recommended. That is, a weak nation would have no incentive to make a subsequent offer if it were understood that the strong nation would then expect the weak nation rapidly to follow this offer by further concessions, until the weak nation's share of the profits dropped to 0. So, our incentive-compatible mediation plan requires that the parties may, in some cases, be steered to expect standoff-equilibrium behaviour in all bargaining that might follow the mediator's deadline for concessions.

In effect, the mediation function must be complemented by an arbitration function in third-party intervention. It is worth noting that mediation is a distinct function from focal arbitration, although these two functions are often performed by the same individual. Mediation means providing a confidential channel for communicating private information, whereas arbitration means evaluating and recommending possible outcomes. In international bargaining, the mediation role imposes different constraints on the qualities of an intervener than does arbitration. An intervener who is only arbitrating has no need for confidentiality. Thus, for example, arbitrative decisions about what should be a fair agreement can be made by a panel of judges. It is not a serious problem if a few of the judges on a purely arbitrative panel are suspected of being partial to one side or the other, as long as the balance of power lies with the judges who are accepted as clearly impartial. However, a mediator must be a single individual who is either acting alone or supported by a tightly disciplined staff. If anyone in the mediator's office is partial to one side, he can undermine the mediation process by leaking information to one side about the other side's concessions. This danger makes it much more difficult to introduce effective mediation into international bargaining.

MULTILATERAL BARGAINING

So far we have only considered bargaining problems that involve two parties. Multilateral bargaining may become even more complicated, but the need for arbitration, to co-ordinate expectations about what each party can demand, and mediation, to facilitate communication of concessions, is no less when many nations are involved.

Game-theoretic concepts like the 'core' and the 'Shapley value' (see Myerson, 1991; ch. 9, for further references) have been developed as tools for analysing the structure of coalitional power in multilateral bargaining problems. An agreement is in the core of a game if there is no coalition that could guarantee a better outcome for all of its members. Unfortunately, for many games with three or more players, the core may be empty. When the core is empty, a general co-operative agreement in multilateral bargaining may none the less be sustained by the perception that no partial coalition will be sustained if any one party withdraws from the general agreement. That is, it may be necessary to link all aspects of a multilateral agreement, so that an attempt by one party to renegotiate one term of the agreement would jeopardize every aspect of the agreement. If any party to a multilateral agreement can upset the agreement between everyone else, however, then the need to have well-coordinated expectations about what each party can reasonably demand is even greater than in bilateral bargaining problems.

REFERENCES

Coase, R. H. (1960), 'The Problem of Social Cost', *Journal of Law and Economics*, 3: 1–44.

Crawford, V. (1979), 'On Compulsory-Arbitration Schemes', *Journal of Political Economy*, 87: 131–59.

—— (1981), 'Arbitration and Conflict Resolution in Labour–Management Bargaining', *American Economic Review: Papers and Proceedings*, 71: 205–10.

Fisher, R. and Ury, W. (1981), *Getting to Yes: Negotiating Agreement Without Giving In* (Boston: Houghton Mifflin).

Myerson, R. B. (1985), 'Bayesian Equilibrium and Incentive Compatibility', in L. Hurwicz, D. Schmeidler, and H. Sonnenschein (eds.), *Social Goals and Social Organization* (Cambridge: Cambridge University Press), 229–59.

—— (1991), *Game Theory: Analysis of Conflict* (Cambridge, Mass.: Harvard University Press).

—— (1992), 'Analysis of Incentives in Bargaining and Mediation', in H. P. Young (ed.), *Negotiation Analysis* (University of Michigan Press, 1994).

Nash, J. F. (1950), 'The Bargaining Problem', *Econometrica*, 18: 155–62.

—— (1951), 'Non-cooperative Games', *Annals of Mathematics*, 54: 289–95.

—— (1953), 'Two-Person Cooperative Games', *Econometrica*, 21: 128–40.

Rubinstein, A. (1982), 'Perfect Equilibrium in a Bargaining Model', *Econometrica*, 50: 97–109.

Schelling, T. C. (1960), *The Strategy of Conflict* (Cambridge, Mass.: Harvard University Press).

Van Damme, E., Selten, R., and Winter, E. (1990), 'Alternating Bid Bargaining with a Smallest Money Unit', *Games and Economic Behavior*, 2: 188–201.

3

International River Basins: Pervasive Unidirectional Externalities

Peter Rogers

INTRODUCTION

The observations on human use of water in this paper fit under the rubric 'transnational commons', which is part of the title of this Conference. We will discuss the large range of possibilities for conflict and co-operation which arise when a peculiarly strong modern social form, the nation-state, super-imposes itself on a geographical, physical, and natural pattern of intense water-resource interdependency—a river basin.

More than 200 river basins,[1] accounting for more than 50 per cent of the land area of the earth, are shared by two or more countries. The more than 280 treaties that have been signed among countries on water issues give evidence of the tensions that divided basins engender. Two-thirds of these treaties have been in Europe and North America, where the problems first became acute (Vlachos, 1990; Delli Priscoli, 1990). In the rest of the world, large-scale development of water resources has only become widespread during the past couple of decades. By the development of water resources, we mean water diversion, and often storage, to serve agriculture, industries, municipalities, and other uses. Water development in our time is driven by population growth and technological advances such as hydroelectric generation and modernized year-round agriculture; under this heading it is fair to visualize multi-billion dollar, often heroic national enterprises such as the Hoover and Aswan dams, and the irrigation of the North China plain. A world-wide perception of global water scarcity, relative to the emerging uses and needs for water of larger populations, is historically new, and the accompanying conflicts have only just begun to manifest themselves. Rapid population and economic growth in many parts of the world are severely stressing natural resources, so much so that water is beginning to have a scarcity value and an emotional intensity resembling that of petroleum.

The author wishes to thank the following persons for their help with this chapter: Dr John Quinn helped with recalculating many of the game solutions; Linda Klaamas worked on editing and bibliographical research, particularly the material dealing with the International Law Commission; Peter Lydon read the manuscript carefully and edited the entire paper; and Professor Robert Dorfman made very helpful suggestions on an early draft.

[1] The United Nations (1978) lists 241 'shared' rivers; 148 flow through two countries, 31 through three countries, and the remaining 62 flow through four or more countries.

The concern with international river basins and the need to move quickly with mechanisms to defuse conflicts before they become deeply entrenched is also part of the current interest in global environmental issues. Most of these are by nature transnational, but the stakes in transboundary water conflicts, being more tangible and closer to home, are perceived more sharply by the individual participants than the stakes in the protection of the global ozone layer. Unlike ozone, water problems also usually present a neighbouring nation or people as an antagonist, which tends to intensify popular emotions, combine water issues with other historical grievances, and favour the combative set of attitudes associated with zero-sum situations. The growth of interest in international rivers is reflected by the dedication of the entire December 1990 issue of *Water International* to international water conflicts.

Table 3.1 shows the details of some of the largest international rivers and Fig. 3.1 shows their locations around the world. Some of the largest rivers have multiple riparians and countries within the drainage basins, like the Danube (with 14 nations), the Nile (with 11), the Niger (with 9), the Zambezi (with 9), the Amazon (with 9), the Congo (with 7), the Rhine (with 7), the Mekong (with 6), the Brahmaputra (with 4), and the Ganges (with 4).

Table 3.1. The largest international rivers of the world

River	Riparian countries	Interesting features
Amazon	Bolivia, Brazil, Colombia, Ecuador, French Guiana, Guyana, Peru, Surinam, Venezuela	The river touches the Colombia border; branches to Ecuador include the Curaray River. The basin borders on French Guiana, Guyana, Surinam, and Venezuela
Amur	China, Mongolia, former USSR	Forms part of the border between China and former USSR. Breaks off into two branches, one of which goes into Mongolia
Brahmaputra	Bangladesh, Bhutan, China, India	
Columbia	Canada, United States	
Congo or Zaïre	Congo, Zaïre	Forms part of Congo–Zaïre border. Tributaries run from Angola, Cameroon, Central African Republic, Zaïre, and Zambia
Danube	Albania, Austria, Bulgaria, Czech Republic, France, Germany, Greece, Hungary, Italy, Poland, Romania, Switzerland, former USSR, Yugoslavia	Forms parts of Bulgaria–Romania and Hungary–Yugoslavia borders
Elbe	Czech Republic, Germany	
Ganges	Bangladesh, China, India, Nepal	Branches from the main river stem into Nepal. Smaller River Alaknanda flows from China into Ganges at western tip

Table 3.1. *(cont.)*

Indus	Afghanistan, China, India, Pakistan	
Mekong	Cambodia, China, Laos, Thailand, Union of Myanmar, Vietnam	Forms parts of Laos–Thailand and Laos–Myanmar borders
Mississippi	Canada, United States	
Niger	Algeria, Benin, Burkina Faso, Cameroon, Côte d'Ivoire, Guinea, Mali, Niger, Nigeria	Forms part of Benin–Nigeria border
Nile	Burundi, Central African Republic, Congo, Ethiopia, Egypt, Kenya, Rwanda, Sudan, Tanzania, Uganda, Zaïre	
Orinoco	Colombia, Venezuela	Forms part of Colombia–Venezuela border
Parana	Argentina, Brazil, Paraguay	Forms part of Argentina–Paraguay border
Rhine	Austria, France, Germany, Liechtenstein, Luxembourg, the Netherlands, Switzerland	Forms parts of Austria–Liechtenstein, France–Germany, and France–Switzerland borders
Salween	China, Thailand, Union of Myanmar	Forms parts of Thailand–Myanmar and China–Myanmar borders
Shatt-al Arab (Tigris, Euphrates, Karun)	Iraq, Syria, Turkey	
St Lawrence	Canada, United States	
Uruguay	Argentina, Brazil, Uruguay	Forms part of Argentina–Uruguay border. Flows from Brazil
Yukon	Canada, United States	
Zambezi	Angola, Botswana, Malawi, Mozambique, Namibia, Tanzania, Zaïre, Zambia, Zimbabwe	Forms parts of Zambia–Zimbabwe and Namibia–Zambia borders

Some major international water conflicts, however, are in the Middle East, where rivers are typically much smaller, and where the region is chronically short of water. Managing the waters of the Jordan is a perennial and growing problem among Lebanon, Jordan, Syria, and Israel (Starr and Stoll, 1988). The Turkish and Syrian developments on the Euphrates are sources of friction between these two countries and downstream Iraq (Tekeli, 1990). The sharing of the Nile waters between Egypt and Sudan has so far proceeded in a relatively co-operative atmosphere, which is now being disturbed by Ethiopia and six other upstream riparians (whose territory generates the bulk of the flow), which are now demanding access to use of the water for their own needs (Smith and Al-Rawahy, 1990; Waterbury, 1979; Haynes and Whittington, 1981; Guariso and Whittington, 1987).

With World Bank assistance, India and Pakistan settled a serious conflict over the use of the Indus which was precipitated by Partition in 1947, although it took until 1960 to arrive at a satisfactory treaty between the countries (Michel, 1967; Kirmani, 1990). India and Bangladesh have had an

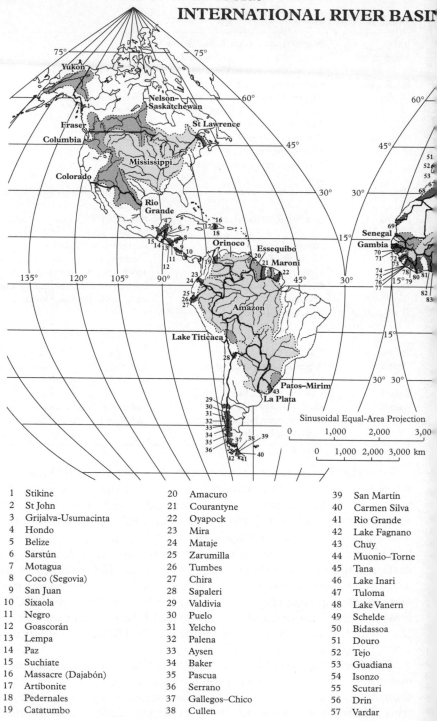

1	Stikine	20	Amacuro	39	San Martín
2	St John	21	Courantyne	40	Carmen Silva
3	Grijalva-Usumacinta	22	Oyapock	41	Rio Grande
4	Hondo	23	Mira	42	Lake Fagnano
5	Belize	24	Mataje	43	Chuy
6	Sarstún	25	Zarumilla	44	Muonio–Torne
7	Motagua	26	Tumbes	45	Tana
8	Coco (Segovia)	27	Chira	46	Lake Inari
9	San Juan	28	Sapaleri	47	Tuloma
10	Sixaola	29	Valdivia	48	Lake Vanern
11	Negro	30	Puelo	49	Schelde
12	Goascorán	31	Yelcho	50	Bidassoa
13	Lempa	32	Palena	51	Douro
14	Paz	33	Aysen	52	Tejo
15	Suchiate	34	Baker	53	Guadiana
16	Massacre (Dajabón)	35	Pascua	54	Isonzo
17	Artibonite	36	Serrano	55	Scutari
18	Pedernales	37	Gallegos–Chico	56	Drin
19	Catatumbo	38	Cullen	57	Vardar

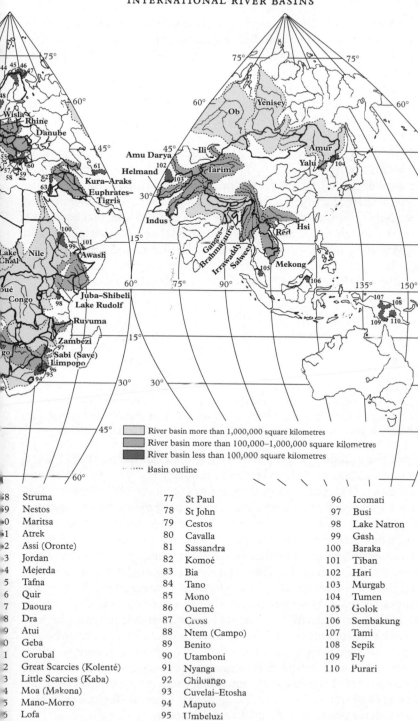

River basin more than 1,000,000 square kilometres
River basin more than 100,000–1,000,000 square kilometres
River basin less than 100,000 square kilometres
········· Basin outline

58	Struma	77	St Paul	96	Icomati
59	Nestos	78	St John	97	Busi
60	Maritsa	79	Cestos	98	Lake Natron
61	Atrek	80	Cavalla	99	Gash
62	Assi (Oronte)	81	Sassandra	100	Baraka
63	Jordan	82	Komoé	101	Tiban
64	Mejerda	83	Bia	102	Hari
65	Tafna	84	Tano	103	Murgab
66	Quir	85	Mono	104	Tumen
67	Daoura	86	Oueme	105	Golok
68	Dra	87	Cross	106	Sembakung
69	Atui	88	Ntem (Campo)	107	Tami
70	Geba	89	Benito	108	Sepik
71	Corubal	90	Utamboni	109	Fly
72	Great Scarcies (Kolenté)	91	Nyanga	110	Purari
73	Little Scarcies (Kaba)	92	Chiloango		
74	Moa (Makona)	93	Cuvelai–Etosha		
75	Mano-Morro	94	Maputo		
76	Lofa	95	Umbeluzi		

Fig. 3.1. International rivers of the world

Source: UN Map no. 1026 rev. 1.

unresolved water dispute since 1975 concerning diversions by the Farakka Barrage on the Ganges in India, and co-operative augmentation of dry-season water supplies in that monsoon zone (Zaman, 1983; Abbas, 1984; Islam, 1987; Begum, 1987). The Bangladesh floods of 1987 and 1988 reopened the question of basin-wide management for high flows between these two countries (Rogers *et al.*, 1989). Problems have already arisen, or are expected shortly, on the Amazon, the Niger, the Senegal (LeMarquand, 1990), and the Zambezi rivers.

Furthermore, water often crosses international boundaries underground, and problems are now arising concerning the use of the North-eastern African aquifer shared by Libya, Egypt, Chad, and Sudan; the Northern Sahara Basin shared by Algeria, Tunisia, and Libya; the Chad aquifers shared by Chad, Niger, Sudan, Nigeria, and Cameroon; the lower reaches of the Rhine recharge aquifers shared by Denmark, the Netherlands, and Germany; and aquifers along the southern border of the United States shared with Mexico. Much of the discussion about international river basins gives insufficient attention to this important ground-water resource.

CAUSES OF CONFLICT: PERVASIVE UNIDIRECTIONAL EXTERNALITIES

An externality occurs whenever an action taken by some economic unit has a direct impact upon the welfare or productivity of some other economic unit. When the medium through which the external effect or externality is transmitted is physical, that medium is a common property resource. (Dorfman and Dorfman, 1972)

In applying this definition to international rivers, LeMarquand (1977) stated that: 'An international river is a common property resource shared among the basin states.' Water used in river basins has the interesting property that both positive and negative externalities usually have their effect in only one direction, that is, downstream. An upstream country affects the volume or quality of a downstream country's water by diverting or polluting it, but the downstream country cannot do the reverse, since it has no access to the water until it has left the upstream country. Since, given enough time, water is the universal solvent and the major geomorphological transport mechanism, the externalities are caused not only by intentional water-uses but also by other natural and human activities occurring in the upstream reaches, such as intensification of agriculture or forestry. This unidirectional feature of water use means that resolution of basin conflicts through mutual control of external effects that work reciprocally is generally ruled out. The downstream partners must often balance the asymmetrical water relationships by the use or exchange of resources from outside the water domain—for example, economic or military power—in the upstream direction.

Table 3.2 gives a list of the major downstream effects of water use and non-water use in upstream reaches. Note that although rivers flow in only one direction, these upstream activities can produce externalities that have a positive as well as a negative impact on downstream users. The traditional uses are hydro-power for peak and base-load power production, irrigation diversions, municipal and industrial diversions, maintenance of flow for navigation or for adequate dilution of waste-water, or for general ecological values, storage for flood control and recreation, and the development of ground-water. The table also lists some of the non-water uses which cause externalities. These typically involve land-use changes occasioned by agriculture, forestry, animal husbandry, filling wetlands, and urban and suburban development. There are also, however, natural processes that cause downstream effects, which are often mistaken for externalities. Large and small landslides, sometimes provoked by earthquakes, in fragile high mountain environments such as the Himalayas, generate huge sediment loads in the

Table 3.2. Downstream effects of upstream water use

Water use	Downstream effect	
	Positive	Negative
Direct		
Hydro-power		
base load	Helps regulate river	
peak load		Creates additional peaks
Irrigation diversions		Removes water from system
Flood storage	Provides downstream flood protection	
Municipal and industrial diversions		Removes water from the system
Waste-water treatment		Adds pollution to the river
Navigation	Keeps water in the river	
Recreation storage		Keeps water out of the system
Ecological maintenance	Keeps low flows in river	
Ground-water development		Reduces ground-water availability; reduces stream flows
Indirect		
Agriculture		Adds sediment and agricultural chemicals
Forestry		Adds sediment and chemicals; increases run-off
Animal husbandry		Adds sediment and nutrients
Filling wetlands		Reduces ecological carrying capacity; increases floods
Urban development		Induces flooding; adds pollutants
Mineral deposits		Adds chemicals to surface and ground-water

rivers that bring drainage congestion and flooding, as well as fertility, down-stream. Natural deposits of salts and heavy metals contaminate ground- and surface-waters by leaching through them. The selenium damage caused by the irrigation drainage waters reaching the Kesterton wildlife sanctuary in California and the increasing salinity of the Colorado River are examples of external effects caused jointly by man and nature.

The sediment–drainage congestion–flooding sequence is often used to call for basin-wide management of land-use practices, but recent literature is equivocal about cause and effect relationships in this regard. Repetto (1987) summarizes studies from Indonesia which indicate substantial downstream damage from agriculture and forestry in the upland areas. It has, however, been claimed by some that for the Himalayan region most of the sediment problems are of natural geological origin, not significantly affected by human land uses.

Most of the literature on externalities in river basins focuses on description of the phenomena and their physical quantification rather than on their economic consequences. It will be shown how navigation, flood flows, and salinity effects can be incorporated into economic analysis without specific knowledge of their economic costs by the use of constraints on their physical magnitudes.

A LEGAL BASIS FOR SHARING THE WATERS OF INTERNATIONAL RIVER BASINS

Resolving water conflicts is complicated by the fact that 'an international legal framework to govern the use and development of international rivers by riparian countries does not exist' (Kirmani, 1990). According to Kirmani, at least four major legal framework doctrines about sharing water in international river basins are available. The first is *absolute sovereignty* over waters flowing within a country. This implies that other riparian countries do not have any right to constrain a country's use of a river within its own boundaries, and is obviously preferred by the upper riparians. The second theory is that *the river belongs to its riparians*; this is of great interest to lower riparians since it implies as much right to the waters for downstream as for upstream users. A third approach can be categorized as *optimum development of the river basin*. This theory is attractive to technical water planners since it allows them to consider the basin as a single hydrological unit and plan accordingly. The fourth approach, *reasonable share or equitable use*, expresses respect for a riparian's sovereign right within its territory, but restricts its uses to ensure reasonable shares for the other riparians. The words describing this theory sound so reassuring and reasonable that it is the obvious choice for non-involved third parties; however, depending upon what the stakes are, it is less attractive to upstream riparians than to downstream riparians.

One other doctrine, which has had widespread application in the US West, has been applied to international river basins; *prior appropriation*. Under this doctrine, water rights go to the first user in time; 'first in time, first in right'. While this doctrine is not being specifically promoted for international water law, it is embedded in most of the definitions of 'equitable use', when they refer to conditioning the definition by 'past utilization of the waters'. It is also often explicitly used by the more advanced, more powerful countries in a basin to deny new uses to co-riparians on the grounds that these will affect existing off-takes or uses.

In addition to private efforts such as those of the Institute of International Law and the International Law Association, since 1971 the United Nations' International Law Commission (ILC) has been attempting to establish, with little success, a set of rules pertaining to the sharing of international water resources for purposes other than navigation (Hayton, 1983; Cano, 1989; Sinclair, 1987).

After years of haggling over definitions, in 1976 the members of the ILC agreed to bypass their disagreements and at its 32nd meeting in 1980, the substantive issues in the regulation of international watercourses were delimited in six articles, which were provisionally adopted by the Commission. By 1984 the six-article draft had grown to 41 articles categorized in six chapters. As of July 1991, 27 articles have been provisionally adopted, but it is fair to say that caution in creating or recognizing obligations upon themselves is the dominant note among governments.

The Special Rapporteur's Report of the 39th session (UN, 1987), for example, addressed the 'general principles of co-operation, notification, and provision for data and information'. Article 9, on the general obligation to co-operate, raised further definitional concerns: should the article be more specific? Some members suggested a revision that would define the obligation as one 'to achieve optimum utilization and protection of the water course, based on equality, sovereignty and territorial integrity of the watercourse states concerned'. Others disagreed, saying that a listing of specific criteria for co-operation would destroy the effect of the regulation.

Articles 11 through 21 address planned measures for international river water-courses, focusing on rules of notification and consultation procedure. Although most ILC members recognized the fact that a state has the right to internal sovereignty over its territories, including water resources, they also noted that this does not permit a state to injure another state indirectly through its internal actions. The ILC defined 'wrongful harm' as injury to another party not consistent with the equitable utilization (Articles 6–10) of the water-course.

Articles 22–5 discuss the protection and preservation of international water-courses; they stress control of ecological disruptions such as pollution and the introduction of new species. Articles 26 and 27 of the draft emphasize the need for emergency procedures to deal with natural causes such as floods, ice-breaks, landslides, and earthquakes. The articles proposed beyond Article 27 have not yet received provisional adoption due to the time-constraints of the Commission. The ILC is, however, hoping to approve the first complete draft of articles by the end of 1991.

However, the legal situation is not without some positive developments. Review papers by Caponera (1983) and Hayton (1983) see substantial agreement on a set of important doctrinal issues. They find that the principles of (1) 'prior consultation', (2) 'avoidance of significant injury', (3) 'equitable apportionment', (4) 'non-discrimination and non-exclusion', and (5) 'provision for settlement of disputes' are widely used in water disputes despite the non-existence of a 'set of laws'. These principles are embedded in the Helsinki Rules formulated by the International Law Association in 1966. The heart of the 37-article Helsinki Rules is Article V, whose recommendations are listed in Table 3.3; they are very similar to Article 7 of the provisionally adopted ILC text.

The World Bank has adopted a policy for financing projects on international waterways called Operational Directive 7.50 (World Bank, 1990).

Table 3.3. Article V of the Helsinki Rules[1]

Article V: (1) What is a reasonable and equitable share within the meaning of Article IV is to be determined in the light of all the relevant factors in each particular case.
(2) Relevant factors which are to be considered include, but are not limited to:

- (a) the geography of the basin, including in particular the extent of the drainage area in the territory of each basin state;
- (b) the hydrology of the basin, including in particular the contribution of water by each basin state;
- (c) the climate affecting the basin;
- (d) the past utilization of the waters of the basin, including in particular existing utilization;
- (e) the economic and social needs of each basin state;
- (f) the population dependent on the waters of the basin in each basin state;
- (g) the comparative costs of alternative means of satisfying the economic and social needs of each basin state;
- (h) the availability of other resources;
- (i) the avoidance of unnecessary waste in the utilization of waters of the basin;
- (j) the practicability of compensation to one or more of the co-basin states as a means of adjusting conflicts among uses;
- (k) the degree to which the needs of a basin state may be satisfied, without causing substantial injury to a co-basin state.

(3) The weight to be given to each factor is to be determined by its importance in comparison with that of other relevant factors. In determining what is a reasonable and equitable share, all relevant factors are to be considered together and a conclusion reached on the basis of the whole.

---

[1] Approved by the 52nd Conference of the International Law Association, Helsinki, 1966.

The Directive is based on two main principles: 'no appreciable harm to downstream riparians' and 'equitable sharing by all riparians'. Although the World Bank's policy encourages riparian behaviour that the ILC is attempting to turn into law, Operational Directive 7.50 requires updating since it completely ignores the important issue of transnational ground-water flows. One need only refer to El-Hindi's (1990) article to gauge the severity with which this type of situation is viewed by riparians.

The Bellagio Draft Treaty (Hayton and Utton, 1989) on transboundary ground-waters specifically addresses this topic. The Treaty was a project instigated and carried out by a group of multi-disciplinary specialists with the intention of improving current international law on the matter. The Bellagio Draft Treaty is based on three major concepts: (1) zoning of ground-water withdrawal regions causing the dispute rather than policing entire border areas; (2) allowing individual nations to administer and enforce their own zones with oversight responsibility given to an already existing international agency (for example, International Joint Commission between Canada and the US); and (3) maintaining sovereignty of nations by giving the governments involved the ultimate approval of actions suggested by the joint Commission. 'The fundamental goal is to achieve joint, optimum utilization and avoidance or resolution of disputes over shared groundwaters in a time of ever-increasing pressures upon this priceless resource' (Hayton and Utton, 1989: 663).

AN ECONOMIC BASIS FOR SHARING THE WATERS OF INTERNATIONAL RIVER BASINS

Economists have a lot to say about the problems of allocating water in river basins (Maass *et al.*, 1962), but they are quick to point out the limitations of their analysis in the presence of external effects. The general economic prescription to deal with externalities is to 'internalize' them. The river basin itself is an ideal unit of analysis to achieve this goal: it can reasonably be assumed most externalities are captured by analysing the river basin as a single unit. This is why the concepts of *integrated river basin planning* and the creation of *river basin commissions* to implement and plan are so popular in the economic and planning literature.

But sorting out externalities among the several nations in one basin is another matter. It is precisely because the international river basin is international that it cannot be readily planned and developed as a single unit unless all of the riparians agree. Only in a few instances has this been attempted, and a leading case, the Columbia River Basin shared by Canada and the US, yielded mixed results (Krutilla, 1967).

If one cannot physically internalize the externalities as between basin countries, what can one do? The economics literature is replete with proposals to tax externalities so that the individuals and groups enjoying them will factor the costs to other people into their calculations. Taxes, or fees, have been widely propounded by US groups such as the Environmental Defense Fund and the World Resources Institute as a way of dealing with transboundary air pollution problems, but this approach requires strong supranational institutions to impose the taxes, and such institutions do not now exist to control transboundary externalities in international river basins.

Pareto-Admissibility

A promising practical approach to dealing with externalities in river basin planning, called 'Paretian Environmental Analysis', was formulated by Dorfman and Jacoby (Dorfman, Jacoby, and Thomas, 1972). They applied Paretian analysis to upstream–downstream conflicts about the management of water quality; their example was within one country, but the conflict of interest was identical to that within many international river basins. Pareto-admissibility emerges as a condition which a water resources development plan for the basin must satisfy in order to be responsive to the basin countries and to the goals of 'reasonableness' and equity.

Let $NB_i(x)$ denote the net benefits accruing to country i if resource allocation plan x is adopted, and assume that each country wishes to maximize its net benefits. Then any allocation x resulting in equal net benefits for some countries and greater net benefits for other countries when compared to resource allocation y will surely be preferred by the countries as a whole over y. Expressed in terms of symbols, $NB_i(x) \geq NB_i(y)$ for all countries i implies that x is preferred over y if the inequality is strict. A resource allocation plan x is Pareto-admissible if there is no allocation plan y which is preferred over x in the sense just described.

> Formally, a Pareto-Admissible allocation is any feasible allocation x such that there is no feasible allocation y making $NB_i(y) \geq NB_i(x)$ for all interest groups i with strict inequality for some i.

Dorfman, Jacoby, and Thomas looked for a non-coercive strategy for a river basin authority that has to persuade its members to agree on a joint solution. The commission could use the threat that if no agreement was reached then the global optimum solution (the maximum benefits available to the entire system ignoring jurisdictional boundaries) would be implemented. The basic assumption is that the upstream polluters and the downstream users would agree upon the reasonableness of the Pareto-admissible strategy and agree to it without undue pressure. But if they were unable to agree, the river basin commission would have the power to enforce the maximum net benefit plan for the basin as a whole. In the context of international river basins, where the individual countries may not wish to give up sovereignty as the global optimum solution would require them to do, but were looking for 'reasonable' solutions, this approach has a lot to recommend it. However, concentrating enough power in an international or bilateral agency to impose such a choice is a very difficult political requirement, at present unlikely to be achieved.

Superfairness

Other approaches to analysing river basin conflicts can be discussed under the general rubric of decision theory. With the increasing emphasis on 'reasonable and equitable share' in the legal approaches to international river basins discussed above, it is necessary to develop operational concepts of 'equity' and 'reasonableness'. The economics profession has recently devoted attention to building theories of 'fairness' and is relaxing its obsession with allocative efficiency. Baumol (1986) provides the most lucid description of this new concern with a book appropriately entitled *Superfairness*.

Superfairness rests upon the Pareto-improvement criterion given above and the concept of 'fair division'.[2] Baumol defines superfairness as follows: 'A distribution is called (nonstrictly) *superfair* if each class of participants prefers its own share to the share received by another group, that is, if no participant *envies* the other' (Baumol, 1986: 15). He augments this definition with a clarification of envy: 'A distribution of n commodities is said to involve envy by individual 2 of the share obtained by individual 1 if 2 would rather have the bundle of commodities received by 1 under this distribution than the bundle the distribution assigns to 2.' In generalizing the two-person equal-division problem to m persons, Baumol focuses upon the distribution of the residue, $(y^\star - y)$, among the remaining $m - 1$ individuals when individual i receives y, where $y^\star$ is the total amount available to be shared. Individual i's fairness boundary for this situation is as follows:

> The equal division of residue fairness boundary for i is the set of vectors (points), y, such that individual i is just indifferent between y and the amounts received by everyone of the $m - 1$ other individuals if the residue $(y^\star - y)$ is divided equally among them so that each receives $(y^\star - y)/(m - 1)$. In other words, y is on i's fairness boundary if, and only if, $U^i(y) = U^i[(y^\star - y)/(m - 1)]$, where $U^i(.)$ is i's utility function.

This definition is based upon the examination of two extreme cases; the first where all the residue goes to one person (the case most likely to arouse individual i's envy), and secondly, the case where the residue is split evenly among the remaining $m - 1$ persons (where i is least likely to envy any other person).

---

2 This is the old children's game of ensuring that two people will divide a cake fairly: one cuts the cake into two parts and the other chooses.

From the set of definitions Baumol demonstrates that if the utility functions are continuous and quasi-concave then there always exists at least one Pareto-optimal solution that is superfair. So far this coincides with Dorfman's use of Paretian analysis; however, Baumol proceeds to show that a superfair distribution may nevertheless be strictly Pareto-inferior to another distribution that everyone considers unfair. This may come about in a two-person case when player 1 likes what he gets at some superfair point Q less than the Pareto optimal point H, but that he likes what player 2 gets at Q even less. He does not envy individual 2 at point Q. Strategic behaviour is the subject of game theory, but as a negotiating or arbitration strategy, superfairness may be of use in modifying the more conventional Pareto-admissible approaches to sharing costs and benefits.[3]

Game Theory

Game theory, which deals with situations ranging from 'pure' conflict to 'pure' co-operation, was given an enthusiastic welcome when it first burst upon the economic scene in 1944 (Von Neumann and Morgenstern, 1944). However, it did not directly yield norms for decisions under conflict of the sort experienced in international river basins. As a result, the field has relied increasingly upon process-oriented approaches such as Alternative Dispute Resolution (ADR; Delli Priscoli, 1990) or the Processes of International Negotiations (PIN; Fisher and Ury, 1981). These aim at getting the parties to arrive at a negotiated solution, making the basic assumption that there is a solution to every conflict and that it can be arrived at by judicious use of a variety of time-tested negotiating strategies (win–win, getting to yes, etc.) administered by a third party.

Despite its early lack of success, game theorists have been pursuing a variety of approaches that are potentially very useful in the case of shared international water resources. In particular, there are a series of recent papers[4] which apply some of the findings of game theory to practical problems of the allocation of benefits and costs between conflicting parties on river basins. All these approaches are based upon analysis of the 'core' of an n-person co-operative game.

---

[3] Dorfman suggested that comparison of Nash equilibria and superfairness might be appropriate for this class of problems. Nash's solution is in terms of strategies, not pay-offs, and is defined as that vector of strategies in a non-cooperative game such that no one player, assuming that the others are committed to their choices, can improve his lot. Algebraically it is the vector of strategies $s_i^\star$ such that the pay-off to player i, $H_i(s_i)$, is for each i,

$$H_i(s_1^\star, \ldots, s_i^\star, \ldots s_n^\star) = \max_{s_i} H_i(s_1^\star, \ldots, s_i, \ldots s_n^\star).$$

This is a generalization of the minimax solution for the two-person zero-sum game.

[4] Young et al. (1982), Young (1985), Dinar and Yaron (1986), Tijs and Driessen (1986), Dufournaud and Harrington (1990 and 1991).

The development and analysis of coalitions is central to game theory. To analyse a coalition structure in a game, it is necessary to assess in a single numerical index the 'value' of the game to each of the coalitions that can form. This is called the 'characteristic function', and is denoted by v, which defines the maximum value of the game which a coalition can guarantee for itself if it forms in the playing of the game. It lists the value of the game to all possible coalitions.

In any n-person game there are potentially $2^n - 1$ coalitions. The games of interest in dividing up water in international rivers are called 'essential' games because there is benefit to co-operation between the players. A well-defined characteristic function, $v(S)$ must satisfy the following condition: If $S \cap T = \Phi$, then $v(S \cup T) \geq v(S) + v(T)$. This 'super-additivity' condition requires that two disjoint sets of players should not suffer by co-operating with each other. If, in addition, $v(1) + v(2) + \ldots + v(n) < v(1,2,3,\ldots n)$, the v represents an 'essential game' in characteristic function form. In other words, the pay-off to the grand coalition is always greater than the sum of individually sovereign solutions; this will always occur in the presence of externalities.

In order to arrive at a 'solution' to a co-operative game some additional requirements need to be placed upon the values of the characteristic function. In particular, we can allow the members of the coalitions to make side-payments to each other; although often and mistakenly disparaged by bureaucrats as 'bribes', such balancing side-compensations almost always play a positive role in supporting co-operation. Taking such side-payments to each member of the coalition into consideration leads to establishing the pay-off to each member of the coalition; this is called an 'imputation', and should meet some logical and reasonable conditions. The three conditions that are most often set are those of feasibility, Pareto-admissibility, and individual rationality. An imputation for an n-person game v in characteristic function form is a pay-off vector $(p_1,\ldots,p_n)$ which satisfies the following two conditions:

1. $p_i \geq v(i)$, for $i = 1,2,\ldots,n$
2. $(p_1 + p_2 + \ldots p_n) = v(1,2,\ldots,n)$

The first condition represents individual rationality and requires that any acceptable pay-off vector must give no player less than what that player can obtain on his own. The second condition corresponds to Pareto-admissibility and also feasibility when the strict equality is replaced by a less than or equals to sign.

The solution concept of the core of the game rests on the idea that there is a set of imputations that leave no coalition in a position to improve the pay-offs to its members. The core of an n-person game in characteristic function form $v(S)$ is the set of imputations which are not dominated by any other imputation. A pay-off vector $(p_1, \ldots, p_n)$ belongs to the core of $v(S)$ if, and only if:

1. $\sum_{i \in S} p_i \geq v(S)$ for all $S \subset N$

2. $\sum_{i \in N} p_i = v(N)$

Condition 1 when applied to $S = (i)$ implies individual rationality. For any proper subset S, condition 1 states that any pay-off vector in the core of a game must give no less total pay-off to each coalition than the total pay-off which that coalition can obtain on its own. Stated in another way, no coalition will accept a pay-off vector that yields less than what that coalition can obtain on its own. In these cases condition 1 now embodies a sense of individual and group rationality. Condition 2 is Pareto-admissibility. Roughly speaking, *the core of an n-person game in characteristic function form is the set of pay-off vectors for which there is no coalition having both the desire and the means of effectuating a change.* The concept of the core is used as the basis to decide on the stability of different pay-off vectors and, hence, coalition structures.

What should now be apparent is the pivotal role played by Pareto-admissibility in the analytic approaches that have been propounded for recommending 'solutions' to the types of problems which are encountered in water allocation in international river basins.

A POLITICAL BASIS FOR SHARING THE WATERS OF INTERNATIONAL RIVER BASINS

Often called the 'queen of sciences', political science is rich in observation but poor in tested predictive theory. Clearly the decisions involved in international rivers are political and can only be adequately addressed in political terms. The problem is to be able to derive a basis for political recommendations and action from political science. Political imperatives contrast to the economic imperatives in three important points:

1. They concretely evaluate the desirability of a policy or an investment on the basis of its value, positive or negative, to a large number of subgroups with varying degrees of interest in the matter.
2. They do not rely solely upon the simplifying quantitative economic measure of money, but are heavily influenced by non-monetizable considerations as well.
3. They are pursued separately and apart from economic objectives, with different personnel and rituals; recruitment to the political arena has a particular history and admission confers a great deal of authority.

The predictive models employed are much more diffuse and less precise than those employed by lawyers and much less quantitative than those used by economists. Political models of bureaucratic and executive politics, pork barrelling, and interest groups tend to be more highly descriptive and idiosyncratic than analogous models in other sciences. The literature on coalition formation is closest to the analytic aspects of game theory mentioned above.

An important work on the political bases for sharing international rivers is the book by LeMarquand entitled *International Rivers: The Politics of Cooperation*. The book discusses both the foreign and domestic policy implications of the decisions to negotiate river basin disputes. Written in 1977, the book tends to relegate international river issues to the 'middle range of objectives', dealing with satisfying domestic social and economic demands, rather than to the 'core objectives' regarding a country's territorial integrity or self-preservation. By 1991 many countries would see themselves entering an era when national sovereignty is now at stake; some countries in the Middle East might claim that national survival is at stake.

LeMarquand suggested the following five aspects of foreign policy as the most influential determinants of a country's position on international rivers.

Image

The concern for national image may be one of the most important factors in deciding how to deal with international water issues, particularly when the issues are considered in the middle-range objectives. The US's decision to build a desalting plant on the Lower Colorado River may have been largely influenced by avoiding the negative image of a large and powerful country pursuing its own national interest heedless of the consequences for a poorer neighbour.

International Law

As discussed above, international law does not provide any strong incentives to behave in any particular way. There is, however, now a widely accepted consensus on a set of principles which, depending upon how much image is important, a country may choose to abide by or not. Hence, the developing and non-binding international legal principles can be important factors in enabling countries to get involved in negotiations.

Linkage

The linkage of river basin settlements to other bilateral or multilateral issues is one way countries may be able to extract concessions from their neighbours. Linkage seems to be used to a certain extent in all of the major river basin negotiations discussed in the literature.

Reciprocity

The desire for mutual commitment and obligation can often have the most bizarre manifestations in negotiating international river basin disputes. LeMarquand cites the case of Switzerland, a land-locked country, insisting that treaties governing the protection of international water-courses against pollution be extended to cover pollution of coastal areas. This demand was, however, not irrational since it was aimed at ensuring that the Netherlands, which would benefit from Switzerland's treatment of its water discharges into the Rhine, could not dump its untreated sewage into the ocean.

Sovereignty

Sovereignty is the major stumbling-block in the path of resolving international river disputes. Given the choice, countries would prefer independent action over international co-operation because of the general loss of sovereignty and independence, and loss of control over domestic resources implied by collective or bilateral constraints.

LeMarquand also cites three factors influencing domestic policy formulation which are salient with regard to international river issues.

Bureaucratic policy formation

He claims that most international river issues are left to bureaucrats in the ministry dealing with foreign affairs. In turn they have to rely upon bureaucrats in the technical water and other resource ministries who often have substantive interest in a particular project, or set of projects, with interest-group support. When the foreign affairs bureaucrats then have to deal with their counterparts in the other riparian countries, negotiations can drag on for years and 'lowest common denominator' agreements are the most likely outcome.

Executive policy formation

When a president or prime minister takes an active interest in the outcome of an international river issue it is generally possible to circumvent recalcitrant bureaucrats and achieve rapid solutions. LeMarquand shows how President Echeverria of Mexico was able to press President Nixon into a rapid resolution of the salinity problems of the Lower Colorado. The current role played by President Ozal of Turkey may give his 'peace pipeline' a better chance of being implemented than if it were left to the usual political channels in the Middle East.

Non-executive policy formation

These essentially deal with the distributive politics of the 'pork barrel' and coalition-building, both features much commented upon with respect to domestic US water policy. Also included are the regulatory politics of environmental management which establish the ground-rules under which much domestic water policy is now governed. Redistributive politics may also enter, as central governments may seek to use international agreements over water as a way of regaining control over regional water use for the purpose of redirecting it towards other social goals.

The most important political basis for sharing water is the 'climate for agreement'. Various authors are cited by LeMarquand for insights into this aspect of the problem. The following conditions are suggested as favourable for successful international agreements concerning water:

1. Countries with the same technical perception of a problem.
2. Similar tastes for consumption of goods and services.
3. When water quality is an issue, the use of similar industrial production technologies.
4. The existence of an extensive network of transnational and transgovernmental contacts between countries.
5. The participation of a small number of countries.
6. The desire of one large country to have an agreement.
7. The necessary development by one country of a good or service for its own use which may benefit other countries.

Domestic and international politics remain the most important features of international river basin development and have to be addressed in any analysis.

SOME CASE STUDIES

We have chosen three real situations to illuminate these issues. They involve, respectively, two countries, three countries, and multiple countries, sharing the waters of a river basin. The basins of the Columbia, the Ganges–Brahmaputra, and the Nile have experienced substantial development pressure, and have given rise to international treaties governing their use. They have been widely discussed in the literature, and some form of analytical study has been performed for each.

The Columbia River

The background of the Columbia Treaty between Canada and the US and the subsequent development of the basin was the subject of an excellent book by Krutilla (1967) and a chapter in LeMarquand's book (1977); the following comments rely heavily upon Krutilla's and LeMarquand's work. Fig. 3.2 shows a map of the basin. After more than 20 years of planning and negotiating, the Columbia River Treaty, which was signed in 1961, called for Canada to provide storage of 15.5 million acre feet (19 billion cubic metres) in three dams and the US was given the option to build a dam in Montana that would flood 42 miles into Canada. In return for providing the storage, Canada received 50 per cent of the increased base power generation at dams downstream in the US, and 50 per cent of the estimated downstream flood control benefits. When the treaty was ratified in Canada in 1964, the Canadians sold their share of the power to the US for a period of 30 years for a lump sum

Fig. 3.2. The Columbia River basin

Source: J. V. Krutilla, *The Columbia River Treaty: The Economics of an International River Basin Development* (Baltimore, Md.: Johns Hopkins University Press, 1967), 90.

payment of $254 million (US), and in addition received $64 million (US) as its share of the flood-control benefits. The treaty is to be in effect for 60 years.

Apart from their social similarity and a long history of good relations, Canada and the US have the unique situation that an International Joint Commission (IJC) was established in 1909 by the Boundary Waters Treaty to deal with conflicts about transboundary rivers. There is a great advantage to having an already existing institution to turn to when a particular river problem has to be resolved. In 1959 the US and Canadian governments requested the IJC to make recommendations on the principles that should be applied in determining:

a. the benefits to result from co-operative use of the storage of waters and electrical interconnection with the Columbia River System; and

b. the apportionment between the two countries of such benefits, more particularly in regard to electrical generation and flood control (Krutilla, 1967: 59).

Eleven months later the IJC promulgated a set of principles, the first two of which are germane to this paper. They are cited by Krutilla (1967: 60) as follows:

General Principle No. 1

Co-operative development of the water resources of the Columbia River Basin, designed to provide optimum benefits to each country, requires that storage facilities and downstream power production facilities proposed by the respective countries will, to the extent that it is practicable and feasible to do so, be added in the order of the most favourable benefit–cost ratio.

General Principle No. 2

Co-operative development of the water resources of the Columbia River Basin should result in advantages in power supply, flood control, or other benefits, or savings in costs to each country as compared with alternatives available to that country.

The application of these general principles could have led to a Pareto-admissible solution if they had been strictly followed. What actually transpired is that the Canadian federal government found itself in major conflict with the provincial government of British Columbia over water resources development. This gave the province a key role in skewing the negotiations in its favour.

Krutilla (1967: 193 ff.) concluded:

It is not at all clear, in fact, that the returns to Canada and the United States combined are greater than they would have been if each country had proceeded independently ... the IJC principles appear to promise that each party to the cooperative venture will receive something that is somehow equal, the circumstances of the case in question permitted a diversion of the real gains predominantly to Canada.

The major reason why the Pareto solution was not obtained appears to be the decision, insisted upon by British Columbia, to share costs and benefits on the basis of a 'grossing' rather than 'netting' formula. The 'netting' approach is favoured by economists and utilities, and was initially favoured by the two governments. Under netting, utilities estimate the least-cost alternative of going alone and then they compare this cost with the cost of co-operative action. The difference between the co-operative case and the least-cost go-it-alone case yields the net value or savings from co-operative action. These net savings from co-operation then become the basis for the equitable sharing of the benefits between them by sharing the costs. Under

the grossing approach each country is responsible for the costs of construct-
ing projects within its own territory and the benefits are then divided equally
between them. Clearly this approach leads to less than optimal basin-wide
net benefits and an arbitrary division of the spoils.

Dufournaud (1982) presents the Canadian side of the Columbia Treaty
and argues that Canada was not the major gainer. He summarizes the arguments of General A. G. L. McNaughton, who negotiated the treaty for the
Canadians, as follows:

McNaughton's concerns are threefold. First, he objects to the Treaty, which, he
argues, underrepresents the United States' eventual gains . . . . He implies that
Canada's gains are smaller than they could have been. Second, he objects to the
requirement that the Treaty imposes upon Canada to unconditionally provide flood
protection to the United States. Third, he objects to the Treaty because he believes
that in the long run this will provide the United States access to Canadian resources
to the detriment of Canada.

General McNaughton, it should be recalled, however, was an ardent propon-
ent of linking the Columbia to the Fraser River and diverting all of the 'excess'
flows away from the US and into an entirely Canadian river basin. It is not
clear that McNaughton could ever have achieved that particular outcome;
however, the very existence of the proposal no doubt figured in the US's
determination to achieve a treaty.

In presenting the Canadian side of the picture, Dufournaud analyses the
Columbia as a two-person non-zero-sum co-operative game and concludes
that Krutilla's analysis does not hold up if the subsequent joint undertakings
are included. He claims (p. 769) that when this is taken into consideration it
'rationalizes an a priori seemingly irrational decision on the part of the
United States'.

The irony is, however, that despite the detailed economic analyses, a variety of circumstances intervened to make Krutilla's pessimistic predictions
obsolete. First, the rapid increase in the value of electricity as a result of the
1973 oil crisis was not predicted by anybody. Hence, the 30-year future sale
of the Canadian share of the power was a great bargain. Secondly, no one predicted the rate of inflation in construction costs that the Canadians had to
face in order to meet their part of the bargain (the 'grossing' formula came
home to roost with a vengeance). Taken as a whole and viewed with hindsight, the US did remarkably well.

In a 1966 paper Krutilla showed how the Kennedy Administration's
urgent desire to find something to compensate Canada for the loss of the sale
of a Canadian-built fighter-plane to NATO in preference to a still un-
produced US plane, influenced Washington's decision to agree to a treaty
that gave Canada an advantage. Such behaviour violates one of the basic
assumptions of most co-operative games: the independence of irrelevant
alternatives. On the surface it appears that real political decisions apparently

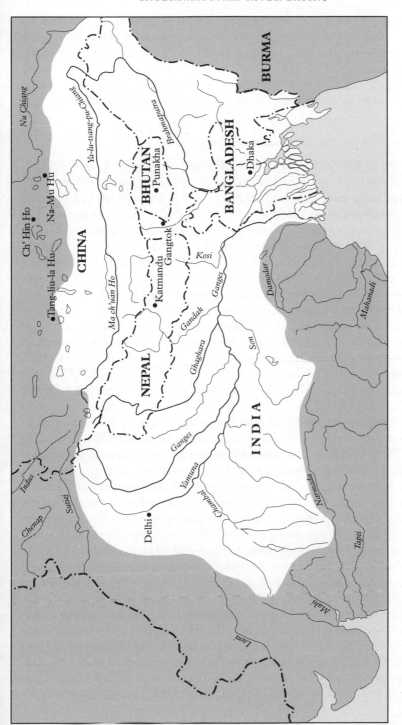

Fig. 3.3. The Ganges–Brahmaputra basin

Source: P. Rogers, D. Seckle., and P. Lyton, *Eastern Waters Study: Strategies to Manage Flood and Drought in the Ganges–Brahmaputra Basin*, prepared for the Office of Technical Resources, Bureau for Asia and the Near East, US Agency for International Development (1989), 2.

pay little attention to the niceties of game-theoretic formulations of decision problems. However, if the range of choices was opened up before the negotiations then the fighter-plane may not have been an 'irrelevant alternative'. This looks like a good example of the linkage discussed above. The strength of the process approaches to negotiation over formal game analysis is that they might identify such alternatives in the process of negotiation itself.

The Ganges–Brahmaputra

Conflict about the development of the Ganges–Brahmaputra river system, which is shared among India, Nepal, and Bangladesh, dates from the 1947 partition of India into India and Pakistan (Fig. 3.3 shows a map of the basin). In the earlier period of British rule, what development there was caused little trouble because the single large nation of India was able to 'internalize the externalities'. With partition, however, came concern about river transport to the Indian state of Assam, which was all but cut off from the rest of India by the territory given to East Pakistan, which in 1972 became Bangladesh. Over time, however, as India began to divert increasing amounts of water for irrigation out of the Ganges system during the dry months, noticeable effects on the hydraulic regime in East Pakistan were observed. The situation was exacerbated by India's resurrection of a nineteenth-century plan to maintain the ocean-going port of Calcutta by diverting large amounts (40,000 cubic feet per second out of a recorded low flow of about 70,000 cfs) of Ganges waters into the Hooghly river during the low flow months (particularly March, April, and May).

In 1975 India completed a barrage across the Ganges at Farakka, close to the Bangladesh border, which gave it that diversion capacity. Since that time there has been a great deal of tension between the two countries about sharing and augmenting the low flows. In 1977 a treaty was signed allocating a little less than two-thirds of the Ganges water to Bangladesh, with the understanding that Bangladesh would co-operate on augmenting the dry season supplies by planning transfers of Brahmaputra water to the Indian Ganges via a canal across Bangladeshi territory. With little co-operation on augmentation coming from Bangladesh, the five-year treaty expired in 1982, and after several shorter extensions, lapsed entirely in 1989, leaving unilateral decisions by upstream riparian India as the mechanism for Ganges water-sharing. In 1987 there was an unusually large flood in Bangladesh, and it was followed in 1988 by an even larger one of catastrophic dimensions. An estimated 10 million people were rendered homeless for up to two weeks, and the country suffered from massive transportation and social disruptions. At that time, Bangladesh newspapers, if not the government, talked about the supposed role of water developments and deforestation by the upstream riparians, Nepal and India, in intensifying the downstream floods (Rogers *et al.*, 1989).

The issue of joint or separate development of the basin had been discussed in the mid-1950s by the UN Mission led by General Krug of the US Army Corps of Engineers. The Krug report came out strongly in favour of basin-wide approaches. Following the 1965 war between India and Pakistan, many countries urged India and Pakistan to try to identify joint development projects as a way of reducing the level of antagonism between the two countries. One such attempt was the study carried out at the Harvard Center for Population Studies under the direction of Roger Revelle. As part of this study Rogers (1969) used a two-person non-zero-sum game to look for solutions to upstream–downstream conflicts on the Ganges and Brahmaputra Rivers between India and East Pakistan. In Rogers's solution only the cases of 'sovereign' and 'optimum development' were strictly considered. An interesting finding of the analysis was that, under the basin optimum, India did no better than she would have done under the sovereignty theory, but lower riparian Bangladesh received substantially more benefits. This would appear to bolster India's claim that the sovereignty theory is the one that she should choose. But since, for Bangladesh, the sovereignty strategy produces substantially lower net benefits, there would seem to be a need for some form of co-operative solution based upon 'reasonable share' if not purely on riparian rights. Bangladesh, however, is currently trying to redefine the 'game', at least in regard to flood control, in such a way that sovereign solutions involving large embankments will bolster its pay-off. Bangladesh also seeks to broaden participation in the game by inducing Nepal to play. The existence of a third player makes the game much more interesting because of the possibility of coalition formation.

The Nile

Flowing 6,825 km. from Lake Victoria to the Mediterranean, the Nile is the longest, and certainly one of the most studied rivers in the world. Historically recorded agricultural settlement has depended upon the river for almost 6000 years. The basin area of just over 3 million square kilometres is split among the nine states shown in Fig. 3.4 and estimates of the percentage of basin area, basin flow contributed, and current water use by each of the riparians are listed in Table 3.4. This table highlights a paradox about the water use of the Nile: the existing treaties and effectively all of the water consumption occur in the two downstream riparians which essentially make no contribution to the river flow. A standard reference on this basin is Waterbury (1979), aptly entitled, *Hydropolitics of the Nile Valley*. However, Waterbury's book focuses on Egypt and Sudan as the main water-users on the Nile, largely ignoring the remaining seven countries, including Ethiopia, which contributes the bulk of the flow. Most of the other recent literature about water sharing on the Nile exhibits the same selective view of the basin (Smith and Al-Rawahy, 1990; Haynes and Whittington, 1981).

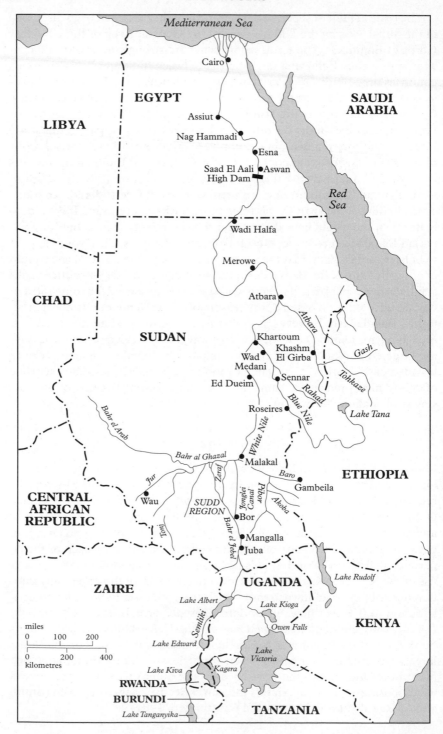

Fig. 3.4. The Nile basin

Source: J. Waterbury, 'Legal and Institutional Arrangements for Managing Water Resoureces in the Nile Basin', *Water Resources Development*, 3/2 (1987), 93.

Table 3.4. Land and water use in the Nile basin

Country	Area (km²)	Flow		Water use (billion cubic metres)
		(% of basin)	(% from country)	
Sudan	1,900,000	62.7	0.0	18.5
Ethiopia	368,000	12.1	86.0	0.0
Egypt	300,000	9.9	0.0	55.5
Uganda	232,000	7.7		
Tanzania	116,000	3.8		
Kenya	55,000	1.8		
Zaïre	23,000	0.8	14.0	0.0
Rwanda	21,000	0.7		
Burundi	14,500	0.5		
Total	3,030,000	100	100	84.00

Source: Based upon Krishna (1988) and Waterbury (1979).

Krishna (1988), however, refreshingly summarizes the history of the Nile treaties with an eye to the basin as a whole, allowing broader concepts of equity to come into play. Table 3.5 is based upon Krishna's summary. The Nile appears to have developed into an extreme case of how to allocate the waters of international river basins in disregard of the Helsinki Rules or other efforts at equity. No single agreement relating to the Nile encompasses all the basin countries, and as mentioned above, nearly all the water is used by the two countries which contribute the least water. In Sudan's defence, it is geographically the largest riparian by far and, hence, under the riparian rights theory should receive substantial amounts of water. Egypt also has substantial claims, based upon having by far the largest population in the basin. 'Prior appropriations', a legal doctrine popular in the western United States but in few other places, are well established going back millennia in the case of Egypt. As the most militarily powerful of the basin states, Egypt does not allow its co-riparians to overlook that fact. According to Krishna (p. 33) President Anwar Sadat said in 1980,

We do not need permission from Ethiopia or the Soviet Union to divert our Nile water ... If Ethiopia takes any action to block our right to the Nile waters, there will be no alternative for us but to use force. Tampering with the rights of a nation to water is tampering with its life and a decision to go to war on this score is indisputable in the international community.

Guariso and Whittington (1987) have attempted to make a formal analysis of the whole Nile basin and look for Pareto-admissible solutions. Their model considered Egypt and Sudan as a unit, since they are linked by their 1959 agreement, and their model considers Ethiopia as if it actually had the four large storage reservoirs of the US Bureau of Reclamation's 1964 plan, and were operating them for hydropower. The model considers only

Table 3.5. Treaty arrangements regarding the Nile

Date	Signatories	Major provisions
1891	Italy, United Kingdom	Government of Italy undertakes not to construct on the Atbara any irrigation or other works that might sensibly modify its flow into the Nile.
1902	Ethiopia, United Kingdom	Emperor of Ethiopia promised not to construct or allow to be constructed any works across the Blue Nile, Lake Tana, or the Sobat, which would arrest the flow of their waters into the Nile except in agreement with the British Government and the Government of the Sudan.
1906 (April)	France, Italy, UK	Tripartite Agreement to protect Egypt's interests.
1906 (May)	The Congo, United Kingdom	Provided that the Independent State of the Congo would not construct, or allow to be constructed, any work on or near the Semliki or Isango rivers that would diminish the volume of water entering Lake Albert, except in agreement with the Sudanese Government.
1925	Italy, United Kingdom	Exchange of notes to protect Egypt's water rights. Granted Britain the right to build a barrage at Lake Thana.
1929	Egypt, United Kingdom	Landmark exchange of notes; called the Nile Waters Agreement. 'Save with the previous agreement of the Egyptian Government, no irrigation or power works or measures are to be constructed or taken on the River Nile and its branches, or on the lakes from which it flows, so far as these are in the Sudan or in countries under British administration, which would, in such a manner as to entail any prejudice to the interests of Egypt, either reduce the quantity of water arriving in Egypt, or modify the date of its arrival, or lower its level.'
1932	Egypt, United Kingdom	Jebel Awlia Compensation Agreement (about a dam in the Sudan).
1949	Egypt, United Kingdom	Agreement on Owen Falls Dam, Uganda, regulating the flow out of Lake Victoria.
1950	Egypt, United Kingdom	Agreement to co-operate in a meteorological and hydrological survey of Lake Victoria.
1952	Egypt, United Kingdom	A reported agreement on the Fourth Cataract Dam. The text of this agreement is apparently not available but is referred to by some authorities.
1959	Egypt, the Sudan	'Full utilization of the Nile waters.' The Sudan agreed to the Aswan High Dam and the Egyptians permitted the Roseries Dam on the Blue Nile. Detailed water-sharing was laid

		out. Financial compensation from Egypt to the Sudan. Mechanisms to deal with claims by other riparians were spelled out. Permanent Joint Technical Committee set up.
1961	Kenya, Uganda, Tanzania	Requested the UN for technical assistance in a hydro-meteorological survey of the Lake Victoria catchment.
1967	Kenya, Uganda, Tanzania	Plan of Operation signed with the UNDP for a hydromet study of lakes Victoria, Albert, and Kyoga with the World Meteorological Organization as the executing agency. Rwanda and Burundi were added later to cover the drainage catchment in those countries.
1977	Burundi, Rwanda, Tanzania	Agreement for the Establishment of the Organization for Management and Development of the Kagera River. Uganda joined in 1981.
1983	Egypt	Egyptian Master Water Plan: a joint effort between Egypt, the UNDP, and the World Bank.
1986	All riparians except Ethiopia	A UNDP Workshop for Nile Countries held in Bangkok endorsed seven principles starting with 'It is essential that the riparian countries cooperate in sharing water resources for the benefit of all on an equitable and mutually beneficial basis for the effective development of the Nile basin.'
1990	Proposal stage only	Proposal to establish a Nile Basin Commission comprising all nine riparians. The proposal wishes to consider the Nile as a hydrological unit to establish the 'best utilization of the waters of the Nile Basin without prejudice to severing the rights of the respective member states.'

Note: For more information on agreements involving the Nile, refer to Waterbury (1987).

Source: summarized from Krishna (1988).

irrigation water uses in Sudan and Egypt, and hydropower in Ethiopia. Guariso and Whittington claim that, contrary to Egypt's belief that any works in Ethiopia on the Blue Nile would necessarily harm the downstream countries, there are potential upstream developments that could expand the amount of water available to the downstream riparians. This is mainly because the evaporation losses in the Ethiopian Highlands are much less than those at downstream reservoirs such as Aswan. They argue that Egypt and Sudan could achieve these benefits without a co-operative agreement with Ethiopia, provided that Ethiopia could be counted upon to act in its own interest. They also claim that their model shows that the developments in Ethiopia would be particularly helpful to the Sudan. All of these claims have to be tempered, however, by ignoring substantial reductions in hydropower at Aswan in Egypt.

The striking aspect of the Guariso and Whittington study is its lack of correspondence with the perceptions of the basin riparians, and the large economic potential it asserts is available to each of them. This leads to questioning whether the nations' perceptions, or the academic analysis in this case, are faulty.

FURTHER EXPLORATION OF THE
GANGES–BRAHMAPUTRA CASE

Although the practical issue of a formula to share the Spring season's low flows at Farakka has often taken over the front pages, the bilateral negotiations between India and Bangladesh have included the issue of augmenting Ganges low flows by transfers from the Brahmaputra. For this, India seeks a canal across Bangladesh to transfer Brahmaputra water from one location in India to another in India on the Ganges. Bangladeshi nationalists are determined to halt this project. At times, India has set this proposal within a broader suggestion to examine very large-scale storages, hydro-electric generation, and diversions of water in the Upper Brahmaputra basin in India (Assam). These would stabilize and support the inter-basin transfer of dry-season water into the Indian Ganges, but in the wet monsoon season, such works would also mitigate downstream monsoon flooding in Bangladesh, which is a major problem for that nation.

At the same time, bilateral exchanges between India and Nepal concerning water have focused upon hydropower production in Nepal's mountains for the Indian market. Recent, and somewhat ephemeral, bilateral Bangladesh and Nepal discussions have focused upon flood control for Bangladesh and access to an ocean port for Nepal. In the Ganges–Brahmaputra basin today there is a great deal of mutual distrust, and what an outsider might call a lack of clear communication between the riparians. If ever there was a situation ripe for multilateral action, this is it.

For the sake of simplicity, in this paper we consider three among the many ways to analyse this problem:

(1) an approach using the 'reasonable and equitable' criterion for sharing the waters;
(2) an approach exploiting Pareto-admissibility; and
(3) a 'game' approach using game theory. Whichever method is chosen, similar sets of information are required. For example, in order to discuss sharing benefits or costs, a method for identifying them must be established. Moreover, if the issue is of sharing the overall benefits due to co-operation, then a reliable method for identifying the optimum allocation also needs to be established. The original Rogers paper in 1969 established a database and ways of identifying the optimum allocation of the resources. Recently, Quinn (1991) recomputed the pay-off matrix for this problem and has explored the implications of 'near optimality' for the originally proposed solutions. Quinn's work is the basis for computing the effects of the legal theories on the distribution of benefits and costs among India, Bangladesh, and Nepal.

Reasonable and Equitable Sharing

Article V of the Helsinki Rules lists eleven factors relevant to determining reasonable and equitable use (Article 7 of the ILC lists six factors). Based upon readily available data, Table 3.6 shows how these criteria apply for the three South Asian riparians in this basin. Using such criteria, about 70 to 85 per cent of the total potential benefits from basin development should go to India, with the remainder roughly equally split between Nepal and Bangladesh. Such an allocation certainly should suit India and would be a reasonable position for it to maintain in international debates over the issue. The 'reasonable and equitable' results, however, do not look so attractive to the other riparians. In particular, they seem to downplay Nepal's potential strategic role in the hydrology, and Bangladesh's very large population, especially in comparison with Nepal, and its strategic vulnerability with respect to India's actions.

Pareto-Admissibility

Using the Ganges-Brahmaputra basin model the global maximum is as follows:

$$\text{Max } [NB_1(x) + NB_2(x) + NB_3(x)]$$
$$x \in X$$

where $NB_1(x)$, $NB_2(x)$ and $NB_3(x)$ are the net benefits accruing to India, Bangladesh, and Nepal. This is equivalent to the grand coalition in game theory terms. To generate Pareto-admissible solutions we followed Dorfman,

Table 3.6. Reasonable and equitable sharing of international rivers

	India	Bangladesh	Nepal	Total
Land area (Mha.)	109.25	15.06	14.08	138.39
	(78.94)	(10.88)	(10.17)	
Cultivable area (Mha.)	73.56	9.51	3.98	87.05
	(84.50)	(10.92)	(4.57)	
Population (millions, 1971)	244.17	70.96	11.29	326.42
	(74.80)	(21.74)	(3.46)	
Population density (per km.^{2})	223.50	471.18	80.18	235.87
Total run-off (Bcm.)	897.0	153.50	225.50	1276.0
	(70.30)	(12.03)	(17.67)	
Irrigation potential (Mha.)	20.23	4.88	1.20	26.31
	(76.88)	(18.55)	(4.57)	
Hydro potential (MW.)	29.20	0.0	85.0	114.20
	(25.57)	(0.0)	(74.42)	
Hydro installations (MW.)	2.09	0.0	0.41	2.50
	(83.60)	(0.0)	(16.40)	
Land per capita (Ha.)	0.45	0.18	1.25	0.42

Note: Figures in brackets represent the percentage distributions.

Jacoby, and Thomas (1972) and chose a set of arbitrary weights W and computed;

$$\text{Max } [W_1NB_1(x) + W_2NB_2(x) + W_3NB_3(x)]$$
$$x \in X$$

where W_1, W_2, and W_3 are weights on the net benefits to each country. Eighteen cases were considered and are listed in Table 3.7. The Pareto-admissible frontier derived from these points for India and Bangladesh is plotted in Fig. 3.5.

A wide range of admissible solutions are possible and, depending upon how one weights the relative net benefits, could be used as starting-points for arbitration. For example, point A weights the net benefits to each equally; the weights are 1.0 for each country. Point D, however, weights India with 1.0 and both of the others with 0.0. Similarly, point E weights Bangladesh with 1.0 and both the others with 0.0. The range of weights are shown in Table 3.7.

In negotiations, however, the net benefits are not the only consideration; politicians are keenly interested in the physical location of investments. Fortunately, the methodology provides detailed descriptions of the entire basin development plans for each point on the graph. For example, points A and F, which are very close to each other in terms of net benefits to each player at the Pareto frontier, have one major difference; in solution F there is no surface storage project in Bangladesh whereas there is one such project in the solution at A. So while the Pareto-admissible solution implies that India and Bangladesh should be more or less indifferent between these two points, it is unlikely that the Bangladesh negotiators would accept a solution at F.

Table 3.7. Pareto-admissibility for Ganges–Brahmaputra models: Net benefits for each country (Rs./Yr)

	Total benefit	India	Nepal	Bangladesh	Weight on objective (India Nepal Bangladesh)	
1)	8.6E + 09	4.9E + 09	1.8E + 08	3.5E + 09	(1 1 1)	
2)	7.3E + 09	5.4E + 09	1.8E + 08	1.8E + 09	(1 .1 .1)	
3)	6.6E.09	5.4E + 09	0	1.2E + 09	(1 0 0)	
4)	7.9E + 09	2.5E + 09	0	5.4E + 09	(.1 .1 1)	
5)	7.9E + 09	2.5E + 09	0	5.4E + 09	(0 0 1)	
6)	7.3E + 09	5.4E + 09	1.8E + 08	1.8E + 09	(1 .5 .1)	
7)	8.6E + 09	5.0E + 09	1.8E + 08	3.5E + 09	(1 .1 .5)	
8)	8.2E + 09	5.1E + 09	1.8E + 08	2.8E + 09	(.5 1 .1)	
9)	7.9E + 09	2.5E + 09	0	5.4E + 09	(.1 1 .5)	
10)	7.9E + 09	2.5E + 09	0	5.4E + 09	(.5 .1 1)	
11)	7.9E + 09	2.5E + 09	0	5.4E + 09	(.1 .5 1)	
12)	8.3E + 09	3.2E + 09	1.4E + 08	4.9E + 09	(.1 3 .5)	
13)	8.6E + 09	4.4E + 09	1.6E + 08	4.1E + 09	(.1 .1 1)	Ind ≥ 4.4E9
14)	8.5E + 09	4.0E + 09	1.1E + 08	4.4E + 09	(.1 .1 1)	Ind ≥ 4.0E9
15)	8.4E + 09	3.6E + 09	0.83E + 08	4.7E + 09	(.1 .1 1)	Ind ≥ 3.6E9
16)	8.2E + 09	3.2E + 09	0.15E + 08	5.0E + 09	(.1 .1 1)	Ind ≥ 3.2E9
17)	8.0E + 09	2.8E + 09	0	5.2E + 09	(.1 .1 1)	Ind > 2.8E9

If the assumption is made that there is no pooling of the riparian countries' financial resources to create a general basin development budget, but that projects built within a country must be paid for by that country, then a different, and potentially smaller, amount of total net benefit is available. In other words, the investment decision is made autonomously with regard to the financial resources, but the location and type of investment are decided on the basis of what is best for the overall basin. This may be much more realistic in many international river basin cases than pooling procedures which would bring about, for example, Bangladeshi payment for a dam in India. The autonomous investment situation is similar to the grossing approach insisted upon by British Columbia in the case of the Columbia River Treaty discussed above. In the case under consideration, the total net benefits dropped from Rs. 8,643 million per year with a distribution to India, Nepal, and Bangladesh respectively of (4,922, 179, and 3,541) to Rs. 8,380 million per year with a distribution of (4,248, 23, and 4,108). One could apply the Pareto-admissibility methodology to this case and look for a frontier of efficient solutions, such as that given in Fig. 3.5 for the complete co-operation with the pooling of resources case. This has not been done yet, but one suspects that the range of interesting solutions will be much smaller than the case of more complete co-operation discussed above.

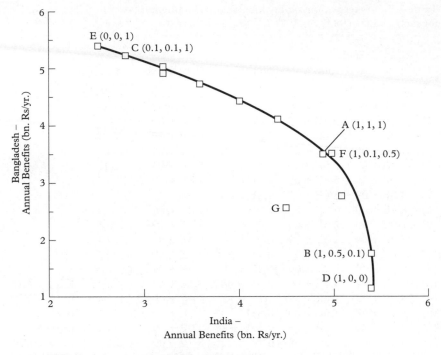

Fig. 3.5. Pareto frontier: India and Bangladesh

In order to assess the value of co-operation, both of these cases need to be compared with the situation where each country is completely autonomous. This is the case of $v(1) + v(2) + v(3)$ from the characteristic function values; it amounts to Rs. 6,961 million per year. This point is also the Nash equilibrium point mentioned earlier. Hence, we could argue that partial co-operation, by merely co-ordinating the investment decisions, leads to an increase of 20 per cent in net benefits. A full integration of the investment decision, without regard to where a facility is installed, leads to a 24 per cent increase in benefits. Does a 4 per cent increase in overall net benefits justify the level of political accommodation needed to achieve the overall optimum solution?

A Game Approach: Superfairness

This situation seems to lead us directly to the concept of superfairness introduced above. The difference between *A* and *F* in Bangladesh's eyes is major and is possibly occasioned by envy of the construction of reservoirs in India. The problem is akin to the cake-cutting example with the cake now having unevenly placed icing, nuts, and raisins. 'You cut, I choose' is no longer a simple proposition. Moreover, with these multiple objectives it is now possible that Bangladesh will prefer a point such as *G*, which is not Pareto-admissible, but at which Bangladesh no longer has reason to envy India.[5] From the point of view of arbitrating this type of conflict the strategic position (strategic position means physical location, economic power, and development options) of the players becomes of paramount concern. For example, it is unlikely that Bangladesh would be very successful in using such an approach in negotiations with India. Hence, the need arises for analyses which take the strategic opportunities of the parties explicitly into account.

If, however, a negotiating approach using Pareto-admissibility is carried out, it is easy to examine each of the proposed outcomes (without any additional data generation) in terms of superfairness, especially the envy criterion.

A Game Approach: the Core

Table 3.8 shows the characteristic function for a three-person game involving resource allocation in the Ganges–Brahmaputra basin. An undominated imputation exists for this characteristic function if there is a feasible solution to the following mathematical programming model based upon the definition of undominated imputations:

maximize any variable p_1, p_2, or p_3, subject to:

$$p_1 \geq 4184$$
$$p_2 \geq 23$$
$$p_3 \geq 2754$$
$$p_1 + p_3 \geq 8,265$$
$$p_2 + p_3 \geq 3,729$$
$$p_1 + p_2 > 4,409$$
$$p_1 + p_2 + p_3 \geq 8,643.$$

This program is feasible and has optimal solutions (4,914, 378, 3,351) when p_2 is maximized (4,914, 23, 3,706) when p_1 is maximized, and (4,386, 23, 4,234) when p_3 is maximized.

The values of the characteristic function can also be plotted to show whether the core is empty or not. Fig. 3.6 shows the core for this game. The core is the area *ABCD*. All points within this boundary are feasible points and represent allocations of benefits and costs to the players that are likely to be accepted. Note that the area is quite small in relation to the total area it might have occupied. The existence of such a tight core should make the task of the negotiators easier than if the range were very large. Within this core, India always receives larger benefits than Bangladesh, but only marginally so. It

[5] Something akin to this may have happened in some of the negotiations in the past with respect to sharing the low flows of the Ganges. It is arguable that Bangladesh's position may have had a lot to do with its unhappiness (envy) over what India was getting rather than any objective additional economic losses due to the actual share.

Table 3.8. Characteristic function of the Ganges–Brahmaputra game (all values are in million 1968 Rupees per year)

$v(1) =$	Maximum net benefits available to India assuming that there is no development in the other parts of the basin. Solve the basin model with separate budget for India and the virgin inflows from Nepal. (Rs. 4,184.)
$v(2) =$	Maximum net benefits available to Bangladesh assuming that Nepal and India are trying to maximize their joint net benefits. Use separate budget for Bangladesh and the border flows derived from the Nepal–India coalition solution. (Rs. 2,754.)
$v(3) =$	Maximum net benefits available to Nepal. Since Nepal is everywhere upstream of India and Bangladesh solve the problem with a separate budget for Nepal and no constraints on the border flows. (Rs. 23.)
$v(1,2) =$	Maximum net benefits for a coalition of India and Bangladesh. Joint budget for these countries and the inflows from Nepal set at the level of no development in Nepal. (Rs. 8,265.)
$v(1,3) =$	Maximum net benefits for a coalition of India and Nepal. Joint budget for the two countries. No constraints on the downstream flows in Bangladesh. (Rs. 4,409.)
$v(2,3) =$	Maximum net benefits for a coalition of Nepal and Bangladesh. Joint budget for the two countries. Assume no developments in India. (Rs. 3,729.)
$v(1,2,3) =$	Maximum net benefits to the Grand Coalition of the three countries. This is the 'optimum use of the basin'. (Rs. 8,643.)

looks like a 50–50 split with only small amounts going to Nepal. However, the amounts going to Nepal vary considerably in percentage terms; they range over a factor greater than 10, from 23 to 378. Nepal's best outcome occurs at the same time as Bangladesh's worst, suggesting that Nepal should 'be nice to India' on issues outside of this river problem to influence the negotiated outcome to this end of the range.

CONCLUSIONS

Without strong and widely accepted international law, the problems associated with the use of water resources in international river basins appear to be quite difficult to resolve unless some form of strong voluntary agreement between the parties concerned is reached. Despite the absence of such international law, however, it is not a Hobbesian jungle. In recent water use conflicts the parties have usually agreed to talk and negotiate. The existence of the various declarations and provisionally approved articles concerning the use of international river basins has indeed helped to create a body of conventions (if not customary law) that inhibit some of the worst aspects of

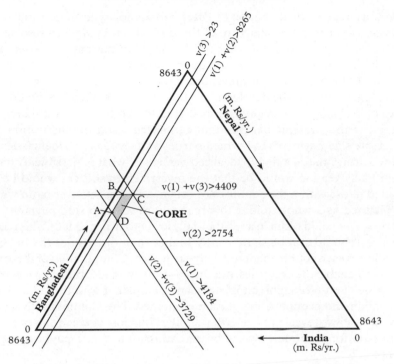

Fig. 3.6. Core for India, Bangladesh, and Nepal game

sovereign behaviour by upstream, and in some cases, downstream, states. It is, therefore, less likely that in the future upper riparians will behave with regard to the lower riparians in the way that the conflicts on the Euphrates among Turkey, Syria, and Iraq have unfolded. Indeed, future developments on the Nile will probably see multilateral negotiations rather than the bilateral negotiations between just Egypt and the Sudan (or their proxies) that have characterized earlier settlements.

The new willingness to negotiate has taken on many different forms. Bilateral arrangements between India and Bangladesh and between India and Nepal concerning the use of the Ganges–Brahmaputra system, and multilateral agreements on the Rhine concerning water quality, and on the Mekong concerning resource development, are examples. The Mekong Committee represents an almost autonomous organization at one end of the spectrum (Kirmani, 1990), and the Joint Rivers Commission on the Ganges, which meets only occasionally, represents a weak structure with effectively no autonomy from the Indian and Bangladeshi governments, at the other end. Whatever the actual organizational structure chosen, this paper argues that in order to make reasonable and equitable decisions regarding resource use an *overall basin-wide study has to be made to establish the range of possible Pareto-admissible solutions.*

Unfortunately, the definition of Pareto-admissibility itself depends upon assumptions about the structure of the institutions created to resolve the problems. In the conventional approach utilized in this paper it is assumed that the Pareto solutions are based upon maximizing the total net benefits that could be derived from the utilization of the basin given the total resources available for the development. In other words, there are no boundaries in the plan, investments are placed in the best geographical areas to maximize the strategic benefits that can accrue, and the institution can effectuate side-payments to harmed parties and charges to beneficiaries. In many settings this is a highly idealized version of what is possible. A much more likely version would be that the investment resources would be restricted to use within the countries of origin, and that the river basin would be planned as a whole under this restriction, with no side-payments or charges. This could result in a substantially lower total net benefit. This result, however, should still be significantly higher than the sum of the benefits accruing to each country acting strictly on its own. Computation of these two cases will enable the countries and the co-ordinating institution to establish the value of co-ordination on its own, and compare it with the value of co-ordination and economic integration combined. The Columbia River case discussed above revealed a somewhat similar situation where the investments were paid for separately by the basin countries but side-payments were allowed.

The derivation of Pareto-admissible strategies for exploitation of the river basin's resources should lead naturally to the key concept that appears to be central to the current thrust of both the Helsinki Rules and the ILC recommendations: reasonable and equitable solutions. This search could be based upon the Pareto solutions discussed above and upon the imputations implied by Core Theory, by asking the following questions:

> Are there decisions (from the set of $x \in X$) which a country would choose if it were acting alone that are also optimal under one of the Pareto solutions?

> Are there side-payments that a country would be willing to accept to avoid choosing an independently optimal solution that would cause harm to a neighbour?

> Are there sets of decisions that when jointly taken will lead to an overall increase in benefits and leave no one country worse off?

Pursuing these types of questions for the Ganges–Brahmaputra river basin we found some interesting results that are not immediately apparent from examination of the river basin development from a strictly national point of view. First, we discovered that the core of the game is not empty; in other words, if a strong river basin authority existed that could allocate the costs and the benefits according to the core, there would be no incentive for coalitions to form that would block these allocations. Even in the absence of such an institution, the core could form the basic arbitration strategy of any third-party approach to resolving the issues.

If it is generally the case that international river basin conflicts have a non-empty[6] core, why should it be so hard to arrive at resolutions of such problems? The existence of imputations in the core implies ease in finding acceptable solutions. It might be that the difficulty arises from some other concepts of nation-state sovereignty which make it difficult for nation-states to negotiate on water issues. The Canadian stance on the Columbia treaty may be one good example of non-economic sovereignty issues intruding and excluding economically good Pareto solutions. Such sovereignty issues certainly are important in the Ganges–Brahmaputra basin.

The Pareto-admissible solutions generated by using arbitrary weights on the benefits to each country could also be used to form the basis of arbitrated settlements. We discovered that there are substantial (in the order of 20 per cent of the total) benefits to co-ordination alone, with only a small increment (another 5 per cent) for full integration in the Ganges–Brahmaputra basin. These results are based upon average flow conditions under which Nepal does not enjoy a particularly important strategic position. However, this might change markedly, if more extreme flow conditions were imposed, when large upstream storages would be required to stabilize the downstream flows.

Finally, the sets of criteria embodied in Article V of the Helsinki Rules for assessing reasonable and equitable allocation of benefits would tend to allocate too much to India and too little to Bangladesh in comparison with the more 'economical' approaches outlined above. This occurs because the Article V approach does not adequately reflect the economic investment opportunities in the basin.

The sheer magnitude of the numbers of actual or potential conflicts over water use around the world, and their intensification in coming years with continuing growth of population, indicates that there is great need to develop a consistent framework and methodology to develop and sort out potential solutions for this class of problems. This paper has been a modest step in that direction.

---

[6] This proposition is not proved in this paper. Chen (1975) showed that the core would always be empty for water pollution games of the type formulated by Dorfman, Jacoby, and Thomas, no matter how many players were involved. This is a strong finding and explains the difficulty that negotiators have in arbitrating and finding agreements between upstream and downstream riparians for this class of problems. For a three-person game, however, Chen was able to show the existence of stable Bargaining Sets.

REFERENCES

Abbas, B. M. (1984), *The Ganges Water Dispute*, 2nd edn. (Dhaka: University Press).

Baumol, W. J. (1986), *Superfairness* (Cambridge, Mass.: MIT Press).

Begum, K. (1987), *Tension Over the Farakka Barrage* (Dhaka: University Press).

Cano, G. J. (1989), 'The Development of the Law of Water Resources and the Work of the International Law Commission', *Water International*, 1.

Caponera, D. A. (1983), 'International River Law', in M. Zaman (ed.), *River Basin Development*, Proceedings of the National Symposium on River Basin Development, Dec. 1981 (Dublin: Tycooly).

Chen, S. H. (1975), 'Application of Some Game Theoretic Concepts to the Bow River Problem', Discussion Paper No. 75-3, Environmental Systems Program (Harvard University; mimeo).

Delli Priscoli, J. (1990), 'Epilogue', *Water International*, 15/4.

Dinar, A. and Yaron, D. (1986), 'Sharing Regional Cooperative Gains from Reusing Effluent for Irrigation', *Water Resources Research*, 22/3.

Dorfman, R. and Dorfman, N. S. (eds.) (1997), *Economics of the Environment* (New York: W. W. Norton).

—— R., Jacoby, H. D., and Thomas, H. A., Jr. (1972), *Models for Managing Water Quality* (Cambridge, Mass.: Harvard University Press).

Dufournaud, C. M. (1982), 'On the Mutually Beneficial Cooperative Scheme: Dynamic Change in the Payoff Matrix of International Basin Schemes', *Water Resources Research*, 18/4.

Dufournard, C. M. and Harrington, J. J. (1990), 'Temporal and Spatial Distribution of Benefits and Costs in River-Basin Schemes: A Cooperative Game Approach', *Environment and Planning* 22.

Dufournard, C. M. and Harrington, J. J. (1991), 'A Linear Constraint Formulation for Spatial and Temporal Cost Imputations in Accord with Shapely Values', *Environment and Planning* 23.

El-Hindi, J. (1990), 'Note, the West Bank Aquifer and Conventions Regarding Laws of Belligerent Occupation', *Michigan Journal of International Law*, 11 (Summer).

Fisher, R. and Ury, W. (1981), *Getting To Yes* (Harmondsworth: Penguin).

Guariso, G., and Whittington, D. (1987), 'Implications of Ethiopian Water Developments for Egypt and Sudan', *Water Resources Development*, 3/2.

Haynes, K. E. and Whittington, D. (1981), 'International Management of the Nile: Stage Three?' *Geographical Review*, 71/1.

Hayton, R. D. (1983), 'The Law of International Water Resources Systems', in Zaman, M. (ed.), *River Basin Development*, Proceedings of the National Symposium on River Basin Development, Dec. 1981 (Dublin: Tycooly).

—— and Utton, A. E. (1989), 'Transboundary Groundwaters: The Bellagio Draft Treaty', *Natural Resources Journal*, 29 (Summer).

Hirshliefer, R., DeHaven, J. C., and Milliman, J. W. (1960), *Water Supply: Economics, Technology, and Policy* (Chicago: University of Chicago Press).

Islam, M. R. (1987), *Ganges Water Dispute* (Dhaka: University Press).

Kirmani, S. S. (1990), 'The Experience of the Indus and the Mekong', *Water International*, 15/4.

Krishna, R. (1988), 'The Legal Regime of the Nile River Basin', in J. R. Starr and D. C. Stoll (eds.), *The Politics of Scarcity:Water in the Middle East* (Boulder, Colo.: Westview Press).

Krutilla, J. V. (1966), 'The International Columbia River Treaty: An Economic Evaluation', in A. V. Kneese and S. C. Smith (eds.), *Water Research* (Baltimore: Johns Hopkins University Press).

—— (1967), *The Columbia River Treaty* (Baltimore: Johns Hopkins University Press).

LeMarquand, D. G. (1977), *International Rivers: The Politics of Cooperation* (Vancouver, B. C.: University of British Columbia and the Waterloo Research Centre, Ontario).

—— (1990), 'International Development of the Senegal River', *Water International*, 15/4.

Maass, A. *et al.* (1962), *Design of Water Resources Systems* (Cambridge, Mass.: Harvard University Press).

Michel, A. A. (1967), *The Indus Rivers* (New Haven, Conn.: Yale University Press).

Quinn, J.T. (1991), 'Analysis of Optimal and Nearly Optimal Plans for Multipurpose River Basin Projects' (Ph.D. thesis, Harvard).

Repetto, R. (1987), 'Population, Resources, and Environment: An Uncertain Future', *Population Bulletin*, 24/2.

Rogers, P. (1969), 'A Game Theoretic Approach to the Problems of International River Basins', *Water Resources Research*, 5/4.

Rogers, P., Seckler, D., and Lydon, P. (1989), *Eastern Waters Study: Strategies to Manage Flood and Drought in the Ganges–Brahmaputra Basin*, Prepared for the Office of Technical Resources, Bureau for Asia and the Near East, US Agency for International Development.

Sinclair, I. (1987), *The International Law Commission* (London, Grotius).

Smith, S. E. and Al-Rawahy, H. M. (1990), 'The Blue Nile: Potential for Conflict and Alternatives for Meeting Future Demands', *Water International*, 15/4.

Starr, J. R. and Stoll, D. C. (eds.) (1988), *The Politics of Scarcity:Water in the Middle East* (Boulder, Colo.: Westview Press).

Tekeli, S. (1990), 'Turkey Seeks Reconciliation for the Water Issue Induced by the Southeastern Anatolia Project (GAP)', *Water International*, 15/4.

Tijs, S. H. and Driessen, T. S. H. (1986), 'Game Theory and Cost Allocation Problems', *Management Science*, 32/8.

United Nations (1978), *Register of International Rivers*, prepared by the Center for Natural Resources, Energy and Transport of the Department of Economic and Social Affairs of the United Nations; pub. in *Water Supply and Management*, 2 (1978).

—— (1987), 'Report of the International Law Commission on the Work of its Thirty-ninth Session', General Assembly Supplement No. 10 (A/42/10), (New York: United Nations).

United Nations (1990), 'Report of the International Law Commission on the Work of its Forty-second Session', General Assembly Supplement No. 10 (A/45/10), (New York: United Nations).

Vlachos, E. (1990), 'Prologue', *Water International*, 15/4.

Von Neuman, J. and Morgenstern, O. (1944), *Theory of Games and Economic Behavior* (Princeton, NJ: Princeton University Press).

—— (1979), *Hydropolitics of the Nile Valley* (New York: Syracuse University Press).

Waterbury, J. (1987), 'Legal and Institutional Arrangements for Managing Water Resources in the Nile Basin', *Water Resources Development*, 3/2.

World Bank (1990), *Operational Directive 7.50: Projects on International Waterways* (Washington: World Bank).

Young, H. P., (ed.) (1985), *Fair Allocation*, Proceedings of Symposia in Applied Mathematics (Providence, RI: American Mathematical Society).

Young, H. P., Okida, N., and Hashimoto, T. (1982), 'Cost Allocation in Water Resources', *Water Resources Research*, 18/3.

Zaman, M. (ed.) (1983), *River Basin Development*, Proceedings of the National Symposium on River Basin Development, Dec. 1981 (Dublin: Tycooly).

4

The Interdependence between Environment and Development: Marine Pollution in the Mediterranean Sea

Ignazio Musu

ENVIRONMENTAL PROTECTION AND ECONOMIC DEVELOPMENT IN THE MEDITERRANEAN BASIN

The Mediterranean basin poses concerns that are at once political, economic, and ecological. The three aspects are interlinked. Moreover, each entails different considerations for the northern and southern shores. In this paper I will address the ecology–economics interface. This is a complex area, and involves a number of issues: marine pollution, the degradation of land resources, and the depletion of fresh-water resources. In what follows, I will limit myself further by concentrating on the first aspect: marine pollution. I shall do this because it is a concern with marine pollution that motivated the design of the institutional framework, known as the Barcelona Convention, that currently deals with the Mediterranean environmental problem.

In fact, the marine pollution problem in the Mediterranean basin can be reduced to a set of regional problems, each involving two or more (but not all) countries bordering the Mediterranean sea. Moreover, there is increasing evidence that most marine-pollution problems originate on land; specifically, coastal zones and their watersheds. It follows that actions at the national level are necessary. Given this fact, the role of international co-operation would be to promote national undertakings and to support each nation with institutional and financial instruments. A considerable portion of this paper will, therefore, be devoted to a discussion of those institutional agreements that are relevant for combating marine pollution in the Mediterranean Sea.

Of course, in referring to 'actions at the national level', I include development policies. The problem is particularly important in the Mediterranean, where countries experiencing different rates and patterns of growth coexist. For example, the less developed among these countries (i.e. those in the south and south-east) have pursued development policies that have been particularly unfriendly towards the environment. They have exacerbated the environmental problems of the basin.

The paper is organized as follows. First, I will review those aspects of the general problem of environmental pollution in the Mediterranean that would appear to be most important. I will then focus on the problem of marine pollution in the basin. Next, I shall make use of the Blue Plan of the United Nations Environment Programme (UNEP) to connect the process of economic development in this region to the evolution of the state of marine pollution in the Mediterranean. Finally, the institutional framework for international environmental action in the Mediterranean will be discussed.

RESOURCE DEPLETION IN THE MEDITERRANEAN BASIN

The environmental problem in the Mediterranean basin can be interpreted as a problem of resource depletion (World Bank–European Investment Bank, 1990).[1] Sea-water, degraded by various types of pollutants, is a re-source that provides multiple services. The Mediterranean Sea is only moderately productive, and the demand for fish in Mediterranean countries substantially exceeds their local supply. The deficit is only partly met by imports from the Atlantic and other fisheries. Bottom-living species, such as mullet and hake, are the most in demand. These species are for the greater part to be found along the northern coast, and they are fully exploited. A number of pelagic fish (anchovy, sardines, mackerel, and so forth) are found in the north-western Mediterranean. Over 80 per cent of these are now caught in the western zone. Owing to the decline in nutrients along the east–west stretch, and to the construction of the Aswan Dam, there has been a severe destruction of the sardine and anchovy fisheries.

Even more serious and widespread are problems of land and soil degradation, in particular, along coastal areas. Urban and industrial development, transport, tourism, and agricultural activity together have contributed to this degradation. Urban development is particularly responsible for the production of solid wastes, although this varies widely across both location and income levels. In the less-developed countries of the region, sewage-collection systems are poorly managed and treatment plants and land-fills are few in number. Industrial development is responsible for a growing number of problems associated with hazardous wastes that are stored in an unsafe way on industrial sites or are dumped illegally into the sea and river basins. (The latter practice contaminates soil and ground-water.) Land and soil degradation and the treatment of waste are all related to marine pollution in the Mediterranean.

In addition, areas of fertile land are continually being developed for urban activities. Land of low capability tends to be over-used for agriculture. This adds to the rate of soil erosion. In one estimate (Mediterranean Action Plan, 1990), soil erosion is 'severe' in 33 per cent of Mediterranean Spain (size:

---

[1] The formal similarity between pollution and resource-management problems was demonstrated in Dasgupta (1982).

5 Mha.); in 25 per cent of Yugoslavia (5 Mha.); in 36 per cent of Greece (5 Mha.); and in 90 per cent of Mediterranean Turkey (16 Mha.). Over-cultivation, over-grazing, and poor land management have increased the risk of soil degradation through salinization and desertification, particularly in the southern coast: in Egypt 30 per cent of the Nile Delta and Valley is estimated to be affected by salinization.

Important aspects of degradation of coastal resources are deforestation and 'wetland-upsetting'. The intensity of forest damage is particularly severe in Yugoslavia, and in the eastern (Turkey) and south-western (Morocco) coast. The sources of the damage here are deforestation, forest fires, and atmospheric pollution; but poor soils and periodic droughts exacerbate the loss in forest productivity in the south-west area of the basin.

Wetlands are an important feature of the Mediterranean coast, particularly estuarine and delta systems, and lagoons. They trap silt and receive organic matter and dissolved nutrients. The supply of nutrients permits plant growth, and the diversity of food sources attracts a large number of fish and a wide variety of wildlife. Ever since ancient times, Mediterranean wetlands have been progressively drained for land reclamation and malaria eradication. The resulting conversion of the wetlands has reduced their ability to sustain wildlife and migratory birds. It has also diminished their capacity to assimilate pollutants.

The depletion of fresh-water resources is likely to become the most important environmental issue facing Mediterranean countries; in particular, their coastal areas. Water scarcity and water pollution together pose an ecological problem that threatens the region in the immediate future. In the extreme, it contributes to economic crises, even famines and regional wars. Examples include the conflict between Egypt and Sudan over Nile-water; between Iraq and Syria over Turkish waters; and the growing demand for the waters of the River Jordan resulting in reduction of ground-water reservoirs.

Access to clean water is not a major problem in advanced countries in the northern reaches of the basin or in Turkey. On the other hand, pollution is a threat there. Furthermore, over-exploitation has resulted in salt-water intrusion and land subsidence in several urban and industrial areas. Close to one-third of the population in the south-east region suffers from inadequate potable water. A still larger proportion suffers from inadequate sanitation facilities. Until the end of this century, more than 75 per cent of the increase in the demand for fresh water will be in the southern countries which even now have fresh-water balances that are fragile.

Many countries in the southern part of the basin use ground-water resources faster than their replenishment rate. According to one influential estimate, the ratio of draw-offs to total water resources is more than one in Israel, Egypt, and Libya; but the ratio of draw-offs to the stable flows of water resources is higher than one in Spain, Italy, Cyprus, Malta, Israel, Egypt, Libya, Tunisia, and Morocco (Grenon and Batisse, 1989).

The problem of fresh-water scarcity is worsened by the fact that the price at which water is sold is significantly below the marginal cost of supply. This practice discourages technological adaptation; and it does not allow for replenishment of aquifers.[2]

MARINE POLLUTION PROBLEMS

The Mediterranean Sea consists of a series of interacting parts and adjacent seas, including two major basins (Western and Eastern). In the Western Mediterranean (about 0.85 million km^2), they include the Alboran Sea, the Algero-Provencal basin, the Ligurian Sea, and the Tyrrhenian Sea. In the Eastern Mediterranean (about 1.65 million km^2), they include the Adriatic Sea, the Ionian Sea, the Aegean Sea, and the Levant (Fig. 4.1).

The surface current system of the Mediterranean involves migration of Atlantic water towards the east. The Mediterranean's circulation pattern has some general features that are stationary; but even they display noticeable seasonal variations. The winter circulation displays a general eastward flow along the North African coast, then a flow along the shore of Asia Minor into the Aegean and then back to the Western Mediterranean as a general westward flow. The summer surface flow is more complex, owing to the more diverse and smaller-scale wind regimes. There is no surface system from the east to the west; the return is by way of intermediate and deep waters, flowing from east to west. The estimated turnover time for the Mediterranean waters is 80 years. The Mediterranean circulation system contains vertical convection components. This affects the distribution of salinity and produces vertical recycling of nutrients and other dissolved substances.

The Mediterranean Sea has a deficient hydrological balance, with losses due to evaporation exceeding recharge through run-off and precipitation. This deficiency is compensated for the most part by Atlantic surface waters flowing into the sea through the Strait of Gibraltar. Roughly speaking, evaporation outflow amounts to 95,000 m^3/s, while precipitation and run-off inflow amount to 50,000 m^3/s. The difference is the net inflow from the Dardanelles and Gibraltar.

By far the greatest volume of waste discharge into coastal waters consists of organic material, which is subject to bacterial attack. The rate of bacterial action depends on the temperature and oxygen availability, among other things. When these factors become limiting, the capacity of the waters to accept organic wastes without damage is reduced. At large rates of discharge, the oxygen demand by bacterial action may exceed the supply of dissolved oxygen. Under these circumstances, further degradation depends on the

---

[2] The marginal social cost of extraction should include the additional future cost of extraction resulting from current extraction. On this, see Dasgupta (1982).

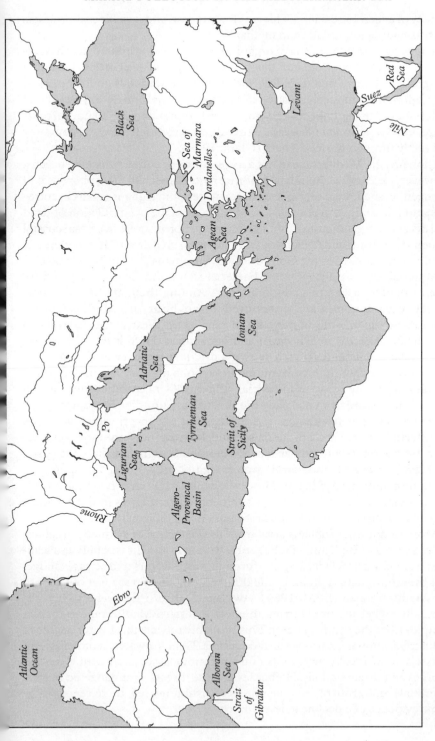

Fig. 4.1. The Mediterranean Sea

activity of anaerobic bacteria. This is a slow process, and it yields end-products such as hydrogen sulphide and methane.

The environmental effects of organic wastes include polluted beaches, inshore waters, and bays; organic deposits in bays and the sea bottom, including sea-grass bed; increased turbidity; and damage to wetlands and submerged vegetation. Both the accumulation of organic material and de-oxydization of waters have strong impacts and impoverish fauna and flora and, furthermore, they cause human diseases, either directly through the water source or indirectly through the food-chain (Clark, 1989).

Globally, the Mediterranean has a lower nutrient content than the oceans. However, excessive accumulation of nutrients (especially phosphorous and nitrogen) in shallow, poorly mixed coastal waters and lagoons results in eutrophication, including 'green tides', 'red tides', and the accumulation of dead and decaying vegetation and fish. The phenomenon is severe in certain coastal lagoons (e.g. Tunis and Alexandria) and in the north Adriatic. It is moderately severe in places such as the Golfe du Lion, Saronikos Bay, and Izmir Bay.

Materials that are not subject to bacterial attack and are not dissipated are often called 'conservative contaminants'. Among them are heavy metals. Mercury compounds are distributed throughout the Mediterranean. Consistently high levels of mercury in tuna in the Western Mediterranean pose health hazards to fishermen and consumers. High levels of mercury occur near point sources, such as rivers draining mercury-enriched areas. High levels of cadmium compounds in lagoons and bays result from discharges of mining-water or industrial effluents. Concentrations in shellfish pose health hazards, but normally the shellfish are unfit for consumption for other reasons. For this reason, cadmium is not a high-priority issue in the Mediterranean. Lead compounds are widely introduced into the Mediterranean by aerial fallout; in particular, automobile emissions have increased lead levels in coastal and marine waters significantly. Local 'hot spots' can result from industrial effluents. However, while lead is known to be a hazardous pollutant in the terrestrial environment, current levels in the Mediterranean marine environment appear to pose no significant hazard.

More significant problems arise from the discharge of synthetic organics. Polychlorinated Biphenils (PCBs) enter the environment via spills and leakages from industrial facilities, and through waste-waters and sewage sludge. But the atmosphere is probably the dominant mode of transport of PCBs to the Mediterranean (EPM, 1989). Average levels of PCBs tend to be substantially higher in samples from the north-western Mediterranean than in samples from the south and east. This probably reflects the greater degree of industrialization in north-western countries. Data for water, sediments, and mussels show locally high PCB concentrations associated with river discharges and urban outfalls. Higher levels pose threats to endangered marine mammals and probably to consumers of fish; however, there seems to be some evidence of a decline in levels since 1978.

DDT compounds are distributed by aerial fallout from regional and continental sources. Local run-off or soil erosion from agricultural or urban areas result in local contamination of sediments, fish, and wildlife. DDT accumulates in biota and poses a threat to fish-eating birds. General background contamination levels are not considered hazardous. However, unrecorded hot spots are thought to exist in areas of heavy use.

Estimates of annual pollution loads of the Mediterranean from land-based sources have been provided by technical agencies of the Mediterranean Action Plan (MAP, 1989). About 60 to 65 per cent of the load of organic matter (expressed in terms of biochemical and chemical oxygen demand) comes from coastal sources. Of this percentage, half originates in industry, and about one-quarter each from domestic sewage and agriculture. Seventy-five to 80 per cent of phosphorus and nitrogen are derived from riverine inputs. One-third of the detergents stem from coastal sewer outfalls and two-thirds are discharges from rivers. Most of the metal loads in the coastal zone come from industry and lesser amounts are contributed by domestic sewage. The loads of persistent pesticides derive from surface run-offs, one-third being DDT compounds, HCH compounds, and other organochlorines.

The high volume of tanker traffic exposes the Mediterranean to continuous risk from massive petroleum accidents: the recent Genoa accident in the Tyrrhenian Sea is an example. Moreover, there is a high level of chronic petroleum pollution, about half of which is caused by the deballasting and tank-washing operations of oil tankers, and by the discharge of oily bilge-water. Discharges of crude oil and refined petroleum products come not only from ships, but also from refineries, coastal facilites, and urban areas, and lead to the presence of oil and tar balls on sea surfaces and on beaches. All these pollutants affect amenities, thus impairing tourism and damaging wildlife.

Non-degradable plastic materials, originating from ships, towns, dumps, and coastal agriculture, float on the surface of the sea and accumulate on beaches. They are now classified as 'severe problems': they reduce the quality of amenities, damage tourism, and harm wildlife.

A tentative analysis of the spatial distribution of marine pollutants in different areas of the Mediterranean Sea was made as a preparatory study for the UNEP Blue Plan (Aubert, 1984). The study refers to ten different zones into which the sea has been partitioned. This is shown in Fig. 4.2. The following indicators have been considered: biochemical oxygen demand, chemical oxygen demand, nitrogen, phosphorus, detergents, mineral oil, and a number of metals (mercury, lead, chromium, and zinc). From this analysis, it appears that the concentrations of pollutants are particularly high (between 25 and 30 per cent) in areas II (the Provencal Basin and Ligurian Sea) and V (the Adriatic Sea). In areas IV (the Tyrrhenian Sea) and VIII (the Aegean Sea), concentrations are more than 10 per cent. In contrast, oil pollution is particularly acute in areas VII, IX, and X.

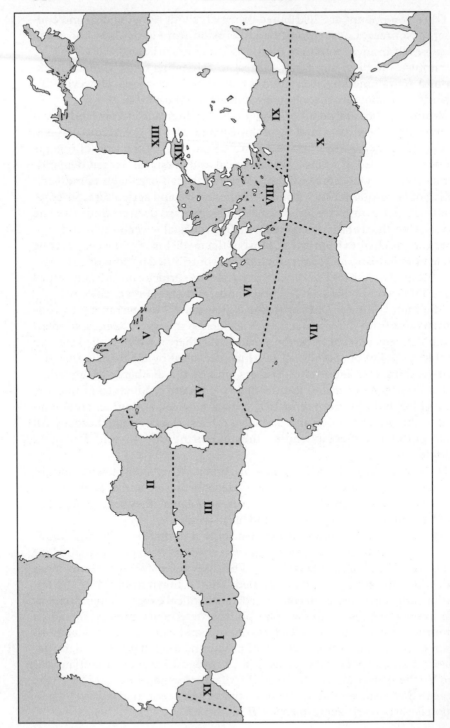

Fig. 4.2. MEDPOL areas

The biological effects of marine pollution are particularly important. Earlier, I mentioned eutrophication; but this is a local, not a regional, problem in the Mediterranean Sea. It is prevalent in the North Adriatic, Izmir Bay, Elefsis Bay, the Lagoon of Tunis, and in all areas where the rate of input of waste-water exceeds the flow into the open sea. The main symptoms consist of the disruption of community structure, excessive micro- and macro-algae production, and the development of anoxicity in the sub-surface layer. However, the open-sea oligotrophic Mediterranean waters remain in sharp contrast to the conditions prevailing in their peripheral parts.

Confined or semi-confined Mediterranean localities that are adjacent to large urban centres appear to be the site of a progressive build-up of pollution. This is a result of continued and uncontrolled anthropogenic releases. The characteristic Mediterranean Posidonia–Oceanica eco-system appears to be heavily threatened and on its way to extinction in the vicinity of large urban centres (the Gulf of Fos–Marseille, the coasts of the Ligurian Sea, and the Saronicos Gulf).

Profound and irreversible changes to the eco-system and the biological economy of the Levantine Sea were caused by two man-made alterations of the environment: the opening of the Suez Canal in 1869 and the building of the Aswan Dam on the river Nile in 1965. Since the opening of the Canal, about 170 Indo-Pacific species have successfully established themselves in the East Mediterranean basin. Meanwhile, the damming of the Nile and the subsequent reduction of its outflow have resulted in a drastic reduction in yields from fisheries.

The primary human-health problems that are associated with marine pollution in the Mediterranean arise from contact with polluted waters and sand in bathing beaches, and from consumption of chemically and micro-biologically contaminated seafood. In both cases the general situation appears to have improved as a result of stricter enforcement of acceptable water quality standards. These standards, coupled with measures to reduce sewage pollution at source, have been introduced at national levels. Adverse health effects caused by the consumption of chemically contaminated seafood appear to be restricted to those who rely extensively on seafood.

THE BLUE PLAN: PROSPECTS FOR THE ENVIRONMENT AND DEVELOPMENT

Eighteen countries lie on the shores of the Mediterranean: Spain, France, Monaco, Italy, Yugoslavia, Albania, Greece, Turkey, Syria, Lebanon, Israel, Egypt, Libya, Tunisia, Algeria, Morocco, Malta, and Cyprus. In 1985 the number of inhabitants in these countries was 351 million, of which 132 million (i.e. 37.5 per cent) lived directly in coastal areas. A high proportion of the younger age-groups live in the south and the east. Life-expectancy at birth in

1985 was approximately 70 years in the countries in the northern part of the Mediterranean, and close to or somewhat below 60 years in the eastern and southern parts (Israel is an exception).

Over the last twenty years, the development of the Mediterranean region has seen a pronounced growth in industry and tourism. This has intensified the trend towards urban agglomeration in the coastal areas and in the immediate hinterland, in particular near major rivers. Wide differences in ecological, political, and economic systems within the region, allied to divergences in resource availability, lie behind the large differences in levels of economic development among the countries in this region. Indeed, the Mediterranean basin contains its own version of the North–South relationship. France, Italy, and Spain are developed industrial countries, while Greece, Yugoslavia, and Turkey are countries in the process of industrialization (but still with a high proportion of their labour force in the primary sector), while countries in the eastern and southern regions (Egypt, Tunisia, and Morocco) are poor.

The future state of the environment will depend on the characteristics of both the demographic and economic development in the coastal areas and their watersheds. The UNEP Blue Plan provides a number of scenarios that describe these evolutionary processes. However, it should be noted that differences in scenarios relate only to economic development: the effects of these different development paths on the environment are considered in a mechanical, deterministic way. The study assumes that every development scenario has a known set of environmental effects. No alternatives are considered for any scenario.

The Blue Plan considers two kinds of scenarios: the T (trend) scenarios and the A (alternative) scenarios. Trend scenarios describe developments that do not differ radically from the trend observed hitherto. Alternative scenarios describe processes characterized by a more goal-oriented approach by governments, both at the domestic and the international levels.

Three trend scenarios are identified. The *reference-trend scenario* is merely a projection of current trends. In the *worst-trend scenario* international economic growth and trade are taken to be weak, and the problems of the less developed countries (e.g. the debt problem) are assumed to remain acute. In the *moderate-trend scenario*, a certain degree of international co-ordination makes it possible to achieve better economic growth.

The Plan considers two alternative scenarios. The *reference scenario* involves the assumption that overall co-operation among Mediterranean countries harmonizes development among them. In particular, it is assumed that there is a strong commitment on the part of the European Union to find a solution to the financial problems of the southern countries.

The *integration scenario* assumes co-operation among groups of countries (e.g. countries of the enlarged European Union, the Maghreb countries, and the Arab East). Under this scenario, the growth pattern is characterized by a comparatively large number of low-productivity activities, and by a better balance between development in rural and urban areas. The environmental impact of this model of development is, therefore, less strong than in the reference scenario.

Human demography is an important factor affecting the state of the environment. Changes from traditional patterns of demographic balance (with high death- and fertility-rates) to modern ones (with low death- and fertility-rates) are taking place at different rates in the countries of the Mediterranean basin. The Blue Plan groups these countries into three regions according to different death-rates and fertility-rates: region A (Spain, France, Greece, Italy, and Yugoslavia), region B (Algeria, Egypt, Libya, Morocco, Syria, Tunisia, and Turkey), and an intermediate region C (small countries: Albania, Cyprus, Israel, Lebanon, Malta, and Monaco). In countries of region A fertility rates have reached levels below the replacement threshold. In countries of region B, fertility rates have been declining, but they remain very high (usually in excess of five). A further characteristic of region B is that fertility rates there are higher in rural areas than they are in urban parts.

Currently the Mediterranean population is divided equally between the northern and southern countries. The Blue Plan envisages that by year 2025 countries in region B will account for more than 60 per cent of the population. Thus, even under trend hypotheses, pressures on the environment are most likely to come from population growth in the eastern and southern parts of the Mediterranean basin, and international migration can be expected to play an important role in the demography of the basin. A considerable number of poorly skilled manual workers are expected to continue to migrate from the southern to the northern countries of the basin; demographic evolution will favour this process. This can be seen if we consider the ratio of entries to withdrawals in the labour market in different groups of countries. In 1980 entries were higher than withdrawals by a factor of 1.6 in northern countries, while the factor was about 2.9 in the southern countries. In year 2025 withdrawals will exceed entries in the north, but entries will remain larger than withdrawals in the south—the ratio is expected to be 1.8 (Grenon and Batisse, 1989). Under each of the scenarios of the Blue Plan, the added urban burden is a significant contributory factor to the deterioration of the coastal environmental (Fig. 4. 3). According to the Blue Plan forecasts, by 2025 the urban coastal population in southern Mediterranean countries will be four times the level of 1985 under the T2 scenario. The increase in the urban coastal population would be lower under the alternative scenario: by 2025 the urban coastal population in the southern part of the basin would be from two-and-a-half to three times higher than in 1985. But population growth will not be the only cause of environmental degradation and of increased pollutant emission into the sea: the development of tourism is also expected to contribute heavily. The number of tourists within the

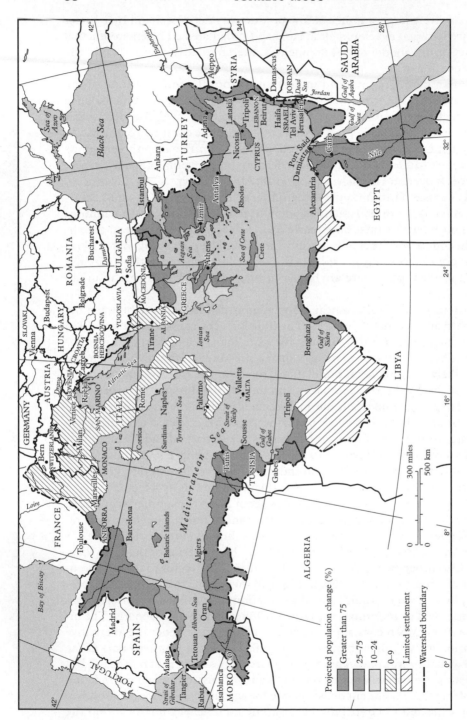

Fig. 4.3. Urban population change: 1990–2025

Source: UNEP (Blue Plan)/US Bureau of Census.

Mediterranean countries is estimated to exceed 200 million per year, of whom some 50 per cent will be from outside the region. The Blue Plan forecasts vary widely under the various scenarios. Under the worst-trend scenario, a growth of 25 per cent is expected from 1985 to the end of the century. Neutral projections indicate a growth of over 60 per cent. Moreover, the number of visitors is expected to double under the alternative scenario (Grenon and Batisse, 1989).

Marine pollution, in the form of material waste from processes of productive economic activity, such as agriculture and industry, will increase. The Blue Plan scenarios contain assumptions about future economic growth-rates. The forecasts are different for northern countries, on the one hand, and for the southern and eastern countries, on the other. The latter group of countries is currently facing structural constraints on growth arising from large foreign debts and from the fact that their exports are more than usually vulnerable to commodity price fluctuations.

The alternative scenarios assume a greater level of international economic co-operation than the trend scenarios. This is responsible for the higher figures for growth-rates in the former. However, as we noted earlier, demographic evolution is assumed to be different under the different scenarios. Differences in growth-rates between southern and eastern countries under trend and alternative scenarios are smoothed out as regards per capita GDP.

The impact of different growth scenarios on the marine environment will depend greatly on the implication of the former on sectoral development. It is expected that the southern and eastern countries will experience greater increases in the industrialization of agriculture. This will be characterized by an increase in the use of fertilizers. The Blue Plan provides forecasts for fertilizer discharge under different scenarios. These forecasts are affected by differences in the efficiency of fertilizer management and erosion control characterizing the different scenarios. Thus, in the worst-trend scenario, discharges rise by a factor of four or five, whereas they fall under alternative scenarios.

The environmental effect of industry will be greater in the southern part of the Mediterranean basin. Major problems will arise from the development of industries that are devoted to the primary processing of raw materials, since these are more polluting than light industries. The southern regions are expected to overtake the northern ones in the production of both steel and cement. The production of organic chemicals will increase in the eastern and southern countries, in the former because they are currently under-equipped (e.g. Greece, Turkey, Egypt, and Algeria); in the latter because they possess oil or gas resources (Algeria, Libya, and Egypt). The production of inorganic chemicals (e.g. ammonia and superphosphates) will continue to shift to the south and east. Refining capacities are likely to increase considerably and could more than double by the beginning of the next century. Much of this increase in capacity will probably occur because of an expansion of existing plants: the demand for new coastal sites could well be confined to a few large complexes in Algeria, Tunisia, and Libya (Grenon and Batisse, 1989). Each of these industrial sectors causes pollution problems that can only be reduced by a reliance on abatement technologies and on cleaner technological processes.

Quite obviously, the nature and extent of energy use will affect the environment. Trend scenarios would lead to a considerable development of coal-fired power-stations, which cause atmospheric pollution. In contrast, alternative scenarios based on rational demand management and on the promotion of natural gas and renewable energy sources would considerably reduce the need for oil and coal as energy inputs. The energy scenarios are directly linked to trends in pollution arising from maritime transport of oil. However, even the most pessimistic Blue Plan scenarios do not envisage significant increases in oil traffic. What they do envisage is a trend, already observed in recent years, towards an increase in the proportion of refined products in the overall traffic. (It should be noted that, when spilled, refined products have a different impact on the environment than crude oil, the former being generally more volatile and soluble, but also more explosive and toxic.)

A long-range study of the pollution of coastal waters due to domestic waste has been undertaken in the Blue Plan. Indicators that have been studied are the volume of waste, biochemical oxygen demand and chemical oxygen demand, suspended solids, and nutrients, such as nitrogen and phosphorus (Grenon and Batisse, 1989). The production of waste in the northern countries is more than four times greater than in the southern ones. As regards changes in pollution indicators in the period 1985–2025, it is an interesting fact that, in the southern region, the alternative scenarios offer a better prospect for organic pollution and suspended solids than the low growth trend. This is not so much due to specific treatment measures that are considered under the alternative scenarios, but rather, to a more rational distribution of the population over the coastal areas. However, under every scenario the south can be expected to produce a greater increase in waste production and pollution than the north during the next thirty years.

Under the Blue Plan an effort has also been made to provide forecasts about pollutant discharges into the Mediterranean. The most interesting results of this analysis are that under the spontaneous and low-growth trend scenarios the reduction in the contribution of economic activities to marine pollution in the northern countries will be partially offset by an increase in the emission of pollution in the southern countries. However, both under the high-growth-trend scenario and under the alternative scenarios, the economic development process in the south is potentially capable of encouraging the adoption of de-pollution techniques. This could lead to a substantial improvement to the entire basin's coastal area (Aubert, 1984).

INSTITUTIONAL ASPECTS OF THE MEDITERRANEAN ENVIRONMENTAL POLICY

The international environmental action for the Mediterranean Sea is an out-growth of a UNEP initiative to address the environmental problems of the oceans and the seas from a regional perspective. There are two elements in UNEP's regional approach to the environmental problem of the seas: (1) co-operation between governments in the region as a way of building an 'action plan', and then adopting and executing it; and (2) co-ordination of technical activities through UN and other intergovernmental technical bodies.

Each UNEP action plan has five constitutive elements:

1. a valuation element, aimed at an assessment of the causes, and the intensity and the consequences of environmental problems;
2. a management element, organized around a set of specific projects to deal with such problems as coastal pollution, waste treatment, and so on;
3. a legal element, based upon a convention and a set of related protocols;
4. an institutional element, to organize the execution of the action plan with the help of national institutions;
5. a financial element, to support the execution of the action plan.

The Mediterranean Action Plan was adopted in 1975 at an intergovern-mental meeting. A conference took place in Barcelona in the following year, where representatives of the coastal countries of the Mediterranean basin adopted a Convention for the protection of the Mediterranean Sea against pollution.

This general objective of the Barcelona Convention can be specified as:

1. the protection of the Mediterranean Sea area from pollution caused by dumping from ships and aircraft, by pollution from ships, by dis-charges from land-based sources, by exploration and exploitation of the continental shelf and the sea-bed and its subsoil, or resulting from emergencies (see below);
2. the establishment of a pollution monitoring system, of co-operation in fields of science and technology, and of an exchange of scientific information, giving priority to the special needs of the developing countries of the region;
3. the establishment of specially protected areas for the preservation of the natural resources, natural sites, and cultural heritage of the Medi-terranean Sea.

The Convention was adopted together with two protocols: one for the pre-vention of pollution of the Mediterranean Sea by dumping from ships and aircraft; the other for co-operation in combating pollution of the Medi-terranean Sea by oil and other harmful substances in cases of emergency.

Two other protocols were added subsequently: the first in 1980 for the protection of the Mediterranean Sea against pollution from land-based sources (which came into force in 1983); the second in 1982 that focused on specially protected areas.

In 1985 the contracting parties to the Barcelona Convention signed (in Genoa) a declaration on the second Mediterranean decade, launching a new phase of co-operative efforts for achieving ten specified targets as a matter of priority. The ten targets were the following:

1. the establishment of reception facilities for dirty ballast waters and other oil residues;
2. the establishment of sewage treatment plants in all cities, of more than 100,000 inhabitants, around the Mediterranean, and appropriate outfalls or treatment plants for all towns with more than 10,000 inhabitants;
3. the use of environmental impact assessment as a tool to ensure proper development activities;
4. an improvement in the safety of maritime navigation, in particular, reducing the risk associated with the transportation of dangerous toxic substances;
5. protection of endangered marine species (e.g. the Monk Seal and the Mediterranean Sea Turtle);
6. achievement of substantial reductions in industrial pollution and solid-waste disposal;
7. identification and protection of some 100 coastal historic sites of common interest;
8. identification and protection of some 50 new marine and coastal sites or reserves of Mediterranean interest;
9. measures to prevent and combat forest fires, soil loss, and desertification;
10. reduction in air pollution which adversely affects the marine environment.

In addition to the above, the Barcelona Convention addressed valuation and legal aspects of the Mediterranean Action Plan, by introducing a Mediterranean Pollution Monitoring and Research Programme, known as MEDPOL; a socio-economic programme aimed at reconciling vital development priorities with a healthy Mediterranean environment. And finally, it established institutional and financial arrangements for facilitating the decision-making process and for providing financial resources towards this end (the Mediterranean Trust Fund).

We have seen how the Barcelona Convention is the constitutive agreement on the basis of which all environmental actions in the Mediterranean Sea are built. It integrates community environmental policies with national actions. However, the Barcelona Convention could not have been implemented without separate and concrete protocols. Among the latter, the most important from the point of view of the problems discussed here is the Protocol on Land-based Sources of Pollution. The protocol identified substances emerging from land-based sources that may be considered pollutants (e.g. 'black-listed' and 'grey-listed' substances). The Protocol also covered the respective duties of the participating countries.[3]

OPEN PROBLEMS IN THE IMPLEMENTATION OF AN ENVIRONMENTAL POLICY FOR THE MEDITERRANEAN

The Mediterranean Action Plan is widely acknowledged to be one of the most successful examples of international environmental co-operation. Not surprisingly, it has been much studied by political scientists (Haas, 1990). However, it is not clear how successful it has been in practice. Of course, there is no doubt that the existence of the Barcelona Convention system, the periodic meetings, and the research activities undertaken both in the economic field and in the natural sciences, have contributed significantly to an improvement in the state of the Mediterranean Sea, while at the same time keeping alive, even promoting, national interests in policies that are in harmony with the objectives and the prescriptions of the plan. On the other hand, as in any other field of policy, there has been a gap between intentions and behaviour here.

A first problem concerns the nature of the Convention itself. The Barcelona Convention and its related protocols may be considered as an international trust of public purpose, beneficial to a community comprising eighteen participating countries. However, the benefit (viz. the protection and promotion of the marine environment in the Mediterranean Sea) is an international public good. If this is accepted, the contracting parties should be seen as public trustees for the entire international community. Consider, for example, a few of the Convention's provisions. Article 3 provides that the Convention shall not prejudice the codification and development of the Law of the Sea by the UN Conference on the Law of the Sea. Article 6 states the intention to establish a process of standardization for regulating pollution from ships consistent with the International Convention for the Prevention of Pollution from Ships, 1973, and its related Protocol, 1978 (MARPOL 73/78). That this reading is correct is attested by the fact that MARPOL 73/78 proclaimed the Mediterranean Sea as a special area. It recognized that,

---

[3] A number of common measures have subsequently been adopted by the contracting parties in terms of the protocol on land-based pollution. They include the establishment of environmental quality criteria for bathing waters (1985); of environmental quality criteria for mercury (1985); of measures to prevent mercury pollution (1987); of environmental quality criteria for shellfish waters (1987); of measures for the control of pollution by used lubricating oils (1989); of measures for control of pollution by cadmium and cadmium compounds (1989); and of measures for control of pollution by organohalogen compounds (1989).

for technical reasons owing to its oceanographic and ecological conditions and to the particular character of its traffic, the adoption of special mandatory methods for the prevention of pollution in the Mediterranean would be required.

A significant problem is that only nine Mediterranean countries have ratified MARPOL 73/78, even though the Third Meeting of the Contracting Parties of the Barcelona Convention, held in Dubrovnik in 1983, recommended that all the Mediterranean countries should become parties to MARPOL 73/78.

A second problem with the qualitative nature of the Barcelona Convention as a public trust relates to the financial autonomy of the system itself. The Mediterranean Trust Fund was established in 1979 for the protection of the Mediterranean Sea against pollution at the First Meeting of the Contracting Parties, held in Geneva. The administration of the fund was entrusted to the Executive Director of UNEP, who has delegated responsibility for its management to the Co-ordinator of the Mediterranean Action Plan. The establishment of the Mediterranean Trust Fund is another sign that the contracting parties have declared themselves as international trustees.

However, although the Barcelona Convention and its related Protocols were constituted as permanent modes of co-operation, the Mediterranean Trust Fund was established for an initial period of two years; and it has to be re-approved every two years. Furthermore, the Fund is entirely dependent on promises. Hence, in its present form, neither predictability nor regularity is secure.

A third issue relates to the enforcement mechanism of the system underlying the Convention. Special powers have been formulated in the Convention that concern the control and administration of the underlying public benefit purpose. Of special importance is the power of the contracting parties to hold ordinary and extraordinary meetings in order to implement the Convention system (Article 14). This allows for an institutional structure for reviewing and adapting the Action Plan and for building up the necessary consensus for action, norms, and policies to be undertaken or established.

The effective administration of the public benefit purpose is also facilitated by the power of the parties to decide at special diplomatic conferences the adoption of additional protocols at the request of two-thirds of the contracting parties (Article 15) and the adoption of amendments either to the Convention or to the Protocols at the request of the same majority (Article 16). With the exception of the amendments to the Annex on arbitration, the meetings of the contracting parties may decide on the more technical issues related to the adoption of annexes or amendments of annexes to the Convention or to any Protocol (Article 17).

An important aspect of the institution established by the Barcelona Convention relates to the powers of the parties to administer disputes between them. Article 22 of the Convention sets out a standard dispute-settlement procedure, typical of almost all treaties. In the case of a dispute, the parties are to seek, first of all, an agreement through direct negotiations. In the case of a deadlock, the parties concerned, by common agreement, are to submit their dispute to an arbitration procedure, the conditions of which are laid down in an annex to the Convention.

However, no specific mechanism is provided for ensuring that participating countries comply with the prescriptions agreed upon by the contracting parties. The lack of an appropriate international authority is a central weakness of the whole institutional system of the Mediterranean Action Plan.

CONCLUDING REMARKS

In order to close the gap between the prescriptions of the Barcelona Convention and their effective implementation, what is required, first of all, is a demonstration of political willingness by the contracting parties. As an intermediate step, regional agreements need to be reached for dealing with those specific problems for which the common interests of two or more nations can be clearly identified (for example the Adriatic problem).

Second, it is necessary to increase the financial resources available for mutually beneficial environmental projects. This means that the Mediterranean Trust Fund should be strengthened and linked directly to other forms of financial support, such as those from the World Bank–European Investment Bank, and from the European Community.

In general the financial programmes should not only aim to support waste treatment and pollution clean-up projects, but should also try to support the implementation of those structural reforms in the development process that are needed in order to make the production and consumption activity more compatible with the preservation of the environmental quality of the Mediterranean basin.

Economic instruments should be given special consideration. In the case of taxes on emissions of particular pollutants, agreement would be required for redistribution of at least some proportion of the tax revenues, in order that countries that would lose are compensated (Mäler, 1989). This is a particularly important issue in the Mediterranean basin, where countries differ widely in their growth level and per capita income. In the absence of compensatory schemes many countries would cease to participate in the co-operative effort.

So much for the politico-economic aspects of the problem; I now turn to ecological matters. A number of methodologies have been developed for monitoring pollution. A large amount of data has been collected in the ten zones into which the Mediterranean basin has been divided. What is lacking, however, is a comprehensive model of physical transport of the various pollutants that is capable of assessing the assimilative capacity of the different areas of the Mediterranean. A model of this kind would allow a better assessment of the effects on the marine environment of the Mediterranean Sea of the different demographic and economic scenarios considered in the Blue Plan. The development of a comprehensive model is a matter of the greatest urgency.

REFERENCES

Aubert, M. (1984), 'Pollutions de la Meditérrannée: situation actuelle et perspectives' (mimeo; UNEP, Nice).

Clark, R. B. (1989), *Marine Pollution* (Oxford: Clarendon Press).

Dasgupta, P. (1982), *The Control of Resources* (Oxford: Basil Blackwell).

EPM, Environmental Program for the Mediterranean (1989), 'Pollution Problems in the Mediterranean: Approaches and Priorities', World Bank, Working Paper No. 1.

Grenon, B. and Batisse, M. (1989), *Future of the Mediterranean Basin: The Blue Plan* (Oxford: Oxford University Press).

Haas, P. M. (1990), *Saving the Mediterranean: The Politics of International Environmental Cooperation* (New York: Columbia University Press).

Mäler, K.-G. (1989), 'International Environmental Problems', *Oxford Review of Economic Policy*, 6.

MAP, Mediterranean Action Plan (1989), 'State of the Mediterranean Marine Environment', UNEP, Athens, Technical Report Series No. 28.

MAP, Mediterranean Action Plan (1990), 'Common Measures Adopted by the Contracting Parties to the Convention for the Protection of the Mediterranean Sea against Pollution', UNEP, Athens, Technical Report Series No. 38.

World Bank–European Investment Bank (1990), *The Environmental Program for the Mediterranean: Preserving a Shared Heritage and Managing a Common Resource* (Washington: The World Bank).

5

The Value of Biodiversity

Paul R. Ehrlich and Anne H. Ehrlich

One of the most vexing problems facing ecologists and economists today is how to measure the value of environmental goods whose destruction (associated with the ever-increasing scale of the human enterprise) generates vast externalities. A prime example of one of those goods is 'biodiversity'—the variety of genetically distinct populations and species of plants, animals, and micro-organisms with which *Homo sapiens* shares Earth, and the variety of ecosystems of which they are functioning parts.

Economists and ecologists are agreed that biodiversity has value to humanity, although whether it has value independent of human needs is less clear. Both groups also agree that the value of biodiversity to humanity has both use and non-use components. Biodiversity can be important because it supplies us with food (fishing and hunting), direct enjoyment (scenic values, bird-watching), or ecosystem services (recycling of nutrients): all use values. It also provides non-use values, especially so-called 'existence' values; for example, the pleasure an American who will never travel to Africa may get from knowing that free-living black rhinos exist there.

This paper does not address the question of how to measure the economic values of biodiversity; that is a task primarily for economists. Rather we wish to summarize two ecologists' views of those values qualitatively to provide economists with the background they need to carry out the evaluation. One can conveniently divide those values into four categories: ethical, aesthetic, direct economic, and indirect economic.

ETHICAL VALUES

The ethical values of biodiversity are based on the religious or quasi-religious feelings of many people in many cultures that other life-forms have intrinsic value and deserve some degree of protection from destruction by humanity. These views differ from society to society and are not applied equally to all

This chapter is dedicated to the memory of our good friend, LuEsther T. Mertz, who did so much to support the efforts of Stanford's Center for Conservation Biology to preserve biodiversity. It has benefited greatly from discussions with Partha Dasgupta (University of Cambridge) and Lawrence Goulder (Department of Economics, Stanford), Lisa and Timothy Daniel (Bureau of Economic Research, Federal Trade Commission), and Harold Mooney and Peter Vitousek (Department of Biological Sciences, Stanford University), all of whom have criticized the manuscript.

organisms. Buddha questioned whether human beings have a right to kill other animals at all. A religious Buddhist may strive to avoid stepping on ants when he walks, since he considers all life sacred. A non-religious American might contend that people should never kill whales, but would swat a mosquito without a second thought.

There has been a historic precedent for extending the notion of 'rights' to include animals other than human beings. Two centuries ago it was permissible to beat your horse to death. Today horses are legally protected against abuse, and regard for other domestic animals is encoded in humane laws. That such sentiments are being extended to non-domestic animals is suggested by increasing opposition to hunting, laws to protect birds, the movement to protect whales and dolphins, and the general revulsion at such spectacles as the Canadian slaughter of baby seals.

Our own view, and that of many biologists and environmentalists, is that, as the dominant species on the planet, *Homo sapiens* has an ethical responsibility to preserve biodiversity. At the very least, this means opposing intentional exterminations of other species, and supporting conservation efforts. One cannot assert this ethical responsibility on scientific grounds. It clearly arises from essentially religious feelings; we believe that our only known living companions in the universe have a right to exist. Biologist David Ehrenfeld, in his thought-provoking book *The Arrogance of Humanism*, called this the 'Noah Principle', naming it after the best-known practitioner of conservation. In Ehrenfeld's view, species and communities should be preserved 'because they exist and because this existence is itself but the present expression of a continuing historic process of immense antiquity and majesty. Long-standing existence in Nature carries with it the unimpeachable right to continued existence.' We suspect that the basic problem of conserving biodiversity is not likely to be solved until and unless a much larger proportion of the human population comes to share this view.

AESTHETIC VALUES

The beauty of birds, tropical fish, butterflies, and flowering plants is widely acknowledged and supports extensive economic activity including bird-watching and feeding, scuba-diving, butterfly-collecting, photography, and the making of nature films. But many less familiar organisms have a little-appreciated beauty. For instance, some tiny wasps and flies, when seen under the microscope, appear to be fashioned out of solid gold. The algae known as diatoms have glass-like shells that are as exquisite and varied as snowflakes. Indeed, all organisms at least exhibit the beauty of design. Even the tiniest beetles, some of which are scarcely bigger than a full-stop on this page, have complete external skeletons, nervous and digestive systems, and complex musculature. Such insects show a degree of sophisticated miniaturization as yet unapproached by human engineers. They also exhibit complicated behaviours and intricate relationships with other organisms, giving them what we have called a 'beauty of interest' (Ehrlich and Ehrlich, 1981). In fact, insects display the kind of beauty, intricacy, and diversity that captivates gun-collectors, aircraft and railway enthusiasts, philatelists, computer hackers, bibliophiles, and so on. Even a single insect species can provide (and has provided) a human being with a lifetime of fascinating study. So even if insects didn't play critical roles in the ecosystems that support humanity, to the degree that we lose their diversity, the world becomes a less interesting place. Each species of bug is, as the great French anthropologist Claude Lévi-Strauss wrote, 'an irreplaccable treasure, equal to the works of art which we religiously preserve in museums.' (Lévi-Strauss, 1975). Each one dwarfs in interest and intricacy works like the Mona Lisa which are valued at tens of millions of dollars—yet humanity exterminates them without a qualm.

DIRECT ECONOMIC VALUES

Natural ecosystems, of course, also directly provide people with food and innumerable materials of all sorts, from maple syrup and truffles to teak. Most notably, a crucial portion of the protein in our diets comes straight from nature in the form of fish and other animals harvested from the seas. This service is provided by the oceans in conjunction with coastal wetland habitats, which serve as crucial nurseries for marine life that is either harvested directly or serves as a food supply for sea-life that we eat.

The timber and other wood products that we harvest from forests are also provided free by natural ecosystems. People do replant trees in managed forests and tree-farms, but the quality and variety of timbers from such sources is generally inferior to that from old-growth forests. Rubber, many kinds of oils and organic chemicals, spices and herbs, wild berries, and game are provided by natural ecosystems. The active ingredients in at least one-third of the prescription drugs used by civilization come directly from, or were derived from, chemical compounds found in wild plants, fungi, or other organisms, especially in tropical forests—digitalis, morphine, quinine, and antibiotics being among the most familiar.

Natural ecosystems maintain a vast 'genetic library' from which *Homo sapiens* has already withdrawn the very basis of civilization and which promises untold future benefits. That library of millions of different species and billions of genetically distinct populations is what biologists are referring to when they speak of biotic diversity, or biodiversity.

Wheat, rice, and corn (maize) were scruffy wild grasses before they were 'borrowed' from the library and developed by selective breeding into the productive crops that now form much of humanity's feeding base. Wild relatives of those and dozens of other crops still represent important reservoirs of genes that are essential for improving the crops or developing new strains to keep them from being overwhelmed by stresses such as changing climate or the evolution of new pests or diseases. All crops and all domestic animals, of course, originated from that library.

The capacity of the genetic library to supply more of the same is still largely untapped. The potential for biodiversity to supply new and vitally needed foods and medicines alone is enormous.[1] Recently, scientists have found another medically useful compound, gliotoxin, among the lowly fungi that gave humanity penicillin and cyclosporin A (the latter is used routinely by surgeons to guard against rejection of organ transplants). Gliotoxin shows promise of providing a way to make transplanted organs 'invisible' to the body's immune system without compromising their other functions (see Waring and Müllbacher, 1990). It could relieve transplant patients of the dangers of taking drugs (like cyclosporin A) that suppress the immune system and protect the transplant but also expose the patient to a serious risk of infection. Gliotoxin also has characteristics that may make it a powerful tool in designing anti-cancer drugs.

Similarly, wild plants and animals could be sources of new foods to augment the human food supply, which in the last generation or two has seen shrinkage in the variety of foodstuffs entering the economy as agricultural systems have shifted to the 'big three' and other widely grown and improved crops at the expense of many traditional varieties and species. The narrowing of the genetic base of major crops is a serious concern that has been addressed (although how adequately is questioned by many agronomists and geneticists). But the neglect of potential food plants that have never been domesticated and of many traditional foods in tropical regions is also a serious matter, especially as tropical forests—the prime potential source of new foods, drugs, and other useful materials—vanish at accelerating rates (Myers, 1989). Furthermore, the tropical regions where such new foods might be found are the regions where people are hungriest and most in need of new food resources (see Ehrlich and Ehrlich, 1990).

INDIRECT ECONOMIC VALUES

Humanity, of course, is dependent for its very existence on other organisms, but in ways that are rarely recognized in formal economic analyses. It must be emphasized that it is not just preserving samples of the world's genetic diversity (as might conceivably, but not practically, be done through a vast network of seed-banks, botanical gardens, and zoos) that is important. Other organisms, in all their extraordinary variety, are part and parcel of a global

[1] For details on the benefits humanity has received and could obtain in the future from the genetic library, see Ehrlich and Ehrlich (1981), and Myers (1979) and (1983).

life-support system that benefits them and humanity as well. We not only sprang from other life ourselves, we are completely dependent on it to maintain the habitability of this planet.

Perhaps the most basic dependence of humanity on other organisms is through the process of photosynthesis. That is the process by which green plants, algae, and some micro-organisms bind solar energy into chemical bonds or carbohydrate molecules (sugars, starches, cellulose). That chemical energy can be used to drive the life-processes of organisms, mostly by combining it with oxygen in a slow burning known as cellular respiration (or just respiration). The vast majority of non-photosynthesizers—human beings and other animals, fungi, and many micro-organisms—must obtain their energy from photosynthesizers, in most cases by eating them.

Members of biological communities, the collection of organisms living in an area, interact continuously with their non-living surroundings, and the interacting complexes are what biologists call ecosystems. Every kind of organism exchanges gases with its physical environment. The rose-bush in your garden takes in carbon dioxide (CO_2) and gives off oxygen when the sun shines (and the reverse at night). Indeed, all photosynthesizing plants remove carbon dioxide from the atmosphere and water from the soil, and use the carbon from the carbon dioxide and the hydrogen from the water to build carbohydrates. The excess oxygen is released to the atmosphere. In contrast, human beings and other animals take in oxygen and carbohydrates (as well as other molecules necessary for life), and give off carbon dioxide, water, and heat. The latter are the exhaust products of respiration; plants also produce CO_2 as they respire and use it in their photosynthesis.

Rooted plants remove a steady stream of water from the soil and release it into the atmosphere as water vapour. The volume of this water flow, which holds plants without woody stems upright and prevents wilting of the leaves of trees and shrubs, is little appreciated. A single corn plant with a dry weight of a pound at maturity transfers some sixty gallons of water from soils to atmosphere during its lifetime of a few months. The amount of water that a single rainforest tree returns to the atmosphere in its lifetime of 100 years or more is truly prodigious—in the order of 2.5 million gallons.

Plants also help to break apart rocks and form soil, and change patterns of low-level winds (as anyone who has moved from an open meadow into a woodland on a windy day can attest). Various organisms, especially bacteria, help run vast chemical cycles in which elements such as carbon, nitrogen, sulphur, and phosphorus circulate on a global scale.

The interdependence of the biological and physical worlds can be seen in the story of how our distant ancestors migrated ashore from the sea. Until perhaps 450 million years ago (about one-tenth of Earth's age), life was confined to the oceans. Then in what, geologically speaking, was a relatively short period—perhaps 40 million years—plants, arthropods (insects and their relatives), and amphibians (ancestors of frogs and salamanders) colonized thc land. That sudden emergence from the deep was made possible by the activities of photosynthesizers in the oceans.

The first photosynthetic bacteria appeared in the sea 3 billion years or more before the land was occupied. Oxygen is a by-product of photosynthesis, and all the oxygen in Earth's oceans and atmosphere was put there by that process. Today oxygen is the second most important gas in the atmosphere (after nitrogen), comprising about one-fifth of it, and it was all put there by living beings over billions of years.

Ozone is a special type of oxygen molecule formed of three, rather than two, oxygen atoms. It is formed in the stratosphere when ultraviolet radiation from the sun splits a normal O_2 molecule and one of the resultant atoms latches on to another O_2 molecule to form a molecule of ozone, O_3. Ozone absorbs solar radiation in a portion of the ultraviolet part of the spectrum known as UV-B.[2] That is lucky for life on land, since UV-B is extremely damaging to life, and no other atmospheric molecule effectively blocks it out (UV-B does not penetrate water beyond 15 to 60 feet, depending on the clarity of the water; see Worrest and Grant, 1989).

It took marine photosynthesizers billions of years to enrich the oceans and then the atmosphere with enough oxygen (and thus ozone) to create an ozone layer high in the stratosphere to shield Earth's surface from most of the incoming UV-B. So early organisms in the oceans critically modified the physical world by giving Earth an oxygen-rich atmosphere. This enabled living things, including our distant ancestors (those amphibians), to leave the sea. And ozone, a product of chemical processes in both living and non-living systems, is itself an important greenhouse gas in the troposphere (lower atmosphere), influencing Earth's surface temperature and climate.

Because of the crucial importance of interactions between living and nonliving portions of the biosphere, they can be viewed as two components of a single worldwide ecosystem. Ecologists consider the entire biosphere to be an ecosystem, and they view local biotic communities and the physical environments with which the organisms in the communities interact as ecosystems as well.

Two kinds of ecosystems are crucial to the functioning of human society today. The first kind is agricultural ecosystems, whose importance to society is obvious. Basically, they are simplified versions of natural ecosystems, artificially maintained by humanity to increase the production of commodities people need and desire. The importance of natural ecosystems is much less widely appreciated, but society depends upon them every bit as much as it depends on agricultural ecosystems. That is true in large part because agricultural ecosystems are embedded in natural ones and depend on the natural components for their sustained productivity.

---

[2] Technically, solar radiation between the wavelengths of 0.23 and 0.32 microns.

Ecosystem Services: Climate and Water

Natural ecosystems provide civilization with a wide array of essential services delivered free and, in most cases, on a scale so large that humanity would find it impossible to substitute for them (see Ehrlich and Ehrlich (1981), and Ehrlich and Mooney (1983)). The most powerful anthropocentric argument for the preservation of Earth's millions of other life-forms is their intimate involvement in the delivery of these services.

An essential ecosystem service is the maintenance of the gaseous composition of the atmosphere. That composition is always changing, as illustrated by the planet-wide buildup of oxygen in oceans and atmosphere over billions of years of Earth's history. Ecosystems prevent changes in the mix of gases and particulate matter from being too rapid.

The slow accumulation of oxygen shifted the dominant life-forms of Earth from 'anaerobic' micro-organisms that obtained their energy without using oxygen to 'aerobic' forms like us and all other animals and all plants. Organisms that use oxygen to 'slow-burn' the energy-rich carbohydrate molecules formed in photosynthesis have long since become the dominate form. Those fascinated by the 'Gaia hypothesis' that Earth is a single, organism-like, self-adjusting system whose life-forms are always improving the physical conditions in which they exist, should contemplate the fate of the anaerobes (see Lovelock, 1988). No Gaia was keeping herself a happy home for them—they started out at the top of the heap, but many were poisoned out by accumulating oxygen. Today their descendants survive in obscure, oxygen-poor environments such as swamps, hot sulphur springs, and termite guts! That life has played a major role in shaping conditions near Earth's surface is indisputable; that Earth itself is 'alive' is indisputably wrong (Schneider, 1990).

But evolving natural ecosystems have generally kept climatic changes sufficiently gradual so that life-forms could adapt to them.[3] The exceptions during Earth's long history were five events that caused sudden mass extinctions, such as the one that exterminated the dinosaurs and many other kinds of organisms 65 million years ago. All were probably due to catastrophic climatic changes. They may have resulted from huge meteor strikes or volcanic eruptions that suddenly changed the atmosphere's composition by injecting vast amounts of dust into the stratosphere and cooling the planet's surface.

The world's climate appears to have undergone other less catastrophic but relatively quick shifts from one pattern to another quite different one in response to continuous slow change in the basic forces that drive it, including small changes in Earth's orbit around the sun, pushing it over some threshold (see Schneider and Londer, 1984). The cycling of the ice ages is the best-known example. Today, the emergence of *Homo sapiens* as a global force

---

[3] This is shorthand for a lot of evolutionary theory. For a summary, see Ehrlich (1986). For details on how the process works, see Futyama (1986).

shows signs of disrupting the climate-control ecosystem service, and the prospect of rapid climatic change in response to increasing concentrations of greenhouse gases is of great concern to scientists. On this, see Houghton, Ephraums, and Jenkins (1990) and Leggett (1990).

The organisms in natural ecosystems influence the climate in many ways besides their role in regulating atmospheric gases. The vast rainforests of Amazonia to a large degree create the moist conditions required for their own survival. Water vapour from the Atlantic condenses into rain that falls on the eastern Amazon basin, is returned to the atmosphere by the vegetation as water vapour, and then condenses as rain again farther west. The moisture is recycled many times as it travels inland. In the western part of the basin, almost 90 per cent of the rain is falling for at least the second time, and quite likely a third or fourth time.[4]

The moist climate in which the rainforest vegetation of the Amazon (and perhaps of Zaïre) thrives depends to a large degree on the water-recycling function of that vegetation. This could have important consequences for the cutting and burning of the Amazon rainforest that has been so much in the news for the past few years. Many biologists believe that a critical threshold of deforestation may be reached beyond which the remaining forest will no longer maintain the climate necessary for its own persistence (see Lovejoy, 1985). After that point, the loss of the entire forest (in anything like its present form) will be inevitable.

Deforestation and the subsequent drying of the climate could have serious regional effects in Brazil outside of Amazonia, conceivably reducing rainfall in important agricultural areas to the south. The degree of impact on global climate is uncertain, but substantial changes in the 'albedo' or reflectivity of the region are likely, and could cause a significant change in the amount of solar energy absorbed by the entire planet. Such changes in albedo are taking place over much of Earth's land surface, and significant local or regional shifts in temperatures and rainfall patterns have been observed to follow. Whether these yet add up to changes that have global climatic consequences is, at the moment, unknown.

Natural ecosystems provide another service related to their climate-control functions, that of regulating Earth's hydrological cycle. In addition to the role that plants play in the cycle by transferring water to the atmosphere that would otherwise flow back into the sea, they also affect patterns of run-off. Trees in forests break the force of falling rain and, at the same time, hold soil in place with their roots. Forest soils are thereby capable of soaking up precipitation, releasing it gradually in streams and springs, or percolating it downward into aquifers (water-bearing rock strata). When a watershed is deforested, the formerly steady flow of surface water is disrupted; rain-water

---

[4] For technical references on recycling of water in the Amazon basin and for an excellent general overview of the role of tropical forests in human affairs, see Myers (1984).

runs off the surface rather than sinking in, leading to an alternation of floods and droughts downstream.

Ecosystem Services: Soils, Nutrients, and Wastes

The generation and maintenance of soils are two more services supplied by natural ecosystems. Soils are much more than ground-up rock, they are themselves complex ecosystems with a rich flora and fauna.[5] The living components of soil ecosystems are crucial to their fertility—to their ability to grow crops and forests. Earthworms are extremely important because they loosen soil and allow oxygen and water to penetrate it. Other animals that help give soil its texture and fertility include insects, mites, and millipedes. The abundance of these animals is difficult to comprehend for anyone who has not spent time sorting them from soil and studying them. In the soils under each square yard of forest in North Carolina were found an estimated 30,000 of these tiny creatures, three-quarters of them mites (miniature relatives of spiders, ticks, and scorpions). But that's nothing. Under a square yard of pasture in Denmark, the soil was found to swarm with as many 40,000 small earthworms and their relatives, nearly 10 million roundworms, and over 40,000 insects and mites.

The number of animals in soils is tiny, however, in comparison to the number of micro-organisms. A gram of forest soil has been found to contain over a million bacteria of one type, almost 100,000 yeast cells, and some 50,000 bits of fungus. A gram of fertile agricultural soil may contain over 2.5 *billion* bacteria, 400,000 fungi, 50,000 algae, and 30,000 protozoa.

But it isn't the numbers of soil organisms that makes them so important to humanity, it is the roles they play in soil ecosystems. Among other functions, micro-organisms are involved in the conversion of the nutrients nitrogen, phosphorus, and sulphur into forms usable by the higher plants that people depend upon. Many green plants enter into intimate relationships with special kinds of soil fungi. The plants nourish the fungi, which in turn transfer essential nutrients into the roots of the plant. In some forests where trees appear to be the dominant organisms, the existence of the trees is utterly dependent upon the activities of these fungi. On farms, other micro-organisms play similar critical roles in transferring nutrients to crops like wheat (Ehrlich 1986).

Organisms are very much involved in the production of soils, which starts with the 'weathering' (wearing away by the elements) of underlying parent rock. Plant roots can fracture rocks and thus help generate particles that are a major physical component of soils; plants and animals also contribute CO_2 and organic acids that accelerate the weathering process. More importantly,

---

[5] For more details on soils and technical citations on what follows, see Ehrlich, Ehrlich, and Holdren (1977); see also, for examples, Alexander (1977), and Thompson and Troeh (1973).

small organisms, especially bacteria, decompose organic matter (shed leaves, animal droppings, dead organisms, etc.), releasing carbon dioxide and water into the soil and leaving a residue of tiny organic particles, resistant to further decomposition, that make up the key soil component known as 'humus'. Humus particles help maintain soil texture and retain water. They play a critical role in soil chemistry, permitting the retention of nutrients essential for plant growth.

Organisms are therefore crucial to the maintenance of soil fertility, and they are also the principal actors in soil conservation. The roots of plants help hold soil in place, slowing erosion by water and wind. In undisturbed ecosystems, the rate of soil loss is usually balanced by that of soil formation (both ordinarily measured on a time-scale of inches per millennium). But if plant cover is removed, as when an area is deforested or overgrazed, soils start to disappear fast. Animals are involved in soil preservation too, as they disperse many seeds and thereby often speed the revegetation of denuded areas. To ecologists, one of the saddest sights in developing countries is the colour of many rivers—brown with silt—which often indicates a haemorrhaging of a prime constituent of any country's natural 'capital'.

Soil ecosystems themselves are the main providers on land of two more essential ecosystem services: disposal of wastes and cycling of nutrients. When organic matter, be it dung, the fallen branch of a tree, or a dead mouse, reaches the soil surface, representatives of that vast category of soil flora and fauna called 'decomposers' invade and devour it. It soon disappears, broken down into simpler constituents that in turn serve anew as nutrients (carbon, hydrogen, oxygen, nitrogen, phosphorus, sulphur, etc.), which are essential to the growth of green plants.

In aquatic ecosystems, bacteria are important decomposers; their waste-disposal capabilities are harnessed by humanity in sewage treatment plants. But most of the action is in the soil. In some cases, the nutrients are taken up more or less directly by plants close to where the decomposers do their work. In others, the products of decomposition may circulate through the global ecosystem in vast 'biochemical cycles' before returning to the soil and being reincorporated into a living plant.

Among natural ecosystems, soils are one of those most taken for granted. This neglect is both sad and potentially disastrous, because soils are among the most threatened systems worldwide and perhaps the ones most vitally needed for civilization's persistence.

Running Biogeochemical Cycles

Biogeochemical cycles are exemplified by the movement of two elements that are necessary components of all living things: carbon and nitrogen. Carbon travels through the atmosphere or oceans as CO_2 until it is taken up by a photosynthesizing plant or micro-organism. Carbon can be thought of as existing in a series of 'pools' through which it circulates at varying rates— the global carbon cycle.[6] One pool is terrestrial 'biomass'—the bodies of all organisms living on land. That pool, roughly 800 billion tons of carbon, is about 100 times as large as the pool of carbon incorporated in the bodies of marine organisms. Recent estimates fix the size of the pool of carbon existing as dead organic matter on land as about one-and-a-half to two times larger than that of living biomass. The pool of carbon in dead organic matter in the oceans is similar in size to that in terrestrial biomass. The amount of carbon stored in recoverable fossil fuels (all fixed by photosynthesis in the distant past) is about ten times as much. The largest pools of carbon exist in oil shale and as dispersed carbon in sediments (also ancient products of photo- synthesis); combined, these amount to 20,000 times the carbon in terrestrial biomass.[7]

Flows between the pools of carbon dioxide in the atmosphere and oceans and in living and dead organic matter were for a long time approximately in balance; photosynthesis removed about as much carbon dioxide from the in- organic atmospheric and oceanic pools as plant and animal respiration and decomposition returned to them. But now the balance has been shifted because the combustion of fossil fuels and the cutting and burning of forests are adding carbon to the atmospheric pool considerably faster than natural systems can remove it. Indeed, deforestation is subtracting a major source of uptake. As a consequence, carbon dioxide is accumulating rapidly in the atmosphere, enhancing the greenhouse effect. The scale of human activities is now so gigantic that *Homo sapiens* is actually altering the composition of the atmosphere in ways deleterious to humanity. Among other consequences, climate change associated with global warming may well both reduce agri- cultural productivity and cause extensive flooding of low-lying coastal areas.

The nitrogen cycle is very complex. Nitrogen (in the form of nitrate or ammonia) in the soil may be recycled immediately by uptake through plant roots; or it can be released into the atmosphere as a by-product of the activ- ities of 'denitrifying' bacteria, which change nitrate into nitrous oxide and nitrogen gas. Nitrogen gas makes up some 78 per cent of the atmosphere, but plants cannot use this critical nutrient in that form. Instead, it must be made available as ammonia and nitrate through a process of 'biological fixation' carried out by several kinds of bacteria in soil or aquatic ecosystems. These organisms can combine atmospheric nitrogen and water to produce ammo- nia and oxygen. The best known nitrogen fixers are bacteria that live in nodules on the roots of legumes (plants of the pea and bean family) and fix

---

[6] This discussion of the carbon and nitrogen cycles is necessarily greatly simplified; for more details, see Ehrlich, Ehrlich, and Holdren (1977).

[7] It is thought that the early atmosphere may have been rich in carbon dioxide and that the vast pool of carbon now sequestered in sediments and oil shales was taken from the atmosphere and deposited by organisms throughout Earth's history: another very significant life-caused modification of Earth by organisms.

nitrogen for their hosts in return for sugars supplied by the plants. The ammonia can then be used by plants to make amino acids, the building-blocks of proteins.

The nitrogen cycle, like the carbon cycle, is being perturbed by humanity. Tens of millions of tons of fixed nitrogen are added to soils each year in the form of inorganic nitrogen fertilizers—about as much as is fixed by the bacteria associated with legumes. This nitrogen is fixed by an industrial process (the Haber process) invented by the Germans during World War I, when they needed nitrate for explosives and were cut off from conventional supplies. Overall, human activities now lead to the fixation of a comparable amount of nitrogen as occurs by natural processes—another indication of the degree to which humanity has become a global force.

Human interference in the global nitrogen cycle has several consequences. Since nitrate is easily leached from soils by water, inorganic nitrogen fertilization has greatly increased the problem of nitrogen pollution of lakes, rivers, streams, and ground-water. It has also increased the flow of nitrous oxide, an important greenhouse gas, into the atmosphere. Fixed nitrogen from fossil-fuel combustion reaches the ground as nitric acid, an important ingredient of acid rain.

Human beings also seriously interfere in the natural cycling of phosphorus and sulphur. But the basic points about these geochemical cycles are illustrated by the carbon and nitrogen cases: first, organisms play vital roles in moving these nutrients around the biosphere; second, humanity is now a major perturbing force in these gigantic cycles.

Pest Control and Pollination

Another critical service provided by natural ecosystems is control of the overwhelming majority—an estimated 99 per cent—of pests and diseases that potentially can attack crops or domestic animals (see De Bach, 1974). Most of the potential pests are herbivorous (plant-eating) insects, and the control is provided primarily by predacious insects that consume them. This service has been disrupted, sometimes spectacularly, by the misuse of artificial insecticides, because insect pests are generally less susceptible to pesticides than are their predators. Populations of pests tend to be large (that is why they are considered pests) and so have a better chance of evolving resistance to pesticides.[8] Herbivorous insects have also long been engaged in a coevolutionary race with plants. Plants have evolved many deadly compounds in attempts to poison their attackers, compounds familiar as the active ingredients of spices (pepper, cinnamon, and cloves, for example), many drugs (marijuana, cocaine, and opium) and medicines (aspirin, digitalis, and quinine). In turn, the insects have evolved resistance to these poisons; this

[8] For a simple explanation of the reasons and of coevolution (discussed below), see Ehrlich (1986).

ability to evolve resistance pre-adapts them for dealing with the insecticides we develop to poison them.

Repeated heavy application of insecticides kills off predacious insects much more effectively than the pests. Pests quickly become resistant to the pesticides and often thrive unless dosages are continuously escalated or different insecticides substituted. Meanwhile, other herbivorous insects, previously not counted as pests because their populations were small, may be relieved of pressure from their predators, and their populations may explode. They are then 'promoted' to pest status. Insecticide resistance has been documented in some 450 species of insects and mites, and is considered one of the most serious threats to both agriculture and public health, the latter because of resistance in malarial mosquitoes and other disease carriers, or vectors (Roush and Tabashnik, 1990).

One example of this failure of the pest-control service of natural ecosystems was the promotion of spider mites to the status of serious pests in many areas of the world when overuse of DDT and other synthetic pesticides killed off their natural insect predators (Van den Bosch and Messinger, 1973). Ill-advised use of pesticides against the fire ant, a nasty pest imported from South America to the southern United States, has brought similar results. Despite numerous warnings from biologists since the 1950s, pesticide spraying has decimated the natural enemies of the fire ant and allowed it to thrive and spread. Professor E. O. Wilson of Harvard, the pre-eminent authority on ants, has called the attempts of eradicate the fire ant by massive aerial spraying 'the Vietnam of entomology'.[9] Mostly, those programmes have simply disrupted the natural ecosystemic pest controls that would have helped keep the ant in check. The fire ant has now spread out of the South, where it has long been established, and occupied a beachhead in Santa Barbara, California. It is expected eventually to reach Oregon and Washington (Lewis, 1990).

While natural ecosystems are providing crop plants with stable climates, water, soils, and nutrients, and protecting them from pests, they also are pollinating many of them—some 90 crops in the United States alone. Although honey-bees, essentially domesticated organisms, pollinate many crops, numerous others depend on pollinators from natural ecosystems. One such crop is alfalfa, which is most efficiently pollinated by wild bees.

We have already discussed the genetic library and its importance as a resource supplying a flow of foods, medicinal compounds, forest products, and materials to human economies, as well as its importance in providing a genetic back-up service for domesticated organisms of all kinds and as a source of potential new resources of unpredictable and immeasurable value.

[9] In 1957 one of us (Paul Ehrlich) wrote to Secretary of Agriculture Ezra Taft Benson, at the behest of our colleague E. O. Wilson, protesting about the first of the Department of Agriculture's ill-conceived plans to 'eradicate' the fire ant. See Ehrlich and Ehrlich (1972), for the text of that letter.

SUBSTITUTING FOR ECOSYSTEM SERVICES

As should be apparent by now, living organisms in natural and agricultural ecosystems play enormous and critical roles in making Earth a suitable habitat for *Homo sapiens*. They have already stored enough oxygen in the atmosphere for us to breathe for thousands of years even if no more were produced;[10] they supply all our food (directly or indirectly), and they help to keep the climate equable and fresh water flowing steadily. Furthermore, these services are provided on such a grand scale that there is usually no real possibility of substituting for them, even in cases where scientists might know how (Ehrlich and Mooney, 1983). In short, their destruction is in large measure irreversible. Even where restoration is possible, it requires a great deal of effort and a long time to accomplish; even then, the result is likely to be an impoverished version of the original. This irreversibility thus raises important questions of intergenerational equity, among others.

People have tried substitutions, sometimes with a measure of success, at least initially. In developing the productive agriculture of the North American Midwest, humanity, with apparent success, has substituted corn and wheat for perennial prairie grasses (plants whose vegetative parts survive several winters and which reproduce over several summers). But the crops are annuals (they go through a complete generation each year, starting from seed), and annuals do not develop the extensive root systems of perennials. They therefore do not participate in the soil-generating service of ecosystems to the same degree as perennials; soil nutrient stores are gradually depleted, and soil itself is more readily eroded away. Inorganic fertilizers are used to replace some important nutrients, but they contribute little towards maintaining the structure of soil or its component micro-organisms. Whether the depth and fertility of the prairie soils can be maintained indefinitely under cultivation remains to be seen. So far, the signs are not encouraging (see National Research Council, 1989; Francis, Flora, and King, 1990). Meanwhile, native prairie grasses that might be essential elements in restoring more productive pastures in the Midwest are barely hanging on in places like cemeteries and railway embankments.

The loss of ecosystem services following deforestation is especially rapid and dramatic. Ecologist F. H. Bormann explained the substitution dilemma as follows:

We must find replacements for wood products, build erosion control works, enlarge reservoirs, upgrade air pollution control technology, install flood control works, improve water purification plants, increase air conditioning, and provide new recreational facilities. These substitutes represent an enormous tax burden, a drain on the world's supply of natural resources, and increased stress on the natural system that re-

---

[10] Of course, if no more oxygen were being produced, photosynthesis would have ceased, and we would all promptly starve to death.

mains. Clearly the diminution of solar-powered natural systems and the expansion of fossil-powered human systems are currently locked in a positive feedback cycle. Increased consumption of fossil energy means increased stress on natural systems, which in turn means still more consumption of fossil energy to replace lost natural functions if the quality of life is to be maintained. (Bormann, 1976).

The loss of the 'genetic library' service is particularly severe when tropical rainforests are cleared, and crops, pastures, scrub, or other types of vegetation substituted for them, since those forests are home to somewhere between 50 and 90 per cent of all of Earth's species (distinct kinds) of organisms.[11]

In fact, one could conclude that virtually all human attempts at complete or large-scale substitution for ecosystem services are ultimately unsuccessful, whether it be substitutions of synthetic pesticides for natural pest control, inorganic fertilizers for natural ones, chlorination for natural water purification, or whatever.[12] Substitutes generally require a large energy subsidy, which adds to humanity's general impact on the environment. And most substitutes are not completely satisfactory even in the short run.

In sum, there is little to suggest that humanity will be able to substitute adequately for the ecosystem services that will be lost as the epidemic of extinctions now under way escalates. And escalate it seems bound to do. No one knows for certain how fast genetically distinct populations and species of other organisms are vanishing, but all biologists who deal with the problem know the rates are far too high and are rising.

THE EXTINCTION EPIDEMIC

How do biologists know? First, they are watching the flora and fauna fading away before their very eyes. Coral reefs on which we studied the behaviour of fascinating fishes have been destroyed by the sewage from 'love boat' cruise ships. Many places where we once studied butterflies have been converted to motorways, car parks, or farm fields. We have searched in vain for once-abundant frogs in Costa Rica. In the last hundred years, ichthyologists have seen 27 species of fresh-water fish become extinct in North America. Ornithologists watch in distress as populations of many forests birds of the eastern United States decline rapidly (Talbot, 1990).

That evidence, however, is anecdotal. More important, and more 'scientific' evidence is what biologists know: that organisms are highly adapted to their habitats.[13] Many eastern warblers require extensive tracts of forest to

---

[11] The percentage depends on the diversity of small arthropods in tropical forests, which at the moment has only been very roughly estimated (see May, 1989).

[12] Chlorination, although clearly an important barrier against water-borne disease where supplies are polluted, does not kill some disease organisms—and chlorine compounds (such as chloroform) formed in the water may be carcinogenic or damaging in other ways (see Wilson and Crouch, 1987).

[13] Much of the material in this section is adapted from Ehrlich and Wilson (1991).

maintain their populations; the neon tetras so prized by aquarists will only breed in acid water (in which trout cannot breed); caterpillars of bay checkerspot butterflies require certain plants to eat, and those plants require certain kinds of soils to grow on. The list is endless: populations of organisms are honed by evolution to thrive in their home environments, and they often have very specific requirements for survival. If a habitat is dramatically changed, most or all the plants, animals, and micro-organisms that once inhabited it will consequently be wiped out.

Humanity today is on a rampage of changing natural habitats dramatically: cutting them down, ploughing them up, over-grazing them, paving them over, damming and diverting water, flooding or draining areas, spraying them with pesticides and acid rain, pouring oil into them, changing their climates, exposing them to increased ultraviolet radiation, and on and on. And the process is accelerating: the rate of destruction of tropical forests almost doubled in the 1980s (Myers, 1989).

Consequently, ecologists know that Earth's biota is being slaughtered at an escalating pace, but it is not possible to count populations and species as they vanish (Raven, 1987). For one thing, the true extent of biodiversity is unknown. Estimates of the total number of existing species range from an extremely conservative 2 million (some 1.4 million have been described and given Latinized names) to well over 50 million.[14] Assuming there are 10 million species more or less, and that on average each species consists of several hundred genetically distinct populations, one can easily postulate the existence of billions of populations.[15]

How fast is this diversity now disappearing? Although it is impossible to say with precision, the answer clearly is 'frighteningly fast'.[16] More than a decade ago, we estimated that mammal and bird species were becoming extinct 40 to 400 times as fast as they normally have since the great extinction spasm that finished off the dinosaurs and many other life-forms 65 million years ago (Ehrlich, Ehrlich, and Holdren, 1977; Ehrlich and Ehrlich, 1981). In 1989 Harvard's Crafoord Laureate ecologist, E. O. Wilson conservatively estimated the annual extinction rate at 4,000 to 6,000 species, some 10,000 times the 'background' rate before *Homo sapiens* started practising agriculture. It is conceivable that the rate is actually 60,000 to 90,000 species annually—150,000 times background. Assuming Erwin's estimates of tropical rainforest diversity are correct (Wilson, 1988), the base of the estimate is a non-conservative total of 30 million species instead of Wilson's 'very conservative' 2 million (see also Ehrlich and Wilson, 1991).

[14] For a fine overview, see Wilson (1989); see also May (1989).

[15] This very rough estimate depends heavily on how one defines both population and 'genetically distinct'. Based on our research group's experience with herbivorous insects (which may themselves number millions of species) and a survey of the literature, this number seems to be in the right ball-park.

[16] A fine book putting the extinction epidemic in a context of human evolution is Diamond (1991).

Of course, biotic diversity is constantly generated by the natural process that eventually creates new species. That process of the differentiation of populations (speciation) normally operates on a time-scale of from thousands to millions of years. All estimates of present-day extinction rates show them to be vastly higher than the rates at which the natural process that creates biodiversity could be expected to compensate for the losses.[17] The extinction 'outputs' far exceed the speciation 'inputs', and Earth is becoming biotically impoverished because of it.

To biologists, perhaps the most ominous data pointing to the urgency of dealing with the extinction problem are those relating to the human impact on the planet's total supply of energy produced in photosynthesis—global net primary production (Vitousek et al., 1986). Net primary production (NPP) is the energy fixed by photosynthesis, minus that required by the plants themselves for their life-processes.[18] One can think of NPP basically as the total food supply of all animals and decomposers. Almost 40 per cent of all potential NPP generated on land is now directly consumed, diverted, or forgone because of the activities of only one of millions of animal species— Homo sapiens. Although the human impact on NPP in oceanic ecosystems is very small (about 2 per cent), that on land is so huge that we appropriate altogether about 25 per cent of global NPP.

Human beings use NPP directly when they eat plants or feed them to domestic animals and when they harvest wood and other plant products. Human beings divert NPP by altering entire systems, redirecting NPP towards human ends, as when natural ecosystems are converted to cropland or pasture. And people reduce potential NPP by converting highly productive natural systems into less productive ones; tropical forests to pastures; savannahs and grasslands to deserts; deciduous forests and prairies to farms; and farms to homes, shopping centres, and car parks.

Since the great majority of the world's species (probably over 95 per cent) now exist on land, the 40 per cent human appropriation and loss of NPP there goes far to explain the extinction crisis. The amount of energy available to support the millions of other kinds of animals on Earth clearly has been drastically reduced. Plant diversity, too, is reduced because much less land, especially land with suitable soils and climates, remains to support plant growth outside human-controlled or degraded areas. One 'probably conservative' estimate made on the basis of this reduction of available energy is that 3 to 9 per cent of Earth's species may be extinct or endangered by 2000, an estimate in the same ball-park as the higher ones above (Wright, 1990). If

[17] For an overview of the differentiation of populations (which leads to speciation), see Ehrlich (1986); a more technical treatment can be found in Futyama (1986).

[18] Technically, NPP is the energy remaining after subtracting the respiration of the primary producers (mostly green plants, algae, and bacteria) from the total amount of energy fixed biologically (virtually all solar). NPP is the energy that supports all organisms—animals, fungi, parasitic plants, and other consumers and decomposers—except primary producers.

the current accelerating trends continue, half of Earth's species might easily disappear by 2050.

The amount of terrestrial NPP available to accommodate further expansion of the human enterprise is not that great, considering that humanity has already taken over some 40 per cent and the human population is projected to double in the next half-century or so. Yet expectations are for massive economic growth to meet the needs and aspirations of that exploding population. One important international study, the Brundtland Report, advocated a five- to ten-fold increase in global economic activity in the next several decades in an effort to eliminate poverty (World Commission on Environment and Development, 1987). What a substantial expansion of both the population and its mobilization of resources implies for the redirection and further loss of terrestrial NPP by humanity is obvious: people will try to take over all of it and lose more in the process.

Harvard policy analyst William Clark was being extremely conservative when he wrote, 'The implications of this desperately needed economic growth for the already stressed planetary environment are at least problematic and are potentially catastrophic' (Clark, 1989). Indeed if anything remotely resembling the Brundtland population–economic growth scenario is played out, we can kiss goodbye to most of the world's biodiversity, and perhaps civilization along with it.

THE ECONOMIC VALUE OF BIODIVERSITY

The ravaging of biodiversity is, in our view, the most serious single environmental peril facing civilization. Biodiversity is a resource for which there is absolutely no substitute; its loss is irreversible on any time-scale of interest to society. The loss can be viewed as one of the (if not *the*) most serious externalities associated with human economic activity. But it is an externality so vast and pervasive that finding ways to evaluate (let alone internalize) it will be difficult in the extreme. All we will offer here are a few comments on possible approaches.

First, there are clearly some species whose value is amenable to rather routine cost–benefit analyses—those, for example that are harvested commercially. The value of species with high aesthetic, interest, or rarity values, such as beautiful birds, *Morpho* butterflies, great whales, or black rhinoceros can also be monetized by techniques such as assessment of willingness to pay travel costs to see them or asking people how much they would be willing to donate to save them. Such methods will provide only partial values for those species, however. They would not ordinarily encompass their roles in food chains or their potential value to future generations.

Furthermore, methods focusing on the values of individual species, especially scarce ones, will not ordinarily capture the critical ecosystem services value of biodiversity in aggregate. For example, one might be able to demonstrate that the role of a given plankton-eating whale species in an oceanic food chain was not critical to the ecosystem's stability. If that species were exterminated, populations of other plankton-feeding whales might increase and fill the role of the extinct species. But the extermination of one such whale species would increase the probability that all the others would become extinct, as whaling pressures were transferred to them. Even the loss of a second whale species might cause significant changes in oceanic ecosystems (perhaps including deleterious impacts on fisheries).

This is an example of what we call the 'rivet-popper' problem (Ehrlich and Ehrlich, 1981). The removal of a single rivet from an aeroplane's wing is unlikely to cause a crash; aeroplanes have fail-safe designs including considerable redundancy. But the continuous removal of numerous rivets will sooner or later lead to disaster. The timing of the disaster would be difficult to predict, since it would depend both on only partially understood structural factors in the wing and on unpredictable future 'environmental' events (for example, rough landings or turbulent flying conditions). For similar reasons, the precise impacts of deleting species (or genetically distinct populations) from an ecosystem are difficult to predict, but the eventual costs of continuing to do so are crystal clear.

Economists, with the help of ecologists, face the unenviable task of assigning value to biodiversity in such a way that the costs of the loss of a small portion of a vast machinery are reasonably assessed. Moreover, they need to account for the enormous losses that have occurred before now, reflecting the reality that the remaining biodiversity is a fast-fading (though otherwise self-renewable) essential resource. When a few hectares of degraded semi-natural habitat, say in the vicinity of Siena, are converted into another road, how can one evaluate the cost in decreased flood control, reduced photosynthesis, increased soil erosion, and disruption of other local ecosystem services? How can one assess the loss of attractive birds to watch, the curtailed opportunities for local children to learn how nature works, and so on? The task may be extremely difficult, but it is also overridingly important. After all, a market system can hardly function to the ultimate benefit of humanity if it must classify the capacity for Earth to support life as an externality that cannot be properly internalized.[19]

REFERENCES

Alexander, M. (1977), *Introduction to Soil Microbiology*, 2nd edn (New York: Wiley).
Bormann, F. (1976), 'An Inseparable Linkage: Conservation of Natural Ecosystems and the Conservation of Fossil Energy', *BioScience*, 26.

[19] This basic point comes from Daly and Cobb, Jr. (1989).

Clark, W. (1989), 'Managing Planet Earth', *Scientific American*, 261.

Daly, H. and Cobb, J. (1989), *For the Common Good* (Boston: Beacon Press).

De Bach, P. (1974), *Biological Control of Natural Enemies* (Cambridge: Cambridge University Press).

Diamond, J. (1991), *The Rise and Fall of the Third Chimpanzee* (New York: Harper and Collins).

Ehrenfeld, D. (1978), *The Arrogance of Humanism* (Oxford: Oxford University Press).

Ehrlich, P. (1986), *The Machinery of Nature* (New York: Simon & Schuster).

—— and Ehrlich, A. (1972), *Population, Resources, Environment*, 2nd edn. (San Francisco: W. H. Freeman).

—— —— (1981), *Extinction: The Causes and Consequences of the Disappearance of Species* (New York: Random House).

—— —— (1990), *The Population Explosion* (New York: Simon & Schuster).

—— —— and Holdren, J. (1977), *Ecoscience: Population, Resources, Environment* (San Francisco: W. H. Freeman).

—— and Mooney, H. (1983), 'Extinction, Substitution, and Ecosystem Services', *Bioscience*, 33.

—— and Wilson, E. (1991), 'Biodiversity Studies: Science and Policy' (mimeo; Stanford University).

Erwin, T. (1988), 'The Tropical Forest Canopy', in E. Wilson (ed.), *Biodiversity* (Washington, DC: National Academy Press).

Francis, C. A., Flora, C. B., and King, L. D. (eds.) (1990), *Sustainable Agriculture in Temperate Zones* (New York: John Wiley).

Futyama, D. (1986), *Evolutionary Biology*, 2nd edn. (Sunderland, Mass.: Sinauer Associates).

Houghton, J., Ephraums, J., and Jenkins, G. (eds.) (1990), *Climate Change: The IPCC Scientific Assessment* (Cambridge: Cambridge University Press).

Leggett, J. (ed.) (1990), *Global Warming: The Greenpeace Report* (Oxford: Oxford University Press).

Lévi-Strauss, C. (1975), 'Discussion of the Special Commission in Internal Pollution', unpublished, London.

Lewis, P. (1990), 'Mighty Fire Ants March out of the South', *New York Times*, 24 July.

Lovejoy, T. (1985), 'Amazonia, People and Today', in G. Prance and T. Lovejoy (eds.), *Key Environments: Amazonia* (Oxford: Pergamon).

Lovelock, J. (1988), *The Ages of Gaia* (New York: Norton).

May, R. (1989), 'How Many Species Are There on Earth?', *Science*, 241.

Myers, N. (1979), *The Sinking Ark* (New York: Pergamon Press).

—— (1983), *A Wealth of Wild Species* (Boulder, Colo.: Westview Press).

—— (1984), *The Primary Source: Tropical Forests and Our Future* (New York: Norton).

—— (1989), *Deforestation in Tropical Forests and their Climatic Implications* (London: Friends of the Earth).

National Research Council (1989), Committee on the Role of Alternative Farming Methods in Modern Production Agriculture, Board on Agriculture (J. Pesek, Chairman).

Raven, P., 'The Scope of the Plant Conservation Problem World-Wide', in *Botanic Gardens and the World Conservation Strategy* (London: Academic Press).

Roush, R. and Tabashnik, B. (eds.) (1990), *Pesticide Resistance in Arthropods* (New York: Chapman and Hall).

Schneider, S. (1990), 'Debating Gaia', *Environment*, 32.

—— and Londer, R. (1984), *The Coevolution of Climate and Life* (San Francisco: Sierra Club Books).

Talbot, F. (1990), 'Earth, Humankind, and Our Responsibility', Plenary Address to the American Association of Museums (unpublished mimeo).

Thompson, L. and Troeh, F. (1973), *Soils and Soil Fertility* (New York: McGraw Hill).

Van den Bosch, R. and Messinger, P. (1973), *Biological Control* (New York: Intext Press). .

Vitousek, P., Ehrlich, P., Ehrlich, A., and Matson, P. (1986), 'Human Appropriation of the Products of Photosynthesis', *BioScience*, 36.

Waring, P. and Mullbacher, A. (1990), 'Fungal Warfare in the Medicine Chest', *New Scientist*, 27 Oct.

Wilson, E. (1988), *Biodiversity* (Washington: National Academy Press).

—— (1989), 'Threats to Biodiversity', *Scientific American*, 261.

Wilson, R. and Crouch, E. (1987), 'Risk Assessment and Comparisons: An Introduction', *Science*, 236.

World Bank (1990), *World Development Report* (New York: Oxford University Press).

World Commission on Environment and Development (1987), *Our Common Future* (New York: Oxford University Press).

Worrest, R. and Grant, L. (1989), 'Effects of Ultraviolet-B Radiation on Terrestrial Plants and Marine Organisms', in R. Jones, and T. Wigley, (eds.), *Ozone Depletion* (New York: Wiley).

Wright, D. (1990), 'Human Impacts on Energy Flow through Natural Ecosystems, and their Implications for Species Endangerment', *Ambio*, 19.

6

Population Growth, Physical Resources, and Human Resources in Sub-Saharan Africa

John C. Caldwell and Pat Caldwell

In terms of both population and economic growth, Sub-Saharan Africa is now the most critical region in the world. In the region as a whole, per capita income has fallen over the last decade (World Bank, 1989: 160). There are no longer the hopes for industrialization that were common 30 years ago. Nor have the production and export of tree crops, with a few exceptions like the Ivory Coast, developed the kind of economic efficiency that has occurred in South-East Asia. Indeed, Ghana's cocoa competed more effectively with production elsewhere 70 years ago than it does today. Africa may have to depend increasingly on the transfer of resources, not only transnationally but transcontinentally, as the continent's population grows, perhaps outstripping economic growth.

The region is demographically much more distinctive now than it was a generation ago. Its annual rate of population growth is around 3 per cent compared with 2 per cent in the developing world as a whole and 0.6 per cent in developed countries. The only other world regions with comparable rates of growth are now North Africa and West Asia, which both record around 2.8 per cent. However, there are real differences. Sub-Saharan Africa achieves this rate of population increase with a birth-rate of 47 per thousand and a death-rate of 17, the latter reflecting a life expectancy still under 50 years. North Africa and West Asia have birth-rates of 39 and 36 respectively and death-rates of 11 and 8, the latter a product of life expectancies near 60 years. This means that Sub-Saharan Africa has a much greater capacity for future population growth for two reasons. The first is that there is little evidence as yet of fertility decline, while the lower birth-rates of the other two regions are evidence of fertility transition well under way. The second reason is that Sub-Saharan Africa's uniquely high death-rate has the potential for very great reduction. In terms of the global situation, there is also another consideration: Sub-Saharan Africa has twice as many people as the other two regions combined.

This potential for growth can be appreciated by looking at the world picture. Sub-Saharan Africa has a birth-rate around 47 per thousand compared

This chapter has benefited from assistance from Wendy Cosford and typing by Pat Goodall.

with 30 in all developing countries and 15 in developed ones. It has a life expectancy of 49 years compared with 60 years in all developing countries and nearly 75 years in developed ones.

At the present time, Sub-Saharan Africa has a population of about 550 million or 10 per cent of the world's population. It is still shown in international projections as reaching more than 11 per cent of the world's population by the end of this decade, and 15 per cent by the year 2020, with around one-and-a-quarter billion persons by that time. As world population growth slows late in the coming century, that proportion could rise to nearly 25 per cent, with perhaps five times the present population. This may not come about. The reason is not faster demographic transition but AIDS, a factor with which the population projection sections of neither the United Nations nor the World Bank have yet been able to cope.

The 550 million people at present found in the region are not evenly distributed: two-fifths are in West Africa, two-fifths in East Africa, and one-fifth in the whole of Middle Africa and Southern Africa combined. Indeed, almost one-quarter of the population may be in Nigeria alone. Both birth- and death-rates are somewhat lower in Southern Africa.

It will be the aim of the rest of this paper to consider what is likely to happen to the demographic forces that drive population and to appraise the impact of population growth on the resources of the region, and on the people themselves.

MORTALITY LEVELS AND TRENDS

Mortality is higher in Sub-Saharan Africa, and life expectancies lower, than in any other world region. With one or two possible exceptions, the only countries in the world with life expectancies under 45 years are now found in Sub-Saharan Africa, mostly in the northern arid area stretching from Mali through Ethiopia to Somalia, and the excessively wet part of the western bulge including Sierra Leone, Guinea, and the Gambia. Nevertheless, it is necessary to dispel a few myths concerning African mortality.

The first point to note is that the high mortality of the region is very largely a result of low incomes and fragmentary health services. The latter are no worse than one would anticipate at these income levels. The problem is not incompetence but poverty. If there has been a failure it has been in the area of economic growth rather than the utilization of resources to provide health services. Per capita income in the region is one-thirtieth of that of developed countries and one-half of that of the developing world excluding China. However, it is estimated to be above both China and mainland South Asia.

In a study which attempted to identify eleven countries in the developing world which had achieved mortality levels much below those which would have been predicted by per capita incomes, Sub-Saharan Africa contributed four of the eleven superior health achievers: Zaïre, Tanzania, Kenya, and Ghana (Caldwell, 1986: 174). Admittedly, it also contributed three of the eleven poorest health achievers: the Ivory Coast, Senegal, and Sierra Leone. The whole study argues that the superior health achievers gained their place because of cultural and social factors, especially high education levels, greater female autonomy, and the product of these two factors, relatively high education levels among mothers. In the whole developing world the level of maternal education is a more powerful determinant of infant and child survival than is either income or the density of health services (Caldwell, 1979, 1986; Cleland and van Ginneken, 1988; Cleland, 1990). The educational factor explains the otherwise surprising contrast between Ghana and the Ivory Coast. The latter has twice the per capita income of the former but exhibits higher mortality. The explanation is that 30 years ago Ghana invested a higher proportion of its per capita income in education than any other country in the world and its mothers still have higher education levels than those of the Ivory Coast.

Another product of the relative autonomy of African women is the lack of any disadvantage, as measured by mortality statistics, that girls have when compared to boys (Rutstein, 1984; P. Caldwell and J. C. Caldwell, 1990). This is a unique situation in the developing world. First, two points should be noted. One is that most age-specific death-rate data are defective because subdividing total mortality is usually done by the use of models. The best comparative data come from the World Fertility Survey with its detailed life-histories and this is the source of the following comparisons. The second point is that we will take as our measure of female disadvantage, toddler mortality (i. e. 1–4 years), because almost universal breastfeeding during infancy has an egalitarian impact in providing both boys and girls with similar amounts of milk and antibodies. The World Fertility Survey showed excess female toddler mortality almost universally through North Africa, the Middle East, and East Asia with a more mixed picture in South-East Asia and Latin America. Only in Sub-Saharan Africa was there no excess female mortality. This is almost certainly a factor in keeping down total mortality.

It also now appears that, at least until the 1980s, Sub-Saharan Africa was more successful in consistently reducing mortality than had previously been feared. This needs some explanation. Death registration in the region hardly exists and our knowledge of levels and trends depends on retrospective data from good surveys and the development of rather radical analytical techniques. For the first time, we have available a large number of analyses of this type for the region (Hill, 1987; Hill and Hill, 1988; Timaeus, 1987). The United Nations used to estimate that developing countries could attain an increasing life expectancy of 0.5 years per elapsed year, and incorporated this assumption into its manual on population projections (United Nations, 1956). Greater experience over the last three decades has shown that 0.4 years is closer to the average experience of developing countries. Admittedly, some do much better, the Maghreb having attained almost one year per year over a quarter of a century (Tabutin, 1990).

It probably comes as a surprise to many that Sub-Saharan African has been close to the developing country average, gaining about one-third of a year for every elapsed year. Perhaps the most instructive aspect of the whole analysis is the identification of the failures that have fallen well behind in terms of the pace at which the death-rate has been reduced. They are not the poor countries, which have done as well as the rich countries although at a somewhat higher mortality level, and they are not the drought-prone countries, which have done as well as those countries not so afflicted but again at a somewhat higher level (Caldwell and Caldwell, 1987a). The failures have been countries where war or civil disturbance has disrupted government services and unsettled individuals and communities. Prime examples are Ethiopia, Angola, and Mozambique.

A central question is whether the situation where health was at least improving changed during the 1980s. UNICEF (1989: 1) claims in *The State of the World's Children 1989*: 'Throughout most of Africa and much of Latin America, average incomes have fallen by 10 to 25 per cent in the 1980s . . . . at least half a million young children have died in the last 12 months as a result of the slowing down or reversal in the developing world.' This conclusion tempts us to acceptance because of our knowledge of the famines, the economic dislocation, and the resultant decay of some health services during the 1980s. But the truth is that only time will prove whether this statement is right or not. In the absence of current data, we can establish African trends only with hindsight through retrospective data in good surveys. UNICEF achieved its estimates by comparing projections for the 1970s, which were perhaps overly optimistic, with a few very small and doubtless unrepresentative populations towards the end of the 1980s. The anticipation that the droughts and famines of the 1980s may have had a major mortality impact must be offset against the fact that those of the 1970s apparently did not.

Apart from famines and AIDS, which we will examine separately, there are other intractable health problems in the region. Malaria still rages through all but the highest and most southerly parts of the region, and there is less optimism now than ten or twenty years ago that a vaccine can be found. Insecticides are less effective against vectors, and falciparum malaria is on the increase. Malaria appears to be responsible for half of all child morbidity and probably a million deaths each year (Bailey, 1990: 1). Its existence is probably an example of transnational commons. African countries are mostly small, typically with land borders, often in forest, with three or more other countries. Any country which acted alone and spent the prodigious investment needed to rid itself of malaria would find the money wasted as disease-carrying mosquitoes and human beings entered the country from its neighbours. Conversely, a regional campaign would omit a single country at its peril.

Toddler mortality (1–4 years) is extraordinarily high compared with infant or adult mortality in terms of the patterns found elsewhere in the world. Cantrelle (1975) attempted to show that this pattern was once more widespread in the tropical world. Nevertheless, the fact remains that in the contemporary world, only one-fifth to one-quarter as many children in Asia or Latin America die between their first and fifth birthdays as during their first year of life. In contrast, in Africa, toddler mortality more often than not exceeds infant mortality. The major explanation does not seem to be malaria, because the phenomenon appears to vary little with the incidence of that disease. It is probably related to the conditions of weaning in a situation where young children not only go straight on to adult food but frequently fend for themselves in the larger family in getting it. Mothers often work in the fields or elsewhere, taking infants with them but leaving toddlers to be looked after by siblings or grandparents. Often toddlers are fostered out, especially when their mothers have remarried: levels reach 10 per cent or more in West Africa (Page, 1989; Bledsoe and Isiugo-Abanihe, 1989).

What can be done? Bailey (1990) has described how the economic strains of the 1980s combined with the new directions set by the 1979 Alma Ata Declaration to bring a halt to the building of health infrastructures which characterized the 1960s and 1970s. There has been an attempt to move towards primary health care as the Declaration recommended, with community-based health care provided by persons chosen and paid by community management councils. This has, however, worked best when higher levels of government have given both leadership and assistance (Bailey, 1990: 4). They can provide training, weeding out unsuitable selected persons, and may help discreetly to find funding to pay the community health workers. The Bamako initiative partly solved the latter problem by leading governments to sell basic drugs to community health services at just above cost price so that resale at a somewhat higher price could generate the funds to finance health care.

The most successful single community-based health initiative has been that of growth monitoring, which has worked well in three or four countries and moderately well in another eight to ten. All children under either three or five years of age are weighed, monthly or quarterly, by trained volunteers. The volunteers identify from charts or tables the most dangerously malnourished and usually either the family or the community does something about it. There are obvious parallels here to the child welfare movements in the West in the early part of this century. The star performer in this programme has been the Iringa region of Tanzania.

Almost half of the children of Sub-Saharan Africa are now covered by DPT immunization; by immunization against polio and measles (with some doubt in the latter case about its efficacy and safety; and immunization against tuberculosis by BCG (about the efficacy of which there are very substantial doubts).

The role of the central health services should not be underestimated even in community-based programmes because leadership, training, and the supply of drugs and equipment are important. In these circumstances, health management training programmes have developed during the 1980s and the results appear to be promising.

Some of the greatest successes have been achieved either by pre-Alma Ata methods or by a mixture of old and new methods. Such approaches have been expensive, however, and clearly cannot be afforded everywhere (Caldwell, 1991). Botswana has adopted an approach very similar to that which has proved to be so successful in Sri Lanka. There is a network of health clinics, the major ones having doctors. Educated young women are selected from each community and are given a two-year health training course. They are then returned to the community where they pay house visits, concentrating on households with young children or pregnant women, and they play a decisive role in encouraging women to have institutional births and to take babies and young children for treatment as soon as they become ill. Dense health services, at least by the standards of the region, have reduced mortality in Zimbabwe, much of central Kenya, and in Chogoria, a part of Kenya where the Church of Scotland provides health and family planning services. All these areas now have life expectancies near 60 years and infant mortality rates down to around 70 per 1000 births or even below. Mortality will probably continue to decline, driven by social change, urbanization, and the growth of the market economy, although this will occur more slowly if economic growth and the development of health services remain static.

THE SIGNIFICANCE OF FAMINE

Much of Africa suffers from periodic famine. This is the result either of recurring droughts as in much of the Sahel, civil wars as in Mozambique and Angola, or both as in Ethiopia, Sudan, and Chad. Indeed, the political situations and system can have a marked impact on the death-rates even in institutions: once famine camps were properly running in the 1973 Sahelian drought, age-specific death-rates within them were below those of the rural population as a whole, while in Ethiopia the camps have had the highest death-rates.

African drought-induced famines give the impression of being Malthusian in the sense of showing that the land can support no more inhabitants, that death-rates are exceedingly high, and that population growth has been reduced to zero or has even become negative. This is probably not true but it is the impression that we first had, and certainly the one we received from the international media, when we began trying to assess the impact of the Sahelian famine (Caldwell, 1975). It was clear that there was a great deal of suffering and also a flight from the worst disaster areas. The latter was alarming but was, of course, part of the answer to the problem.

The basic problem is that societies where droughts kill people are also societies where the statistical base is too weak to be able to measure the excess mortality. Richer societies, which have adequate statistical systems, tide themselves over drought years by means of the savings of individual farmers and of the nation, as happens in the drylands of both Australia and the United States. Even India is moving toward this situation and recent severe droughts appear to have resulted in little excess mortality (Caldwell, Reddy, and Caldwell, 1986; Chen, 1990). We do know that where mobility is limited, or authoritarian governments misunderstand the magnitude of the problem, or the societies are very poor sedentary farming areas, then mortality can rise to a point where population growth is halted. We know this happened in 1959–61 in China at the end of the Great Leap Forward because the record is embedded in the 1964 and 1982 censuses single-year age data. This is usable for such retrospective analysis because, unlike the situation in most of the Third World, the identification of Chinese birth-year animal signs allows an accurate assessment of what happened to each single-year age group. We also know that growth was halted by the 1943–4 Bengal famine because of the recently analysed household survey carried out by the Indian Statistical Institute in the latter part of the famine (Greenough, 1982; Caldwell, 1983). And that there was an approach to this situation in the fully measured and monitored population in the Matlab district of Bangladesh during 1973–4 as recorded by the Demographic Surveillance System of the Cholera Research Laboratory, now the International Diarrhoeal Disease Research Centre, Bangladesh (Chowdhury and Chen, 1977). Pre-modern famines or outbreaks of disease quickly produced population declines because they started with stationary or slowly growing populations, but it is very different when the initial rate of population increase is 2.5 or 3 per cent per annum.

In 1973 we discovered quickly that there was no statistically satisfactory base for the mortality estimates being made for the Sahel, or indeed for Ethiopia (Caldwell, 1975). It took longer to conclude that the suggested death-rates were much too high and that, even at the height of the famine, population was probably still growing at 2 per cent per annum. These estimates were greeted with some scepticism at the time, but further data have led to this conclusion becoming the established view (Hill, 1988: 114–15). Indeed, the West African droughts cannot subsequently be detected in the retrospective demographic record provided by censuses or surveys, but this may be partly due to poor age statement.

There was agreement among the older residents of savannah and Sahelian West Africa that the drought of the early 1970s had killed large numbers of animals but not people, in contrast to the man-killing drought of 1913, although the rainfall deficit appeared to be much the same. Clearly in 1973 there was little grass and, over great areas, almost total crop failure, so how had the people saved themselves? The greatest African defence has always been mobility, partly because neither nomads nor shifting cultivators have the same fierce determination or need to stay with a specific parcel of family land that the Asian peasant has. The African family structure also makes it easier to shed single men or most women for long periods. In normal times only single men move south in the hungry season preceding the harvest to-wards the West African forest and coast, but, in 1973, the migration stream—no longer seasonal—contained, in addition, many middle-aged and married men and some women and children. There were places to go in 1973 which did not exist in 1913: large towns with jobs or government assistance, tree-crop estates, and relief camps. Some of the migrants sent back remittances from Kano, Ibadan, Abidjan, or even Europe. There were greater possibilities of selling up both animals and household or personal possessions than in the past. Older methods of defence were also used and there was a resort to bush food and to hunting, although these resources are declining. Perhaps the greatest change was the growth of the market and of communications, in terms of roads and lorries as well as newspapers and radios reporting hard times in the savannah. Long before international aid arrived, lorries full of food were appearing from further south because of the news that prices had risen dramatically in the famine area and that a lorry-load of food would yield a good return. Even in the savannah, even if it meant some belt-tightening, high prices made food flow from the least badly hit areas. Ultimately, inter-national aid arrived, again a product of the communications explosion.

What effect does drought have on the countries prone to it? So far, pasture recovery in good seasons appears to be largely complete, and soil deteriora-tion is probably more the result of growing new crops and shortening the fallow than of misuse of soil during famines. A comparison over the period 1965–85 of ten drought-prone and famine-prone countries with those not so affected shows that the former had lower per capita incomes and slower rates of economic growth (Caldwell and Caldwell, 1987a). They also had some-what higher mortality, but no more than would be predicted by their income and educational levels. However, the rate at which their life expectancy was rising was almost identical between the two groups of countries, and the margin in the rate of population growth was very narrow.

What is the future of these areas and why do they not adopt the methods of the plains farmers of Australia or America? With regard to the latter question, the answer is that they are largely subsistence farmers and they cannot em-ploy bank accounts to carry them over bad periods. They could grow and store more food, but savannah farming is hard, unpleasant work and the idea of doing perhaps unnecessary extra work each year and throwing away the surplus through a series of good years is abhorrent. Those who did maintain stored surpluses would be under tremendous social pressure (including accusations of witchcraft) if they did not diminish those stores by sharing them with the needy. The only way out of the bind is through the growth of commercial farming and this means general development, which is not an easy prospect for these resource-poor countries. Ultimately, population growth-rates will have to be curtailed, but, at present, this has little to do with the fundamental need for development, the growth of the market economy, and diversification in primary production. Indeed, with life expectancies around 45 years, mortality is so high and capricious, that even moderately large families would stand some chance of being wiped out. The situation is, first, that even the Sahelian population is not faced by Malthusian checks, and secondly that curtailing population growth is not likely to be the fundamental solution nor to succeed until incomes grow and mortality falls.

THE IMPACT OF AIDS

The major unknown with regard to future population growth in the region and population pressures on resources and the environment is the AIDS epidemic. At present the most affected area stretches north to south from southern Sudan to South Africa and west to east from Zaïre to the East African coast. In this area, there is evidence that around 7.5 per cent of the population of Uganda is HIV-positive and there is probably a similar incidence in Rwanda, Burundi, and eastern Zaïre. Levels may well be over 5 per cent in many other areas such as Zambia, Malawi, the rest of Zaïre, and perhaps Kenya and Tanzania. Levels are much lower in most of West Africa, although there are major pockets of infection in Abidjan and the Ivory Coast more generally, in Dakar, and more recently in southern Ghana. Levels are low in Nigeria.

The total impact of the epidemic on the region depends very much on what happens in West Africa, and predictions vary according to the explanation put forward for the relative protection of the area so far. One explanation is that West Africa is further from the original areas of highest infection, but this explanation is not completely credible. Lagos is one of the crossroads of Africa and an early major outbreak might well have been anticipated there. Another explanation is based on the incidence of male circumcision. There is now evidence that uncircumcised males are more easily infected (Bongaarts and Way, 1989), a finding that may be relevant when we take into account the fact that male circumcision is almost universal in West Africa while the pattern is much more heterogeneous by ethnic group in the rest of Sub-Saharan Africa. There do not appear to be significantly different levels of sexual activity between West Africa and the rest of the continent (Caldwell, Caldwell, and Quiggin, 1989; Caldwell, Caldwell, and Orubuloye, 1990), but there may be different emphases which help to explain the AIDS pattern. In much of East, Middle, and Southern Africa, city populations are characterized by a substantial predominance of men. This has often been explained in terms of colonial restrictions on wives and other women joining men in mining areas and administrative centres. However, the pattern is found even in cities where no such restrictions applied and it is probably largely the result of the fact that women in these parts of Africa have worked mostly in farming and have not been independent traders. Usually African men or Asians are the traders and hence women have little employment in town except in commercial sex or illicit beer-brewing, two occupations that are often interrelated. In contrast, West African women are traders, with the consequence of near parity of the sexes in most urban areas. Although there is a good deal of pre-marital and extra-marital sex in West Africa, it is more widely diffused than in the urban areas further east, where there is more concentration on prosti-tutes and probably severer foci of infection (Larson, 1989). It is probably no accident that the two most infected cities in West Africa, Abidjan and Dakar, are the two most similar to East or Southern Africa in their sex-ratios, since their incoming migrant streams are predominantly male because they come from the Muslim savannah.

AIDS in Sub-Saharan Africa is very largely heterosexually transmitted. This has the effect that, unlike the situation in most of the rest of the world, there are as many infected women as men, perhaps more. Thus, although Sub-Saharan Africa currently contains about 55 per cent of all infected per-sons, it is probably the home of around 83 per cent of infected women and over 90 per cent of infected children, the latter figure being partly a product of the high birth-rate. When it is realized that the region is home to only about 10 per cent of the world's population it can be seen that the AIDS epidemic in Africa is an all-enveloping tragedy on a scale which makes the situation elsewhere appear almost trivial. The reason for the high level of heterosexual transmission in Africa is probably the product of two factors. The first is a level of pre-marital and extra-marital sexual relations which is higher than that found in most of the Third World's old peasant societies. The second is a high incidence of uncured ulcers and lesions from other sexually transmitted diseases, explained partly by the pattern of sexual relations and partly by the very low level of health services.

Africa's uniqueness arises from two institutions which may be interlinked: polygyny and long female post-partum sexual abstinence. This may be made clearer if we concentrate on modelling the Yoruba population of Nigeria, whose demographic patterns probably still resemble those found across the region at the beginning of the century. The Yoruba, like most of the patrilineal societies of West Africa, still typically have 45–50 per cent of married women in polygynous marriages at any one time (Lesthaeghe, Kaufmann, and Meekers, 1989). This situation can be attained only if men first marry on average at an age around ten years older than women. With the present popu-lation age-structure and the current age at first marriage of women, that means that around half of post-puberty males remain unmarried at any given time. Until the last few decades, Yoruba women refrained from sex during most of pregnancy and for three years after the birth. In 1973, even in the city of Ibadan, that period had only fallen to just under two years and remained at almost three years where the couple were illiterate (Caldwell and Caldwell,

1977; 1981: 186). Wives were available for sex for only 39 per cent of their re-productive span, and even a man with two wives had access to any wife for less than two-thirds of the time. Thus a conservative picture of the whole society would have been one where three-quarters of men had at any one time no access to marital sex. It was generally assumed throughout most of the region that any prohibition on male sexuality would destabilize the society and alienate those whose role was to be warriors. The real debate was how this immense amount of male sexuality was absorbed. There were great variations across the region in just how permissive societies were with regard to either pre-marital or extra-marital female sexual relations. However, even in societies well known for punishing females or their partners for pre-marital or extra-marital sex, these punishments were often exacted only for transgressions against powerful or wealthy families. Many women came from poorer families who were in a weaker position and, in any case, knew that their women needed what assistance they could get. In spite of strong pressures for the divorced and widowed to remarry, there were always women who were separated or had broken with their families who desperately needed support.

Underlying this system was the fact that the focus of morality in African religion was on fertility rather than female chastity. The reason was probably that most of Africa's poor lands were not suited to the plough, and sedentary cultivation with private land ownership had not developed. Thus, there was none of the fanaticism of old Eurasia about land inheritance, marriage alliances with similarly endowed families, and female chastity that prevented pre-marital or extra-marital sexual relations disturbing inheritance plans, or the setting-up or maintenance of those alliances (Goody, 1976; Caldwell, Caldwell, and Quiggin, 1989). In parts of East and Southern Africa young men and women were encouraged to participate in rather intense sexual relations short of breaking the hymen, but, with social change, this was easily transformed into full penetration. The major social change everywhere was colonialism, not so much in its excesses, but in its protection of women from the physical punishments which had restricted sexual straying, and in its determination to shield women from what was seen as the horror of polygyny, even to the extent of allowing women from the beginning of the present century easy and cheap divorce (Caldwell, Orubuloye, and Caldwell, 1990). The Christian religion also forced unmarried young men's sexuality outside the family by regarding as incest the previously licit, if discreet, relations with the younger wives of their elder brothers or fathers. These changes, coupled with the growth of the towns, probably resulted in some increase in sexual activity, but what they certainly did was to enlarge sexual networks to the point where they greatly overlapped and set the stage for increasing venereal disease and ultimately for AIDS.

Most African women have lower levels of pre-marital or extra-marital sexual relations than do men. Indeed, the majority of HIV-infected women have probably caught the disease from their husbands. But, because women are at least three times as likely as men to be infected by each sexual act with an HIV-positive partner, and because wives have little control over relationships even with an infected husband, the women are at least as exposed as the men.

What, then, are the likely demographic effects? The African epidemic will probably prove to be the greatest calamity of our time. In one sense it will exceed the Black Death in Europe in the fourteenth century, in that, over the next half-century, it may well kill 250 million Africans or more than five times the toll of the Black Death. In another sense it will be very different. The Black Death struck when European population growth was stationary, and immediately numbers began to decline, to the extent of perhaps one-third by the end of the epidemic.

The contrast can be understood if we take the case of Uganda, where we can predict the next decade fairly accurately. Current United Nations and World Bank population projections show the Ugandan death-rate as declining to 12 deaths per 1000 people about a decade from now, with a resulting rate of natural increase around 3.5 per cent. Instead, we now know that the death-rate will be closer to 23 per 1000 with almost half of all deaths attributable to AIDS and three-quarters of the deaths caused by AIDS in the 15–59 age-group. This will clearly be a disaster of enormous magnitude and will dominate the society. Nevertheless, the impact will be far from Malthusian and the hapless population will still be growing at a rate of about 2.2. per cent per annum.

There are two unknowns. First, there may be major behavioural changes. African society may be puritanized in the sense desired by missionaries and many colonial administrators at the beginning of the century, with most sex kept within marriage, the near-disappearance of polygyny, and the much earlier marriage of males to wives of similar age. Spousal relationships and family economics may be transformed, perhaps even with a resultant fertility decline. Neither a fertility transition nor a Westernization of the African family under the whiplash of enormous AIDS mortality is a pleasant thought, and Africa might well resist it. Except in some élite groups, and possibly in Kinshasa, there is as yet little sign of massive behavioural change. The other possibility is that there will be secondary effects on marriage and family formation which will reduce fertility, and secondary effects on general health care which will raise mortality further. There is already evidence in the worst-affected parts of Uganda of the collapse of widow inheritance by brothers of men who have died of AIDS. There are many other unknowns. Many governments and much of the population are still reluctant to recognize AIDS for what it is and to discuss it. Many men either think they are unlikely to get it or regard the matter as something not under their personal control. There is certainly no universal recognition that it is incurable.

Huge numbers of Africans are now seropositive compared with the numbers who have already died of AIDS. We do not yet know the full impact on societies but it is clear that AIDS will dominate other issues and will absorb resources that could have been used in other ways. Those resources will be needed not merely for the dying but for many other groups. Family care systems for orphans are already breaking down in substantial parts of Uganda, not merely when both parents die but also when the father dies, and the mother, not now reabsorbed into the family by remarriage, leaves the locality to look for support elsewhere. All we know about population projections is that the existing authoritative ones will be far wrong. We do not know whether a tragedy on this scale will make societies and their governments more careless about how they harbour other resources.

THE PERSISTENCE OF HIGH FERTILITY

Much of the following discussion is derived from a series of studies on the subject (Caldwell and Caldwell, 1985, 1987c, 1988; Caldwell, 1991). Sub-Saharan fertility is high, but not unprecedentedly so. Characteristically, birth-rates are in the high 40s per 1000 and women bear between six and seven children each in a lifetime. What is unique to the region is that, until very recently, no independent, mainland country had evidenced any sign of fertility decline. That situation may now have passed as there is new evidence of early fertility decline in Botswana, Zimbabwe, and Kenya. This first evidence should be treated carefully. The extent of Botswana's decline was at first overstated because of confusion about the analytical methods that had been employed. The Kenyan decline was little more than a fall from a recent upswing and the Zimbabwe decline is based on somewhat imperfect survey data. As in the case of the rest of the region, there are no birth registration systems to confirm these trends.

There has been a heated debate about whether Sub-Saharan Africa is different in terms of the persistence of high fertility and whether the forces that operate in much of Asia and Latin America to reduce fertility have much less strength in Sub-Saharan Africa. The chief proponents of the view that it is one world in terms of the gains and losses from high fertility at the family level have been Boserup (1985) and the World Bank (1986, 1989), especially in the 1986 publication, *Population Growth and Policies in Sub-Saharan Africa*. The argument here was that Africa was merely poorer and at an earlier stage of development than these other societies. We have disagreed with this view (Caldwell and Caldwell, 1987a, 1988, 1990) as have Frank and McNicoll (1987), Cleland and Wilson (1987), Page (1989), Lesthaeghe (1989) and a recent publication by the World Bank (Cochrane and Farid, 1989).

A comparison (Caldwell and Caldwell, 1988) of seven African countries (Ghana, Nigeria, Kenya, Tanzania, Zambia, Senegal, and the Ivory Coast) with four Asian ones (India, Indonesia, Thailand, and China) showed that in the mid-1970s the former were no poorer than the latter, obtained no more of their GDP from agriculture, were as urbanized, and had almost as many children in school. They fell behind somewhat at the secondary-school level, especially in terms of girls. Mortality levels in India and Indonesia were similar to the African ones. India's government family planning programme dates back to 1952, but those in Indonesia and China started in 1969, the same period as the Ghana and Kenya programmes began, and that of Thailand in 1974, not long before the Senegal programme and six years before the Zambian one. But, while the Asian countries exhibited fertility levels in the 1960s similar to those in Africa, by the 1980s they had recorded falls in the range of 29–57 per cent, while there had been either no change in Africa or some rise in fertility. The Asian family planning programmes have been described as more efficient, but efficiency often arises from the fact that there is a demand for the services.

African fertility levels are achieved by near-universal marriage of women during the reproductive period, a product of early marriage, rapid re-marriage after widowhood or divorce, and the securing of husbands for all women by means of polygyny. Fertility would be higher still but for the practice of post-partum sexual abstinence in order to maximize the chance of child survival (P. Caldwell and J. C. Caldwell, 1981). This phenomenon may hide for some time the beginning of a fertility transition. The reason is that in many African countries the main reason for married couples adopting contraception is to substitute this imperfect method of fertility control for the complete control provided by abstinence. This may be sufficient to offset the effect of others attempting to control fertility and may result in no change at all in the birth-rate of the whole community.

West African studies have shown that the major reason for the failure of fertility to fall lies in the nature of family economics. Because of both the lineage system and polygyny, wives and husbands have separate budgets and different responsibilities. Mothers bear most of the cost of raising children but fathers in old age and earlier receive a great deal of assistance from the children. This upward flow of assistance to elders is sustained by respect for ancestors, whether living or dead, and was shaped by the traditional religious system.

In a system where men are likely to spend less on children than they gain, there is little reason for them to restrain fertility. Furthermore, they and their families of origin control fertility because of the institution of bride-wealth and the attitudes that accompany it. A study of Ibadan, Nigeria, showed that women had considerable control over their own sexuality but very little over their reproduction (Caldwell and Caldwell, 1987b). Even independent women with their own unions and tenuous relations with their husbands believed that they had no right at all to decide on sterilization or even the insertion of an IUD.

The usual paradigm of family economics and fertility is further confused by an additional weakening of the relationship between reproduction and economic responsibility, for, in much of West Africa, around one-third of children are fostered from one family to another at any given time. It might be noted that this willingness to take in additional children is hardly evidence that children are an economic burden. Indeed, both polygyny and fosterage suggest that neither wives nor children are a burden, a situation explained by the prime role they play in agriculture, especially in the cultivation of tubers as in West Africa (Clignet, 1970). It is significant that where subsistence, hoe-based farming has declined, as it has in Botswana with the advent of the plough, commercial livestock-raising, and diamond-mining, it is not fertility which has collapsed but marriage (Lesthaeghe, Kaufmann, and Meekers, 1989; Timaeus and Graham, 1989).

There are qualifications which must be made to this picture. The first is that there is a strong relationship between mortality levels and insistence on high fertility, probably stronger than anywhere in the world. One reason that fertility remains high is that high mortality does not merely erode a larger fraction of a family but is very capricious and may completely wipe out even moderately large families. This possibility is an abiding fear among African women. The centrality of fertility to traditional religion meant that childless women were regarded as wicked and usually as in league with evil forces; as a result they were badly treated and their lives were, and usually still are, wretched (Caldwell and Caldwell, 1987c). The position of a woman who has borne children but has subsequently lost them all is nearly as bad. When fertility began to fall in France in the late eighteenth century, French women were willing to take a one-in-five chance of a three-child family being wiped out. African women are not willing to take a one-in-eighty chance of a four-child family disappearing. It is no accident that the only parts of the region to report fertility declines—Botswana, Zimbabwe, and central Kenya—are the only areas where infant mortality has been reduced to 70 per thousand births or lower, and where only about one-seventh of births result in deaths by 5 years of age. The second qualification is that the centrality of fertility to African traditional religion, and the fact that there are no traditional national élites with ancient histories of providing moral as well as political leadership, means that no African government could institute a coercive family planning programme like that of China, or even the types found in Indonesia or in India during the Emergency. If they tried to do so, they would certainly be overthrown. The first Sub-Saharan African government to establish a national family planning programme found it difficult to justify its programme to other African politicians who regarded it as 'un-African'. Now that most African countries accept the need to restrain population growth and many have instituted family planning programmes, there is no such problem. Perhaps this is an example of transnational commons. There is a parallel at the local level: now that the Nigerian government is enthusiastic about fertility control, local administrators and hospital doctors no longer feel at all defensive about offering and advocating contraception, even to unmarried women.

The picture might change, but probably not at the pace suggested by international population projections which tend to adopt Asian analogies. Nevertheless, East and Southern Africa are characterized by certain modifications of the West African situation which we have described in some detail, and these differences may have potential importance for fertility decline. Postpartum sexual abstinence is already short in much of East Africa and so the substitution of contraception will not obscure the beginning of fertility transition. Polygyny is now at more moderate levels in East Africa and low in Southern Africa. Separate spousal budgets are not characteristic of East and Southern Africa, and child fosterage is at lower levels. If fertility decline begins, it will probably do so first in Southern and East Africa. The United Nations Population Projects are almost certainly wrong in suggesting that much of the early fertility fall will occur in coastal West Africa.

POPULATION GROWTH AND ITS IMPLICATIONS

There is probably a closer interrelation between mortality and fertility decline in Sub-Saharan Africa than in any other region of the world. Fertility decline depends on mortality decline and may not begin anywhere until around 93 per cent of births can be guaranteed survival to the first birthday and 86 per cent to the second. In much of Africa this will not happen for another 20 years, and in parts for 50 years, even with the sustaining of recent rates of mortality decline. We are not yet sure what effects the structural adjustment programmes of the 1980s had on mortality declines, but field experience of the greater difficulties in paying for modern medical treatment suggests that they may have had an impact. If this has really been the case, then long-term development priorities suggest that ways must be found for exempting health services from the rigours of these programmes. Indeed, the relationship between parental education and child survival suggests that education, too, should be exempted.

Two points should be made with regard to the structural adjustment programmes. The first is that they are a response to economies in great difficulties. Most Africans regard the assault on the social infrastructure as being due solely to these programmes, without admitting that a deepening of the economic problems may have had much the same result. The second point is that the programmes themselves may have some impact on fertility. Nigerians continually report that SAP or the economic structural adjustment programme (in reality they are also talking about the end of the oil boom) has resulted in higher costs for feeding and educating children, and has accordingly placed great pressure on high fertility. There is very recent evidence that there may have been some decline in fertility in south-western Nigeria, although it appears to arise from a postponement of the beginning of reproduction, and probably of marriage, rather than the limitation of family size.

The great unknown with regard to future mortality trends in the region is the long-term impact of AIDS. It is already clear that the epidemic in East, Middle, and Southern Africa is going to have the seriousness of the Black Death. Posterity will judge our generation by what we did to help in this situation. They will not easily forgive us if we look the other way in embarrassment because we feel that this is an unfortunate event which may distract attention from our population or environmental priorities.

The family planning programmes are already facing this difficulty. If there is a move towards the conjugal family, there is a role for them in substituting contraception for post-partum sexual abstinence and in showing that fertility can be controlled in the new economic situation of these families. There is an immediate role in terms of condom usage. Yet, if the programmes are not to incur hatred, they must refrain from ignoring or resenting AIDS and admit publicly that the situation has changed and that the very existence of many families and some communities is threatened even at present levels of fertility.

Existing economic-demographic theory of the type that argues that high fertility is almost invariably unrewarding, does not work at the family level, particularly in West Africa. Those who make the fertility decisions, namely men and their families of origin, do not suffer from high fertility. Indeed, they usually gain from it. It is even probable that large families have disproportionate success because of the political and commercial pressures they can exert on others (Imoagene, 1976). When an African demographer or economist disagrees with a Western colleague about the likely impact on the economy of high fertility and high levels of population growth, the fundamental reason for the disagreement is that the African's experience is that high fertility has not been financially harmful to himself while the Westerner's personal experience has been very different.

Much economic-demographic theory suggests that the experience should be very different at the national level. This has been put very clearly by Coale and Hoover (1958) and spelt out starkly by Enke (1960, 1968). However, there is practically nothing in the historical experience of the real world to provide empirical support for the argument (Caldwell, 1991).

The experience of Sub-Saharan African countries between 1965 and 1980 showed that countries with higher rates of population growth also had higher incomes, higher proportions of children in school, and denser health services (Caldwell, 1991). Of course, the higher income largely explained the better health services and better education, which in turn yielded lower mortality and greater population growth. More unexpectedly, these countries also exhibited the highest levels in per capita income growth over the period 1965–87. This finding was confused by the higher rates of immigration into these countries, and, when the measure was not population growth but the rate of natural increase, and when a simple dichotomy was employed to divide the countries, there was a little evidence to show that lower levels of natural increase brought some economic benefit at the level of individuals.

Most of us find it difficult to accept that Africa could absorb the huge projected population increases without substantial reductions in per capita food supplies. The problem is that much of the forest land is lateritic and there are hardly any of the great alluvial valley bottoms that support much of Asia's population. There are those who argue that the levels of rainfall and insolation found in most of the region mean that these populations can be adequately supported. Indeed, the major international report on the subject said so (Higgins, 1982), but the more optimistic projections incorporated assumptions about improvements in agricultural technology which may not come to pass. Certainly, population growth is shortening the fallow period, perhaps dangerously so (see Allan, 1965), and this will continue to be the case unless the farming system changes.

It is possible that the savannah systems can change so as to support in an equilibrium system substantially higher populations, as has occurred around Kano in northern Nigeria (Mortimore, 1968) and is beginning to occur around some other towns in the same area. The present economic policies of Nigeria have resulted in the growing of substantial amounts of wheat in northern Nigeria and a major increase in hill-rice production in southern Nigeria. However, the former has been achieved with substantial indirect subsidies and the latter at the expense of more destruction of the forest.

There are a number of simplistic ways by which the claim can be made that African food production is outstripping food supplies. One can point to the substantial food imports, but these are mostly groceries not produced by Africa's poor secondary industries, or sugar, wheat, or rice produced more efficiently elsewhere. One can also point to estimates of declining per capita food availability, but these are based on estimates of subsistence food production which are very dubious.

The most clearly dwindling resource in the region is the forest. The true forest with its large trees has been mostly destroyed in southern Nigeria over the last quarter of a century. However, it is doubtful whether this has been a product of population growth, as the main driving force was the demand for wood by commercial timber firms rather than the demand for new farmland. It was economic growth during the oil-boom years with the resulting building of access roads through the forest, and the finance available for investment in the timber industry, which led to the destruction of the forest. The destruction was a method of temporarily raising living standards.

The famines of the 1970s and 1980s appear to be the product of weather changes and civil wars rather than population growth. At their height, the troubles were possibly aggravated by human numbers and certainly by animal numbers, although the steep rise in the latter was clear evidence of rising living standards. There is little evidence of permanent damage to the countryside, and most of the reports of advances of the Sahara Desert were exciting tales generated to meet media and ideological demand.

Our own estimate is that per capita incomes will rise and economic development proceed in Sub-Saharan Africa if fertility falls, child survival improves, polygyny declines, spousal relations strengthen, and resources are largely concentrated within nuclear families. This programme is, however, not merely one of economic and demographic change, but of cultural and social transformation, and it is a matter for Africans to decide if that is what they really want.

Africa does possess assets of great value extending over many borders with a significance for all mankind: the tropical forest, the Sahara Desert, which is the archetypal sandy desert of our folk memories, and its unique large wild mammals, whose passing would greatly impoverish us all. If mankind wishes to preserve the remaining forest and the African animals, then the richer countries of the world will have to pay the full cost of maintaining what would be in essence global national parks, which could otherwise be employed to raise the living standards of some of the world's poorest people through the sale of timber and the creation of farmland. The situation is much more complex than it is in Brazil's Amazonia. In the latter, the preservation of the forest benefits most of the people who are already there because they are hunters and gatherers whose animal and plant foods prosper in unchanged habitats. In Africa, the forests and game-parks are the frontier lands for slash-and-burn agriculturalists. Furthermore, most of the forest is the traditional land of clans or families with rights long antedating those of the new states. They, and not the whole country, will suffer most from any preservation orders made on that land in the interests of all mankind, and, unless all transactions are very carefully monitored, little of the international compensation paid to national governments for the protection of these transnational commons is likely to reach them.

It is important that the remainder of Africa, which lies outside these global forest and animal parks, should be assisted in its economic development, and in its attainment of health services sufficient to reduce the transmission of AIDS, and to achieve infant and child mortality rates sufficiently low to encourage fertility decline as well as improving the quality of life. Otherwise, its poor people will not allow its governments to concede their immediate future, in the form of agreeing that some resources are of global importance, for their longer-term future. Otherwise, too, the population of Sub-Saharan Africa may become a permanent global burden of great transnational consequence if they form one-quarter of the human race.

REFERENCES

Allan, W. (1965), *The African Husbandman* (Edinburgh: Oliver and Boyd).

Bailey, K. V. (1990), 'Health Issues in Africa South of the Sahara', paper presented at Australian African Studies Association Conference.

Bledsoe, C. and Isiugo-Abanihe, U. (1989), 'Strategies of child fosterage among Mende grannies in Sierra Leone' in Lesthaeghe, 1989.

Bongaarts, J. and Way, P. (1989), *Geographic Variation in the HIV Epidemic and the Mortality Impact of AIDS in Africa*, Population Council Research Division Working Papers No. I (New York: Population Council).

Boserup, E. (1985), 'Economic and Demographic Interrelationships in Sub-Saharan Africa', *Population and Development Review*, 11.

Caldwell, J. C. (1975), *The Sahelian Drought and its Demographic Implications*, Occasional Paper No. 8 (Washington, DC: Overseas Liaison Committee).

—— (1979), 'Education as a Factor in Mortality Decline: An Examination of Nigerian Data', *Population Studies*, 33.

—— (1983), 'Review of Paul R. Greenough, *Prosperity and Misery in Modern India: The Bengal Famine of 1943–1944*', *Population and Development Review*, 9.

—— (1986), 'Routes to Low Mortality in Poor Countries', *Population and Development Review*, 12.

—— (1991), 'The Soft Underbelly of Development: Demographic Transition in Conditions of Limited Economic Change', in World Bank, *Proceedings of the World Bank Annual Conference on Development Economics, 1990*, supplement to the *World Bank Economic Review* and the *World Bank Research Observer* (Washington, DC: World Bank).

—— and Caldwell, P. (1977), 'The Role of Marital Sexual Abstinence in Determining Fertility: A Study of the Yoruba in Nigeria', *Population Studies*, 31.

—— —— (1981), 'Cause and Sequence in the Reduction of Post-Natal Abstinence in Ibadan City, Nigeria', in Page and Lesthaeghe, 1981.

—— —— (1985), *Cultural Forces Tending to Sustain High Fertility in Tropical Africa*, PHN Technical Note, 85(16), (Washington, DC: World Bank).

—— —— (1987a), 'Famine in Africa', paper presented to IUSSP Seminar on Mortality and Society in Sub-Saharan Africa, Yaoundé, 19–23 Oct.

—— —— (1987b), 'The Limitation of Family Size in Ibadan City, Nigeria', in E. van de Walle and J. A. Ebigbola (eds.), *The Cultural Roots of African Fertility Regimes* (Philadelphia: University of Pennsylvania, and Ile-Ife: Obafemi Awolowo University).

—— —— (1987c), 'The Cultural Context of High Fertility in Sub-Saharan Africa', *Population and Development Review*, 13.

—— —— (1988), 'Is the Asian Family Planning Program Model Suited to Africa? A Comparison of India and sub-Saharan Africa', *Studies in Family Planning*, 19.

—— —— (1990), 'Cultural Forces Tending to Sustain High Fertility', in G. T. F. Acsadi, G. Johnson-Acsadi, and R. A. Bulatao (eds.), *Population Growth and Reproduction in Sub-Saharan Africa: Technical Analyses of Fertility and its Consequences* (Washington, DC: World Bank).

—— —— and Orubuloye, I. O. (1990), 'The Family and Sexual Networking in Sub-Saharan Africa: Historic Regional Differences and Present Day Implications',

Health Transition Working Paper, No. 5 (Canberra: Health Transition Centre, Australian National University).

Caldwell, J. C., Caldwell, P., and Quiggin, P. (1989), 'The Social Context of AIDS in Sub-Saharan Africa', *Population and Development Review*, 15.

—— Orubuloye, I. O. and Caldwell, P. (1990), 'Changes in the Nature and Levels of Sexual Networking in an African Society: The Destabilization of the Traditional Yoruba System', *Health Transition Working Paper*, No. 4 (Canberra: Health Transition Centre, Australian National University).

—— Reddy, P. H., and Caldwell, P. (1986), 'Periodic High Risk as a Cause of Fertility Decline in a Changing Rural Environment: Survival Strategies in the 1980–1983 South Indian Drought', *Economic Development and Cultural Change*, 34/4: 677–701; repr. in J. C. Caldwell, P. H. Reddy, and P. Caldwell, *The Causes of Demographic Change: Experimental Research in South India* (Madison: University of Wisconsin Press, 1988).

Caldwell, P. and Caldwell, J. C. (1981), 'The Function of Child-Spacing in Traditional Societies, and the Direction of Change', in Page and Lesthaeghe, 1981.

—— —— (1990), 'Where there is a Narrower Gap between Female and Male Situations: Lessons from South India and Sri Lanka', *Health Transition Working Paper*, No. 7 (Camberra: Health Transition Centre, Australian National University).

Cantrelle, P. (1975), 'Mortality: Levels, Patterns and Trends', in J. C. Caldwell *et al.* (eds.), *Population Growth and Socioeconomic Change in West Africa* (New York: Columbia University Press).

Chen, M. (1990), 'Drought and Famine in Gujarat, India', PhD diss. (University of Pennsylvania).

Chowdhury, A. K. M. A. and Chen, L. C. (1977), 'The Dynamics of Contemporary Famine', in International Union for the Scientific Study of Population, *International Population Conference, Mexico, 1977*, i (Liège: IUSSP).

Cleland, J. (1990), 'Maternal Education and Child Survival: Further Evidence and Explanations', in J. C. Caldwell *et al.* (eds.), *What We Know About Health Transition: The Cultural, Social and Behavioural Determinants of Health* (Canberra: Australian National University).

—— and van Ginneken, J. K. (1988), 'Maternal Education and Child Survival in Developing Countries: The Search for Pathways of Influence', *Social Science and Medicine*, 27/12: 1357–68; repr. in J. C. Caldwell and G. Santow (eds.), *Selected Readings in the Cultural, Social and Behavioural Determinants of Health* (Canberra: Australian National University).

—— and Wilson, C. (1987), 'Demand Theories of Fertility and Transition: An Iconoclastic View', *Population Studies*, 41.

Clignet, R. (1970), *Many Wives, Many Powers: Autonomy and Power in Polygynous Families* (Evanston, Ill.: Northwestern University Press).

Coale, A. J. and Hoover, E. (1958), *Population Growth and Economic Development in Low-Income Countries: A Case Study of India's Prospects* (Princeton, NJ: Princeton University Press)

Cochrane, S. H. and Farid, S. M. (1989), *Fertility in Sub-Saharan Africa: Analysis and Explanation*, World Bank Discussion Paper No. 43 (Washington, DC: World Bank).

Enke, S. (1960), 'The Economics of Government Payments to Limit Population', *Economic Development and Cultural Change*, 8.

—— (1968), 'Raising per Capita Income through Fewer Births', *68TMP-9* (Santa Barbara, Calif.: Tempo, General Electric Company).

Frank, O. and McNicoll, G. (1987), 'Fertility and Population Policy in Kenya', *Population and Development Review*, 13.

Goody, J. R. (1976), *Production and Reproduction: A Comparative Study of the Domestic Domain* (Cambridge: Cambridge University Press).

Greenough, P. R. (1982), *Prosperity and Misery in Modern India: The Bengal Famine of 1943–1944* (New York: Oxford University Press).

Higgins, G. M. (1982), *Potential Population Capacities of Land in the Developing World: Technical Report of Project INT/75/P13 - Land Resources for Populations of the Future* (Rome: FAO in Collaboration with IASA and UNFPA).

Hill, A. G. (1987), 'Trends in Childhood Mortality in Sub-Saharan Mainland Africa', paper presented to IUSSP Seminar on Mortality and Society in Sub-Saharan Africa, Yaoundé, 19–23 Oct.

—— (1988), 'Famine in Africa: The Most Dreadful Resource of Nature', in van de Walle *et al.*, 1988.

—— and Hill, K. (1988), 'Mortality in Africa: Levels, Trends, Differentials and Prospects', in van de Walle *et al.*, 1988.

Imoagene, O. (1976), *Social Mobility in Emergent Society: A Study of the New Elite in Western Nigeria*, Changing African Family Monograph No. 2 (Canberra: Australian National University).

Larson, A. (1989), 'The Social Context of HIV Transmission in Africa: Review of the Historical and Cultural Bases of East and Central African Sexual Relations', *Reviews of Infectious Diseases*, 11.

Lesthaeghe, R. J. (ed.) (1989), *Reproduction and Social Organization in Sub-Saharan Africa* (Berkeley: University of California Press).

—— Kaufmann, G. and Meekers, D. (1989), 'The Nuptiality Regimes in Sub-Saharan Africa', in Lesthaeghe, 1989.

Mortimore, M. J. (1968), 'Population Distribution, Settlement and Soils in Kano Province, Northern Nigeria 1931–62', in J. C. Caldwell and C. Okonjo (eds.), *The Population of Tropical Africa* (London: Longman).

Page, H. J. (1989), 'Childrearing versus Childbearing: Coresidence of Mother and Child in Sub-Saharan Africa', in Lesthaeghe, 1989.

—— and Lesthaeghe, R. J. (eds.) (1981), *Child-Spacing in Tropical Africa: Traditions and Change* (London: Academic Press).

Rutstein, S. O. (1984), 'Infant and Child Mortality: Levels, Trends and Demographic Differentials', *Comparative Studies: Cross-National Summaries* (rev. edn.), no. 43 (London: World Fertility Survey).

Tabutin, D. (1990), 'Evolution comparée de la mortalité en Afrique du Nord de 1900 à nos jours', *Working Papers* (Louvain-la-Neuve: Demography Programme, Louvain University).

Timaeus, I. (1987), 'Adult Mortality in Sub-Saharan Africa', paper presented to World Bank Seminar on Disease and Mortality in Sub-Saharan Africa (Tunbridge Wells).

—— and Graham, W. (1989), 'Labor Circulation, Marriage and Fertility in Southern Africa', in Lesthaeghe, 1989.

UNICEF (1989), *The State of the World's Children 1989* (New York: Oxford University Press).

United Nations, Population Division (1956), *Methods for Population Projections by Sex and Age* (New York: United Nations).

World Bank (1986), *Population Growth and Policies in Sub-Saharan Africa* (Washington, DC: World Bank).

—— (1989), *Sub-Saharan Africa: From Crisis to Sustainable Growth: A Long-Term Perspective Study* (Washington, DC: World Bank).

7

Global Commons: Can They Be Managed?

A. L. Hollick and R. N. Cooper

A common property resource is available to multiple users without exclusion. That is, the use of the resource by one party does not preclude use by another. The term 'resource' implies either realized or potential scarcity which results from a situation of actual crowding or potential competition.

The opportunities for managing global commons are diminished by the absence of community. There is no overarching authority to provide dispute-settlement mechanisms. The problem of management is made more complex by the fact that states are technologically and economically disparate, yet the international system retains the legal fiction of sovereign equality for all states. As a result, the use of global commons resources remains an ongoing source of dissension among nations.

Not all uses of the oceans or of outer space constitute a resource use. The geostationary orbit, for example, is a resource because with existing technological capabilities it can accommodate only a finite number of telecommunications satellites. There is no competition, however, over sending research satellites into deep space.

Certain patterns of development have characterized global as well as other common property resources. In the first stage, technological change makes new areas or opportunities available and, in effect, creates new resource opportunities. Commons resources that are currently at this early stage of exploration and development include Antarctic minerals, deep sea-bed manganese nodules, and polymetallic sulphide brines. The second stage is one of active exploitation of the newly available resource. Among the resources in this category are Antarctic krill, offshore oil and gas, geostationary and elliptical earth orbits for space satellites, the radio spectrum, and some aspects of the atmosphere. In the third and final stage, demand generated by the rapid growth of world population and income leads to over-exploitation and in some cases depletion of the commons. Well known examples are the over-fishing of regional fishery populations or of certain types of pelagic whales. Similarly, disposal of human wastes puts pressure on jointly used lands, rivers, or atmosphere in the form of unwanted pollution.

This chapter begins with a brief general discussion of ways of managing global commons. It then discusses in more detail existing arrangements for the oceans, Antarctica, space, and the atmosphere. It takes up in depth the prospect of greenhouse warming as an issue requiring international management, and ends with a few concluding observations.

MANAGEMENT OPTIONS

Efficient management of global commons, a form of international public good, requires joint action by several or many nations. Often international public goods involve joint or at least co-ordinated expenditure, as in UN peace-keeping missions or the eradication of smallpox. Such financing can be done either by formula, such as that mandated for United Nations assessments, or by voluntary contributions, or by some combination of the two. The UN assessments are based on each member country's share of world income, calculated by converting national income over the last ten years into a common currency at market exchange-rates, and then adjusting for differences in per capita income and other factors that, in the judgement of a committee of experts, should influence the results. There is a minimum contribution from each member country of 0.01 per cent of the total UN budget, which is paid by 79 of the 159 members, and a ceiling of 25 per cent that at present applies only to the United States, but would presumably apply also to the European Union if it one day evolves into a United States of Europe. Table 7.1 shows the shares of UN assessments for 1989–90.

Global commons differ from other kinds of international public goods in that they require restraining actions rather than jointly agreed expenditures. Of course, at a certain level of generalization, restraints and budgeted expenditures can be made economically equivalent, but the decision dynamics are quite different. Jointly agreed expenditures require national appropriations of funds, whereas restraints require jointly agreed rules of self-restraint and possibly restraint on private citizens. These restraints may affect only a few parties, as in the case of Antarctica, or may affect many, as in the case of emission of CO_2 and other greenhouse gases.

International commons have the characteristic that parties from two or more countries can 'graze' them, thereby imposing costs, or negative externalities, on other users. Optimal use of the commons requires some cutback in use, but that imposes costs on at least some users in the short run, until the

Table 7.1. Share of United Nations assessments, 1989–1990 (%)

EC member states	29.5
United States	25.0
Japan	11.4
Other OECD	8.3
USSR	11.6
Other Eastern Europe[a]	3.5
China	0.8
Rest of world	10.0
Total	100.0

[a] Including the German Democratic Republic

commons recovers and settles into a long-run managed equilibrium. Management of the commons therefore has the property of a Prisoners' Dilemma: both parties can gain through mutual restraint, but one party can gain more if the other party restrains alone.

Three management options exist for dealing with global commons resources: *laissez-faire*, exclusive management via partition, or joint management by more than one nation. Of the three approaches, that of *laissez-faire* has been the most often practised, and has resulted in over-exploitation. The classic cases are Europe's offshore fisheries and worldwide whaling. The Second World War temporarily limited European distant water fleets and allowed fish and whale stocks to revive. On the other hand, the sardines off the shores of California became extinct. In yet another case—severe atmospheric and river pollution in Europe—national and regional measures have relieved the problem and allowed these resources to revive. The 1976 Outer Space Treaty and the 1958 Geneva Convention on the High Seas also reflect the *laissez-faire* approach, although they call for due regard for other users and set general rules of the road.

The second management option—partition, or the establishment of property rights—has been most often adopted for many domestic commons. In the 1982 Treaty on the Law of the Sea, the international community agreed to partition certain offshore resources. Ocean areas that were formerly part of the ocean commons were carved into 200-mile economic zones belonging to the coastal states. This represents an allocation of property rights to nation-states according to a concept of geographical rights based on proximity or on historic claims. The possible partition of the Antarctic is in a state of suspension as important state members of the Antarctic Consultative Group have refused to recognize the claims to slices of Antarctic territory made by seven claimants. Perhaps the most striking effort to partition a common property resource is represented by the effort of equatorial countries to lay claim to the airspace above their countries to an altitude of 22,300 miles, to include the geostationary orbit which lies over the equator.

The third approach to managing a global commons—joint management— may make the most sense economically for some resources and areas.[1] Joint management does not necessarily require the establishment of supranational international organizations. It is none the less politically difficult. Joint management approaches may encompass a range of possible schemes—from consultation, liability, and regulatory approaches at one extreme, to comprehensive management and centralized resource allocation at the other. Apart from the 1911 Fur Seal Treaty, early examples of joint management efforts include the international whaling organizations of the 1930s as well as a series of post-war regional fisheries commissions. In the 1972 Convention on

---

[1] An early and successful example is the Fur Seal Treaty of 1911 between Canada, Japan, and the United States for the Pribiloff Islands.

Antarctic Seals and in the 1980 Antarctic Living Marine Resources Agreement, joint management approaches are still being tested. The Mediterranean Action Programme is developing a mixed system of regulation and liability. The World Administrative Radio Conference (WARC) has evolved towards a regime that in some regions calls for pre-planned allocation of satellite orbit and frequency spectrum resources. The 1982 Law of the Sea treaty seeks to resolve the hotly disputed issue of access rights to deep sea-bed manganese nodules by creating a complex system for centralized management and allocation of sea-bed resources.

The choice among these three types of approach is made either deliberately or by default. The process of choosing raises difficult political, institutional, and economic questions. The political difficulties are usually equity issues. In determining which approach to pursue, decisions must be made as to who will participate and in what manner, how decisions will be made, and who should benefit.

Economists have tended to favour assignment of property rights, on the assumption that owners will best manage their property; or, where that is difficult or impossible to achieve, to limiting access by charging an appropriate access fee, on the grounds that market principles will be allocatively superior to administrative fiat. Governments, in contrast, under public pressure, have typically rejected access fees and allocation of a common resource to those who can pay for it in favour of administered access, on grounds of 'equity' towards historical users.

The perennial management question is what issues should be grouped or linked. For example, should all ocean issues be dealt with in a single UN Conference on the Law of the Sea? Or would it be better to tackle ocean issues along regional or functional lines? Should fisheries management be linked to other food regimes, and sea-bed minerals issues be linked to Antarctic and other land-based minerals regimes? These types of decisions are typically made on political rather than scientific or technical grounds, as one group perceives a negotiating advantage in one or another form of linkage.

The economic questions of how to exploit and maintain a resource most efficiently are generally among the last to be addressed. In the case of each resource, there are often physical and technological attributes which determine how the fewest factor inputs (capital, labour) can be expended in order to preserve or recover the common property resource. Clearly, the design of an elaborate and costly International Seabed Authority was intended to meet political rather than economic or efficiency goals. On the other hand, the partition of the continental margins among coastal states allows a government to extend its existing national regulatory framework to the new areas. In this context, the factors of production used to develop each oil-pool or coastal fishery can be judiciously limited if the government in question is concerned with efficiency.

The national partition approach has not worked economically for the fisheries above the continental margin. The United States, for example, has created a monopoly for domestic fishermen based on hidden and overt subsidies and an expensive management scheme. Foreign fishermen were excluded from access to the surplus catch, when it existed. Now there is no surplus and US fishermen are over-fishing coastal stocks. Foreign processing has been excluded also. This reduces the welfare of the US taxpayer, who both covers the cost of the subsidies and pays higher prices for fewer fish.

In the case of living resources as well as the marine environment, the actions of neighbouring coastal states in managing the 200-mile zones affect the management of resources on the other side of the boundary line. As with the atmosphere, the movement of ocean waters and the creatures in them generates certain unavoidable interdependencies. One lesson that emerges is that an economically efficient solution to common property resource management will depend upon the attributes of the resource in question.

OCEANS

Among the global commons, the seas and oceans have possibly the longest history of international use, crowding problems, and regime negotiation. The Third United Nations Conference on the Law of the Sea (UNCLOS III) was the last in a series of attempts to codify the rules governing exploitation of ocean resources. Through a combination of customary law and successive codification efforts, the law of the sea has evolved towards a mixed management regime—partition of coastal resources, navigation with few constraints, mutually agreed national approaches to vessel-source pollution, and proposed joint management of deep sea-bed mineral resources. The ocean resources of immediate economic value are located in coastal waters or on the continental margin. In these areas, partition has prevailed.

Fishing

Fishing, together with navigation, is an ancient ocean activity. Most fisheries are located in near-shore areas due to the coastal upwelling of phytoplankton or to the effect of shallow continental margins on the food-chain. Before the adoption of the 200-mile 'exclusive economic zones' (EEZ) by UNCLOS III, the response to crowding beyond the narrow territorial sea was a weak form of joint management based on regional fisheries commissions. Lacking enforcement capabilities, the commissions were unable to limit access to the resource, much less to enforce compliance with agreed rules restricting gear or limiting the duration of the fishing season.

Regardless of equity considerations, coastal states were determined to assert their special interest in offshore areas. Countries with the longest coastlines are the major beneficiaries of partition into national zones. Although the 200-mile zone concept originated in Latin America,[2] developed countries on the whole benefited more than the developing world. For example, one-fifth of world fisheries, by value of catch, lie off US and Canadian shores. On the other hand, Asian and African states often have short coastlines or small offshore areas that are abutted by other states. And most land-locked countries are in the developing world.

The problem of equity was solved (or ignored) in UNCLOS III by simply moving national boundaries 200 miles out to sea with rules to determine adjacent claims. Some hortatory provision was made for land-locked and geographically disadvantaged states to camouflage this imbalance. Each country was called on to manage the living resources within its EEZ. While this solution might be viable in the short term for countries with long coastlines fronting on open ocean, it will have to be modified where the fisheries of a region are ecologically interlinked across the new watery national boundaries. On the coast of West Africa and in South-East Asia, the activities of each nation in its narrow zone directly affect neighbouring states. In North America, where consolidating national jurisdiction has been a principal preoccupation, the United States and Canada are already plagued with conflict over 'straddling stocks' and will eventually have to revert to joint approaches to manage these fisheries.

Two unique high-value fisheries pose special management problems—tuna and salmon. Tuna is a highly migratory fish that moves at great speed both within and beyond 200 miles of shore. The fact that tuna migrate across national zones and into open ocean leads to conflicts between distant water and coastal fishing nations. UNCLOS III sought, unsuccessfully, to grapple with tuna management. The UNCLOS treaty reflects the developing-country preference for controlling tuna on a zone-by-zone basis, which is especially significant for the island nations of the Pacific. In 1990 the United States accepted this approach in the revised Magnuson Act,[3] regulating tuna within the 200-mile EEZ. Despite coastal state preferences, the long-run survival of the fishery will require a co-operative approach to managing the tuna throughout its migratory range. However, states will come to this conclusion only after the resource has been depleted and other alternatives have been exhausted.

The behaviour of salmon is equally problematic. The salmon is an anadramous species, which means that it spawns in fresh water and travels far out to sea to feed. Beyond 200 miles, salmon may be subjected to over-fishing that undercuts the effort of the coastal state to maintain the spawning streams. Here, as in the case of tuna, fishery management must be undertaken on a co-operative basis unless agreement is reached that all salmon

[2] On the origins of this concept, see Hollick (1981).
[3] Fishery Conservation and Management Act Amendments of 1990.

fishing is restricted to streams of origin. This, not surprisingly, has been the clear preference of the host states.

Co-operative management approaches develop slowly at best. Most often co-operation is forced by adversity. Only after over-fishing or pollution has caused negative transboundary impacts do nations come reluctantly to accept and act on their mutual vulnerability and interdependence. Regional commissions working under the auspices of the UN Food and Agricultural Organization (FAO) or the UN Environmental Programme (UNEP) could play an important role in facilitating co-operation. Because co-operative approaches are politically costly, however, semi-crisis conditions will be needed to encourage their adoption and only after efforts at unilateral action have failed.

Navigation

Navigation, like fishing, is a historic use of the oceans. Over the centuries, navigation regimes have been based on customary practice and treaty law (e.g. the 1958 Geneva Conventions on the Territorial Sea and the High Seas). The territorial sea, in which the coastal state is sovereign (with the exception of the right of innocent passage for surface ships and aircraft), evolved from 3 to 12 miles in UNCLOS III. This posed potential transit problems through and over international straits. UNCLOS III resolved this through the development of the concept of 'transit passage'. Since commercial navigation spans the globe, regulatory regimes must be developed on a worldwide basis. Because all countries engage in international trade, they share an interest in avoiding piecemeal national environmental and regulatory schemes for navigation.

UNCLOS III was not the forum for serious efforts to develop international regulatory and liability regimes. The focus was rather on the balance of rights between coastal states and navigation interests. UNCLOS III settled on a 12-mile territorial sea with transit passage assured through and over international straits less than 24 miles wide. Coastal states claiming 'archipelagic' or 'straits states' status, such as Indonesia and the Philippines, insisted on the right to determine shipping lanes, but were not successful. In the case of ocean pollution, the coastal state was given some right *vis-à-vis* a proven violator of environmental standards. For the most part, however, the Intergovernmental Maritime Organization (IMO) retains responsibility for developing codes of conduct for navigation. By the end of the century, IMO will have to come to terms with the need to regulate traffic in highly congested areas, such as the English Channel and the Straits of Malacca. While straits states will play a major role, this matter will be better handled by the international community of users that has a stake in assured passage through these areas.

Offshore Oil and Gas

In the case of offshore oil and gas, partition is a viable management option as long as two problems are properly handled: (1) recovery from a common pool that spans national boundaries; and (2) attention to pollution impacts on adjacent states. As our capability to drill and recover hydrocarbons has moved to greater depths, offshore oil and gas have come to provide roughly one-third of the world's oil supply. The prevailing view is that offshore hydrocarbons will be limited to the continental margins. It is also likely that there will be a correlation between onshore and offshore deposits. Thus, a division of marine oil and gas resources among the coastal states ensures that countries that already have substantial onshore resources, such as Mexico, the United States, and Saudi Arabia, will have more offshore.

In UNCLOS III political expediency dictated that coastal states would divide these resources among themselves. The conference provided that continental margins would extend to 200 miles, or even beyond that to the outer limit of the geological slope and rise. This was a geographically extreme evolution of the continental-shelf regime. The legal concept of the continental shelf provides for coastal state jurisdiction over the living and non-living resources of the area.

Fortuitously, partition of the continental margin among coastal states is likely to be the most economically efficient way to recover oil and gas. When a single state has clearly defined property rights in its offshore deposits, it should seek to encourage its operators to recover these deposits with a minimum investment of labour and capital, subject to environmental regulations. Thus, the coastal state can ensure that, in the development of each pool of oil and gas, appropriate factor inputs and appropriate rates of recovery are used. Difficulties arise, however, if an oil or gas deposit crosses a national border. As we have seen in the North Sea, a state may engage in competitive drilling in order to take the most oil out of the pool before its neighbour does. The initial pattern of Norwegian drilling, for instance, was only along its boundary with the United Kingdom. The preferred approach would be to manage the common pool jointly to limit factor inputs and to share recovery costs and benefits, as is done by Japan and Korea in the Strait of Tsusuma.

Similarly, states must be attentive to the environmental impact of their drilling activities on their neighbours. While one state may wish to concentrate on a rapid exploitation of its offshore hydrocarbon resource, a neighbour may prefer to focus on tourism, recreation, fishing, and other activities that require preservation of the marine environment. It may, therefore, adopt more stringent safety and environmental measures than its oil-hungry neighbour. A case in point was the blow-out of Mexico's Ixtoc well in the Bay of Campeche. The United States found itself at the mercy of Mexican safety and environmental policies and procedures, and the state of Texas suffered substantial financial losses in tourism and fishing.

Due to the strong emphasis on coastal states' rights rather than respons-ibilities at UNCLOS III, there are no provisions in the Law of the Sea Convention that would serve as a basis for legal action or co-operative man-agement of the EEZ or continental shelf. However, the UNEP regional seas programme has begun to develop action programmes to fill the void. And as the pace of offshore activities increases, more and more incidents will under-score the mutual vulnerability of coastal states, and regional and global liabil-ity and regulatory schemes will be developed to address the question.

Pollution

Pollution issues also arose at UNCLOS III with regard to shipping. As with resource exploitation in national zones, the Conference was torn between contradictory impulses. In the case of shipping, coastal states have clearly wanted to protect themselves from pollution caused by vessels transiting near their shores. On the other hand, all nations perceive an interest in ocean shipping whether they are exporters, shipping nations, or simply dependent upon ocean-borne imports.

In this situation, the Conference sought to avoid a piecemeal approach to regulation of shipping through national or economic zones. Instead, the UNCLOS text tries to balance the environmental concerns of the coastal states with the general interest in navigation by maintaining the principle of flag-state enforcement. The coastal state may lodge complaints with a vessel's state of destination. That port state has the right to impose standards higher than those agreed internationally on ships entering its ports. It is empowered to take the appropriate verification steps and to bring specific types of action against the offending vessel if the charges are deemed valid. The coastal state may take certain enforcement action in its territorial sea and EEZ depending on the severity of the pollution offence. However, flag-state enforcement rights against violations can supersede all other legal actions if the flag state has developed a credible record of punishing infractions of safety and environmental rules.

The Deep Sea-Bed

In addition to navigation, the major exception to the partition approach was the negotiation of a management regime for the deep sea-bed. The resources of principal interest in the sea-bed are manganese nodules and polymetallic sulphides. Nodules of greatest commercial value (e.g. with the highest cop-per, nickel, and cobalt content) are found in the deepest part of the oceans, largely in the Pacific Ocean, well beyond the limits of national jurisdiction. Because of early visions of vast mineral wealth, the United Nations General Assembly passed a resolution in 1970 declaring the sea-beds beyond na-tional jurisdiction to be the 'common heritage of mankind'—a concept that has never been defined. The most notable impact of that resolution was that many coastal states immediately laid claim to 200-mile zones and to the continental margins where they extended beyond 200 miles, radically accelerating trends that had been under way for decades. Coastal states thereby succeeded in removing most valuable common resources from prospective international management.

In subsequent negotiations to develop a regime to mine what remained of the sea-bed, potential mining states recommended an economically efficient approach based on a minimum of regulation. This would in essence allow miners to explore and lay claim to sea-bed sites. Conflict with other miners would be resolved through dispute-settlement procedures among the mining states. Revenues from resource exploitation would be shared with the international community in deference to the disputed 'common heritage' principle.

Developing countries, on the other hand, interpreted the common heritage concept to mean something quite different. Lacking the technology and capability to mine the sea-bed directly, the Group of 77 developing countries proposed that a sea-bed mining body call the 'Enterprise' be set up under the auspices of an International Seabed Authority (ISA) which they would control. The Enterprise would mine the sea-bed directly, to the exclusion of all national mining, with technology and financing provided by the developed states.

The UNCLOS III treaty sought a compromise between the positions of the developed and developing countries. The compromise was based on the concept of the 'parallel system', as it came to be called. On one track, private or state companies would be able to mine part of the sea-bed, provided they fulfilled certain conditions that would allow the Enterprise to go into business at the same time. These conditions began with the requirement that each company explore and submit to the ISA the co-ordinates for two sites of equal value. The Authority would then select one for the Enterprise. Other conditions included substantial up-front financial contributions to the ISA by governments, limits on sea-bed production to protect competing land-based mineral producers, and mandatory transfer of technology to the Enterprise and to developing countries if the mining technology is not available on the open market. In the view of the developed nations, this 'compromise' imposed too many onerous and economically costly burdens and set unacceptable political and economic precedents. Unable to negotiate the necessary changes within the UN context, the United States, Germany (FRG), and the United Kingdom, among others, decided not to sign the treaty.

The developed countries have since worked to create a basic approach to sea-bed mining that addresses problems as they arise. In 1984, after resolving claims to overlapping mine sites, the United States, Britain, France, Japan, the FRG, Belgium, Italy, and the Netherlands (collectively, the 'reciprocating states') agreed to respect existing and future claims on the basis of first in time. These claims were then published in the UN LOS Bulletin. In 1987, after negotiations with the Soviets to resolve claims conflicts, the Soviet and Western claims were reissued to reflect the agreed revisions.

While the reciprocating states were pursuing a pragmatic approach, the 'preparatory committee' of the proposed sea-bed mining Authority was meeting periodically to prepare for the entry into force of the UNCLOS treaty. Two of the reciprocating states, Japan and France, and the USSR participated in discussions about the areas they would offer as a mine site to the Authority. Given the size of the prospective sea-bed mining area (600,000 sq.km.), each claim had to be compressed in the negotiation. Each consortium applied for a 150,000 sq.km. area. Collectively, they were able to offer only one mine site to the Authority of 75,000 sq. km., with each of the three ending up with a like amount. This is far from the one mine site per national claim that was envisaged by the treaty drafters.

In the intervening years, reality has further intruded on the sea-bed mining part of the UNCLOS convention. The visible failure of centrally planned economic systems in Eastern Europe had an impact on the UNCLOS preparatory discussions, and a number of countries have indicated a willingness to revisit and revise the sea-bed portions of the UNCLOS treaty. Many are urging that the entirety of Chapter XI be frozen, with only limited monitoring of exploration of existing claims. The mining regime could then be renegotiated in 20 to 30 years, when sea-bed mining may be a more realistic proposition, since the economics of sea-bed mining has proven to be much less attractive than was thought to be the case in the 1970s.

In summary, there is a variety of approaches to the management of ocean resources. The partition approach has prevailed in UNCLOS III for fisheries and offshore oil. Navigation and environmental resources have been left to existing international regulatory institutions with some increased obligations for coastal states. And sea-bed mining has been addressed in a flawed effort at comprehensive management. The general trend in management of oceans resources has been to promote national control through partition, where possible. Where politically expedient, namely in case of deep sea-beds, joint management approaches have been urged. However, in regional situations, such as the Mediterranean or the Baltic, co-operative management efforts are growing out of near-crisis conditions in fisheries and marine pollution. Multilateral approaches have been used only where physical realities impose themselves on policymakers.

ANTARCTICA

The Antarctic and its resources are at an earlier stage of resource exploitation than the oceans. This is due in part to the difficult physical environment, and now also to the complex political regime that governs the Antarctic. Here the approach has been to respond to resource issues as they develop on a joint or co-operative basis, but with an emphasis on national enforcement and self-policing.

Arrangements for Antarctic resource and other issues are developed by a twenty-five-member Antarctic Consultative Group. This institutional mechanism has evolved from the political and scientific history of the area. In 1957–8 the International Geophysical Year included an Antarctic research phase. The twelve countries that participated in Antarctic scientific research included seven states that claimed territory in the Antarctic (Argentina, Australia, Chile, France, New Zealand, Norway, and the United Kingdom) and five countries which neither claimed nor recognized claims to territory (Belgium, Japan, South Africa, the United States, and the Soviet Union).

In 1959 the twelve researching governments institutionalized their co-operative scientific relationship in a treaty. The resulting Antarctic Treaty of 1961 applies to the area below 60° south latitude. Territorial claims are set aside while research activities are continued. Research plans and scientific findings are freely exchanged. The area is to be used only for peaceful purposes and treaty state observers have free access and inspection rights to all installations and equipment. The treaty further provides for peaceful dispute-settlement and for an ongoing consultative mechanism.

Additional countries may accede to the Treaty: 27 countries have chosen to do so since 1961. Of these new members, thirteen became Consultative Parties by undertaking substantial scientific research in Antarctica: Poland (1977), the Federal Republic of Germany (1981), India and Brazil (1983), China and Uruguay (1985), the former German Democratic Republic and Italy (1987), Spain and Sweden (1988), and Finland, the Republic of Korea, and Peru (1989). Consultative parties are entitled to vote at biennial consultative meetings. Other states may participate in the discussions as observers and in meetings called to deal with resource issues. Consultative parties, however, enjoy special status as decision-makers in the treaty system.

As resource questions have arisen, the consultative parties have handled them on a case-by-case basis. Two broad types of resources have been at issue—living and non-living. The basic political issues have been those of claimants versus non-claimants and, where claims overlap, claimants versus claimants. An important factor in overcoming these tensions within the consultative group has been the eagerness of other members of the UN to have a role in managing the Antarctic. The prospect of UN involvement has been an important incentive to maintaining the cohesion and the viability of the Antarctic consultative process. At the 1983 General Assembly, the United Nations first resolved to study the Antarctic issue and has kept it on the agenda since then.

Living Resources

Antarctic resource issues became central concerns of the consultative parties early in the life of the treaty. In the 1960s living resources were in the forefront. Nations had already grappled in the 1930s with how to regulate the harvest of Antarctic whales. The International Whaling Commission restricts whaling on a global basis consistent with the dispersal and range of the resource. The consultative parties, however, have addressed only resources limited to the Antarctic. In 1964 'Agreed Measures for Conservation of Antarctic Fauna and Flora' (Recommendation III-8) was adopted, and in 1966 the 'Interim Guide-Lines for the Voluntary Regulation of Antarctic Pelagic Sealing' (Recommendation IV-21). The latter served as the basis for the 1972 Convention on Antarctic Seals (CCAS), which was negotiated in a wider framework that reflected the wide migratory range of seals.

By the late 1970s the displacement of Soviet and Japanese distant-water fleets from the newly claimed 200-mile zones was putting greater pressure on Antarctic living resources, in particular krill. In 1980, after difficult negotiations, the Antarctic Consultative Group concluded the Antarctic Living Marine Resources Agreement (CCALMR). The problem of how to deal with the seven territorial claimants was handled by expanding the resource management area to encompass an ecological unit known as the 'convergence zone'. This ecosystem contains all interrelated Antarctic species; it contracts and expands with seasonal change. The zone is important from a political perspective, because it encompasses islands which are under recognized national jurisdiction, such as Kerguelen. Thus it has been possible to develop a formula that begs the issue of national claims to the Antarctic mainland by referring to recognized areas of national jurisdiction.

The treaty relies on data collection by participating states to keep informed about the condition of the resource. Assuming that all participating scientists agree that the data suggest the need to cut back on the level of fishing, consensus decision-making is required to bring a system of allocation into effect. It is difficult to achieve agreement on the scientific evidence when that can lead to management decisions that there needs to be a reduced level of harvest of a particular species. The 1980 Agreement takes the initial steps in laying the foundation for co-operative management. These groups have been set up under the Scientific Committee to collect and assess data on krill, fish, and ecosystems. A number of conservation measures have been taken ranging from minimum mesh sizes and total allowable catch, through closed seasons for certain fisheries, to limits and even prohibitions on fishing of certain species in designated areas. The consensus decision-making process (whereby all parties must agree, or at least acquiesce) has predictably slowed the process of adopting the necessary conservation measures. There is, however, no alternative to consensus decision-making and the linkage to scientific research progress has helped.

Non-Living Resources

The non-living resources of the Antarctic, particularly offshore oil and gas, became the focus of attention by the 1980s, following a decade of oil price increases. Little is known of the mineral potential of the continent, although it is expected that the Antarctic contains minerals similar to those found in Australia, South Africa, and the Chilean–Argentine peninsula. In 1981 the Antarctic consultative parties committed themselves to negotiating a minerals regime for the continent.

By 1988 the consultative parties adopted by consensus the Convention on the Regulation of Antarctic Mineral Resource Activities (CRAMRA): 33 states participated in the final meeting (twenty consultative parties) and are eligible to ratify the treaty. CRAMRA covers three stages of mineral activity: prospecting, exploration, and development. Exploration and development activities are subject to prior authorization, but prospecting may be undertaken with advance notice and subject to regulations adopted by the Commission. CRAMRA provides for the establishment of a plenary commission with general authority, regulatory committees (ten members each) to manage each of the geographical areas yet to be identified, and a scientific and environmental advisory committee to provide expert advice. As envisaged by the drafters, each committee would proceed in stages to (1) promulgate general requirements, (2) review and approve applications, and (3) monitor activities to ensure conformity with requirements set out by the Commission.

CRAMRA was carefully crafted to take account of the different interests in the Antarctic. For it to come into effect, sixteen of the twenty consultative parties who were at the final negotiations must ratify the agreement. These states must include those needed for the regulatory commissions to function —the United States, the Soviet Union, and the seven claimants; and they must also include five developing countries and eleven developed countries.

The treaty was designed neither to encourage nor discourage exploration and development. However, unlike the living resources convention, activities (except prospecting) are prohibited until decisions are taken to ensure that mineral activities will take place in an acceptable form. In particular, opening a specific area for consideration of exploration and development proposals would require a consensus. Specific proposals would then be decided by qualified majorities. Environmental protection is an integral part of CRAMRA. An environmental impact assessment is among the requirements to initiate exploration, as is agreement on a liability protocol. A system of inspection and reporting is provided for, as well as procedures for compulsory settlement of disputes.

These safeguards have not been sufficient to allay the concerns of the environmental community. Immediately upon completion, some environmental groups set about a major campaign to see that CRAMRA did not come into force. While special concern was expressed about the decision not to require prior authorization for prospecting, there was also a desire on the part of some to ensure that no mineral mining activities would ever take place. As a result of domestic pressure, the governments of France and Australia have advocated a permanent ban on all mineral activity in the Antarctic. United States environmental lobbies have generated draft legislation calling for an indefinite ban on mining. The danger of UN intervention if stalemate persists suggests a compromise in the form of a ban of limited duration, possibly linked to acceptance of CRAMRA, as well as a separate agreement on the environment.

OUTER SPACE

In outer space, the international community is facing many of the same political and management problems that it confronted in the oceans and the Antarctic. The resource in question includes the use of geostationary and other orbits for activities such as telecommunications, meteorology, resource surveys, or solar power transmission. Initially, a few technologically advanced countries had the capability to launch and maintain satellites. In the 1960s the situation was one of relatively few users operating in space and the legal regime was much like that for navigation on the high seas.

The 1967 Outer Space Treaty[4] was agreed among the major actors in space. Few developing countries took part in negotiating this treaty. The treaty adopts the *laissez-faire* approach of allowing free exploration and use of space, subject to the proviso that space activities be carried out for the benefit and in the interest of all countries in accordance with international law. Activities are to be pursued on the basis of equality and international cooperation on scientific research. Weapons of mass destruction are proscribed, as are military installations in space. The treaty also bans national appropriation of celestial bodies.

Although space still remains an uncrowded and under-exploited area, a number of developing countries became apprehensive in the 1970s that certain space resources were, in fact, finite and that the developed countries would appropriate available resources operating under the first-come-first-served principle. In particular, they were concerned about future access to geostationary orbits and the allocation of the radio spectrum.

The geostationary orbit is located 22,300 miles above the equator. At this altitude satellites can remain in a fixed position above the earth to carry out a number of telecommunications and other activities. The minimum distance which should separate satellites in geostationary orbit to avoid interference with one another has been a function of technology. The technology

---

[4] Treaty on Principles Governing the Activities of States in the Exploration and Use of Outer Space Including the Moon and Other Celestial Bodies.

used at present would allow in the order of 200 geostationary satellites to operate in the same frequency band without interfering with one another. However, the use of directed beams and improved stabilizers, as well as other new technologies, could permit hundreds more satellites to be stationed above the equator in the near future, depending on the geographical areas being served. Clearly, the possibility of allocating a thousand or more satellite positions would pose far fewer problems than the prospect of only a few hundred. Foreseeable technological advances can increase the number of available satellite slots even further.

Although there has been no internationally agreed definition of where national air space ends and outer space begins, it has been widely accepted that earth orbiting satellites move in outer space. The lowest orbit for maintaining a satellite in orbit is 62 miles (apogee) to 28 miles (perigee). By this definition, the geostationary orbit would fall well beyond national air space. Despite the generally accepted norm for defining outer space, eight equatorial nations (of eleven) agreed in the Bogotá Declaration in 1976 to claim the geostationary orbit as part of their national territory. They argued that, since there is no explicit definition of outer space, the ban on national appropriation does not apply to them, even though their claims extend to a volume 22,300 miles above the Earth. The eight countries stated that satellites stationed over their countries must receive their prior authorization. The geostationary orbit over the oceans was part of the common heritage of mankind, and, in their view, an appropriate regime should be developed. The Latin American claimants declared that they were willing to negotiate regional agreements with other Latin Americans to provide access to the geostationary locations over land.

The claims of the equatorial states have been largely ignored in practice both within the International Telegraphic Union (ITU) and the Committee on Peaceful Uses of Outer Space (COPUOS). None the less, they provide a striking example of the partition approach carried to an extreme. They also illustrate the anxiety of developing countries that they will be too late to benefit from common property resources when the technological capabilities are initially in the hands of a few developed countries.

Similar anxieties are apparent in the negotiations over the allocation of the radio spectrum at the meetings of the World Administrative Radio Conference (WARC). The WARC process of spectrum and orbit allocation is an example of nations negotiating to allocate a scarce resource through an international decision process. In the discussions, the developing countries favour reserving frequency spectra and orbital positions for themselves, even though they currently have no plans to use them. The developed countries argue that this is a waste of the spectrum. Instead, they point to the fact that technological progress has continued to allow an increase in the number of frequency bands available to all users. At the 1977, 1981, and 1983 WARC negotiations, the developing country perspective prevailed and certain portions of the spectrum were assigned *a priori* for direct broadcasting satellites. During the 1985 and 1988 WARC negotiations, a complex plan was devised to assign each ITU nation a specific orbital location for fixed satellite services in certain newly allocated, lightly used frequency bands. This counterbalanced the desire of developed countries to maintain an 'as-needed' assignment methodology in the bands heavily used for commercial and military or government satellites.

THE ATMOSPHERE

In many respects our atmosphere can be viewed as a resource and as such raises global commons problems. National activities affecting the atmosphere and the stratosphere can have direct and indirect impacts on the climate, weather, health, and resources of other countries.

A variety of ostensibly domestic or local activities may adversely affect the atmosphere or the stratosphere. The conversion of forest lands to agriculture, as well as heavy reliance on fossil fuels, can increase levels of CO_2 production and increase the absorption of infra-red radiation by the Earth. Emissions such as CO_2 will promote a 'greenhouse effect' by trapping the sun's energy. Carried out on a massive scale, such changes will raise the Earth's temperature. Similarly, national policies on the use of chlorofluorocarbons (CFCs) have become a matter of international concern since the release of these chemicals reduces the capacity of the stratospheric ozone to protect creatures, including people, from ultraviolet radiation from the sun.

Environmental problems affecting the atmosphere and stratosphere may have local impacts and relatively short gestation periods, or they may build gradually into global problems. The easiest to recognize are the relatively localized problems, where pollutants and particulate matter have direct and visible effects. In addition, local emission of chemical gases may contribute to acid rains and other pollution in a region. The Nordic countries experience acid rain originating from the factories of the United Kingdom, while the US and Canada contribute acid rain to one another from their industrial areas. We have learned that the Arctic haze found over Point Barrow, Alaska originates with the factories of Western Europe. Where these cause–effect relationships can be determined, there are still significant political and economic reasons for resisting the scientific finding, especially when there are significant costs to reducing the pollution.

It is even more difficult to secure international agreement on the long-range atmospheric or stratospheric impacts of national activities. To verify a trend towards the warming of the Earth would not be sufficient to induce governments of poorer nations to modify their policies on deforestation, particularly where these offer short-term economic benefits. A vivid example of the way policy determines the response to scientific findings is apparent in the shifting national responses to evidence on CFCs. The first National Academy of Sciences' analysis of the impact of CFCs on the ozone layer was not accepted initially by the European scientific and policy communities, although it was taken very seriously in the United States. Then, after the Reagan Administration reviewed the issue, the US government adopted the position that we do not know enough to act on CFC emissions. If the findings were accepted, they would clearly require changes in the use of aerosols, nitrogen fertilizers, and refrigerants. The economic costs were recognized as substantial. At about the same time, the European scientific community became more concerned with ozone depletion and European governments took the lead in pressing for measures to reduce CFC emissions.

Then a startling and alarming confirmation of what hitherto had to most people been somewhat theoretical occurred: scientists discovered late in 1985 a large and unexpected 'hole' in the stratospheric ozone layer over Antarctica. While it could not be traced with certainty to CFCs (that was definitively confirmed by late 1987), it provided strong circumstantial evidence that the emission of CFCs was causing a potentially dangerous effect on a global scale. That finding galvanized governments into action, and in September 1987 they agreed, in the Montreal Protocol, on a halving by the year 2000 of production and consumption of CFCs in the industrialized countries, from their levels in 1986. Special, but transitional, arrangements were made for developing countries, at their insistence.[5] Further work on substitute products along with continuing scientific concern about the persisting level of chlorine compounds in the upper atmosphere led governments of the industrialized countries to agree, in 1990, on the elimination of consumption of CFCs by 2000.

GLOBAL CLIMATE CHANGE

The salient international 'commons' issue at present is concern about so-called 'greenhouse warming' of the earth as a consequence of the collective production of greenhouse gases by economic activity around the world. Some foresee disaster for mankind if the process is not halted or at least substantially slowed. Here, partition in the traditional sense will not work, since gases produced anywhere are fairly quickly diffused throughout the upper atmosphere, where they perform their greenhouse function. As with CFCs and ozone, here is another truly global externality. But how serious is it? And what can or should be done about it at the international level? The answer to the first question is unfortunately unclear, at least for a time horizon that is relevant for making decisions in the near future.[6] The answer to the second

---

[5] For a detailed account of the discussion and scientific developments leading to the Montreal Protocol, see Benedick (1991a and b).

[6] There is something to be said for letting each generation make its own strategic decisions,

question is obviously dependent in part on the answer to the first, but also on the capacity of the international system to manage the commons. What follows offers a tentative response to both questions.

A Digression on Scientific Background

How serious is the problem of global climate change due to greenhouse warming? The basic science with respect to greenhouse warming is straightforward and uncontroversial. The Earth absorbs energy from the sun and reradiates it to space at a lower frequency. The molecules of certain gases, notably CFCs, methane, water vapour, and carbon dioxide, absorb energy of the frequency the Earth radiates, and in so doing they heat the lower atmosphere to the point at which it can radiate enough energy to equal the incoming radiation. (Of these gases, CFCs are the most potent per molecule, but CO_2 is the most abundant.) This 'greenhouse effect' makes possible life as we know it, for the Earth would otherwise be uninhabitably cold. Since the beginning of the Industrial Revolution, however, people have been cutting trees and burning coal, oil, and natural gas at an ever-greater rate, producing carbon dioxide faster than the Earth's natural processes can recapture and sequester it. The result has been an increase in atmospheric concentration of carbon dioxide from about 275 parts per million (ppm) two centuries ago to 350 ppm today, and the increase is continuing. The extension of agriculture through cutting trees, which decay into carbon dioxide, cultivating wetland rice, and establishing large herds of cattle, both of which produce methane, has also contributed greenhouse gas emissions, although the net contribution of the latter two is unclear, since many methane-producing swamps have also been cleared, and natural herds of ruminants have been depleted.

Increasing the concentrations of greenhouse gases in the atmosphere should be expected, on the grounds of basic physics, to increase atmospheric temperature. The controversy begins over estimating the rate at which greenhouse gas concentrations will increase, on the one side, and on the impact that any given increase in concentration will have on surface temperature. The first issue arises because nearly half of the carbon dioxide that has been produced through human activity in the last 200 years, mainly through burning fossil fuels, cannot be accounted for. If the 'sink' that has been absorbing the missing carbon is becoming saturated, a given level of emissions may result in more rapid concentration in the atmosphere in the future; but since we do not know where it is going, it has become conventional to assume that in the future, as in the past, half the carbon released finds its way into the atmosphere.

since both preferences and opportunities will differ from generation to generation. Each generation's moral task is to leave to the next generation a set of opportunities that is no worse, and preferably better, than its own and an institutional set-up for generating more technical knowledge.

On that assumption, and on plausible projections of fossil fuel use and other relevant human activity during the next century, atmospheric concentrations of carbon dioxide and its equivalent in other gases can be expected to reach twice their 1800 level, i.e. 550 ppm, in the middle of the twenty-first century. What effect is that likely to have on global temperature and on other features of global climate?

There is much less agreement on the temperature impact of a doubling of carbon dioxide than there is on the basic science, and still less on the climatic effects of a given temperature change. Current consensus on the former point suggests an increase in average equilibrium temperature of the surface of the Earth ranging between 1.5 and 4.5 degrees centigrade, with 2.5 degrees representing a best guess. Average precipitation will rise with increasing temperature, sea-levels will probably rise due partly to some melting of glaciers and mainly to thermal expansion of surface water (the consensus range is 29–90 centimetres, 11–35 inches, by 2090), and the temperature increases will be greater toward the Earth's poles than at the equator, leading to lower temperature gradients between equator and poles than now exist.

The projected temperature change is wide because many secondary consequences of warming come into play, some of which reinforce it (e.g. warming increases the water vapour content of the atmosphere, and that in turn enhances warming) and some of which attenuate it (e.g. increased cloud formation at certain altitudes increases reflection of the sun's energy, and thus reduces the amount of energy reaching the Earth's surface). Many of these secondary effects have been identified, but their detailed operation and magnitude are poorly understood. But details are important.

There is another source of uncertainty. The basic analysis relies on equilibrium states. Yet it may take some length of time, called the transient, between the arrival of the stimulus (e.g. a doubling of carbon dioxide equivalent) and the attainment of the new equilibrium. The transient in the case of global warming is unknown; it may be as little as a decade, or as long as two centuries. The key variable here is how much heat the oceans absorb, and that in turn depends on how rapidly the oceans churn up their deep, cold waters, a process about which little is known. If the oceans churn very little (which is possible, because cold water sinks), the relevant transient will be relatively short; but if churning is great, the transient could last for decades, running into centuries, as the water of the oceans absorbs heat from the surface.

The major analytical tool for studying climate change is the global climate model (GCM), of which five were functioning in 1990. These are large-scale mathematical and numerical models of the world's climate that can simulate climate change for many notional decades on large-scale computers following some autonomous change, such as increased carbon dioxide introduced into the atmosphere. These models are intellectually very exciting, but they remain relatively primitive (a single point of 'observation' on the Earth's surface is roughly the size of Colorado, for instance), and there is low agreement among them on crucial details, particularly on the regional effects of increased average surface temperatures. Yet these regional effects are crucial for assessing the impact on society. Also, since the computational time required for each simulation is enormous, less sensitivity analysis to alternative assumptions has been done than would be desirable.

In short, our conjectures about future warming of the Earth's climate are based on some fundamental physics, combined with known and forecast increases in emissions. The detailed projections rely on simulations of large-scale numerical models that have been calibrated against reality only roughly, and which have no forecasting history because of their relative newness.

One way to test a model is to forecast a historical period with known exogenous variables (e.g. change in carbon dioxide concentration) and compare the results with what actually happened. Such forecasts have not actually been undertaken because of the expense involved, but if performed in 1890 they would probably have predicted a rise in equilibrium average surface temperature of the earth by 1990 in the vicinity of 1.5–2 degrees centigrade. How does that compare with what actually happened?

Unfortunately, and perhaps surprisingly, we do not know exactly what happened to the average global surface temperature over the past century. The reason is that three-quarters of the Earth's surface is water, some of it remote from places of habitation and major trade routes, and our measurements of water temperature a century ago are erratic and inaccurate. None the less, a best guess is that the Earth's temperature rose by about 0.5°C. over this period. What interpretation can we put on that increase, assuming it took place? First, it is positive, but substantially below the likely forecast increases. By itself, that suggests either that the forecasts are too high, especially the high end of the range;[7] or that the transients are quite long, since we are comparing forecasts of equilibrium temperature changes with observations (more accurately, estimates) of actual temperature changes. Moreover, most of the increase observed over the last century occurred in the first half of that period; average temperatures showed no trend between the 1930s and the 1970s, contrary to the pattern that would be expected on the basis of ever-increasing greenhouse gas emissions. The 1980s, however, were the warmest decade of the century.

Interpretation of such data is complicated, however, by the fact that there are large year-to-year variations in average temperature, much greater than the observed trend; and average temperatures changed over time before mankind arrived on the scene, so the presumption of no temperature change

[7] Indeed, Wigley and Raper (1991) suggest that if warming since 1860 is attributed to the enhanced greenhouse effect alone, the implied equilibrium temperature increase for the equivalent of doubling carbon dioxide is in the range 1.3–1.6 degrees centigrade, considerably lower than the consensus range. But they caution that this strong assumption cannot be made confidently.

over the century in the absence of greenhouse gas emissions may be erroneous. In particular, if the Earth is once again on a natural cooling trend, the estimated rise in temperature from that trend would be higher than 0.5°C. Moreover, other human activities, such as the emission of sulphur dioxide and other pollutants, may have reduced the incidence of the sun's energy on the surface enough to obscure a stronger effect from greenhouse gas emissions. So the historical results do not strongly support the use of GCMs as forecasting tools, but there are many reasons for regarding that test as inconclusive, and hence they cannot be decisively rejected.

Social Impact

The social impact of a global increase in temperature over the next century is similarly uncertain. Temperature increases in the consensus range have been alleged to entail mass dislocation, especially along coastal areas, and mass starvation due to declines in staple food output, which in turn is due to desiccation of the major grain-producing areas (see, for example, the TV documentary, *Race to Save the Planet*, 1990). Such outcomes are no doubt possible. But they are far from certain, and indeed are improbable. Carbon dioxide is itself a critical ingredient in photosynthesis, the process whereby plants make food. An increase in atmospheric carbon dioxide, especially if combined with increased precipitation, which is also a likely consequence of surface warming, will more likely permit an increase in total food production, compared with what would be possible otherwise, especially when allowance is made for the improvements in plant and animal strains that we know are possible over a century, permitting adjustment to the changed circumstances. Of course, considerable adaptation would be required, and some of the areas that are highly productive of food today may become less so with alterations in patterns of temperature and rainfall. But overall conditions would be more propitious for food production, unless by bad luck the additional rainfall all occurred over oceans, and rainfall over agricultural areas actually declined. Moreover, with a reduced temperature gradient between equator and poles, major storms, hence storm damage, would possibly become less severe, although again patterns would change and some areas not today subject to major storms might become so.

Rising sea-levels would require construction of sea-walls in inhabited lowland areas, or would require migration to higher ground. Some uninhabited low-lands would become inundated, i.e. would revert to salt marsh or mangrove.

Human adaptation to gradual climate change over the next century would seem to be possible without undue hardship or excessive cost for those societies sufficiently wealthy to make the expenditures required for adjustment. Indeed, it is likely to fall well within the compass of adaptations to many changes, such as rapid population growth and technical developments, that have taken place over the last century. Very poor societies, however, might find it impossible to make the required expenditures, for example on sea-walls or irrigation facilities, and some countries might simply have inadequate land to provide for their populations if significant areas became inundated or desiccated. The result could be mass migration of desperate people searching for a viable place to live. Moreover, some natural ecological systems, particularly forests, might not be able to move on their own rapidly enough to adapt to the changing temperature and patterns of rainfall, or they might encounter barriers of inland water or inhospitable soil that prevent further migration. They would not be able to survive without human assistance.

The Scope for International Action

Is international action to forestall greenhouse warming warranted in the near future? If so, is it possible? The answer to both questions is a highly qualified affirmative. The scientific uncertainties are such that it is difficult to make a compelling case for urgent, costly action by the international community to reduce greenhouse gas emissions. Moreover, some warming would actually be beneficial, at least to some parts of the globe; and adaptation to modest warming by most nations will not apparently be difficult. Obviously, beyond some point warming could endanger civilization as we know it, but that appears to be more than a century away. Furthermore, future generations will enjoy greater possibilities for dealing with it—particularly if the present generation leaves an appropriate legacy—through energy sources that substitute for fossil fuels at moderate cost. These greater possibilities may also include actions to offset the tendency towards greater warming through various kinds of geo-engineering, such as encouraging and controlling the growth of algae in parts of the ocean which are barren at present, or reducing the incident radiation of the sun by placing reflective particles in the upper atmosphere. Part of the legacy the present generation should leave is more information on these and other possible courses of action.

Equally obviously, however, if actions to mitigate greenhouse warming are relatively inexpensive, a precautionary move by the current generation might be to take such actions—if for no other reason than to prolong the period for adaptation to whatever warming does occur, since the rate of change is an important factor determining the costs of adaptation. Furthermore, actions to mitigate greenhouse warming would be desired by highly risk-averse individuals against the possibility that reality is considerably worse than now appears to be likely.

The logical way to reduce greenhouse gas emissions would be to place a tax on CO_2 emissions and their greenhouse equivalent in methane and CFCs, global in scope, at a uniform rate. This would represent the 'access fee' to use of the atmosphere as a disposal medium for greenhouse gases. In practice, such a tax would not be difficult to impose, with international agreement, on coal, crude oil, and natural gas, all of which have limited loci of production or sale. But it would be virtually impossible on local fuel substitutes, mainly wood; and of course on breathing by human beings and other animals. It would also be extremely difficult to levy a tax on methane (apart from the technical problem of finding an appropriate equivalency to CO_2),[8] since it is produced by many different processes: certain kinds of farming (especially rice), raising cattle and sheep, decomposition of city dumps and other sources of waste, and so on. Moreover, it would be difficult to tax the decomposition of cut forests.

Of course, before considering levying a tax on CO_2 emissions, it would be desirable to raise energy prices around the world to their equilibrium market prices, since both coal and oil are highly subsidized in some parts of the world, particularly in China and OPEC countries.

If there were to be a carbon tax, what should it be? That is not an easy question to answer. It depends first on the global objective with respect to carbon emissions, and at present there is no basis for establishing an acceptable limit. It depends further on how any given tax influences human behaviour with respect to consumption of the taxed item (fossil fuels, in this case, based on their carbon content), and there is little agreement on that. The oil price increases of the 1970s offer some experimental evidence in those countries that passed the price increases to the users of oil.

One economic study has suggested that it would take a carbon tax of $400–550 a ton, the equivalent of over 300 per cent per barrel of crude oil (at $20/bbl, and the equivalent for other fossil fuels) to reduce US CO_2 emissions to 80 per cent of their 1990 level by the year 2020.[9] Even if such a tax were introduced gradually, to avoid transitional disruption, it would slow economic growth within the framework of the model, and reduce US GNP by about 3 per cent.

On the other hand, a bottom-up approach to mitigation suggests that substantial amounts could be achieved at relatively little social cost, largely by encouraging society to move more rapidly to current best practice in energy conservation, where 'best practice' means that the technology has been demonstrated to be both technically and economically feasible. This is in addition to the elimination of CFC emissions that has already been agreed among the industrialized nations. Taken together, such actions could conceivably (if the response were widespread) lead to CO_2-equivalent emissions in the United States that were no greater in 2010 than they are in 1990, despite a 60 per cent real growth in the US economy over the intervening 20 years, at a cost no greater than $35 per metric ton of carbon, under one-tenth

---

[8] Methane is a more potent greenhouse gas per molecule than CO_2 by a factor of about 13, but it has a much shorter life in the atmosphere, and the results of its chemical decomposition are complex and difficult to predict.

[9] Manne and Richels, 1991.

the cost estimated by Manne and Richels, and with net benefit deriving from many of the actions.[10] But the methodology of both studies is controversial, and neither can be taken as definitive.

Interestingly, a poll of American adults taken by the Alliance to Save Energy (1991) showed that two-thirds felt that steps should be taken soon to reduce CO_2 emissions. The median respondent was willing to pay a maximum of \$132 a year to do so. This works out to 0.4 per cent of family disposable income, and the equivalent of a 4.4 per cent tax levied directly on household consumption of energy (including electricity) in 1989; the tax-rate would be lower if levied on industrial consumption of energy as well. This expressed willingness to pay falls far short of the tax the Manne–Richels objective and analysis would require, but represents the upper range of the low cost options outlined in the Evans Report.

A global CO_2 tax raises the question of who gets the revenue. Simplest and politically easiest would be for it to go to the country of consumption, since it is a tax on consumption. But that would imply rights to atmospheric disposal proportional to consumption, and that could, and almost certainly would, be questioned on grounds of international equity, since the bulk of the revenues would accrue to the high fuel consumption countries, i.e. to the rich countries. Furthermore, OPEC could argue, on administrative as well as equity grounds, that a tax on the carbon content of crude oil could be more easily levied by the country of production, and that such countries should keep the revenue. Alternatively, one could imagine at least some portion of the revenue being paid into a global fund, to be devoted to internationally agreed purposes. These purposes should certainly include financing basic and applied research on the origins and effects of climate change, improved global weather forecasting and dissemination of the forecasts (timely notice of storms can do much to save lives and some property), and research and development of non-fossil sources of energy. But it could also go further afield and finance public health or infrastructure improvements in poor countries, on the grounds they will lead to higher productivity, and higher productivity leads to higher real incomes and greater capacity to adapt to all kinds of change, including climate change.

Is it possible to get international agreement on significant efforts to mitigate greenhouse warming? Again, the answer is a highly qualified affirmative. Greenhouse warming, like ozone depletion but unlike acid rain, is obviously a global problem, in principle affecting all societies. Similarly, preventive action, to be effective, must take place on a global scale, although actions by individual countries can serve to mitigate the greenhouse effect. It is true that in the late twentieth century most fossil fuel consumption takes place in the rich countries of Europe, North America, and Japan, plus the formerly centrally planned economies. But even then, emissions from deforestation and

---

[10] NAS, 1991 (Evans Report).

rice cultivation occur mainly in developing countries. Moreover, on current projections, developing countries as a group will be major consumers of fossil fuel in the twenty-first century, so their co-operation will eventually be essential if emissions are to be reduced.

There is increased consciousness among leaders and intellectual élites in developing as well as developed countries of environmental degradation as a result of human activity, not least because some of the large urban areas in developing countries have become so unattractive from an environmental point of view. But, while there is increased consciousness of environmental degradation compared with ten to twenty years ago, other issues command much more attention. Leaders in developing countries must deal with the fact that (in general) the 1980s were not a good decade in terms of economic development. Large external debts continue to weigh heavily on many countries. And a number of governments are politically shaky, in part (but only in part) for economic reasons; some are even embroiled in civil war. These are much more pressing issues than the environment, even taking the possibility of dramatic climate change in the next century into consideration.

Developing countries are not likely to constrain their economic growth, and hence their demand for energy, for the sake of environmental improvement. Furthermore, they will argue with some plausibility that apart from local air and water pollution, the contribution to global environmental degradation is made overwhelmingly by the rich countries, with significant help from the recently centrally planned economies. Despite smaller populations, these countries use much more energy and generate much more waste. This position is largely correct with respect to present and past conditions, although as Table 7.2 shows, by 1988 five developing countries were among the top twenty emitting countries, and they tended to use energy less efficiently than the rich countries, but more efficiently than the centrally planned economies. The fact that the relative contributions can change markedly with successful economic development (contrast 1960 with 1988), is a matter that they are likely to be willing to take into consideration only after that development has actually occurred.

The bottom line is that many developing countries will co-operate with developed countries in reducing the emission of greenhouse gases into the atmosphere so long as it does not require great commitment on their part (e.g. in terms of domestic political conflict), and so long as the developed countries incur the extra costs associated with that co-operation.

Indeed, developing countries, individually or as a group, may attempt to extract a price from co-operation on environmental matters beyond the incremental costs of changing their behaviour, to the extent that they detect that the environment has become a priority issue for the developed countries. Developing countries have long felt frustrated over their lack of adequate 'bargaining leverage' with respect to the rich countries, many of which were former colonial powers.

Table 7.2. Carbon dioxide emission estimates

	1960	1988	
		Total	Relative to GNP
United States	2858	4804	0.98
USSR	1452	3982	1.50[a]
China	789	2236	6.01[a]
Japan	234	989	0.35
Germany (West)	545	670	0.56
India	122	601	2.52
United Kingdom	590	559	0.80
Poland	202	459	2.66[a]
Canada	193	438	1.00
Italy	110	360	0.43
Germany (East)	264	327	2.05[a]
France	274	320	0.34
Mexico	63	307	1.74
South Africa	99	284	3.60
Australia	88	241	0.98
Czechoslovakia	130	234	1.90[a]
Romania	54	221	2.77[a]
South Korea	49	205	1.19
Brazil	47	202	0.63
Spain	13	188	0.55

[a] Coefficients for centrally planned economies are likely to err on the low side, because of generous estimates of GNP.

Note: Units in million metric tons of CO_2, or in metric tons CO_2 per $1000 of GNP.

Source: NAS (1991), 7–8.

Under the heading of greenhouse gas emissions, the question of property rights over the atmosphere as disposal medium will be raised. Indeed, an opening salvo has already been fired by Anil Agarwal, an Indian environmentalist, who argues that greenhouse gas emission rights should be based on population, and should be transferable among countries (why not among individuals?). At least for the next several decades, the rich, energy-consuming countries would therefore have to buy emission rights from the poor countries, leading on to his estimate of payments by the United States of $38 billion a year into a global environmental fund, from which India would be entitled to draw several billion dollars a year.[11] One problem with the atmosphere is that there is no logical basis for establishing property rights, and there is unlikely to be a global consensus around any of the

[11] Anil Agarwal, 'The Emerging Global Environmental Agenda: Is the Third World Being Taken for a Ride?', a lecture given on 7 February 1991 and widely and approvingly cited in the Indian press.

'reasonable' but non-logical bases, e.g. historic use, GNP, area of national territory, or population, as these may or may not be modified by national temperature range or average humidity.

Even when the governments of developing countries agree on the desirability of improving the environment, or restraining its deterioration, their priorities will be elsewhere, and it would not be surprising to find them trying to extract some quid pro quo for their environmental co-operation in some other area in which developed countries can be helpful to them.

For these reasons, the international negotiating environment for mitigation actions is likely to be very complicated, to say the least. One strategy is for the OECD countries to take on the assignment among themselves, in the hope that developing countries will later join the consensus actions after their incomes and their fossil fuel consumption have risen considerably. This strategy does not exclude action within developing countries, provided the OECD countries are willing to pay for it, for example through World Bank loans that take climate change considerations into their design. The problem with this strategy is that there seems to be no right time for a country to graduate from developing to developed status, especially if it is costly, as we have seen in resistance to being graduated from eligibility for highly concessional IDA loans or from tariff preferences under the Generalized System of Preferences.

Even among developed countries there is likely to be serious debate over how costly actions should be shared among countries. This source of contention is present in the best of circumstances whenever a collective good is involved, since there is no obviously correct principle for burden-sharing. Contribution to the problem, ability to pay, and accrual of future benefits all vie for consideration, along with the diverse practical political constraints that countries face. But it is especially a source of contention when ignorance about the nature and distribution of the 'good' in question—in this case, the benefits from mitigation actions—is as great as it is at present. Moreover, some countries may be expected to benefit from at least a modest amount of warming (e.g. the weather might become less uncertain in the grain-growing areas of the Soviet Union), and this possibility may also induce reluctance to contribute to an international effort. International co-operation in other fields has progressed most successfully when there was agreement not only on the objective, but also on how best to achieve it. As the prolonged and sometimes acrimonious history leading to international co-operation in the non-controversial objective of containing contagious diseases suggests, absence of scientific consensus on key aspects of how greenhouse gas emissions translate into global temperature changes will make even more difficult agreement on how to share costly actions, or indeed on what actions should be taken (Cooper, 1989).

These various considerations will tend to push countries away from mitigation actions towards reliance on adaptation, where the actions are in response to identifiable localized problems (e.g. a shore being inundated, or croplands being flooded), and where the expenditures are willingly made by the direct beneficiaries. 'Property rights' have thus been established. Even foreign aid in this case can be focused on well-defined mitigation of visible hardship, a factor that makes garnering foreign support easier. In short, the need for international co-operation, while frequently present on a regional basis, will be much less acute with a broad strategy of adaptation than for a major commitment to mitigation.

CONCLUDING OBSERVATIONS

As long as scientific findings on environmental problems are inconclusive, calculations of the economic, political, and social costs and benefits of action will determine the policy response. Equally apparent is the fact that no environmental problems can be successfully addressed until all those countries principally responsible for the problem are prepared to act. Before national governments will be willing to take on the costs of change, the scientific community must establish an agreed basis of facts that again will be sufficiently convincing.

In the case of the environment, the non-divisibility of the seas or the atmosphere may drive nations reluctantly in the direction of joint management. Before international agreement to act on long-term trends can be reached, the problem must be serious, the findings of the scientific and technical community must be compelling, and the costs of action must be proportionate to the nature of the problem. Policy-makers will not adopt costly environmental protection measures without a strong case.

In those cases where a common property resource cannot be managed by dividing the resource among interested states or by allowing its use on a first-come, first-served basis, joint management approaches have evolved. The intergovernmental institutions that have been created in response to commons problems range from bilateral agreements, such as the US–Canada Commission on the Great Lakes, to global international organizations, such as the IMO, which develops rules for international shipping. Regional and global institutions can be complementary and mutually reinforcing. The regional seas programmes, for example, benefit from the umbrella oversight role performed by UNEP. And UNEP's broad environmental goals have been furthered by devolving responsibility on to these regional groups.

An overview of the diverse institutional arrangements that have been sparked by the need to manage common property resources indicates how difficult it is to make prescriptive generalizations about commons management. Each particular commons question has distinctive technical and political attributes which will strongly condition any successful solution to emerging problems. It is difficult, therefore, to propose a concrete solution that would bear on all commons problems. An issue facing governments and interested organizations is how to make existing institutions more effective in dealing with the commons problems that they have been designed to manage.

The essential first step in tackling commons issues is to determine whether a problem exists and how severe it is. This requires an improved capability to monitor and plan for an emerging problem—whether it is a greenhouse effect or increased fishing pressure on Antarctic krill. It also requires a capability to diagnose the cause of existing commons problems such as acidification of lakes and forests by acid rain. A well-developed base of information is a vital first step, to be followed by the development of scientifically persuasive cause–effect analyses.

The second step in effective response is the development of a viable regime to deal with the problem. It is preferable to act before the problem becomes acute; in practice, action is usually taken only after a situation is severe enough to generate political attention. In order for a response to a problem to be effective, all the parties that are directly concerned—whether the issue is environmental pollution or the emplacement of satellites—should be part of the decision-making process and part of the agreed response. By the same token, the inclusion of actors whose direct interest in the issue is marginal runs great risk of impeding a successful outcome, for they will tend to use their influence to pursue other objectives that are more important to them.

Successful regimes and institutions build on the best available information and shared concern about the need to deal with a problem. Financial and decision-making responsibility must be correlated, and a regime must be able to adapt to new problems and to accept new participants as appropriate. Any institutional structure that does not maintain the support of the major parties to a commons problem is bound to fail.

In the broadest terms, commons regimes are sparked by problems that cannot be ignored even though the preference of most governments is to maximize sovereign autonomy and limit financial responsibility. Promising research might usefully focus on a comparative analysis of the international organizations and institutions that have developed to manage common property resources. The questions to be answered are how well these regimes have coped with the issues they were asked to address, and what accounts for the differences in success.

REFERENCES

Alliance to Save Energy (1991), *America at the Crossroads: A National Energy Strategy Poll* (Washington, DC).

Benedick, R. (1991*a*), *Ozone Diplomacy* (Cambridge, Mass.: Harvard University Press).

—— (1991*b*), 'Protecting the Ozone Layer: New Directions in Diplomacy', in J. Mathews (ed.), *Preserving the Global Environment* (NewYork:W.W. Norton).

Cooper, R. N., *et al.* (1989), *Can Nations Agree?* (Washington, DC: Brookings Institution).

Hollick, A. L. (1981), *U.S. Foreign Policy and the Law of the Sea* (Princeton, NJ: Princeton University Press).

Manne, A. S. and Richels, R. G. (1991), 'Global CO_2 Emission reductions—the Impacts of Rising Energy Costs', *The Energy Journal*, 12/1:87–107.

National Academy of Sciences (1991), *Policy Implications of Greenhouse Warming* (Evans Report), (Washington, DC: National Academy Press).

National Academy of Sciences (1991), *Policy Implications of Greenhouse Warming— Report of the Mitigation Panel* (Washington, DC: National Academy Press).

Wigley,T. M. L., and Raper, S. C. B. (1991), 'Detection of the Enhanced Greenhouse Effect on Climate', *Proceedings of the Second World Climate Conference* (Cambridge: Cambridge University Press).

8

How Should International Greenhouse Gas Agreements be Designed?

Michael Hoel

INTRODUCTION

One of the most serious environmental problems in the next century may be climatic changes caused by the greenhouse effect. Increased atmospheric concentration of greenhouse gases, of which CO_2 is the most important, may increase the average temperature by 1.5–5 degrees within the next century. The greenhouse problem is a typical global environmental problem: climatic changes throughout the world depend on world-wide aggregate emissions of climate gases, and not on how these emissions are distributed between countries. The consequences of climatic changes may, of course, differ greatly between different countries, but the climatic changes themselves depend only on world-wide emissions.

Global environmental problems are difficult to solve. Each country's own contribution to world-wide emissions is small, and there is therefore little each country can do by itself. Although each country benefits from reduced emissions from all other countries, it is in no country's interest to make significant sacrifices through large reductions in its own emissions. The reason is that, given the emissions of other countries, any single country's own emissions contribute only negligibly to aggregate emissions. So we are faced with a 'Prisoners' Dilemma' type of situation. This situation is given a brief formal presentation in the following section, where CO_2 emissions are modelled as the outcome of a non-cooperative game. The non-cooperative outcome is compared with the first best social optimum.

Due to their nature, global environmental problems need co-ordinated action between countries. For such co-ordinated action to be taken, one must have some kind of international agreement. International co-operation often takes the form of an agreement among co-operating countries to cut back on emissions by some uniform percentage compared with a specific base year. However, work in the field of environmental economics has indicated that equal percentage reductions of emissions from different sources give an inefficient outcome, in the sense that the same environmental goals can be

This chapter has arisen from the research project 'Energy and Society' at the Centre for Research in Economics and Business Administration (SNF), Oslo. I am grateful to Rolf Golombek and Karl-Göran Mäler for useful comments on an earlier version of the paper.

achieved at lower total costs through a different distribution of emission reductions. As argued below, participation in agreements of the 'uniform reduction' type may also be quite low.

The next section discusses three types of taxes on CO_2 emissions:

1. a domestic CO_2 tax to achieve a domestic emission goal (which may or may not be derived from some international agreement);
2. international agreement which harmonizes domestic CO_2 taxes; and
3. an international CO_2 tax. It is shown that an international agreement of this last type may give an allocation of emissions which is (almost) equal to the first best social optimum. Harmonization of domestic CO_2 taxes, on the other hand, is for several reasons shown to be inferior to an international CO_2 tax.

Then I show that an international agreement with tradable emission permits has very similar properties to an international CO_2 tax. In particular, both types of agreements have built-in mechanisms for side-payments, so that the distribution of the burdens of reducing emissions may be chosen independently of the allocation of emissions.

The formal model used in this chapter is very simple. In particular, the objective function of each country includes only total income and some measure of environmental costs. Moreover, no types of domestic or international institutional constraints are explicitly included in the analysis. These restrictive assumptions are later relaxed, and it is then shown that the main results also remain valid in a more complex setting. In particular, it is shown that a uniform international CO_2 tax, or a system of tradable emission permits, is efficient even in the presence of more complex objectives and institutional constraints. However, an efficient allocation of emissions between countries does not necessarily imply that domestic CO_2 taxes should be the same in all countries.

Future climatic changes depend on emissions of other climate gases (CFC, CH_4, O_3, N_2O) as well as on CO_2. A fully efficient agreement should therefore be related to emissions of all climate gases, and not only CO_2. Some of the complications which arise when greenhouse gases other than CO_2 are included in an agreement are discussed towards the end of this chapter.

CO-OPERATIVE AND NON-COOPERATIVE OUTCOMES

Consider N countries, each with a income function $r_j(v_j)$, where v_j is the emission of CO_2 from country j. Other inputs are held constant, and the income function is assumed to be increasing (up to some level v_j^{max}) and strictly concave in v_j. $r_j(v_j)$ measures income in excess of the income level associated with no emissions, i.e. $r_j(0) = 0$. It is also assumed throughout the paper that all $r_j'(0)$ are so large that corner solutions may be disregarded.

Total CO_2 emissions (V) are given by

$$V = \sum_i v_i, \tag{1}$$

and each country is assumed to have an increasing and strictly convex environmental damage function $d_j(V)$.

The net benefit of country j is

$$b_j = r_j(v_j) - d_j(V). \tag{2}$$

Consider first the non-cooperative Nash equilibrium of the one-shot game in which all countries choose their CO_2 emissions simultaneously. The non-cooperative Nash equilibrium implies that b_j in (2) is maximized with respect to v_j, taking the other emission levels v_i ($i \neq j$) as given and with (1) inserted into (2). This gives

$$r_j'(v_j) = d_j'(V); \tag{3}$$

i.e. each country chooses its emission level so that the marginal income of emissions is equal to the country's own marginal environmental damage.

The sum of net benefits for all countries is

$$B = \sum_j [r_j(v_j) - d_j(V)]. \tag{4}$$

A first-best social optimum follows from maximizing (4) with respect to CO_2 emissions, which gives

$$r_j'(v_j) = D'(V) \qquad j = 1,..,N, \tag{5}$$

where we have defined

$$D(V) = \sum_i d_i(V). \tag{6}$$

In other words, marginal incomes are equal for all countries, and equal to the sum over all countries of the marginal damage of CO_2 emissions. Notice that (5) gives a particular distribution of CO_2 emissions, and thus a particular distribution of net benefits between countries in the absence of side-payments. With side-payments, however, the conditions (5) do not restrict the possible distributions of net benefits between countries. It is therefore only when side-payments of some form are permitted that (5) is the obvious candidate for a co-operative equilibrium. Moreover, it is only when all countries have the simple objective function of total income measured in international currency that the social optimum is given by (5). The issue of more complex (and more realistic) objective functions will be taken up in more detail later.

Comparing (3) with (5) it is easily verified that the sum of emissions from all countries is lower in the first best optimum than in the non-cooperative equilibrium. To prove this formally, use superscripts $\star$ and o for the non-cooperative and co-operative outcome respectively. Assume $V^o \geq V^\star$. Since this gives $D'(V^o) > d_j'(V^o) \geq d_j'(V^\star)$, it follows from (3) and (5) that $v_j^o < v_j^\star$ for all j, which implies $V^o < V^\star$. This contradiction proves that we must have

$V^o < V^*$. Intuitively, we might expect that emissions from all countries are lower under the first best optimum than they are in the non-cooperative case. For the general case, however, this need not be true (see Hoel (1991b) for a counter-example).

EQUAL PERCENTAGE REDUCTIONS OF EMISSIONS

International co-operation often takes the form of an agreement among the co-operating countries to cut back emissions by some uniform percentage rate compared with some base year. This type of agreement has two disadvantages. In the first place, equal percentage reductions of emissions from different countries usually give an inefficient outcome, in the sense that the marginal incomes $r_j'(v_j)$ will differ between countries. The same environmental goals could therefore have been achieved at lower cost through a different distribution of emission reductions.

A second problem with agreements of equal percentage reductions is that not all countries will find it in their interest to participate in such agreements. A likely minimum requirement for a country to participate in an agreement is that the country is better off under the agreement than it is without any international agreement. The reason for such a requirement is that as long as there is no international law to force countries to participate in an agreement, each country can choose to be a free-rider outside the agreement instead of participating in the agreement. If the country stands outside the agreement, it can enjoy (almost) the same benefits of reduced emissions as if it participates in the agreement, while it doesn't bear any of the costs of reducing emissions. An important motive for a country to participate in an agreement instead of being a free-rider is that by being a free-rider it increases the risk of the whole agreement breaking down. This motive for participating in the agreement is stronger the more the country has to lose from the agreement breaking down. Obviously, a country which doesn't lose anything from the agreement breaking down has no incentive to participate in the agreement, and it will therefore choose to be a free-rider instead.

Even with a relatively modest reduction in emissions, some countries might be better off without any agreement than they are with the agreement of uniform emission reductions. It is unlikely that these countries will participate in the agreement. But if some countries don't participate, the benefits of the remaining countries are also reduced, so that some of this latter group of countries might be worse off with the agreement than they are without, and therefore would choose not to participate. In this way the whole agreement might unravel. To illustrate this point, consider the following example: there are three equal sized groups of countries, A, B, and C. With the proposed agreement of a uniform reduction of emissions, the C-countries are better off without than with the agreement; the A- and B-countries are better off with an agreement than without, provided all countries participate. However, B-countries are better off without than with the agreement if C-countries don't participate; and A-countries are better without an agreement than with if they are the only countries which participate. In this example, a majority of the countries are thus better off with the agreement (with full participation) than without. Nevertheless, it is clear that no country will join the agreement in this example, provided countries only participate if they are better off with the agreement than without (see, for example Hoel (1992a) for a further discussion of this issue).

A CO_2 TAX

It is important to distinguish between cost efficiency at the national and at the international level. At the national level, cost efficiency for CO_2 emissions implies that whatever the total CO_2 emissions from the country are, the marginal costs of reducing CO_2 emissions should be equalized across different domestic sources of such emissions. The most obvious way to achieve such cost efficiency is to impose a domestic tax on all domestic CO_2 emissions. In practice, this means taxes on all types of fossil fuels, with tax rates depending on the amount of CO_2 released through combustion.

Even if all countries use cost-efficient policies to achieve their goals for total domestic CO_2 emissions, global cost efficiency is only achieved if the international CO_2 agreement is appropriately designed. As explained above, global cost efficiency requires that CO_2 emissions are distributed among countries in such a way that the marginal cost of reducing them is equalized among countries. A possible candidate for an international agreement is an agreement to harmonize domestic CO_2 taxes across countries. However, it is not clear what such an agreement implies, in particular if some of the participating countries are non-market economies. Even in market economies, it is not clear whether such a harmonized CO_2 tax should be in addition to various other domestic taxes on fossil fuels the countries might have, or instead of all existing taxes on fossil fuels. If existing taxes reflect domestic externalities in transportation etc., an internationally agreed CO_2 tax ought to be an addition to existing taxes, while one could argue that the CO_2 tax should take the place of other taxes on fossil fuels if these taxes are pure revenue-raising taxes.

A problem with an international agreement requiring equal domestic CO_2 taxes is the free-rider problem: it is in each country's interest to have few or no restrictions on their own CO_2 emissions, given the CO_2 emissions from other countries. If a country is required to have a CO_2 tax through an international agreement, it is therefore in the interest of the country to try to make this tax as ineffective as possible. One way to do this is to reduce other domestic taxes on fossil fuels, e.g. taxes on petrol, which several countries have for domestic purposes. Even if a country doesn't directly reduce such domestic taxes, it might raise them less than it would have done, had it not been for the imposed CO_2 tax. Another way to reduce the effect of the imposed CO_2 tax is to manipulate the prices of other domestic goods. Roughly speaking, a country should tax close substitutes to fossil fuels and subsidize complements. Obvious examples are taxes on other types of energy (e.g. hydroelectric power), and subsidies on automobiles and air conditioning. This type of price policy will reduce the effect of an imposed CO_2 tax on a country's consumption and production pattern, and thereby reduce the cost to the country, even though in a formal sense it is sticking to the international agreement. In spite of the possibility that each country will reduce the effect of a CO_2 tax, any realistic goal for global CO_2 emissions could probably be achieved with a sufficiently high CO_2 tax. The point is, however, that each country's attempts to reduce the effect of such a tax lead to inefficiencies at the national level: each country could have achieved whatever emission level it has in equilibrium at a lower cost had it been allowed to reduce the CO_2 tax and at the same time remove all counteracting policies of the type mentioned above.

In addition to this efficiency argument, an international agreement to impose a specific domestic CO_2 tax in each country will have only a small chances of encouraging wide participation. I will return to this point later.

Instead of harmonizing domestic CO_2 taxes, an international agreement could introduce an international CO_2 tax. This tax should be imposed on each country (through its central government) by some international agency according to each country's CO_2 emissions. Assume that emissions from country j are taxed at a rate t_j by the international environmental agency. The tax revenue is reimbursed to the countries in fixed ratios $\beta_1, \beta_2, ..., \beta_N$, where $\sum_i \beta_i = 1$. (The determination of the β_j's will be explained below.) Since each country is assumed to care only about its total income measured in domestic currency (in addition to the environment), the net benefit of country j is

$$b_j = r_j(v_j) - [t_j v_j - \beta_j \sum_i t_i v_i] - d_j(V). \tag{7}$$

The term in square brackets represents taxes minus reimbursements for country j, and may be positive or negative.

Consider the non-cooperative Nash equilibrium of the game in which all countries choose their CO_2 emissions simultaneously, regarding tax-rates and the reimbursement vector β as given. The non-cooperative Nash equilibrium implies that b_j in (7) is maximized with respect to v_j, taking the other choices v_i $(i \neq j)$ as given and with (1) inserted into (7). This gives

$$r_j'(v_j) = d_j'(V) + (1 - \beta_j)t_j. \tag{8}$$

Comparing (8) with (5) reveals that the taxes giving the social optimum must satisfy

$$d_j'(V^o) + (1 - \beta_j) t_j = D'(V^o) \tag{9}$$

or

$$t_j = [D'(V^o)] \left\{ \frac{1 - \left[\frac{d_j'(V^o)}{D'(V^o)} \right]}{1 - \beta_j} \right\}. \tag{10}$$

It is clear from (10) that if and only if

$$\beta_j = \frac{d_j'(V^o)}{D'(V^o)} \tag{11}$$

for all j, is it possible to find a uniform tax-rate which makes the Nash equilibrium coincide with the social optimum. In this case the optimal tax rate is given by

$$t = D'(V^o); \tag{12}$$

i.e. the tax rate is equal to the sum of marginal environmental damages.

Whether or not the condition (11) holds depends on the β vector. In principle, the β vector could have been chosen so that (11) holds in equilibrium. With arbitrary d_j-functions, however, this could violate the requirement that all countries are at least as well off in this first best optimum as they are in the non-cooperative case without any CO_2 tax. In particular, there could be a country which would not be negatively affected by the climatic changes following from increased atmospheric concentration of CO_2, i.e. $d_j' \leq 0$ for this country. Clearly, such a country would need to have $\beta_j > 0$ to be willing to participate in an arrangement with a positive tax on CO_2 emissions, i.e. $\beta_j > d_j'(V)/D'(V)$.

Even if (11) doesn't hold, the tax given by (12) will be a close approximation to the ideal taxes given by (10), at least for small countries: for small countries both β_j and d_j'/D' are close to zero, so that the ideal tax for such a country is close to D'. For large countries, such as, for example, the USA and the former USSR (which are responsible for 23 and 18 per cent of total CO_2 emissions, respectively), d_i'/D' and β_i cannot be approximated by zero. Nevertheless, $(1 - \beta_j)/(1 - d_j'/D')$ may also be close to 1 for such countries.

Although the tax given by (12) is a good approximation to the first best optimum, it is usually not the best uniform tax. If one, for practical purposes, must stick to a uniform tax, a second best social optimum can be found by maximizing (4) with (8) and $t_j = t$ as constraints. This second best tax-rate is derived in Hoel (1992b), where it is shown that this tax may be lower or higher than $D'(V^c)$, where V^c is the second best optimal total emission level.

Let us finally consider once more an international agreement requiring each participating country to impose a CO_2 tax on all domestic emissions. Such an agreement gives a specific distribution of costs between countries. In fact, disregarding the counteracting policies discussed previously, an agreement of this type is identical to an international CO_2 tax with reimbursement parameters chosen so that each country's reimbursements in equilibrium are exactly equal to the tax it pays to the international agency.

This particular set of reimbursement parameters may very well make several countries worse off with the agreement than without any agreement. Participation in such an agreement may therefore be rather limited.

TRADABLE EMISSION PERMITS

For domestic environmental problems, it is well known from the literature on theoretical environmental economics that a system of tradable emission quotas under certain conditions has similar desirable efficiency properties to those of a system of emission taxes. Practical experience with tradable quotas is, however, somewhat mixed; see, for example, the discussions by Hahn (1989), Pearce (1990) and Tietenberg (1990).

For domestic environmental problems, it is well known that a system of tradable emission permits has the same desirable cost efficiency properties as a system of emission taxes. For global environmental problems there is a strong similarity between a global emission tax and internationally tradable emission permits. An alternative to an international CO_2 tax is therefore a system of CO_2 emission permits which each country is free to use itself or to sell to other countries which can use them instead.

When there are many countries participating in the CO_2 agreement, and each country is relatively small, a competitive market for CO_2 emission permits is likely to develop. In this case each country will regard the price of CO_2 emission permits as independent of its own CO_2 emissions. Denoting this price by q, the net benefit of country j is thus

$$b_j = r_j(v_j) - q(v_j - \beta_j V) - d_j(V). \tag{13}$$

Country j is assumed to receive an initial allocation of emission permits equal to $\beta_j V$. In (13) the term $q(v_j + \beta_j V)$ therefore gives the payment from country j to buy additional emission permits (i.e. if this term is negative country j is a seller of emission permits).

The expression (13) is valid for all countries. In a non-cooperative equilibrium, each country chooses v_j so that b_j is maximized. In this maximization, V is taken as given, since it is determined by the total number of emission permits which are allocated to the countries. A small country will also regard the market price of emission permits (q) as exogenous, so that maximization of (13) gives

$$r_j'(v_j) = q. \tag{14}$$

Assuming for a moment that all countries consider q as exogenous, the equilibrium price q is determined by (5.2) and $\sum_i v_i = V$. Notice that whatever V-value one chooses, (14) implies that all countries have the same marginal incomes of CO_2 emissions. In other words, total income is maximized subject to the constraint on total emissions. Moreover, if V is chosen equal to the socially optimal level V^o, it is clear that the present non-cooperative equilibrium coincides with the first best optimum.

Notice the similarity between a system of tradable emission permits and an emission tax. Provided all countries are small, so that optimal tax-rates for all countries are (approximately) given by (12), it follows from (4) and (12) that $r'_j(v_j) = t$ in the tax case. From (14) it is therefore clear that the price of tradable permits plays the same role as the tax-rate. The tax scheme and the system of tradable emission permits are thus isomorphic: the gross CO_2 tax paid by a country corresponds to the market price of CO_2 emission permits multiplied by the country's CO_2 emissions, while the country's reimbursement corresponds to the market price of CO_2 emission permits multiplied by the initial emission permits the country gets. A tax scheme with an emission tax t^o giving total CO_2 emissions equal to V^o and tax reimbursements to the N participating countries proportionally to the vector $(\beta_1, \ldots, \beta_N)$ with $\sum_i \beta_i = 1$ is thus equivalent to a system of tradable emission permits where the initial emission permits to the N countries are $(\beta_1 V^o, \ldots, \beta_N V^o)$. In this system of tradable emission permits the market price of the emission permits becomes identical to the emission tax t^o in the corresponding tax scheme. The exact equivalence between a CO_2 tax and a system of tradable emission permits no longer holds when some of the countries involved are large. For a further discussion of this issue, see Hoel (1991a).

Since the initial distribution of tradable CO_2 emission permits corresponds exactly with the reimbursement parameters in the CO_2 tax scheme, the preceding discussion of how reimbursement parameters should be determined in a tax system is valid also for the determination of the initial CO_2 emission permits.

DISTRIBUTION OF TAX REVENUE OR INITIAL EMISSION PERMITS

As with all distributional issues, there are no principles which are generally agreed upon that can be used to determine how the total net gains from a CO_2 agreement should be distributed among the participating countries.[1] However, as mentioned previously, a reasonable minimum requirement is that all participating countries should be better off under the CO_2 tax scheme than without any international agreement.

The minimum amount of reimbursement a country needs in order to be better off with the CO_2 tax scheme than without any agreement is higher (a) the larger the costs the country has in reducing its CO_2 emissions, and (b) the smaller the negative consequences for the country of climatic changes

---

[1] For discussions of the distributional issues involved, see e.g. Grubb (1989), Kverndokk (1992) and Pearce (1990).

caused by increased atmospheric concentration of CO_2. The sum of the minimum amounts of reimbursement the countries need in order to be better off with the CO_2 tax scheme than without any agreement must be lower than the total gross CO_2 taxes paid by the countries. This is a direct consequence of the tax-rate being chosen according to some agreed total CO_2 emissions, so that there is a positive net gain from the tax scheme to be distributed among the participating countries. Nevertheless, we cannot theoretically rule out the possibility that there exists a group of countries for which the sum of minimum amounts of reimbursements in order for them to be better off with than without the CO_2 tax scheme exceeds total gross CO_2 taxes paid by all participating countries. This group of countries would typically be characterized by high costs of reducing CO_2 emissions, and/or modest concern over possible climatic changes. If such a group of countries exists, the sum of the tax reimbursements to the remaining participating countries would have to be negative, i.e. some or all of these countries would have negative β_i-values. In spite of these countries having to pay taxes in addition to the CO_2 tax, these countries would benefit from the CO_2 tax scheme, due to the reduction in global CO_2 emissions.

These principles could be applied when determining the reimbursement parameters if costs of reducing emissions and the costs of climate change were common knowledge. This is, however, far from the case. In practice, these costs cannot be measured objectively with any precision, although some rough indicators of them are observable.

Consider first the costs of reducing CO_2 emissions. Countries in which a large fraction of their electric power generation and other stationary energy use is coal-based (e.g. the UK and Germany) can reduce CO_2 emissions at relatively low cost by switching to natural gas or (to a smaller extent) to oil. On the other hand, countries which use practically no coal initially and have no natural gas grid, and in which a large part of the oil consumed is used in transportation (e.g. Norway), can only achieve significant reductions in their CO_2 emissions at quite a high cost.

Turning to the consequences of climatic change, some island and coastal countries (e.g. the Maldives, the Netherlands, Egypt, and Bangladesh) are very exposed to a rising sea-level due to global warming. On the other hand, one could argue, for example, that significant parts of the former USSR would benefit from a warmer climate. Since the regional effects of a warmer global climate are extremely uncertain, however, trying to guess the consequences for different countries of climate changes must be very speculative.

If, in practice, one tried to determine reimbursement parameters according to the principles above, it would be in each country's interest to claim that it had high costs of reducing emissions, and that the expected climate change in the absence of an agreement would not have any serious impact on the country. The negotiation process would be very difficult, and it is doubtful whether any agreement would be reached. Moreover, if the size of the tax-rate was determined simultaneously or prior to the negotiations about reimbursements, countries would go for a low tax-rate in order to make credible their arguments about high costs of emission reductions and/or small adverse effects of a climatic change. Even if an agreement was reached, one would therefore probably get a lower tax rate, and thus higher CO_2 emissions, than the socially optimal level.

For the above reasons, the reimbursement parameters for most countries would in practice have to be determined by relatively simple criteria which leave little scope for objections from individual countries. Three obvious criteria are reimbursements in proportion to (1) historical CO_2 emissions ('grandfathering'), (2) GNP (in the current year of CO_2 taxation or some fixed base year), and (3) population (in the current year of CO_2 taxation or some fixed base year[2]). One obvious objection against using historical emissions as a reimbursement criterion is that it punishes countries which have unilaterally cut down their CO_2 emissions long before any CO_2 agreement.

Current CO_2 emissions per unit of GNP differ significantly between countries, with, for example, emissions from China being about seven times higher than emissions from the USA (relative to GNP). However, the introduction of a CO_2 tax will induce high emission countries such as China, which use coal as a major energy source, to reduce their CO_2 emissions relatively more than low emission countries. Under a CO_2 tax scheme, CO_2 emissions per unit of GNP will probably differ far less between countries than they do today. Reimbursement proportional to each country's GNP therefore implies that most countries will pay or receive relatively small net amounts to or from the international agency in charge of the CO_2 tax. A CO_2 tax/GNP-reimbursement scheme would probably be preferred by most countries to a situation without any international CO_2 co-operation. The exceptions would be countries which at present have relatively high CO_2 emissions per unit of GNP and relatively high costs of reducing CO_2 emissions, and/or countries with modest concern over possible climatic changes.

For the LDCs, it would obviously be better if the tax revenue was reimbursed according to population rather than according to GNP (or historical emissions). Current CO_2 emissions per capita differ sharply between countries—from 1 tonne for Africa to 20 tonnes for the USA, with a world average equal to 4 tonnes. This pattern will most likely remain after CO_2 emissions are reduced due to a CO_2 tax. Reimbursement proportional to each country's population therefore implies large net payments from the industrialized countries and large net payments to the LDCs. While the LDCs will certainly benefit from such a tax scheme, several industrialized

---

[2] In order not to give countries incentives to increase their population, it seems better to use population in some historical base year rather than current population as the criterion. Grubb (1989), who also discusses these three criteria, suggests that one should use the current population as the criterion, but only counting population above a specific age.

countries will probably be worse off under such an arrangement than without any international CO_2 co-operation.

It follows from the discussion above that all of the three mentioned reimbursement criteria have weaknesses. An obvious possibility is to use some combination of the three criteria, i.e. let reimbursement be proportional to an index including historical emissions, GDP, and population. If countries could agree to this, the negotiation process would be limited to the two weights of this index, as well as to the size of the tax (i.e. the total level of emissions). Such negotiations would be difficult enough, but it at least seems conceivable that an agreement could be reached with relatively large participation.

Even if historical emissions, GNP, and population are the main criteria for tax reimbursements, one could save some of the tax revenue to be reimbursed according to special considerations. Obvious candidates for such special treatment are LDCs with high costs of reducing CO_2 emissions and for which climatic changes don't have an obvious strong negative impact.

Even if one can reach an agreement on reimbursement parameters making most countries better off with the agreement than without, the free-rider problem remains: a country may be better off participating in an agreement than it would be without any agreement. But it will often be even better off if the other countries co-operate, while the country itself stands outside the agreement and pursues its self-interest. The free-rider problem obviously complicates negotiations, and reduces the chance of reaching an agreement with broad participation. For further discussion of the free-rider problem in the context of international environment problems, see, for example Barrett (1991a, 1991b), and Mäler (1991).

A CO_2 TAX OR TRADABLE QUOTAS IN A WORLD WITH MORE COMPLEX OBJECTIVE FUNCTIONS

So far, each country has been assumed to maximize its revenue, measured in international currency, minus net tax payments to an international agency.[3] This is obviously a drastic simplification compared to real world policy goals. An important question is therefore to what extent our conclusions from previous sections remain valid with more complex preferences and/or various market failures and constraints on economic policy. In particular, how robust is the conclusion that an international CO_2 tax (combined with some reimbursement rules) gives an efficient allocation of CO_2 emissions between countries, as long as countries are 'small' in the sense that they regard total emissions as given?

[3] In this section it is assumed that all countries are small, in the sense that they regard total emissions (V) as given in the tax case, and the market price q as given in the case of tradable quotas. Since each country regards V as (approximately) independent of its own emissions, we need not include the environmental cost functions $d_j(V)$ in the countries' objective functions.

Intuitively, one might expect that various distortions in domestic and international markets, as well as objective functions including more than the countries' total income, would imply that a uniform international CO_2 tax is no longer an efficient type of greenhouse gas agreement. Arguments along this line have been made in a recent study by Haugland and colleagues (1990):

cost efficiency is not necessarily assured by internationally uniform CO_2 taxes, as is frequently suggested. Clearly an efficient set of taxes will have to be adjusted in accordance to the initial differences in energy prices. Similar problems occur in a system of tradeable emission permits; if all countries are charged the same price for CO_2 permits, and the domestic energy prices differ considerably, agents face different costs of acquiring fossil energy. This situation is of course not globally efficient.

To see whether or not a uniform international CO_2 tax is efficient, one must start by specifying a welfare function for each country. A general welfare function is $w_j(v_j, s_j)$, where v_j is emissions from country j, while s_j is net transfers to country j from other countries. This function is defined as follows:

$$w_j(v_j, s_j) = \max_{x_j}[u_j(x_j) \text{ s.t. } x_j \in X_j(s_j); \quad v_j = f_j(x_j)]. \tag{15}$$

Here x_j is a vector of economic variables, such as production and consumption of different goods, employment in particular sectors, various prices, policy instruments such as taxes and subsidies, etc. The objective function of the country is $u(x_j)$, and may depend in a complex way on all variables included in the vector x_j. The feasible set X_j of possible x_j-vectors may depend on the net transfers from abroad. Finally, total emissions depend on the vector x_j, usually in a very simple way.[4]

Since $u_j(x_j)$ is a very general function, and the constraints implied by $X_j(s_j)$ may include all relevant institutional constraints, the welfare function $w_j(v_j, s_j)$ is very general. A reasonable assumption is that w_j is strictly increasing in s_j. Moreover, we assume that w_j is increasing in v_j for v_j-values below some critical value.

Given a constraint on total emissions ($= V$), an optimal $(v_1, \ldots, v_N, s_1, \ldots, s_N)$ vector is defined by the following maximization problem:

$$\text{Maximize} \quad \sum_i \alpha_i w_i(v_i, s_i) \tag{16}$$
$$\text{s.t.} \quad \sum_i v_i \leq V$$
$$\text{and} \quad \sum_i s_i = 0,$$

where the α_i's are some non-negative weights. The solution to this maximization problem of course depends on the vector $\alpha = (\alpha_1, \ldots, \alpha_N)$. Whatever the α-vector is, the solution to (16) must satisfy the condition

---

[4] If one only considers CO_2 emissions from fossil fuels, the function f_j will be a linear function of the use of different types of fossil fuels.

$$\frac{w_{1v}}{w_{1s}} = \ldots = \frac{w_{Nv}}{w_{Ns}}, \tag{17}$$

where $w_{jv} = \partial w/\partial v_j$, etc. All allocations of $(v_1,..v_N,s_1,\ldots,s_N)$ satisfying (17) are thus efficient in standard economic terminology. Which of these efficient allocations is regarded as best depends on the α-vector.

Notice that if the w_j-function is $r_j(v_j) - s_j$, as in the previous sections, the condition (17) is identical to the first part of (5), which requires that the marginal income of emissions, $r_j'(v_j)$, should be equal for all countries. For this special case there is thus a unique efficient emission vector $(v_1,\ldots,v_N)$, while the vector $(s_1, \ldots ,s_N)$ will depend on the α-vector. For more general w_j-functions, however, the vector $(v_1,\ldots,v_N)$ will depend on the α-vector.

Consider an international tax on CO_2 emissions. Country j pays a tax equal to tv_j, and is given a reimbursement equal to $\beta_j t V$. Without loss of generality we may ignore other transfers between countries,[5] so that $s_j = - tv_j + \beta_j t V$ and $w_j = w_j(v_j, - tv_j + \beta_j t V)$. By assumption, country j regards t, β_j, and V as exogenous, so that maximization of $w_j(\cdot)$ implies

$$w_{jv} + w_{js}(- t) = 0$$

or

$$\frac{w_{jv}}{v_{js}} = t. \tag{18}$$

It is immediately clear from (17) and (18) that as long as all countries face the same CO_2 tax t, an efficient allocation of emissions is reached.

Notice that any efficient allocation $(v_1^\star,\ldots,v_N^\star, s_1^\star,\ldots, s^\star)$, i.e. a solution to (16) for any non-negative α-vector, may be reached by an international CO_2 tax and a suitable β-vector. The appropriate CO_2 tax follows directly from (17) and (18):

$$t = \frac{w_{jv}(v_j^*,s_j^*)}{w_{js}(v_j^*,s_j^*)}, \tag{19}$$

and the appropriate tax reimbursement vector β follows from the equality

$$s_j^\star = - tv_j^\star + \beta_j t \sum_i v_i^\star,$$

giving

$$\beta_j = \frac{s_j^* + tv_j^*}{t \sum_i v_i^*}. \tag{20}$$

In particular, all efficient allocations satisfying the constraint

$$w_j(v_j^\star,s_j^\star) \geq w_j^o \qquad \forall j \tag{21}$$

may be reached through a suitable choice of (t,β), where w_j^o is country j's welfare level under the non-cooperative equilibrium.

[5] As long as any other transfers are regarded as independent of emission levels, there is no loss of generality if these are assumed to be zero.

For some of the efficient allocations the β-vector implied by (20) may have some negative elements. It may even be the case that all allocations satisfying the constraint (21) imply β-vectors with negative elements. If one restricts oneself to non-negative tax reimbursements, it may therefore not be possible to design a tax scheme making all countries better off than they are in the absence of any agreement.

Instead of an international CO_2 tax, an efficient allocation $(v_1^\star, \ldots, v_N^\star, s_1^\star, \ldots, s_N^\star)$ could be reached through tradable emission permits. If the market price of emission permits is t, and country j initially gets $\beta_j V^\star = \beta_j \sum_i v_i^\star$ permits, it faces exactly the same maximization problem as it does in the case of a corresponding international CO_2 tax. In the case of tradable permits, however, it is difficult in practice to imagine that $\beta_j < 0$ for any country.[6] One may therefore have to supplement a system of tradable permits with some side-payments in order to be able to reach an allocation satisfying the constraint (21).

An international CO_2 tax (or a corresponding system of tradable emission permits) makes each country choose a particular emission level. How should a country implement its emission goal? This question cannot be answered without a more detailed description of the country's objectives and constraints. For simple economies with competitive markets and no distortionary taxes, it will be optimal simply to have a domestic tax on CO_2 emissions which is equal to the international tax t. For more complex economies, this need not be the case. Due to various distortions in the domestic economy, it may be (second best) optimal for a country to tax CO_2 emissions at a rate which differs from the international tax-rate. To illustrate this, the rest of this section treats one particular type of distortion: we consider a simple competitive economy which must raise a specific tax revenue by distorting taxes.

Without any international CO_2 tax, the revenue function of country j is $r_j(v_j) - c_j(h_j)$, where h_j is tax revenue raised by taxes other than a domestic CO_2 tax. The term c_j represents the deadweight loss of non-CO_2 taxation, and it is assumed that $c_j(0) = 0, c_j' \geq 0$, and $c_j'' \geq 0$. There is a domestic tax on CO_2 emissions equal to τ_j, and the equilibrium CO_2 emissions are given by

$$r_j'(v_j) = \tau_j, \tag{22}$$

so that $v_j = v_j(\tau_j)$.

The country faces an international CO_2 tax equal to t, and a tax reimbursement equal to z_j. Its objective function is thus $r_j(v_j) - c_j(h_j) - tv_j + z_j$. The country is assumed to have an exogenous tax revenue requirement g_j for

<hr />

[6] Theoretically, one could have a system of tradable emission permits in which $\beta_j < 0$ for some countries. The interpretation is that a country with $\beta_j < 0$ would have to buy emission permits (in the magnitude $-\beta_j V$) from other countries and return them to the international agency even if it has zero emissions. With positive emissions, it must of course purchase more than $-\beta_j V$ from other countries.

domestic purposes. We therefore have $h_j = g_j + tv_j - z_j - \tau_j v_j$, where the sum of the first three terms is total revenue requirement, and $\tau_j v_j$ is tax revenue from the domestic CO_2 tax. Country j's objective function is therefore

$$w_j = r_j(v_j) - c_j(g_j + tv_j - z_j - \tau_j v_j) - tv_j + z_j \tag{23}$$

and $v_j = v_j(\tau_j)$ follows from (22). Country j regards g_j, z_j, and t as exogenous, and chooses τ_j to maximize w_j. Differentiation of (23) gives

$$[r_j' - c_j' \cdot (t - \tau_j) - t]v_j'(\tau_j) + c_j' \cdot v_j(\tau_j) = 0;$$

or, inserting (22) and rearranging

$$\tau_j = t + \frac{c_j'(1 + c_j)}{-v_j'/v_j}. \tag{24}$$

From (24) we immediately see that $\tau_j = t$ if there is no marginal deadweight loss associated with non-CO_2 taxation (i.e. $c_i' = 0$). For $c_j' > 0$ we have $\tau_j > t$, and the difference $\tau_j - t$ is larger the larger is the ratio between the relative marginal deadweight loss of non-CO_2 taxation $[c_j'/(1 + c_j)]$ and the relative sensitivity of CO_2 emissions to the domestic CO_2 tax. To interpret (24) it is useful to rewrite it as

$$(\tau_j - t) \cdot \frac{-v_j'}{v_j} = \frac{c_j'}{1 + c_j}. \tag{25}$$

The left-hand side of (25) expresses by how much CO_2 emissions are reduced (in relative terms) as a consequence of the domestic tax exceeding the international tax. In a second best optimum this relative reduction of CO_2 should be equal to the relative marginal deadweight loss of non-CO_2 taxation. There is no reason to expect the second term on the right-hand side of (24) to be equal for different countries. In general, an efficient allocation of CO_2 emissions between countries therefore implies different domestic CO_2 taxes for different countries.

The conclusion from this section is thus that a uniform international CO_2 tax, or a system of tradable emission permits, is efficient even in the presence of more complex objectives and institutional constants. However, an efficient allocation of emissions between countries does not necessarily imply that domestic CO_2 taxes should be the same in all countries.

The conclusion of this section thus contrasts with what one might intuitively expect, as expressed in the quotation from Haugland and colleagues above. One reason for this difference is that the present analysis takes objectives and constraints as given. In contrast, Haugland et al. seem to have some kind of first best optimum as their point of reference when they write of efficiency 'a CO_2 tax should ideally correct for initial "taxes" or "subsidies" ' and 'price differences caused by existing trade barriers, in combination with differences in costs in various regions should also be taken into consideration when designing a globally efficient system.' It is obviously true that an international CO_2 tax—uniform or not—cannot in itself eliminate all types of domestic and international inefficiencies. What the present analysis has shown is that if one takes these types of inefficiencies as given constraints—or as given elements of the countries' objective functions—a uniform international CO_2 tax gives a (second best) efficient allocation of CO_2 emissions between countries.

OTHER GREENHOUSE GASES

Future climatic changes depend on emissions of other climate gases (CFC, CH_4, O_3, N_2O) as well as on CO_2. A fully efficient agreement should therefore in principle be related to emissions of all climate gases, taken together with their impact on the climate. One practical complication with greenhouse gases other than CO_2 is that emissions of most of these gases are considerably more difficult to monitor than CO_2. Although efficiency considerations suggest agreements encompassing all climate gases, practical considerations might therefore force one to limit an agreement to CO_2, at least initially. Nevertheless, it is useful to see how other greenhouse gases should be treated, if the monitoring problem were solved.

If the environmental effects of greenhouse gases other than CO_2 were limited to the greenhouse problem, extending a CO_2 agreement to a full greenhouse gas agreement would be trivial. Instead of a CO_2 tax or CO_2 emission permits, one would have a greenhouse gas tax or greenhouse gas emission permits. For a particular gas, the international tax per unit of emission, or the number of permits per unit of emission, would be proportional to the greenhouse effect per unit of this particular gas.

A complicating factor is the fact that emissions of some gases (e.g. some CFCs) contribute both to the greenhouse problem and to other environmental problems (e.g. depletion of the ozone layer). To illustrate this issue, let us assume there are three types of gases, A, B, and C, and two global environmental problems, P and Q. Problem P is affected by emissions of the gases A and C, with one unit of C having the same effect as x units of A. Problem Q is affected by emissions of the gases B and C, with one unit of C having the same effect as y units of B. In this case the appropriate international taxes in a tax scheme would be t_P and t_Q. Emissions of the three gases A, B, and C should be taxed at the rates t_A, t_B, and $xt_A + yt_B$ per unit of emission, respectively. The values of t_A and t_B depend on the goals for total emissions affecting the P- and Q-problems, respectively. These goals should in turn be decided by equating the marginal cost of emission reduction with the sum over all countries of the marginal environmental cost (cf. (5)-(6)). Similarly, in an international agreement with tradable emission permits, one 'A-permit' should be required per unit emission of the A-gas, and one 'B-permit' should be required per unit emission of the B-gas. For one unit emission of the C-gas, the emitting country should be required to use x 'A-permits' and y 'B-permits'.

A much larger complication arises if some of the greenhouse gases give rise to international environmental problems in which it is not only the sum of emissions which matters for the environment, but also which countries the emissions come from. In this case it is obvious that it will not be optimal for all countries to face equal international emission taxes for the gases with these properties. Similarly, unrestricted trading between countries of emission permits for such gases will give rise to an inefficient allocation of emissions. The integration of agreements for this type of general transnational environmental problem with an agreement covering the greenhouse problem is quite a complex issue, and will not be pursued here.

CONCLUSIONS

International agreements are necessary to achieve significant reductions of emissions of CO_2 and other greenhouse gases. Traditional agreements of the type 'uniform percent reductions' have two disadvantages. In the first place it would probably be difficult to get a sufficiently large participation in such an agreement, since it gives a distribution of costs of reducing emissions which may differ strongly from the advantages the countries have from avoiding climatic changes. In the second place agreements of this type are generally not efficient, i.e. the same environmental goal may be achieved at lower total costs with a different allocation of emissions between countries.

An international CO_2 tax and tradable CO_2 quotas are two systems which are almost[7] efficient under quite general assumptions, and which can be designed so that a large participation is likely. The difference between agreements of this type and traditional 'uniform percent reduction' agreements is larger the higher are the costs of reducing emissions. This means that as long as one is considering only modest reductions in CO_2 emissions (relative to a 'business as usual' scenario), the loss associated with a simple 'uniform percent reduction' agreement will be relatively small. In order to avoid serious climatic changes in the next century, it is probably necessary to curtail CO_2 emissions substantially. The costs of such emission reductions will be relatively high even if costs are minimized. If one does not reach an efficient agreement, the costs of reducing global CO_2 emissions may be so high that it will be impossible to agree upon a reduction of emissions which is sufficient to avoid serious climatic changes.

Disregarding large countries, a CO_2 tax scheme and a system of tradable CO_2 quotas are equivalent. However, there are some practical differences between the two systems. An obvious objection to CO_2 tax is that it is difficult to know exactly which tax-rate corresponds to an agreed level of total CO_2

---

[7] The 'almost' is due to large countries, which take into consideration that they can influence total emissions and total tax revenue in the tax case, and the market price of quotas in the tradable quota case.

emissions. However, for the case of CO_2 one is not particularly concerned about the exact emissions in any particular year, but rather about the development over several years. Once one has agreed upon a desirable development of CO_2 emissions, one can decide upon a corresponding initial CO_2 tax-rate and a tentative future development of the CO_2 tax. If it turns out that the initial CO_2 tax gives a different level of CO_2 emissions than expected, the CO_2 tax at later dates can be adjusted up or down compared with the original plan for the CO_2 tax development. Through this type of procedure, one should relatively quickly be able to reach a path of CO_2 emissions which is close to the desired path.

With CO_2 quotas, the desired path of CO_2 emissions can be obtained accurately and immediately. However, in this case the problems are pushed over to each individual country. It is difficult for each country to achieve CO_2 emissions which are exactly equal to its quotas. If unused quotas become worthless after the year they are issued for, most countries will not design their CO_2 policies with a large security margin relative to their CO_2 quotas. One must therefore expect frequent cases of CO_2 emissions in excess of the quotas. Unlike the CO_2 tax scheme, the system of CO_2 quotas has no built-in mechanism for treating CO_2 emissions in excess of what a country had planned.

If a country in a particular year has lower emissions than it has quotas for (through initial distribution and additional net purchases), one can allow the country to transfer its excess quotas to later years, since there are no negative consequences to the climate of postponing emissions. If a country in a particular year has higher emissions that it has quotas for, the international agency in charge of the quotas can sell the necessary supplementary quotas to the country. The price of such supplementary quotas could be set somewhat higher than the market price for the relevant year, in order to avoid a tendency for total emissions to exceed the emission goal one has for each year.

The main advantage with tradable quotas compared to an international CO_2 tax is that the first system resembles more closely traditional agreements of the type 'uniform percent reductions'. It might therefore be easier to get acceptance for this system than for a system of an international tax.

An agreement of 'uniform percent reductions' is an agreement about a distribution of emission quotas based on the historical emissions of the countries. Allowing these quotas to be traded between countries is only a minor modification of such an agreement. The special case of tradable quotas where the initial distribution of quotas is proportional to historical emissions is thus very similar to traditional agreements of the 'uniform percent reduction' type. Compared to an agreement with 'uniform percent reduction' with non-tradable quotas, the system with tradable quotas gives a gain to all participating countries (or at least no loss to any country). No country is forced to buy or sell its emission quotas, and therefore no country can be worse off when trade is permitted than when it is not. So it ought to be possible to achieve wider participation in a system of this type than in a system of 'uniform percent reductions' without tradability. However, one can probably achieve even higher participation in an agreement where the initial distribution of quotas is based on criteria other than historical emissions alone.

REFERENCES

Barrett, S. (1991a), 'International Environmental Agreements as Games', in R. Pethig (ed.), *Conflicts and Cooperation in Managing Environmental Resources* (Berlin, Springer-Verlag).

—— (1991b), 'The Paradox of Global International Environmental Agreements' (mimeo; London Business School).

Grubb, M. (1989), *The Greenhouse Effect: Negotiating Targets* (London: Royal Institute of International Affairs).

Haugland, T., Olsen, Ø., and Roland, K. (1990), 'Stabilizing CO_2-Emissions by Carbon Taxes—A Viable Option?', Report 1990/11 (Oslo, Fridjof Nansen Institute).

Hahn, R.W. (1989), 'Economic Prescriptions for Environmental Problems: How the Patient Followed the Doctor's Orders', *Journal of Economic Perspectives*, 3.

Hoel, M. (1991a), 'Efficient International Agreements for Reducing Emissions of CO_2', *Energy Journal*, 12/2.

—— (1991b), 'CO_2 and the Greenhouse Effect: A Game Theoretical Exploration' (mimeo; Department of Economics, University of Oslo).

—— (1992a), 'International Environment Conventions: The Case of Uniform Reductions of Emissions', *Environmental and Resource Economics*, 2.

Hoel, M. (1992b), 'Intertemporal Properties of an International Carbon Tax', *Resource and Energy Economics*, 2/1.

Kverndokk, S. (1992), 'Global CO_2 Agreements: A Cost Efficient Approach', *The Energy Journal*.

Mäler, K. G. (1990), 'Incentives in International Environmental Problems' (mimeo; Stockholm School of Economics).

Pearce, D. (1990), 'Greenhouse Gas Agreements: Part 1' (mimeo; University College London).

Tietenberg, T. (1990), 'Economic Instruments for Environmental Regulation', *Oxford Review of Economic Policy*, 6/1.

9

The International Protection of the Environment: Voluntary Agreements among Sovereign Countries

Carlo Carraro and Domenico Siniscalco

INTRODUCTION

A large quantity of pollutants are discharged into the environment as a result of human activity in each country. Some emissions are transported in the atmosphere and in the water and affect other countries as well as the global environment. There are many examples of such trans-frontier and global pollution. The current policy debate mainly concerns atmospheric emissions and the associated damage: carbon dioxide and other greenhouse gases in relation to global warming; CFC and the ozone layer; sulphur doxide and nitrous oxide, which are mainly responsible for acid depositions.

The transportation of pollutants in the environmental media is a source of substantial interdependence among countries: each country benefits from using the environment as a receptacle for emissions and is also damaged by environmental degradation. While the benefit is related to domestic emissions only, the damage is also related to foreign emissions which reach the country from other countries. Hence there arises a problem of international externalities which, in the present institutional setting, can be solved only by international agreements among sovereign countries.

Such agreements involve several difficulties related to the asymmetries of the countries concerned: the attitude towards the environment differs greatly between countries according to their preferences, their level of development, and their environmental endowment. An additional difficulty is created by the incentive to free-ride: each country would like to enjoy a cleaner global environment without paying for it, and this behaviour can directly damage the co-operation between other countries. Hence, there is a problem of potential instability in any agreement.

This chapter presents a general framework with which to analyse the profitability and the stability of the international agreements to protect the environment in the presence of trans-frontier or global pollution. The analytical work is based on a game-theoretical framework, where sovereign countries bargain over emissions in a common environment. The agreements can be co-operative or can simply reflect non-cooperative behaviour.

The interdependence of decisions depends on a small set of fundamentals, such as preferences and technology, and on the transportation of emissions in the environmental media. With reference to the recent literature (e.g. Barrett, 1991; 1992; Bohm, 1990; Hoel, 1991; 1992; Kaitala, Pohjola, and Tahvonen, 1992; Mäler, 1989, 1991; Newbery, 1991), the analysis provides a sort of taxonomy of different agreements and explores new strategies to protect the international or the global environment.

The main analytical conclusions can be summarized as follows:

1. the strategic interaction among countries in a common environment does not lead necessarily to the 'tragedy of commons' (Hardin, 1968; Hardin and Baden, 1977; Ostrom, 1990) but there is a full range of voluntary agreements to control emissions, even if co-operation among countries is typically unstable;
2. beyond non-cooperative emission control (which can be effective in some circumstances) there exist co-operative agreements among subgroups of countries which are not undermined by free-riding;
3. the partial coalitions mentioned above tend to be small; in such cases, however, gains from partial co-operation can be used to sustain much broader coalitions by inducing other countries to co-operate through self-financed utility transfers. To sustain broader coalitions, however, two conditions must be met: environmental policy must be backed by other policy instruments, and a minimum degree of commitment must often be introduced into the game.

Some applications and simulations make it possible to qualify the analytical results mentioned above: in the presence of high environmental interdependence, non-cooperative emissions are not much higher than co-operative emissions and represent a much easier way to protect the environment. As the interdependence decreases, non-cooperative emission control becomes less effective, but partial co-operation becomes easier. Partial coalitions tend to involve a small number of countries. These coalitions, however, can be expanded through appropriate changes in the strategies to sustain environmental co-operation. This route to environmental protection seems to be much simpler to achieve and maintain than full cooperative agreements among all countries. It could therefore provide an alternative and more pragmatic blueprint for environmental negotiations, which usually seek full co-operation.

The paper is divided into three sections. The next section introduces the analytical framework and defines the main kinds of agreements which can lead to pollution control; it also provides three main results on stable coalitions. We then argue that the various kinds of agreements examined in general terms may correspond to possible outcomes in plausible situations and discuss the main implications of the proposed analysis.

THE ANALYTICAL FRAMEWORK

Players, Pay-offs, and Strategies

Consider n players ($n \geq 2$) who interact in a common environment, and bargain over emissions of specific pollutants. We interpret players as countries. As usual, each country i benefits from using the environment as a factor of production and as a receptacle for emissions. Its welfare, however, is negatively affected both by its own emissions x_i and by a given share α_i of other countries' emissions $X - x_i$, where $X = x_1 + \ldots + x_i + \ldots + x_n$. Parameter α_i is computed using a pollutant-specific transportation model; α_i can be interpreted as an aggregate parameter derived from a general transportation model (e.g. the RAINS model developed at the International Institute of Applied Systems Analysis in Austria) that identifies the amount of pollutant a_{ij} transported from country j to country i. We focus on a single, aggregate parameter for simplicity's sake.

Country i's benefit and damage enter a welfare function

$$P_i(x) = B_i(x_i) - D_i[x_i, \alpha_i(X - x_i)],$$

where $B_i(x_i)$ denotes benefits arising from the use of the environment for production and consumption activities, $D_i[x_i, \alpha_i(X - x_i)]$ denotes damages (utility losses) determined by pollution emissions, and $x = (x_1 \ldots x_n)$.

Consider the benefit function $B_i(x_i)$: a reduction in pollution, which can be achieved through domestic environmental policies, is costly and therefore reduces benefits. The benefit function, which depends on abatement costs, is country-specific and is related to technology, economic structure, the level of development, and environmental endowments. By technology we mean more than the mechanical process of turning inputs into outputs; we mean useful knowledge and experience, institutions and organizational form, as well as norms and values that impinge upon and govern the processes of production and exchange.

The damage function $D_i[x_i, \alpha_i(X - x_i)]$ depends on a country's perceived effects of emissions of a given pollutant, as well as on the evaluation of such effects. It is thus mainly based on a subjective, country-specific, evaluation of environmental goods. The parameter α_i, $0 \leq \alpha_i \leq 1$, reflects pollution externalities. It is equal to zero if the pollutant has only local effects, i.e. when foreign emissions do not reach country i; it can be equal to one if domestic and imported emissions have equal weight for country i, as in the case of global pollutants such as greenhouse gases. The specific functional form of $D_i(.)$ can be determined using appropriate models of Environmental Impact Evaluation (EIE). Such models usually contain both the measurement of the relevant physical damage and its evaluation, the two values being summarized in an index.

Let δ_i be the maximum level of pollution emission for country i. This value, taken as a bench-mark, is computed by maximizing environmental benefits

$B_i(x_i)$ without taking into account the associated costs evaluated through the function $D_i(.)$; δ_i is also a measure of country dimension and development.

The 'emission game' between the n countries is thus defined by a triple (N,S,P), and by appropriate rules; as usual, $N = \{1 \ldots n\}$ is the set of players, $S = S_1 x \ldots x S_n$, where $S_i = (0, \delta_i)$ is the strategy space, $P = [P_1(x) \ldots P_n(x)]$ is the pay-off vector. Complete information is assumed. Problems arising in the presence of asymmetric information will be mentioned briefly below.

In this context, a country may decide whether or not to co-operate with other countries in order to reduce total emissions (by taking into account reciprocal externalities). Co-operative agreements are assumed not to be binding. As in the actual practice, countries consider one pollutant at a time. The decision whether or not to co-operate is the outcome of a 'meta-game' in which each country anticipates the choice (co-operative or non-cooperative) of the other countries, and the relative outcomes in terms of emission levels.

We restrict the analysis to one-shot games. Analysing repeated games would be relevant (in terms of additional equilibrium outcomes) only if appropriate trigger or stick-and-carrot strategies could sustain co-operation as an equilibrium outcome. Emissions, however, can hardly be conceived as a trigger variable which is expanded in response to other countries' defection. Emission reduction, in most cases such as CO_2 or CFCs, involves substantial irreversible investments. Expanding emissions as a retaliation, in cases such as SO_2 or NOX, would cause environmental damage primarily to the triggering country. Finally, emission expansions can hardly be used as a selective punishment. Other effective punishments (e.g. trade protectionism) could be even more costly for the triggering country and therefore not credible. For these reasons trigger or stick-and-carrot strategies seem to be of little help in sustaining co-operation, and the equilibria of the repeated game would coincide with the equilibria of the one-shot game. We thus concentrate our attention on the latter. In further analytical work, of course, it would be worthwhile to explore repeated games, too. Note, however, that in the real world no environmental issue has yet been dealt with by means of trigger or carrot-and-stick strategies.

Let us solve the game by analysing its outcomes under alternative strategic combinations. First we assume that countries play simultaneously, and non-cooperatively. In this case, country i's optimal level of emissions is determined by equating marginal benefits and marginal costs, given the emission levels set by the other countries. The solution of the system of first-order conditions determines the Nash equilibria of the game. For simplicity's sake, we assume the equilibrium to be unique.

The Nash equilibrium of the non-cooperative game can also be determined by computing the fixed point of countries' best-reply functions. Let $R_i(x)$, $x = (x_1 \ldots x_n)$, be country i's best-reply function, where

$$R_i(x) = x_i : P_i(x_i, X - x_i) \geq P_i(s_i, X_s - s_i),$$

$$X_s = x_1 + \ldots + x_{i-1} + s_i + x_{i+1} + \ldots + x_n, \quad \text{for all } s_i \in S_i.$$

The non-cooperative equilibrium x^o is defined by $x^o = R(x^o)$, where

$$R(x) = [R_1(x) \ldots R_n(x)].$$

Alternatively, countries can decide to set emissions co-operatively. In this case, we assume that a bargaining process takes place in order to achieve a Pareto-optimal outcome. The bargaining process may lead to the formation of a coalition among j countries, where j goes from 2 (the smallest feasible coalition) to n (when all countries set emissions by taking into account reciprocal externalities). We name full co-operation a coalition formed by n countries.

In this work we determine the co-operative outcome of the game by using the Nash bargaining solution. This is meant to capture a dynamic bargaining process in which countries alternate offers until an agreement is reached, and in which the time-interval between successive offers is arbitrarily short. As argued by Binmore, Rubinstein, and Wolinsky (1986), the outcome of such a dynamic bargaining process coincides with the Nash bargaining solution of the one-shot game.

Moreover, we use the non-cooperative equilibrium $x^o = (x_1^o \ldots x_n^o)$ as the threat point of the bargaining process. This means interpreting the alternating offers model as a model in which players face a risk that, if the agreement is delayed, then the opportunity they hope for, to exploit it jointly, may be lost.

More formally, using the Nash bargaining solution corresponds to saying that, when j countries reach an agreement, they set emission levels in order to maximize the joint product of the difference between $P_i(x)$ and P_i^o, the non-cooperative welfare.

Before setting emission levels each country must therefore decide whether to act co-operatively or not. We model this decision problem by defining a 'meta-game' in which countries choose between the co-operative and the non-cooperative strategy anticipating the outcomes of the related emission game. Most environmental studies model this 'metagame' as a one-shot 'Prisoner's Dilemma' in which non-cooperation is the dominant strategy. As we show in the next section, there are many environmental problems that do not correspond to a 'Prisoners' Dilemma'.

Profitability and Stability

Let $P_i(j)$ be the welfare obtained by country i when it decides to co-operate, and $Q_i(j)$ be its welfare when it does not join the coalition formed by j countries. Moreover let $\mathcal{J}$ be the set of co-operating countries, whereas $\mathcal{J}^o$ denotes the set of countries that play non-cooperatively. Let us suppose, for simplicity, that all countries are symmetrical; that is, the welfare function $P_i(x)$ is not country-specific. We do not therefore index the welfare functions P and Q and their parameters.

The minimum requirement to be imposed for an environmental coalition to be formed is that the welfare of each country signing the co-operative agreement be larger than its welfare under no co-operation. In other words, country i gains from joining the coalition, with respect to the non-cooperative welfare, if $P(j) > P^o$. This leads to:

> Definition 1. *A coalition formed by j players is* profitable *if $P(j) > P^o$ for all countries belonging to $\mathcal{J}$.*

This is, of course, a minimum requirement that may not suffice to induce countries to sign the agreement (Barrett, 1989, 1990). As stated in the introduction, the main problem preventing the formation of any coalition is the free-riding behaviour by some countries. The usual explanation is the following: as one country can profit from the reduction of emissions by co-operating countries, it has an incentive to let other countries sign the co-operative agreement, without paying any cost (benefit reduction) for the cleaner environment. If all countries are symmetric, no co-operation takes place. In other words, the 'metagame', in which countries choose between cooperation and non-co-operation, is represented as a Prisoners' Dilemma. In such a game, co-operation is profitable, but each country has an incentive to defect once the other countries co-operate. This leads all countries not to cooperate. As we will see, however, this representation of countries' strategic choice may not be appropriate if countries' best-reply functions are near-orthogonal.

Let us define the problem formally. For each country, the crucial comparison is between $P(j)$, the pay-off it gets if it joins the coalition, and $Q(j-1)$, a country's pay-off when it chooses not to sign the co-operative agreement. Let us define by $L(j)$ the function denoting a country's incentive to defect from a coalition formed by j players, i.e. $L(j) = Q(j-1) - P(j)$. Moreover, let $P(j+1) - Q(j) = -L(j+1)$, be the incentive for a non-cooperating country to join a j coalition (that therefore becomes a $j + 1$ coalition).

> Definition 2. *A coalition formed by j players is* stable *if there is no incentive to defect, i.e. $Q(j-1) - P(j) < 0$, for all countries belonging to $\mathcal{J}$, and there is no incentive to broaden the coalition, i.e. $P(j + 1) - Q(j) < 0$, for all countries belonging to $\mathcal{J}^o$.*

This leads directly to:

> Proposition 1. *A stable coalition is defined by the largest integer j lower than or equal to $j^* = \arg \min_{j} [\sum_j L(j)]$*

This proposition can easily be proved by noting that a coalition is stable for all j^* such that $L(j^*) < 0$, and $L(j^* + 1) > 0$.

We will later argue that for given, sufficiently general, welfare functions, stable coalitions exist. This is not, however, a satisfactory response to the problem of protecting international commons because, as we will discuss, stable coalitions are generally formed by $j^\star \leq n$ players, where $j^\star$ is a small number, whatever n. We are therefore concerned with the following question: can the $j^\star$ players who co-operate expand the coalition through self-financed utility transfers to the remaining players who, by definition, have no incentive to join it?

In order to add one player to a j-coalition, the gain that the j players obtain from moving to a $j + 1$-coalition must be larger than the loss which the $j + 1$ player incurs by entering it, i.e.

$$\sum_{i \in \mathcal{J}}[P_i(j + 1) - P_i(j)] > Q_j + 1(j) - P_{j+1}(j + 1). \tag{1}$$

This condition makes it possible to self-finance an enlarged coalition. Is the broadened coalition stable? The $j + 1$ player does not defect if the transfer is larger than

$$Q_j + 1(j) - P_j + 1(j + 1).$$

However, as by definition of stable coalition,

$$P_i(j + 1) < Q_i(j + 1), \qquad i \in \mathcal{J},$$

the j players of the original coalition have an incentive to defect; this incentive is larger because of the transfer to the $j + 1$ player. Hence the $j + 1$ coalition is unstable. This leads to the following conclusion: *utility transfers from countries belonging to a stable coalition to non-cooperating countries cannot be used to expand the initial coalition (because the larger coalition would be unstable), unless the rules of the game are changed.*

Suppose that some countries, but not all, are committed to carrying out the environmental policy. This obviously changes the rules of the game. The questions to be answered are the following: if all players of the initial, stable, coalition are committed to co-operation, how many other countries can be induced to join the coalition through appropriate monetary transfers from the initial coalition to the newly entered countries? What is the minimum number of countries that must be committed to co-operation if full co-operation (a situation in which all countries sign the co-operative agreement) is to be achieved? The answer is provided by the following two propositions:

> Proposition 2. *If j countries are committed to carrying on the co-operative agreement whatever the number of countries in the coalition, and if $P(j + s) > P(j)$, $Q(j + s) > Q(j)$ for all positive s, $s \leq n - j - 1$, then at most r countries can be induced to join the initial coalition, where r is the largest integer satisfying:*

$$r < j[P(j + r) - P(j)] / [Q(j + r - 1) - P(j + r)]: \tag{2}$$

This is proved by the fact that the initial j countries can use their gain from broadening the coalition to finance other countries' co-operation. This gain is $j[P(j + r) - P(j)] > 0$ if $P(j + r) > P(j)$. For a transfer to be self-financed, it must be larger than the incentive to defect for the r countries that have to enter the coalition. This is $r[Q(j + r - 1) - P(j + r)]$. Hence:

$$j[P(j + r) - P(j)] > r[Q(j + r - 1) - P(j + r)]. \tag{2'}$$

Moreover, the maximum transfer $j[P(j + r) - P(j)]$ must be larger than the loss that the total entering countries suffer; this is $r[Q(j) - P(j + r)]$, i.e.

$$j[P(j + r) - P(j)] > r\{[Q(j) - Q(j + r - 1)] + [Q(j + r - 1) - P(j + r)]\}. \tag{3}$$

Notice that $[Q(j) - Q(j + r - 1)] < 0$ and $[Q(j + r - 1) - P(j + r)] > 0$. Hence, (2') implies (3). As (2) implies (2'), the proposition is proved. The newly entered countries have no incentive to defect, and gain from joining the coalition; the initial co-operating countries gain from expanding the coalition, and are committed to co-operation. The new equilibrium constitutes a Pareto improvement.

Proposition 3. *If $Q(n - 1) > Q(j)$ for all positive $j < n - 1$, the minimum fraction of countries that must be committed to a co-operative strategy for all n countries to co-operate is defined by the lowest ratio j/n such that:*

$$j/n > [Q(n - 1) - P(n)] / [Q(n - 1) - P(j)]. \tag{4}$$

To prove this, we assume that j countries are committed to carrying out the co-operative strategy whatever coalition is formed. Given the assumed bargaining process, their emissions are still a function of the fraction of players in the coalition. Suppose the j players accept to transfer part or all of the gain from moving to an n-coalition to the $n - j$ players who do not co-operate. This transfer should compensate the $n - j$ players for the loss due to joining the coalition, and should also offset their incentive to defect from the n-coalition. In order to compensate the $n - j$ players for the loss due to joining the n-coalition we must have:

$$j[P(n) - P(j)] > (n - j)[Q(j) - P(n)]. \tag{5}$$

This condition ensures that the enlarged coalition is self-financed. It can be rewritten as:

$$j[Q(j) - P(j)] > n[Q(j) - P(n)]. \tag{5'}$$

In order to offset the incentive to deviate from the n-coalition the gain $P(n)$ plus the transfer $j[P(n) - P(j)]/(n - j)$ must be larger than the defector's welfare $Q(n - 1)$, i.e. re-arranging the equation:

$$j[Q(n - 1) - P(j)] > n[Q(n - 1) - P(n)], \tag{6}$$

which is equivalent to (4). Notice that both sides of the equation are positive. Eqn. (6) can be rewritten as:

$$j\{[Q(n-1)-Q(j)]+[Q(j)-P(j)]\} > n\{[Q(n-1)-Q(j)]+[Q(j)-P(n)]\}. \quad (6')$$

Let us show that (6') implies (5'). Assume that (6') holds as an equality and solve it with respect to $Q(j)-P(j)$. Then replace this expression into eqn. (5'). We get

$$(n-j)[Q(n-1)-Q(j)] > 0$$

which is satisfied for all positive $j < n-1$. Hence, condition (4) guarantees that both the financing condition (5) and the no-defection condition (6) are satisfied. As a consequence, the $n-j$ players joining the initial coalition have no incentive to defect. The initial j players are, instead, committed to co-operation. Notice that the fraction of players that must be committed to co-operation decreases as the gain from full co-operation increases, and the incentive to deviate from full co-operation decreases. Finally, the move to the n-coalition is a Pareto improvement. This proves the proposition.

There exists another possibility to expand an environmental coalition. As non-cooperating countries gain when the co-operative agreement is broadened (because they receive a lower level of emissions), they could use their own additional gains to induce some countries to enter the coalition. Suppose therefore that *non-cooperating countries agree to finance environmental co-operation* (emission reduction in other countries). Which is the largest number of countries that can be induced to join a stable j coalition?

Proposition 4. *A stable outside supported coalition formed by $j + r$ players exists if $P(j + s) > P(j)$ and $Q(j + s) > Q(j)$ for all positive $s \leq n - j - 1$, and:*

$$(j + r)/n < 1/(1 + \theta), \qquad \text{where } \theta = \frac{Q(j+r-1)-P(j+r)}{Q(j+r)-Q(j)} \qquad (7)$$

To prove this we assume a stable j-coalition. Countries which do not join the coalition gain from financing, through appropriate transfers, a larger coalition, if $Q(j + r)$, their pay-off when the $j + r$-coalition is formed, less

$$[Q(j+r-1)-P(j+r)](j+r)/(n-j-r),$$

the transfer to the $j + r$ co-operating countries, is larger than $Q(j)$, their pay-off before broadening the coalition. This is true if (7) holds. Moreover,

$$Q(j+r)-[Q(j+r-1)-P(j+r)](j+r)/(n-j-r)$$

must be larger than $P(j + r + 1)$, i.e. no more countries want to joint the coalition. This is true if:

$$(n-j-r)[Q(j+r)-P(j+r+1)] > (j+r)[Q(j+r-1)-P(j+r)], \qquad (8)$$

which can be written as:

$$n[Q(j + r) - P(j + r + 1)] > (j + r)[Q(j + r) - P(j + r)$$
$$+ Q(j + r - 1) - P(j + r + 1)]. \tag{8'}$$

Comparing (7) and (8'), it is easy to see that (7) implies (8') (and therefore (8)).

We are left with the proof that the players in the $j + r$ coalition have no incentive to defect. This is true if $P(j + r)$, the welfare when the $j + r$ coalition is formed, plus $Q(j + r - 1) - P(j + r)$, the transfer each co-operating country receives, is not lower than $Q(j + r - 1)$, the welfare that each co-operating country would receive by defecting from the coalition. This implies $Q(j + r - 1) \geq Q(j + r - 1)$, which obviously holds (we assume that when a country is indifferent between co-operation and defection, it co-operates). Morcover, $P(j + r) + [Q(j + r - 1) - P(j + r)]$ is larger than $P(j)$, the welfare that countries in the stable coalition received before its expansion, because $P(j + r) > P(j)$ by assumption and $Q(j + r - 1) - P(j + r) > 0$ by the instability condition; it is also larger than $Q(j)$, the welfare that countries entering the coalition received before, because $Q(j + r - 1) > Q(j)$ by assumption.

As a consequence all players in the $j + 1$ coalition do not defect, all players outside the coalition do not want to join it, and the move to a $j + 1$ coalition constitutes a Pareto improvement. This completes the proof.

We have thus proposed two ways of expanding a stable coalition. In the first one, we determine the minimum number of countries that must commit themselves to a co-operative behaviour in order to achieve an equilibrium in which more countries cooperate. We call this a *minimum commitment* to co-operation. In the next section, we show that the commitment of a few countries may lead to a stable coalition formed by all countries. Then we consider the incentive that non-cooperating countries may have to finance other countries' co-operative behaviour (emission reductions). We call this *outside support* to co-operation. In the following section, we show that in this type of monetary transfer, the number of players belonging to a stable coalition may be doubled or even tripled. Two important points must be made in order to clarify some implications of previous results:

1. When the coalition is sustained by a minimum degree of commitment, or when it is sustained by transfers from non-cooperating to co-operating countries, an additional policy instrument has to be introduced. Utility transfers are indeed impossible and/or inefficient if exclusively based on emission contractions. *Large profitable and stable coalitions can therefore be obtained only if countries bargain over different policy instruments.* Some examples could be the co-ordination of environmental and trade policies, or environmental and debt policies when LDC countries are concerned.

2. If stable coalitions exist, the 'metagame' in which countries decide whether or not to co-operate is not a Prisoner's Dilemma. Let us assume that a j-stable coalition is formed: by definition, no incentive to defect exists $[Q(j - 1) < P(j)]$. All countries, however, have an additional incentive not to

co-operate. Since non-cooperating countries gain from the others' co-operative behaviour, each country has an incentive to let other countries form the coalition $[Q(j) > P(j)]$. This is not a Prisoner's Dilemma because the situation in which one group of countries co-operates and the others do not is an equilibrium of the metagame. This is shown by the following 2×2 matrix illustrating environmental coalitions as chicken games:

Country h

		C	N
Country i	C	$P(j+1), P(j+1)$	$P(j), Q(j)$
	N	$Q(j), P(j)$	$Q(j-1), Q(j-1)$

In this matrix, C and N denote the co-operative and non-cooperative strategy respectively, and the pay-off pairs indicate countries' welfare, as defined in the previous section. It represents a situation in which $j - 1$ countries co-operate. A stable coalition is formed by j countries. Countries i and h are the marginal countries with respect to the stable coalition. Both i and h have an incentive to join the coalition (by definition of stability). However, country i's most preferred outcome is the one in which it lets h co-operate. However, if country h does not act co-operatively, country i will choose to do so, in order to belong to the stable coalition (by definition of stability). Formally, this is implied by the following inequalities:

$$Q(j) > P(j+1) > P(j) > Q(j-1).$$

The first and the last inequalities are implied by the stability of the j-coalition; $P(j+1) - P(j)$ holds by assumption (as shown above). Hence, non-cooperation is not the dominant strategy. This game is known as a 'chicken game' (a game belonging to the class of co-ordination games). There are two equilibria (N,C) and (C,N), but all countries have an incentive to let the others co-operate. The game has no dominant strategy; countries' attempts to choose non-cooperation, in order to let the others co-operate, may lead to the worst possible outcome (N,N). The co-operative outcome (C,C) is not Pareto-optimal.

The impasse is solved by the introduction of asymmetries into the game. If countries have different preferences, technologies, or environmental endowments, it is possible to figure out which countries are likely to form a coalition. For example, in the case of outside supported stable coalitions, countries with higher abatement costs are likely to finance emission reductions in countries with lower abatement costs which therefore form the coalition. In the case of stable coalitions with minimum commitment, countries in which environmental policy is part of a package of co-ordinated policies, or large countries that heavily affect the global environment, are more likely to commit themselves to co-operation, thus attracting other co-operators. If the game were repeated, countries with a higher discount rate would be more likely to form a coalition.

MAIN RESULTS AND POLICY IMPLICATIONS

Non-cooperative vs. Co-operative Emission Control

The analysis presented so far has been carried out by means of a general framework, without assuming any particular form for the benefit and damage functions of the different countries. Analytical work and simulations we have carried out show that the various outcomes examined in general terms may correspond to plausible situations (see Carraro and Siniscalco, 1991). In general, they show that the various results are closely related to the structure of the pay-off and of the corresponding best reply functions, which can vary substantially across countries and particularly among various pollutants. For this reason one should not discuss environmental negotiations as such, but should place the analysis in a context, paying attention to the specific pollutant involved and to the corresponding pattern of interdependence.

To argue this point let us consider first non-cooperative emission control. Countries which interact in a common environment with mutual externalities set their emissions by equating their own marginal benefit to marginal damage, given the emissions set by the other countries. In this context, country i's actual emissions are generally lower than emissions δ_i which maximize the benefit; but non-cooperative emissions are increasingly reduced if the transportation of the pollutant is high, the damage is high, and the benefit (abatement cost) is low. (These conditions of course depend on the specific pollutant involved.) The non-cooperative reduction of emissions, in other words, is greater the higher the interdependence, i.e. whenever the best-reply functions are mutually elastic and negatively sloped.

The reason behind this result is intuitively simple. The best reply functions reflect, *inter alia*, the marginal damage which is determined by foreign countries' emissions. If foreign countries' emissions determine a substantial marginal damage to country i, the best non-cooperative response of country i to foreign expansion is an emissions contraction. This contraction will be higher if the benefit of domestic emission is low. For any given foreign expansion, the contraction will be greater the higher is the elasticity of the best-reply function, and vice versa. The difference between δ_i and the actual non-cooperative emissions of country i is therefore positively related to the slope of country i's best-response function.

There are reasons to believe that some international agreements to protect the commons in the case of some specific pollutants are to be obtained (or

have been obtained) as non-cooperative outcomes, and that the corresponding negotiations can be seen as pre-play communications in order to reach a
Nash equilibrium.

Now, consider co-operation. Countries, in this case, bargain over emission
levels in order to achieve an optimal aggregate outcome; they set emissions by
taking into account reciprocal externalities. As is well known, co-operation
among all countries is profitable and optimal, but it is intrinsically undermined by free-riding behaviour. If the best-reply functions are orthogonal or
near orthogonal, however, there is some scope for partial co-operation, and
partial co-operative agreements among small groups of countries can be
profitable and stable.

The reason, again, has to do with free-riding behaviour, as reflected by the
best-reply function of a country which does not belong to the partial co-
operation. If this best-reply function is negatively sloped, the non-cooperating
country will expand its emissions if the coalition restricts them, off-setting
the effort of the co-operating countries. If, on the contrary, the best reply
functions are orthogonal or near-orthogonal the free-rider will simply enjoy
the cleaner environment without paying for it, but will not offset the emission
contraction by the co-operating countries.

The above considerations suggest that, in environmental agreements,
there is a sort of trade-off. When the best-reply functions are negatively
sloped there is a high degree of interdependence and non-cooperative emissions control can lead to substantial results. But if one or more countries unilaterally or co-operatively reduce emissions, this contraction is offset by an
expansion by the non-cooperating countries. This kind of interaction under-
mines all kinds of co-operation, as the free-riding behaviour implies a substantial loss for countries which wish to co-operate. With an orthogonal or
near-orthogonal best-reply function the situation is somehow the opposite.
Non-cooperative emissions control leads to small emissions reductions,
but the scope for co-operation is now greater: if a number of countries co-
operatively reduce their emissions, this reduction is not offset by free-riders,
who simply enjoy a better environment but do not directly damage the countries which co-operate. In this case, therefore, there are 'stable coalitions'.

Starting from a stable coalition, the gains from partial co-operation can be
used to finance broader agreements. We explored two possibilities which we
named 'coalitions with minimum commitment' and 'outside-supported
coalitions'. In the first case, a stable coalition can use the gains from partial
co-operation to induce other countries to enter the coalition, by compensat-
ing the gains from free-riding. In the case of outside-supported coalitions,
a group of non-cooperating countries can subsidize from the outside a co-
operative reduction of emissions in other countries.

Both examples of expanded coalitions, which can be self-financed up to a
certain number of players, require that environmental policy be backed by
other instruments (e.g. trade or financial policy) to transfer welfare. This

requires a change of strategy *vis-à-vis* the typical environmental negotiation, where countries bargain only on emissions. In addition to this, an expanded coalition may also require a commitment by a certain number of countries; this commitment, which is much less demanding than a commitment by all countries, may even lead to full co-operation. Some first calculations we carried out on the assumption of symmetrical countries show that stable coalitions can be made of two or three players only, depending on the slope of the best-reply functions, and irrespective of the number of players; that coalitions with minimum commitment and outside-supported coalitions can include up to eight players starting from three; that the critical coalition to reach full co-operation must include about 50 per cent of the players. We expect more favourable results by simulating the interaction among asymmetrical players, perhaps by modelling players who to some extent reflect the characteristics of the main countries involved in the actual negotiations.

The Determinants of Interdependence

The choice between co-operation and non-cooperation, as well as the level of emissions in each case, are the key decisions of the game. As we just recalled, they crucially depend on the slope of countries' best-reply functions, i.e. on the structure of pay-offs. As the relative slope of the best-reply functions, and more generally the structure of pay-offs, is so important, let us reconsider, from the economic point of view, the main conditions which lay behind the different cases.

As we recalled, the slope of the best-reply functions tends to decrease under some sufficient conditions:

(1)   as the transportation parameter α_i, $0 \leq \alpha_i \leq 1$ decreases;
(2)   as the ratio between the damage and the benefit function becomes small;
(3)   as the pay-off function becomes separable in domestic and imported emissions.

The first condition is quite easy to understand: with a low transportation parameter α, a small proportion of foreign emissions affects country i, which therefore reacts very little to greater foreign emissions. The second condition (a low ratio between the damage and the benefit functions) is equally intuitive. If the abatement cost (benefit) is very high relative to the damage, country i will be very reluctant to respond to a foreign expansion with a domestic contraction, and vice versa.

The above examples, of course, are only sufficient conditions, because orthogonal best-reply functions can be obtained even if the pay-off function is separable in domestic and imported emissions. This is the case, for example, of a damage function separable in domestic and foreign emissions. This specification, which is quite common in the literature (for example Mäler,

1991; Hoel, 1991; 1992), implies that, at the margin, country i will not respond to other countries' emission variations (each country has a dominant strategy in terms of emissions).

How often can environmental interdependence be captured by orthogonal, rather than negatively sloped, reaction functions? Given the relevance of their slope, we believe that the crucial parameters and functions in a model of environmental policy co-ordination can only come from serious applied work.

Estimates of the international transportation of pollutants can be obtained with specific models, such as the RAINS model of SO_2 and NOX developed by IIASA. They can also be based on judgemental evaluations: in the case of pollutants with only global effects, such as CO_2 or CFC, for example, parameter α implies a full transnational effect.

Estimates of the abatement costs of various emissions (i.e. the estimate of the parameters entering the benefit function) do not involve any special difficulties, and can be based on single-country or on multi-country econometric models, which consider a full range of macroeconomic feedbacks. An interesting OECD paper (Holler, Dean, and Nicolaides, 1990) surveys a dozen recent models which assess the cost of abating greenhouse gas emissions. The paper is relevant because it contains a very detailed discussion of the problems that can be met in such an assessment. For our purposes, it is sufficient to recall that the benefits from pollution and the associated abatement costs are related to the level of development, to the economic structure, and, most of all, to the specific pollutant involved. (Compare, for example, the abatement costs of CFC and CO_2: reducing CFC is a matter of changing technologies in sprays and refrigerating devices; reducing CO_2 affects energy consumption, which is closely related to development and to life-style.)

The most serious difficulties arise in estimating a damage function. On empirical grounds, a damage function can be obtained econometrically, by estimating the first-order conditions, under several, rather heroic, assumptions. Alternatively, it can be calculated by means of appropriate environmental evaluation models, which summarize in an index the physical damage of a given pollutant and its evaluation. Taking into consideration several types of damage, adaptation costs, and the like, the indexes produced by ecological models embody a sort of utility function, which simply reflects the model-builder's (or the user's) preferences, but are far from being objective. In this field, therefore, much work has still to be done to merge the economic and the ecological approach.

Over and above the difficulties we just mentioned, a further problem arises from the lack of reliable statistical data on the environment and emissions at the international level.

Despite all these problems, we believe that a meaningful analysis of a country's interaction in environmental policy cannot be carried out without empirical data. Only empirical work can justify alternative specifications of a country's interdependence. Only empirical work, moreover, can support our intuition: while in the traditional case of common-property goods (fisheries, pastures, forests, etc.) the pay-off functions give rise to non-orthogonal best-reply functions, in the case of some global pollutants, e.g. CO_2, the best-reply functions are probably orthogonal (or near-orthogonal), because the damage function is plausibly non-linear but separable. In other words, the damage resulting from various emissions is associated with the total amount of pollutant that affects country i, as a sum of domestically produced and imported emissions.

Of course, this intuition needs further investigation on empirical grounds. But if it proves correct, the analysis of co-operative agreements we gave above may become relevant to some current policy discussions. The use of the analysis is enhanced if one takes a group of countries—such as the EU, the USA, the former USSR, Eastern Europe, China, or the NICs and LDCs—as the relevant players. In this case, our simulations show that a stable coalition of three commited players could even reach full co-operation.

To elaborate this point, assume that a small group of big players—say the seven big groups mentioned above—bargain over the reduction of a specific pollutant, say CO_2, in the presence of near-orthogonal best-reply functions. Non-cooperative control, in this case, implies a limited reduction of emissions. There is some scope, however, for partial co-operation. Let three countries form a stable and profitable coalition. If these countries commit themselves to co-operation, they can 'buy' all the other players and reach full co-operation by self-financed utility transfers.

Another possibility is to create coalitions that are sustained by transfers from non-cooperating to co-operating countries. In this case, too, utility transfers are viable and efficient only if an environmental policy is backed by other policy instruments. This case provides a rationale for the European proposal of subsidizing a reduction of pollution in some areas, e.g. Eastern Europe or the LDCs, especially if they have relatively lower abatement costs. This proposal has been the object of much analytical work (e.g. Newbery, 1989; Mäler, 1991).

It may be interesting to note that the possibility of partial agreements, which is seldom considered in models, is often advocated in applied policy proposals (Nitze, 1990). This case provides a rationale for the advocates of a progressive extension of environmental co-operation from Europe, to the OECD, China, Russia, and the NICs and the LDCs. To extend co-operation, however, environmental policy ought to be linked to other policies, such as technology transfers, debt policy, development aid, trade policy, etc.

Conclusions and Scope for Further Work

In the next few years, the international protection of the environment will increasingly rely on international agreements, which seem to face substantial difficulties in reaching a co-operative agreement among a great number of countries. To what extent can the proposed analysis be useful, and how can it be extended?

The analytical framework we proposed is highly simplified and any result must be taken with great caution. However, given the difficulties and failures of many attempts to reach comprehensive agreements, it seems a promising route for research. First, it shows that it is quite sterile to study optimal agreements among all countries if such agreements are profitable but intrinsically unstable. The structure of such agreements can be useful as a bench-mark, but it is very unlikely to be accepted. Secondly, it shows that there is a full range of agreements among sovereign countries to protect the international environment. When environmental interdependence is high, effective protection can be obtained by non-cooperative emission control. As the degree of interdependence decreases, environmental protection can be reached only through co-operative agreements. Co-operative agreements among all countries are typically undermined by free-riding. In fairly general cases, however, there exist partial coalitions which can be expanded through appropriate self-financed transfers. To expand co-operation, however, environmental policy must be linked to other policies, such as technology transfers, debt policy, development aid, trade policy, etc. Partial co-operative agreements can also be seen as a first step towards more appropriate institutions to manage the international environment.

We can now suggest some important issues for further work. First, it is essential to provide a taxonomy relating the various pollutants to appropriate damage functions. Only with such a taxonomy will it be possible to contextualize policy analysis, obtaining meaningful results for each case. Secondly, it is necessary to reappraise the instruments for implementing co-operation. Emissions, in many cases, are very difficult to monitor. The various economic instruments needed to implement an agreement must therefore be designed in order to prevent cheating. So far, the literature has compared the various agreements in terms of efficiency, i.e. maximum profitability. Our analysis proposes another criterion: an instrument must be efficient, but must also be effective in preventing or discouraging free-riding. In other words, it must also be designed to promote the stability of the agreements.

Finally, we should work on two extensions. First, asymmetric information. As we have already mentioned, preferences cannot be observed. If we remove the assumption of complete information, each country that is induced to enter a coalition would be tempted to overstate the cost and claim for greater incentives. The solution to this problem is to embody an appropriate information or self-selection premium in the incentive to each country that enters the coalition. Secondly, the benefit function must account for the effects of transfers. This prevents the analysis of environmental policy as such, but requires its integration into a wider analysis which considers other economic variables in the pay-off of each country.

REFERENCES

Barrett, S. (1991), 'The Paradox of International Environmental Agreements' (mimeo; London Business School).

—— (1992), 'International Environmental Agreements as Games', in R. Pethig (ed.), *Conflicts and Cooperation in Managing Environmental Resources* (Berlin: Springer Verlag), 18–33.

Binmore, K., Rubinstein, A., and Wolinski, A. (1986), 'The Nash Bargaining Solution in Economic Modelling', *Rand Journal of Economics*, 17; 176–88.

Bohm, P. (1990), 'Efficiency Aspects of Imperfect Treaties on Global Public Bads: Lessons from the Montreal Protocol' (mimeo, Department of Economics, University of Stockholm).

Carraro, C. and Siniscalco, D. (1991), 'Strategies for the International Protection of the Environment' CEPR Discussion Paper, no. 865 (London: CEPR).

—— —— (1992), 'Transfers and Commitments in International Negotiations', paper prepared for the ESF Task Force 3 on Environmental Economics; repr. in K. G. Mäler (ed.), *International Environmental Problems: An Economic Perspective* (Dordrecht: Kluwer).

Grubb, M. (1989), *The Greenhouse Effect: Negotiating Targets* (London: Royal Institute of International Affairs).

Hardin, G. (1968), 'The Tragedy of Commons', *Science*, 162; 1243–8.

—— and Baden, J. (1977), *Managing the Commons* (New York: Freeman & Co).

Hoel, M. (1991), 'Global Environmental Problems: The Effects of Unilateral Actions Taken by One Country', *Journal of Environmental Economics and Management*, 20/1; 55–70.

—— (1992), 'International Environment Conventions: The Case of Uniform Reductions of Emissions', *Environmental and Resource Economics*, 2; 141–60.

Holler, P., Dean, A., and Nicolaides, J. (1990), 'A Survey of Studies of the Costs of Reducing Greenhouse Gas Emissions', OECD Economics and Statistics Department, Working paper no. 89.

Kaitala, V., Pojola, M., and Tahvonen, O. (1992), 'Trans-boundary Air Pollution and Soil Acidification: A Dynamic Analysis of Acid Rain Game between Finland and the USSR', *Environmental Resource Economics*, 2; 161–82.

Mäler, K. G. (1989), 'The Acid Rain Game', in H. Folmer and E. Ierland (eds.), *Valuation Methods and Policy Making in Environmental Economics* (New York: Elsevier).

—— (1991), 'Environmental Issues in the New Europe', in A. B. Atkinson and R. Brunetta (eds.), *Economics for the New Europe* (London: Macmillan).

Newbery, D. M. (1991), 'Acid Rains', *Economic Policy*, 1; 42–88.

Nitze, W. A. (1990), *The Greenhouse Effect: Formulating a Convention* (London: Royal Institute of International Affairs).

10

Protecting the Transnational Commons

Robert Dorfman

For the past twenty years or more, concern has been rising about the damage inflicted on the environment by a wide range of activities associated with modern technologies and increasing population pressure. Recently, attention has been shifting from activities that disrupted relatively localized portions of the environment to those with more widespread effects, some extending to the entire globe. These activities, with consequences that cross national boundaries, inject a new and unwelcome complication into the already sufficiently complicated problem of controlling human abuses of the environment.

This complication arises from the circumstance that the world is divided into entities called 'sovereign nations', each of which is entitled to use, or misuse, the transnational commons in whatever way it considers advantageous, unless it agrees voluntarily to forgo some or all of these rights. Since no one nation's abstention is enough to protect transnational commons, nothing can be done without the awkward, uncertain, and nearly interminable process of international negotiation. Meanwhile, the damages accumulate and the transnational commons deteriorate.

We can take as just one example the Montreal Protocol limiting discharges that erode the protective ozone layer. It is held up as a distinguished achievement in defence of environmental integrity, and indeed it is. But it is distinguished only because our expectations about what such negotiations can achieve are so very low. We should not forget that some sixteen years elapsed between the time when Molina and Rowland established the danger to the ozone layer and the date that the protocol was signed. Nor should we forget that the protocol adopted after so many years of painful compromises and negotiations was found to be inadequate within a year of its signature.

The problem of protecting the transnational commons is, thus, less a natural scientific problem of understanding the physical and biological processes that disrupt the environment or of developing appropriate protective techniques, than it is a social scientific problem of devising procedures to expedite international co-operation in protecting the transnational commons. We generally know what should be done (or not done); we do not know how to agree to do it (or not do it).

That is the problem I address in this chapter. My suggestion is a simple one. It is that the procedures of international negotiations be altered so as to make more use of relevant economic concepts and insights. In particular, I shall recommend an approach based upon the benefits principle of public finance, advocated particularly by Knut Wicksell (1896) and Erik Lindahl (1919).[1] In an unpublished memorandum on the costs of reducing sulphur emissions in Europe, submitted to the Economic Commission for Europe in 1989, Klaassen and Jansen (1989) used an approach very similar to the one I am about to describe. That is the only previous application of the benefits principle to international problems that I have encountered.

In order to be concrete, I shall describe the recommended procedure as it would apply to abating discharges of some harmful pollutant. It is easy to see how the procedure could be extended to reducing other types of environmental abuse.

To apply the benefits principle, it is necessary to know how each individual affected (in our case, each nation) perceives the benefits it would receive from a reduction in the harmful discharges. To this end, the recommended procedure begins by requesting each participating nation to report the greatest amount that it would be willing to contribute to an international undertaking to reduce emissions of the target pollutant by, say, X thousand tonnes per year. X should be given five or six values, ranging from a nearly negligible decrease from the current level to a cutback more severe than anyone would contemplate in reality. A curve fitted to these half-dozen values would then be an estimate of the country's demand curve for reduced emissions of the pollutant. This curve will be denoted $b^i(X)$, defined formally thus:

$b^i(X)$ = the most that country i is willing to contribute to an international undertaking to reduce emissions of the target pollutant by X thousand tonnes per year. The contributions are measured in millions of constant-value dollars, or other monetary units, per year.

Obviously, the answers to such a question cannot be taken automatically at face value. A country has too much to gain by understating its interest in reducing the emissions and, besides, its response will be a political document reflecting the pull and tug of political forces within the country. The problems raised by the difficulty of eliciting truthful responses will be discussed at length below.

The global demand curve for reductions in emissions of the subject pollutant, denoted $B(X)$, is simply $\sum_i b^i(X)$, the aggregate of the values of a reduction of X thousand tonnes per year to all the countries involved.

Costs must also be taken into account in applying the benefits principle. The procedure is similar to the procedure just described for the demand side, but with a slight complication. First, each participating country is asked to

---

[1] At the conference in Siena, Professor Stefano Zamagni pointed out that U. Mazzola and M. Pantaleoni had previously published similar ideas.

estimate the costs it would incur if it reduced its discharges of the target pollutant by x thousand tonnes per year for a half-dozen values of x, spread over the range of plausible reductions for the country responding. A curve fitted to these values would be the country's cost curve, denoted $c^i(x_i)$ and defined formally by

> $c^i(x_i)$ = the total annual cost to country i (interpreted as social opportunity cost) of reducing its discharges of the target pollutant by x_i thousand tonnes per year. Alternatively, $c^i(x_i)$ could be defined as the smallest compensation for which country i would be willing to reduce its output of the pollutant by x_i tonnes per year.

Then, if x_i denotes the amount by which country i reduces its emissions, the total reduction, X, will be $X = \sum x_i$. The aggregate cost of a reduction of X tonnes per year is given by the solution of the following Kuhn-Tucker problem:

> Minimize $\sum c^i(x_i)$ with respect to the x_i, subject to the constraints $x_i \geq 0$, all i, and $\sum x_i \geq X$.

The solution, the global cost of reducing discharges by X thousand tonnes per year, will be denoted $C(X)$.

Gathering and collating the estimates of benefits and costs for the individual countries is an arduous and time-consuming task, though it is only the first stage of the procedure recommended here. Before advancing to the next stage, the formal negotiation stage, we should consider it a bit further.

The data-gathering stage actually has two purposes. The first is the obvious one of acquiring the data needed for a well-informed negotiation. The second, nearly as obvious, purpose is educational. It is not necessary to document the statement that the best way to understand a problem is not to read a report about it, but to write the report.[2] The educational purpose is served by having every nation involved participate in writing the report. This is accomplished by having each nation perform several functions.

The first of these functions is to develop the benefit and cost estimates pertaining to its own society. Estimating benefits is not a task to be delegated to a few specialists and their computers. The benefits of an environmental improvement are an expression of social concerns and preferences; to ascertain them, some professional analysis is in order, but ultimately the society has to be consulted. This can be done by scrutinizing revealed preferences, by polling, by political debate, or, almost inevitably, by an interplay of all these methods. In the course of such an inquiry, members of the public as well as the staffs of the relevant government agencies become both aware of the

---

[2] For an extended example of the benefits of involving participating nations in studies of a shared environmental problem, see Haas (1990), esp. ch. 8.

environmental problem and informed about its implications for their welfare, economic and otherwise; they also learn about alternative ways of coping with the problem and their implications, and so forth. The estimates that result when the divergent points of view have had an opportunity to be heard will inevitably be compromises. Certainly, no great precision can be expected in answers to such questions.

The cost estimates do not present as many difficulties as the benefit estimates, but they are hard enough, and so expensive to prepare that I do not believe that any country has had an estimate made of its cost curve for any important type of environmental improvement. In the United States, for example, the cost of reducing carbon dioxide emissions has been estimated only for a rather arbitrarily selected 20 per cent cut-back.

Concentrating attention thus on a single level of environmental protection has the decisive drawback that it pre-empts one of the most important issues to be decided. In order to make an intelligent choice about how stringently emissions should be constrained, it is clearly necessary to have some appreciation of the costs of the available alternatives. Besides, providing estimates of the cost of different levels of restriction does not magnify the task. To estimate the cost of a single level of abatement, one must obtain data on the current level of emissions, on alternative technologies for curbing emissions, and on the costs of applying those technologies. By the time those data are acquired for one level of restriction, the great bulk of the work for any other level has been performed.

Economic and technological expertise play more prominent roles in the cost estimates than on the benefit side, but still policy considerations arise that are beyond the purview of the experts. To some extent, the interested public has to be consulted on the cost side too.

In short, gathering information from the public and informing the public about the problem go hand in hand in all participating nations. But that is not all that goes on during the preparatory stage. The nations cannot prepare their estimates of the benefits and costs of restricting the harmful emissions in isolation from each other. At the very least, they must base their estimates on assumptions about population growth, economic expansion, technological advance, and so on, that do not conflict with those of other nations. The different nations must also frame their analyses and estimates using concepts and categories that, if not identical, are at least readily translatable into each other. There must therefore be a substantial amount of international contact and co-ordination at the staff level, which will be an important educational aspect of the work.

Part of the international exchange during the preparatory stage should be devoted to reconciling the estimates prepared by the different countries. To a large extent they will be estimating similar things; the costs of scrubbing flue gases, for example, or the benefits of reducing the incidence of specific diseases. This is the stage at which conflicts in assumptions can be discussed profitably, and either eliminated or justified. In general, just as each country has a strong incentive to minimize its stated willingness to pay for abatement and to exaggerate the costs of curbing its emissions, so also each has an incentive to challenge discrepancies in other countries' estimates and to demand explanations.

Thus, even before the formal negotiations are convened, a great deal has been accomplished. The participants have established a common vocabulary, they have become acquainted with each others' points of view, and they have ironed out many discrepancies at the technical level. All this takes time—at least a year, I should guess, and perhaps two or even more. But there is no reason to think that it takes any more time than the current style of negotiation; indeed, I should expect it to take a good deal less.

We can now advance to the formal negotiation stage. The principal tangible result of the preparation stage is the national and global benefit curves, $b^i(X)$ and $B(X)$, respectively, and the national and global cost curves, $c^i(x_i)$ and $C(X)$. These are intended to form a common ground for the discussion at the negotiation stage and cannot help in framing that discussion to any considerable extent. (It should be noticed at this point that for each level of aggregate abatement, X, the calculation of the cost, $C(X)$ entails the estimation of x_i, the level of abatement of country i's emissions that is consistent with achieving X at the lowest aggregate cost. Thus the x_i's can be regarded as functions of X.)

In order to help visualize those curves and to discuss them it is necessary to introduce a few plausible assumptions. We shall assume that the basic functions, $b^i(X)$ and $c^i(x_i)$, are non-negative, non-decreasing, continuous, and differentiable throughout the non-negative domains of their arguments. In addition, we assume that for all countries, $b^i(X)$ is concave (i.e. exhibits decreasing willingness to pay for marginal decreases in environmental contamination) and $c^i(x_i)$ is convex (i.e. exhibits increasing cost of marginal reductions in harmful discharges). These assumptions, though unsupported by any research, seem reasonable.

An immediate consequence of the assumptions is that $B(X)$ has all the properties assumed for the $b^i(X)$ and $C(X)$ has all the properties of the $c^i(x_i)$. Then graphically, $B(X)$ and $C(X)$ can assume either of the two configurations shown in Fig. 10.1. In the case of configuration (a), the cost of any positive amount of reduction exceeds the amount that all the nations together are willing to pay to achieve it; no positive level of abatement is deemed worth the cost. In the other, and more interesting, configuration (b), $B(X)$ is greater than $C(X)$ for a range of values of X. If we denote by X^* the value of X for which the excess of $B(X)$ over $C(X)$ is greatest, X^* can be regarded as the optimal value of X, the number of tonnes per year by which emissions are reduced, because for all increments beyond that level of abatement, the additional costs exceed the value of additional benefits. Not only is that level of aggregate abatement optimal, but it is achieved in the most economical

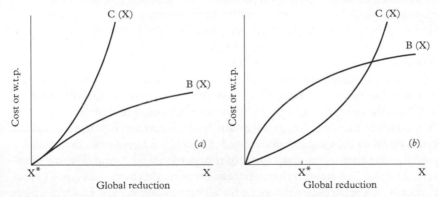

Fig. 10.1. Possible configurations of aggregate benefit and cost curves

way by using the abatement targets for the individual nations recommended by the solution to the Kuhn–Tucker problem.

In addition to finding the optimal level of abatement and the optimal allocation of the reductions among the participating nations, the problem of distributing the costs of abatement equitably has to be faced. On the benefits principle, each country's contribution to the annual costs should reflect the value that it places on the result. One way, but not the only one, to obey this principle would be for a typical country, i, to contribute $[C(X^\star)/B(X^\star)]$ $b^i(X^\star)$. This typical country will incur a cost of $c^i(x_i)$ to abate its emissions by the efficient amount, and that cost will equal its equitable assessment only by coincidence. A cost equalization fund is therefore needed, probably managed by the UNEP, the IMF, or some similar international agency. Our typical country should contribute a net assessment of

$$\frac{C(X^\star)}{B(X^\star)} b^i(X^\star) - c^i(x_i^\star)$$

to the equalization fund. The net assessment could be negative for some countries. When this occurs, the country would be reimbursed for the excess costs of meeting its abatement target over the value it placed on the benefits it derived from the overall reduction in pollution.

I have called the foregoing scheme for choosing the level of reduction and allocating the tasks among participating nations 'optimal' because it selects the level of abatement that the participating nations value as much in excess of the cost of attainment as possible. But legitimate questions can be raised about that criterion of optimality. It requires us to conceive that the willingnesses to pay of different nations, large and small, rich and poor, democratic and otherwise, can be added together meaningfully dollar for dollar. We often do that for individuals; it has a rough-and-ready plausibility. But this procedure does not stand up under close inspection. I therefore present an alternative decision criterion, closely related to Lindahl's proposal for determining the scale of provision of public goods inside a single nation or jurisdiction (Lindahl, 1919). Lindahl's proposal has the virtue of not requiring any assumptions about the comparability of willingnesses to pay or other measures of utility in different nations.

Lindahl's criterion employs the same data and construction as the one just sketched, but instead of using them to derive a purported global optimum, it simulates the operation of a perfect market. One virtue of a perfect market is that it leads to a price at which the quantity of the commodity that is supplied in it is equal to the quantity demanded. Lindahl's scheme does the same for public goods such as the abatement of transnational pollution. The novel aspect of Lindahl's scheme is that, whereas a true market attains its equilibrium by means of a price that is the same for all buyers and sellers, Lindahl's plan operates by allocating the cost of the public good among its beneficiaries in such a way that they all desire the same level of provision.

It works as follows. We have already defined $C(X)$ to be the aggregate cost of the level X of pollution abatement. Now we assume that the participating nations will contribute to meeting this cost according to the rule that nation i will contribute the portion h_i of the total, i.e., the amount $h_i C(X)$. The proportions h_i have to meet three demands. The first two are easy:

(1) none of the h_i can be negative, i.e. no nation can be bribed to cooperate even though it does not regard the result as being at all useful;
(2) the total of the assessments has to equal the aggregate cost: $\sum h_i C(X)$ = $C(X)$.

The third demand is the ingenious one. It is that the shares, h_i, shall be such that all nations, regarding them as established, shall desire the same amount, X, of abatement. It is easy to see that if the h_i satisfy this requirement, the amount of abatement that will be supplied will also be the amount demanded by every nation.

This third requirement can be stated algebraically by imagining that the net value, or utility, of any level of abatement to country i depends on the level itself and on the amount of the country's net national product remaining at its disposal after it has paid its assessment. Let us write the posited relationship for country i as $V^i[\text{NNP}_i - h_i C(X), X]$. The h_i are to be chosen so that if X_i denotes the level of abatement that country i would prefer, taking the assessment it entails into account, the X_i for all participating countries will be equal and can be denoted by a common value, $X^\star$. That is, suppose that for each country i, X_i is the value of X that satisfies

$$V^i[\text{NNP}_i - h_i C(X_i), X_i] = \sup_x[\text{NNP}_i - h_i C(X), X].$$

Then the formal problem is to find $h_i \geq 0$, with $\sum h_i = 1$, such that all the X_i have the same value, $X^\star$. Regarded as a mathematical problem, finding this equilibrium level is a bit more complicated than finding the level that maximizes the excess of aggregate benefits over aggregate costs, but still it is not a formidable task.

The level of abatement and the allocation of costs produced by the Lindahl procedure can be shown to be Pareto-efficient. (The same is true of the other scheme described.) In addition, it minimizes the amount of dissatisfaction, since every nation experiences the amount of abatement that it prefers, taking account of the assessment associated with that level, whereas all that could be claimed for the earlier scheme was that no nation could claim that it was being charged more than the results justified.

I am not going to try to adjudicate between these principles. In fact, with a little ingenuity a good number of other plausible principles could be proposed. The possibilities I haven't mentioned are not necessarily inferior to these two; I just haven't thought of them. These two suggestions are enough to indicate that the supply and demand data that I have described provide a basis for rational negotiations.

It is not to be expected that the quasi-mechanical results of this work of compilation and computation will be accepted with docility. Too much will be at stake. Even though a good deal of reconciliation has been undergone during the preparations, when the overall results are calculated and revealed, searching questions are sure to arise. The preliminary work should then prove its value by focusing and constraining the debate when the negotiators are finally brought together. I have tried to visualize the nature and tenor of the ensuing discussions, but have finally concluded that only experience can show.

A few things are clear. For one, doubt will (and should) be cast on the numerical estimates. No one will, or should, have much faith in them, not even in his or her own country's estimate of its benefit curve. So sensitivity testing and revisions will be needed in the course of the negotiation meetings. They can easily be provided.

In the past, non-governmental organizations have played prominent and constructive roles in international environmental negotiations, and I should expect them to contribute even more effectively to the recommended procedures, since so much pertinent information will be made public. They should participate both in arriving at the estimates of the national benefit and cost curves and in the international negotiating sessions.

I have a few suggestions about procedural matters that should be decided during the negotiations. First, the estimates of the $b^i(X)$ and $c^i(x_i)$ curves will doubtless be inaccurate, sometimes wildly so. Experience will soon reveal any gross inaccuracies in the estimates of $c^i(x_i)$. There should be provision for revising the annual contributions to, and withdrawals from, the equalization fund when substantial inaccuracies are revealed. There is an even more important provision that should be made for correcting errors in assigning abatement targets and financial burdens to individual countries. The abatement targets should be transferable. That is, a nation that expects to have great difficulty in living within its discharge quota should be permitted to purchase additional discharge rights from nations that were willing to sell them at mutually agreeable prices, provided that the change in the locality of the emissions would not harm the environment significantly. Such transferability would provide a safety-valve to relieve the costs of errors in estimating national costs of abatement or willingness to pay for it, and the welfares of all would be increased by mutually advantageous exchanges.

There should be provision for a modest secretariat and for periodic meetings of participating nations to review progress in tackling the environmental problem that brought them together in the first place. Between the meetings, the participating nations should monitor their progress and report their findings to the secretariat at least annually. The secretariat should also keep track of technical and scientific developments relevant to the initiating environmental problem, and should publish progress reports at least annually, as well as emergency bulletins when appropriate. These activities could be financed by a small addition to the equalization fund contributions. The secretariat's budget might also provide for some monitoring, research, transfer of abatement technologies, and educational activities that contribute to contending with the environmental problem.

Finally, there is the problem of enforcing the obligations that the nations have accepted by signing the conventions and protocols designed to curb abuses of the transnational commons. Each signatory should be responsible for compliance on the part of its own nationals. If the progress reports or environmental monitoring should indicate lapses, the secretariat should be empowered to require the nations involved to explain the indications and to present satisfactory plans for correcting the situation if necessary. In such a case, the secretariat might arrange for an international committee of technical and legal specialists to advise the nations that are encountering difficulties and assist in formulating plans for correction. Such procedures have proved effective in the work of the International Monetary Fund and other international regulatory agencies. Of course, they require a modicum of co-operative intent on the part of participating nations, but that is a *sine qua non* for the success of any scheme of joint effort.

Nothing is perfect. One basic shortcoming of this approach should be made explicit. It is that the procedure suggested treats the abatement of abuses of the environment as if it were a static matter, whereas it is intrinsically dynamic. To be more specific, the basic data include estimates of how much it would cost country i to restrict its emissions of a specified substance to a specified amount, or to reduce its emissions by a specified percentage. But reliance on those data ignores the fact that years will be required to achieve the specified reduction, during which substantial transition costs will be incurred and only partial benefits will be realized. Thus the difficult dynamic problem of ascertaining acceptable transition paths has been replaced by the more manageable problem of finding a good ultimate steady-state policy, though the steady-state may be in the distant future.

I see no way out of this drastic simplification. Probably, in practice the negotiation would have to contemplate two stages. First, the ultimate level of abatement would be decided, as described above. Second, there would have to be agreements about the time-paths by which the nations would approach the targeted steady-state.

There, in brief, is my proposal for a more rational, less adversarial approach to negotiating multinational policies for abating abuses of the transnational commons. It may sound visionary, but the alternative is nightmarish. Thus, my basic conclusion and recommendation is the familiar call for more research. Specifically, I believe that the need for a drastic improvement in negotiating procedures is great enough to justify conducting pilot trials in one or two relatively manageable cases. Three attractive opportunities for such trials come to mind at once:

- Protocols on specific substances to be controlled as part of the Mediterranean Action Plan.
- Control of discharges into the Baltic Sea.
- Restriction of atmospheric emissions of sulphuric and nitrogenous acids in North-Eastern Europe.

Any or all of these would be useful exercises. They would be worth the effort intrinsically, and would help indicate the conditions under which it would be feasible and useful to apply the suggested benefit–cost approach.

REFERENCES

Benedick, R. E. (1991), *Ozone Diplomacy: New Directions in Safeguarding the Planet* (Cambridge, Mass.: Harvard University Press).

Haas, P. M. (1990), *Saving the Mediterranean: the Politics of International Environmental Cooperation* (New York: Columbia University Press).

Klaassen, G. and Jansen, H. M. A. (1989), 'Economic Principles for Allocating the Costs of Reducing Sulphur Emissions in Europe', paper submitted to the Group of Economic Experts on Air Pollution, Economic Commission for Europe, 26–8 June.

Lindahl, E. (1919), 'Just Taxation—A Positive Solution', in Musgrave and Peacock (1967), 168–76.

Mazzola, U. (1890), 'The Formation of the Prices of Public Goods', in Musgrave and Peacock (1967), 37–47.

Musgrave, R. A. and Peacock, A. T. (eds.) (1967), *Classics in the Theory of Public Finance* (New York: St Martin's Press).

Pantaleoni, M. (1883), 'Contribution to the Theory of the Distribution of Public Expenditure', in Musgrave and Peacock (1967), 16–27.

Wicksell, K. (1896), 'A New Principle of Just Taxation', in Musgrave and Peacock (1967), 72–118.

11

Implications of a World Economy for Environmental Policy and Law

Lynton Keith Caldwell

The interpretation of the influence of an emergent world economy on environmental policies I present in this chapter follows a logical topical sequence. Beginning with a description of the techno-economic developments that are shaping the present world the principal environmental issues that have consequently arisen are identified. Then follows a synthesis of economic-environmental interrelationships that form the present context for national and international environmental policy and law. Following this, I analyse alternative strategies—administrative, fiscal, diplomatic, legal, and ethical—through which transnational issues of global change are being addressed. Finally, the implications of policy choices for the future of the world economy and of the human condition in the biosphere are conjectured.

I view global change as a holistic, systemic process in which physical and societal elements interact—often in ways that are poorly understood. The transnational economy is a world-shaping societal factor in this system of systems, no part of which operates in isolation from the rest. We may distinguish, however, between the geo-biophysical systems which comprise the planet Earth, and the artificial or cultural systems which we call the World. That these systems interact in ways that determine the future has been tacitly recognized, especially in those so-called 'primitive societies' whose economies are tied closely and visibly to the Earth. In modern society techno-economic achievements, applying science as a servant, have abetted a conceit that man can 'conquer' nature, and that technology can overcome all obstacles to human economic advance. But, in reality, modern society has been utilizing natural laws and forces to redirect nature to satisfy human needs, preferences, and ambitions. 'Obedience' to natural laws, however, does not ensure against their misuse. Domination, or attempted domination, of nature should not be taken as an excuse for abuse. Such misconception opens the way to self-destructive consequences.

In this hubris of human domination over nature we find the roots of the so-called environmental crisis of our times, which in many respects has led to an economic crisis, notably in the world of techno-economically less developed nations (see White, 1967). In reality, the alleged crises are misnamed. They are not sudden critical events, but rather the culmination of decades, even centuries, of unperceived developments reaching in our times a point of climacteric, at which our artificial systems, running contrary to the limiting factors in nature, can no longer sustain themselves (see Ashby, 1918). Recognition of this reality has not come easily to modern society and is still denied by technocratic optimists who refuse to abandon illusions which heretofore have been mistaken for reality. But new ways of understanding the world have emerged, expressed in such concepts as ecological economics, sustainable development, and organic or contained growth, as contrasted with indiscriminate exponential growth. We are at present in a period of discontinuity between conventional modern assumptions and emergent insights which, if they become dominant, presage a reshaping of a post-modern world. New globe-spanning transboundary technologies, notably in communications and transportation, have radically altered relationships among nations and have allowed the emergence of a global economy (see Mowlana and Wilson, 1990).

CAUSAL ISSUES

First, we examine the environmental issues that have arisen as a result of the kinds of techno-economic developments that have shaped the modern world. The salient questions under this topic are:

(1) What issues have arisen to induce international concern for the environment?
(2) What has caused these issues to arise at this time?
(3) What is their relative significance for public policies, both national and transnational?

There is no single best way to categorize these issues. Classifications de-pend upon how the selected phenomena interrelate with other phenomena and are thus perceived as particular subjects of concern or 'issues'. For our purposes, four main groupings of environmental issues will be identified, all of which interrelate with economic activities and policies. These groupings are, respectively, air, water, land, and biota.

Atmospheric issues include global warming and climate change; disintegration of the protective stratospheric ozone layer; atmospheric contamination by chemical pollutants and particulates. A fourth group of atmospheric issues not commonly appreciated includes the effects and uses of wind, relevant to agriculture, energy, aeronautics, and building construction. Ecological and socio-economic problems have arisen under each of these topical issues as consequences of modern economic-industrial development. Each has significant implications for economic activity in relation to both causes of industrial and commercial developments and consequences of their environmental and social impacts.

Issues pertaining to water—the essential fluid of life—are inextricably linked with the economy at all organizational levels, from households to multinational corporations. Different aquatic issues arise depending upon the location and properties of water. A natural resource in at least four circumstances, water presents distinctive issues for the economy and the environment, most of which occur without regard to jurisdictional boundaries (a circumstance with obvious implications for transboundary political issues). These circumstances are fresh surface-water in the form of lakes and rivers; ground-water, especially in aquifers; oceanic saline water—covering 70 per cent of the world's surface; and water in the atmosphere in the form of rain, snow, ice, or water vapour (e.g. fog).

Water issues divide between considerations of quantity and quality, of domestic and industrial uses, of purity and contamination. With the growth of transnational economic relationships, the status of water as a common property resource becomes a policy issue. For example, the free-trade agreement between Canada and the United States has enlarged an old debate regarding the transboundary diversion of water as a commodity transaction, and is discussed in Cole-Misch (1988). And degradation of international river systems in many parts of the world has important biological and economic consequences that translate into national and international policy and environmental and economic legislation (see chapter 3, above).

Land and its uses comprise the oldest and most obvious set of policy issues in which economics and environment, in effect, appear to be opposite sides of the same coin. Land as a resource has been basic to human social organization and behaviour since the migrations of peoples as early as the Stone Age. The movements of peoples have responded to changes in climate, population increase, food supply, and aggressive tendencies within societies. From the early wanderings of hunting-gathering tribal bands to the recent preemption of all habitable areas of the Earth by humans, land has been the basic economic resource.

With the development of hydraulic technologies even the initial absence of water has not precluded human settlement and economic development. Water transport technologies, exemplified by dams, canals, irrigation, aqueducts, and waste-disposal systems, were an absolute prerequisite to the emergence of urban settlements and the growth of food supply through the expansion of agriculture and a more efficient processing of grain through water-power. The economic effects of political control over water supply have obvious implications for land use because, when flowing water can be managed, those who manage have potential control over those who do not, but who must nevertheless have access to the water. Indeed, the historian Karl Wittfogel interpreted the emergence of despotic regimes in the governance of the ancient Orient as a consequence of what he called hydraulic civilization (Wittfogel, 1957). Much of the history of Egypt, Mesopotamia, India, and China turns upon the relationship between the control of

hydraulic systems by governing classes and control over the uses and ownership of land. In principle this situation has not changed. Where water is a pre-
condition of wealth, security, and even survival, politics becomes a factor in
economics and environment.

How humans have used the land in relation to the natural forces of water
and wind has had major economic and environmental consequences. Over-
grazing, unwise tillage, deforestation, and motorized recreation have resulted in soil erosion, diminishing the productivity of land and contributing
to the sedimentation of lakes and streams, with deleterious effects upon food
supply, commerce, and health.

For example, the economics of once-thriving ports on the Mediterranean
Sea were destroyed by the siltation of their harbours by sediment-bearing
streams. In addition, the health of their inhabitants was apparently jeopard-
ized by the spread of malaria following the transformation of formerly clear
estuaries into stagnant marshes. A Roman architect and engineer in the reign
of the Emperor Augustus, Marcus Vitruvius Pollio, recounts the petition of
the inhabitants of Old Salpia in Apulia to remove their town to a site free from
the 'heavy, unhealthy vapours' of the adjacent marshes.[1] Today we overcome
such environmental effects through the control of disease vectors, and it is no
longer necessary to remove settlements. Still, the control of malaria and
other environmentally conditioned pathologies has economic and behavioural costs which are in some cases considerable. Schistosomiasis, for example, is a debilitating illness that has spread in the wake of water-resource
development. As human settlements spread into previously unexploited environments, the list of environmentally influenced diseases has lengthened,
affecting domesticated animals as well as humans, with obvious consequences for economic productivity.[2]

All of the foregoing environmental-economic cause–effect relationships
have had measurable consequences for the biota, i.e. for living species of
plants, animals, micro-organisms, and ecosystems. The epitome of the
species diversity issue today is the fate of the tropical rainforests. But there
are endangered species in all environments—in deserts, mountains, the sea,
and even in formerly remote polar regions. Ecosystem destruction leads to
economic impoverishment or disaster, with consequent social and political
disruption. Examples of ecological–economic–political linkages are all too
apparent in Ethiopia, Haiti, El Salvador, Nepal, and Uzbekistan, just some of
the countries or regions threatened by socio-ecological bankruptcy.
Reconstruction of ruined environments and their economies can be costly in
all meanings of the word. Contamination of lakes, rivers, and coastal seas,
and loss of fertility in cultivated lands have deprived humans of natural
sources of nutrition and diminished economic productivity.

---

[1] On the effects of siltation on the economy and environment, see also Demand (1990).
[2] See World Bank (1974) and Caldwell (1990a); also, Pavlovsky (1966).

CONTEXTUAL RELATIONSHIPS

At this point we need to examine briefly the circumstances, geophysical and societal, in which the issues identified have arisen. Not all of these circumstances are generally thought to be specifically environmental or economic. Yet there is growing recognition that they interrelate with, and influence, both economic and environmental trends. These relationships are contextual, in the sense that they set the conditions under which all of the foregoing issues have arisen, and are parameters, or limiting factors, which influence the strategies that may be adopted to cope with their consequences.

Each of our designated environmental-economic issues relates in some respect to each of the following contextual circumstances: population dynamics; depletion of natural materials; and misapplication of technology. An attribute of these contextual relationships, and their problematic aspects, is the unevenness of their distribution. These relationships make for the wealth, poverty, and power of nations; they influence political agendas and have often been factors in diplomacy, war, revolution, and invariably in international commerce.

We have identified human population dynamics as a contextual parameter, not to discount the ultimate problems of absolute numbers in any finite environment, but because the more pressing problems of population relate to the effects of growth, decline, and mobility and to the rapidity with which each of these processes occurs. Densities *per se* are not necessarily causes of environmental over-stress or of poverty, although they often may be.

For example, the Netherlands and Bangladesh are among the world's most densely populated nations. Yet the former is relatively rich and has a well-managed environment whereas the latter is poor and vulnerable to environmental and economic disasters. One factor in the contrast is the informed and effective use of technology in the Netherlands and technological and informational deficiencies in Bangladesh, where land and economic possibilities are limited. Rapid population growth, through births or immigration, stresses economies, socio-political relationships, and environments. The effects are often broadly destabilizing and the deteriorating social consequences often exacerbate political tensions. Ethnic diversity tends to exaggerate social conflict and complicate economic relationships throughout much of the world.

The uneven distribution of materials, especially of arable soils, forests, minerals and, in a larger sense, of configurations of the land, also affects all environmental and economic circumstances. These natural factors have particular economic significance when materials become resources, and more so when materials become scarce. For example, uranium and petroleum were present in the material environments of the ancient world, but had no economic value as resources. No technologies were available to apply them to human purposes. But forests, cultivatable soils, and deposits of copper, iron, and tin were natural resources and were commodities for exploitation, fabrication, and trade. Vegetable and animal products such as frankincense, myrrh, cotton, silk, and ivory were articles of commerce and often objects of policy. In the ancient world, societal pressure on natural resources was relatively light during any limited period of time. Cumulatively, however, the continuing attrition of forests, soil fertility, and wildlife led to environmental impoverishment and hence to economic decline. North Africa, and especially the Nile Valley, was once the 'granary of the Roman Empire', but today this region does well to feed its inhabitants poorly and it is hardly a factor in world trade in grain (on this, see Brice, 1978; Murphy, 1951; Marsh, 1965; Thomas, 1965).

Relationships between resources, environments, and economies have been observed and recorded, but until very recent times were rarely addressed as issues for conservation management or foresighted rational development. These relationships, although now widely publicized and understood by many people, are still being ignored, denied, or alibied by the greater part of the world's political leadership. Technological innovations in agriculture, mining, energy production, manufacturing, and transportation have enlarged human capabilities for resource exploitation and economic growth. They have also contributed to a technocratic hubris which obscures the ultimate consequences of exuberant growth on economies and human populations.

That humans are in important respects a unique species in the living world has been misconstrued as the belief that humans are exceptions to the so-called 'laws of nature'. The apotheosis of this assumption to an article of faith has been the belief that ultimately mankind will be able to do anything that it can imagine. The ability to send computerized probes deep into outer space and to land astronauts on the moon gave credibility to an exaggerated expectation of possibilities in a universe in which all things were not actually possible. The ways in which the universe works appear to have evolved over billions of years and by means that humans may never fully understand. As Buckminster Fuller (1969) observed, we do not yet know what our forward capabilities may be and where we may encounter ultimate limits. We may still be a long way from the end of history. Yet we are hardly entitled by what we know of life and the cosmos to assume that there are no ultimate limits, and that humanity enjoys a perpetual dispensation from those 'laws' that govern the rest of nature.

The rational view of reality is therefore to assume that we live in a world of limits even when their boundaries are not discernible. The Earth is not infinitely malleable to human purposes, and there are possibilities in nature and in human artifice that are inimical to human welfare and survival. To identify and cope with these possibilities and to safeguard and advance the quality of life on Earth will require for the future (as it has in the past) strategies and policies that will ensure, as best we may, the continuation and improvement of environmental and economic conditions. But because of our limited ability to foresee and predict, we live in a world of many uncertainties. Our social strategies must therefore undertake to prepare us to cope with events at present unforeseen, as well as with trends that we can ascertain and possibly control.

This context of uncertainty implies a need for the identification of feasible alternatives for addressing the future. To this end it is imperative that we close the artificial gap in our modern perception of ecological and economic phenomena. The gap exists only in the way in which we have understood the world. As we understand it better, the rationale for the gap diminishes. We are approaching a point in our intellectual evolution when the 'disciplinarity', academic exclusiveness that has characterized the universities, is no longer justifiable. We may, of course, continue to factor out of the total system (which exceeds the ability of the human mind to comprehend) those particular subsystems which are essentially economic or ecological in substance. But to do so prudently and consistently with the way the world works, the reality of the comprehensive whole must be kept in mind. Our failure to appreciate the contextual relationships among things has led us into mistaken assumptions about the consequences of our policies, and into misapplications of our technologies. Thus humanity has too often been its own worst enemy, as destructive to its happiness and welfare as are the indifferent forces in nature.

The integrative circumstance in which all of the foregoing relationships occur is the emergence of a global economy transcending cultural, political, and ecosystemic boundaries. The origins of this world economy can be traced to the formation of companies of merchant-adventurers at the beginning of modern times. Advances in navigational technology, cartography, and shipbuilding permitted the expansion of the West European economy through exploration and colonization. This expansion led both to economic and scientific advance and to socio-ecological destruction. By the twentieth century a world economy existed, rapidly expanding despite great wars, through unprecedented innovations in transportation, communication, computation, and environmental sensing. Techno-economic globalization preceded transnational and global environmental concern. The history of the European Community affords an example of the way in which economic multinational integration induces corresponding environmental policies. A parallel development is appearing as a consequence of the implementation of free trade in North America. In sum, a world economic order induces a world order of the environment—each ultimately dependent on the other for sustainability.

STRATEGIC ALTERNATIVES

Within the emergent dual order of the world (natural and artificial), what strategies are available for reducing risk, avoiding error, and coping with the uncertainties and hazards of unprecedented innovation? What assumptions do rational analyses of the interrelationships of the globalized systems entitle us to adopt? How may we validly ascertain and evaluate the consequences of the alternatives available to us? What do we need to learn to guide the course of our social development towards higher levels of moral, intellectual, and material achievement?

We live in a world of nation-states through which our collective and often private affairs have been governed. This form of political organization is far from inherent in human societies. It has emerged and become dominant as a governing system only during the past 500 years. Historians in the future may define the period that we call 'modern' as the era of the national state, roughly demarcated chronologically by the years 1492–1992.

In examining alternative strategies for redefining economic–environmental–political relationships few useful generalizations are available to guide policy choice. To be achievable, alternatives must take account of existing systems of governance (if only to propose their modification). The feasibility of strategies depends greatly upon the status and receptivity of the dominant political order. The national state is, and has been, the basic unit of governance, but, as we shall see, its unique status is being compromised by both internal and external political forces. The inequality of national states by size and circumstance precludes identifying a simple, logical set of clearly marked choices through which environment and ecology can be brought together in pursuit of environmentally sustainable economic development, which must also be sustainable social and moral development.

The political structures of ancient and medieval times—city-states, empires, theocracies, and dynastic regimes—were not nations. Today the attrition of the nation-state is apparent. Transnational forms of governance are emerging and subnational jurisdictions are asserting autonomy over policies formerly administered from national capitals. Organizations conventionally regarded as non-governmental (NGOs) are increasingly playing roles that are significantly political.

Environmental NGOs are numerous and are greatly varied in status, scope, and function. In addition, beyond direct administration by national states, their structures are often international (for example, the World Conservation Union, Greenpeace, Friends of the Earth). There has been a proliferation of transnational organizations that are less than governments but more than private institutions.[3] Their emergence and growing importance has stimulated a new field of political science called 'regime theory'. The presence and functions of these public quasi-governmental organizations have complicated international policy and law, and blurred conventional distinctions between political, economic, and environmental affairs.

In this late modern world near the end of the twentieth century the structure of actual governance has become varied and complex beyond precedent.

[3] On this, see e.g. issues of *International Associations*, and Skjelsbaek (1971).

It is difficult to describe or to comprehend, and its realities are seldom consistent with traditional assumptions. Governance now frequently occurs in ways unfamiliar to conventional political science. Economic policies are made as often outside conventional government as within it, and what are often taken to be the official policies of government are, in fact, formulated outside 'normal' political systems, for example, by corporations, occupational associations, and social service and scientific organizations formulating their own policies and applying them to the general public.

The emergence of large and often transnational environmental organizations is especially relevant to our subject. They undertake to influence and to work through normal governmental and international agencies and to interact with multinational corporate enterprise as well. They also engage in nongovernmental diplomacy (e.g. the World Conservation Strategy and the WFN Network on Conservation and Religion) and some have recently become involved in international financial affairs (e.g. buying up national debts in exchange for national commitments to environmental conservation). In certain countries NGOs have, in effect, become partners in resource management, providing funds to supplement national budgets for wardens and guards in national parks and nature reserves. They have founded or undertaken environmental research that national governments lack the means or motives to initiate. In less developed countries some have become intermediaries between local and national authorities and international funding institutions. The Fundación Moises Bertoni in Paraguay is a case in point.

In these and other ways environmental and scientific NGOs are playing roles that could be described as quasi-political. Not only do they seek to importune their official governments to adopt preferred policies, but they also form coalitions (sometimes across national boundaries) to persuade governments to adopt parallel or common policies and to enforce international agreements. Some NGOs have transnational memberships (e.g. Greenpeace, Friends of the Earth, and the Cousteau Society). Federated NGOs— professional, philanthropic, and scientific—play similar roles. Prominent in environmental policy-shaping are the International Union for Conservation of Nature and Natural Resources (IUCN), now the World Conservation Union, the International Council of Scientific Unions (ICSU), and the World Wide Fund for Nature (WWF). Environmental issues have also been on the agendas of international professional societies such as the European Federation of National Engineering Societies (FEANI).[4]

Business firms have also established environmental organizations, especially to deal with environmental issues affecting their economic interests. Examples include the International Environmental Bureau (a division of the

[4] See, for example, *Engineering and Education for Environment* (Proceedings of a seminar co-sponsored by FEANI and UNESCO, held at Stockholm, Sweden, 1–3 March 1976). Stockholm: Sveriges Civilingenjorsforbund, CF-STF.

International Chamber of Commerce), the business-supported World Environment Center in NewYork, and the International Petroleum Industry Environmental Association. Relatively few people are aware of the scope and complexity of the matrix of organizations now concerned transnationally with the interactions of economic and environmental affairs.

The larger transnational and international federated NGOs have established consultative and co-operative relationships with official international-intergovernmental organizations within the United Nations system. These relationships are essential to the strength and outreach of every UN Specialized Agency. This is notably the case in environmental policy, especially for UNESCO, the World Meteorological Organization (WMO), the Food and Agriculture Organization (FAO), the World Health Organization (WHO) and the International Maritime Organization (IMO) (which has important linkages with international shipping interests). An NGO environmental liaison centre has been established in Nairobi for direct interaction with the United Nations Environment Programme. NGO environmental forums have now paralleled every major UN environmental conference. Even World Bank policies have now been influenced by NGO pressure, directly as well as through member governments (see, for example, Shabecoff, 1986 and Wirth, 1986).

A complex and pervasive structure of intergovernmental–nongovernmental organizations increasingly defines the direction and limits of national policies. Although national governments remain the ultimate source of political authority, their choice among policies has been influenced increasingly by external quasi-political forces (e.g. other governments, international nongovernmental organizations, including multinational corporations, and organized transboundary public opinion). Cases in point have been the acquiescence of long-resistant governments to international agreements to protect the ozone layer, to reduce acidic deposition, to protect endangered wildlife, and to prevent the continuing pollution of regional seas and the open ocean by oil, industrial chemicals, and hazardous wastes. Implementation as enforcement of rhetorical commitments is quite another matter. Such evidence as we have suggests that the promises of governments are more often pro forma than pro actions. The more common strategies for dealing with transnational global issues, and environmental issues in particular, have been through treaties, charters, and declarations, as well as through joint programmes of which the UNEP Regional Seas Programme is a prominent example. Alternative strategies would include direct administration of transnational policies by quasi-autonomous authorities. Such bodies do exist in embryonic form for some international bodies of water such as lakes and river systems (see Caldwell, 1990b).

Jealousy of national governments for political sovereignty, and of national bureaucracies for their functional self-interests, partially explains an ambiguity characterizing the policy roles and jurisdictions of many UN secretariats and commissions, and of international conferences. There are, moreover, often discrepancies between policy and action authorization on paper, and administration in practice. Budgetary constraints are common explanatory factors where multi-national authorities depend on funding from voluntary contributions by national governments, and have no independent sources of revenue under their control. Even within national governments where an intergovernmental agency functions at a sub-national level (as in the American Tennessee Valley Authority), political manœuvres by central bureaucracies may gradually erode the organization's effectiveness. There is some informed opinion to the effect that Canadian and United States bureaucracies have constrained the potential effectiveness of the bi-national International Joint Commission in policy development relating to the transnational boundary waters (especially regarding the Great Lakes).

To assess the effectiveness of alternative strategies it is necessary to examine each alternative in actual or probable performance over a period of time appropriate to its mission, along with the declared policies of governments, the role of related nongovernmental bodies, and activated public opinion. Given the complexity of the large issues no feasible strategy is likely to be simple. Taking the text of a treaty at apparent face value is likely to lead to a misconstruction of the actual situation. Even more than with national law, international legal commitments are subject to various interpretations. Not all parties to a treaty (or comparable agreement) interpret their obligations in the same way. Some governments ignore their treaty responsibilities altogether, and some have been guilty of flagrant violation. A notorious case in point was the deliberate discharge of crude oil into the Persian Gulf by the government of Iraq during the 1991 war over Kuwait.

A common failure in international negotiations and arrangements for environmental protection is the absence of any effective provision for monitoring and obtaining national compliance. Failure to comply is not always fairly attributable to deliberate national dereliction. It is sometimes the consequence of administrative incompetence, of insufficient resources for surveillance and policing, of exigencies of immediate human need (as in famine or environmental disaster), or of *sub rosa* connivance by local officials who are susceptible to bribery or intimidation. Even with the best intentions, Third World governments are often incapable of enforcing their own laws when lawbreakers, looters, poachers, and timber thieves are secretly protected by highly placed but not necessarily official personalities. For example, although the government of Kenya was officially committed to enforcement of the Convention on International Trade in Endangered Species, it was alleged that a ring of poachers and smugglers of wildlife products was protected by one of the wives of the president. Moreover, if not all nations adhere to a treaty intended to protect natural species or cultural artifacts, merchants in non-complying nations may enjoy a lucrative trade in illegally obtained commodities.

These and other miscarriages and abuses of international intent prompted a former vice-president of Argentina to propose an inter-American system for tracking the observance of environmental agreements (Martinez, 1987). Many governments, however, would not welcome intrusion into what they regard as their internal affairs. For some environmental issues—notably deforestation, desertification, air and water pollution over land and sea— surveillance by orbiting satellites has become a technology of potential enforcement. Closing off the market for prohibited natural products may be an effective alternative to policing. Yet as long as there are eager and affluent buyers of such products as rhinoceros horn, elephant ivory, the feet and hands of gorillas, and skins of the spotted cats, evasion of international law will be a continuing problem.

There is both the need and the opportunity for the development of new forms of governance over some areas of land and sea which cannot or will not be adequately protected under the national state system. A major step towards creating a universal regime for the oceans has been taken through the UN-sponsored Law of the Sea Convention. Some of the major maritime powers, however, have refused to ratify it—sometimes, as in the case of the United States because of objection to a single provision. The question of who controls deep-sea mining is the obvious sticking-point for the technologically advanced states. But the economic benefits are uncertain and adverse environmental effects seem probable. Here, as in many maritime issues, obsolete economics appears to override ecological rationality. To cite another case in point, although most maritime states have adopted a ban on commercial whaling, a few nations with investments in whaling claim immunity from international conformity under the subterfuge of taking whales for research.

Human nature, political realities, and the short-term economic interests of commercial enterprises make self-policing alone a dubious alternative to economically disinterested negotiation and enforcement of environmental and resources protection measures. For example, it is not apparent that the International Tropical Forest Agreement and Action Plan of 1985 has significantly slowed the destruction of tropical forests, nor that the quotas and allocations by the several international fisheries commissions (many sponsored by FAO) have significantly prevented depletion of fish stocks. The numerous conventions ostensibly for protection against the pollution of the oceans by oil, suggest a continuing 'rear-guard' resistance by petroleum shipping interests and their governmental sponsors. Self-policing and bureaucratic co-option have proved to be ineffective alternatives to disinterested control, independent of overt or convert shielding by political agencies acting under the influence of the very enterprises which government is attempting to regulate.

In the so-called 'common spaces' of the high seas, outer space, and Antarctica, the logic of circumstances calls for quasi-autonomous governing

regimes. Antarctica in particular is insufficiently protected against environmental pollution, depletion of marine life, and over-exploitation of its coastal
waters. The Consultative Committee of the governments with a presence in
Antarctica has not yet freed itself from the jealousy and ambition of member
states.[5] Legal conservatism, political coaptation, and obsolete, self-serving
nationalism have slowed the course of institutional innovation.

SOCIETAL IMPLICATIONS

It appears that in this era of discontinuities the policy alternatives before us
are not clear. Humanity faces a test of whether or not it can shape its future
by considered choice and action. If alternatives are not sufficiently clear to
permit rational choice, can methods towards clarification be found?
Extensive conjectures as to the direction in which the world is moving have
been undertaken, illustrated by various models of world dynamics.[6] Even in
an era of social transition there are residual continuities, so we cannot be sure
that all of the determining factors in our present circumstance have been
identified nor their potential significance assessed.

Would such essentially physical-mathematical conjectures as chaos theory
and catastrophe theory enable us to identify some apparently insignificant
elements in our present techno-economic-environmental situation that
might be nuclei of unforeseen turns of events in human history? Our mind-
sets or the ways in which we think about our problems influence our methods
of investigation, and thereby risk imprinting a predetermined bias on conclusions that have not been verified by objective analysis. In our policy de-
liberations, and especially in economic and political affairs, the wish is still
the father of the thought.

In the context of the massive and pervasive transition in our world, the
basic problems of policy are conceptual and moral. Modern society has generated a set of conditions that have become increasingly inconsistent with
many of the ways in which members of the society see their world.
Contradictions have emerged between definitions of the ecological and economic problems of which we have become aware and our approaches to their
solutions. Even when we think that we know how these problems might be resolved, our governments and universities have moved only slowly and reluctantly towards development of the methodological and institutional means to
resolve them.

Our difficulties in effectively addressing our problems follow from our persistent reliance upon concepts and policies that, while appropriate to past
circumstances, are inappropriate to the challenges that now confront us.
Modern society has been the architect of its own difficulties. It is attempting

---

[5] For a survey of governance for the common spaces, see Caldwell (1990b) and Trigg (1987).
[6] See Toth, Hizsnyik, and Clark (1989); and Barney (1980).

to address novel problems with traditional assumptions and institutions maladaptive to emerging conditions.

Our very successes have sometimes illuminated our failures. For example (allowing for the unforeseen) our ability to analyse trends and to forecast futures through computerized technologies has revealed the unsustainability of many persisting practices and arrangements. Regardless of their reliability in detail, the several reports to the Club of Rome on the predicament of our times set in motion a series of inquiries that informed the recommendations of the World Commission on Environment and Development (Bruntland Commission, 1987). These are reflected in the UN World Charter for Nature and in numerous resolutions and declarations at the highest levels of international politics (Burhenne and Irwin, 1986; Caldwell, 1990b). And so we have the paradox of widespread informed agreement regarding goals and preferred outcomes, but we lack consensus regarding what is necessary to their attainment.

The cause of this dichotomy is the incongruity between assumptions and practices that have made the world modern, and the science-based intimations of what must be done to ensure a sustainable society in the future. The dominating assumptions of modern times have been those of a commercial society in which almost every activity results in one or more exchange transactions. Prevailing economic theory has developed around these practices of production and consumption that have defined the character of modern society. Allowing for exceptions that may be more apparent than real (e.g. communalism, socialism, and militarism), the human individual has been the basic unit of theory in politics and economics. Particularly in the democratic market economics of Western society, the individual is the repository of wants and rights, but the production and consumption of goods and services cumulates to an essentially social process. Modern society has achieved the highest standard of material affluence that humans have attained—the persistence of poverty not withstanding,—but it now appears that it has done so by heavily discounting the future, initially by failing to internalize the external or residual effects of economic processes upon both people and their environments.

The conventional market-structured economy of the modern era failed to provide for the future in two important respects. Focused on the needs and wants of individuals, social and economic policies were developed around assumptions limited by the actuarial life-span of individuals. Policies, both public and private, were even more delimited by the narrower span of the active working life of individuals, and limited further by the fixed periodicities of economic and political institutional arrangements (e.g. elections to public office, fiscal years, and mandatory retirement requirements). Thus, consistent with its essential dynamics, modern society could not adapt its behaviours to future needs. Transgenerational equity and the environment were discounted (Brown Weiss, 1989; Daly and Cobb, 1989).

Anticipated future problems of equity and environment can only be avoided by action in the present. There has been little incentive or reward for present political or economic leadership to invest in a future that is far beyond their time horizons; nor for the general public to forbear from present indulgence in the interest of a future that they will never live to see. But this negative prognosis appears to be partially off-set by a transnational environmental movement that seeks behavioural changes needed to attain a sustainable future of high environmental quality. Among professional economists, ecological and long-range considerations are now more often built into economic analysis.[7] Moral and prudential values are beginning to modify, perhaps ultimately to displace, contemporaneous expediency. Why is this happening?

At least two developments in the modern world have induced these re-orientations. First, history is accelerating and the future arrives ahead of its anticipated schedule. The rapidity of technological innovation and of changes in economic processes and facilitating structures means that the discounted future may soon indeed become our present. The emergence of a popular literature of 'mega-trends' and 'future shock' documents a recognition that to discount the future is no longer practical or prudent. But that is not to say that these future prognoses are reliable indications of what may happen. Our foregoing identification of critical environmental issues demonstrates that we must cope now with problems created during or culminating in our own lifetimes. Experience has become a persuasive teacher even to reluctant learners. Not everyone, of course, has been persuaded to learn.

A second development has been the major advance in the science and technology of cause–effect analysis and forecasting. Major global issues such as 'greenhouse' climate change, stratospheric ozone depletion, and loss of natural biological diversity have arisen out of scientific investigation. Computer simulation makes possible the projecting of alternative scenarios of possible futures. Critics of systems modelling are probably right in warning against placing too much confidence in their prognoses when formulating present policies. But they would be wrong to underestimate their cautionary value for alerting policy-makers to possible problems that may be gestating. Computer technology is surely in the early stages of development. In view of the unprecedented speed and power with which humans may now impact upon nature (and upon themselves) it has become an imperative of human and biospherical survival that we choose our policies on the assumption that we are now, or soon will be, living in the future.

CONCLUSION

The advent of a transnational world economy has induced developments in environmental policy and law, and in ethics, because these aspects of our lives

[7] See, for example, articles in the journal *Ecological Economics*. Also, Boulding (1981; 1985).

are integral to the management of the 'household' (*oikos*) of humanity and involve far more than production, consumption, and investment. The house is now the planet; its material properties, both animate and inanimate, are the environment; and its management, to be prudent and sustaining, must be future-directed and ethical.

Symbolic of an emerging synthesis of things that belong together was an event occurring appropriately in the town of Assisi in central Italy in September 1986. Here, on its 25th anniversary, the Worldwide Fund for Nature (WWF) convened a meeting of representatives of five of the world's great religions.[8] The purpose was to form an alliance and establish a network on conservation and religions. This movement has continued and grown. Religion has traditionally set the assumptions and concepts by which mankind's relationships with the natural world have been guided, and those relationships are expressed most explicitly in the conduct of the economy.

Historians in the more distant future may interpret the pervasive disorders and discontinuities of our times as consequences of a loss of societal and moral integrity. Our long-trusted assumptions and institutions no longer serve our new circumstances and the needs that they have generated. We thus experience a discontinuity between our customary ways of believing and behaving and our ability to cope with new and pressing problems of environment, economy, equity, and ethics. A consequence has been loss of confidence in our institutions in an age of anxiety. Confidence cannot be regained nor institutions reconstituted, without an intellectual and moral regeneration and synthesis that is based on respect for the cosmos as we have been able to understand it. Were this to be achieved, it would set the direction of the post-modern age and establish a new and higher level of civilization.

REFERENCES

Ashby, E. (1918), *Reconciling Man with the Environment* (Stanford, Calif.: Stanford University Press).

Barney, G. (ed.) (1980), 'Analyses of the Projection Tools: Other Global Models', in *The Global 2000 Report to the President*, ii. *Technical Report* (Washington DC: US Government Printing Office).

Boulding, K. (1981), *Ecodynamics: A New Theory of Societal Evolution* (Beverly Hills, Calif.: Sage).

—— (1985), *The World as a Total System* (Beverly Hills, Calif.: Sage).

Brice, W. (ed.) (1978), *The Environmental History of the Near and Middle East since the Last Ice Age* (New York: Academic Press).

Burhenne, W. and Irwin, W. (1986), *The World Charter for Nature: A Background Paper*, 2nd edn. (Berlin: Erich Schmidt).

[8] See *The New Road*, 1.

Caldwell, L. (1977), '1992: Threshold of the Post-modern World', in *A Time to Hear and Answer: Essays for the Bicentennial Season*, the Franklin Lectures in the Sciences and Humanities (Taskuloosa, Alabama: University of Alabama Press for Auburn University).

—— (1990a), *International Environmental Policy: Emergence and Dimensions*, 2nd edn. (Durham, NC: Duke University Press).

—— (1990b), 'International Commons: Atmosphere, Outer Space, Oceans, Antarctica', in Caldwell (1990a).

Cole-Misch, S. (1988), 'Great Lakes Diversions: A Conflict Assessment', in L. K. Caldwell (ed.), *Perspectives on Ecosystem Management for the Great Lakes* (Albany, NY: State University of New York Press).

Daly, H., and Cobb, J., Jr. (1989), *For the Common Good: Re-directing the Economy toward Community, the Environment, and a Sustainable Future* (Boston: Beacon Press).

Demand, N. (1990), *Urban Relocation in Archaic and Classical Greece* (Norman, Okla.: University of Oklahoma Press).

Fuller, B. (1969), *Operating Manual for Spaceship Earth* (Carbondale, Ill.: Southern Illinois University Press).

Krier, J. and Clayton, P. (1985), 'The Un-easy Case for Technological Optimism', *Michigan Law Review*, 84.

Marsh, G. (1864), *Man and Nature: or Physical Geography as Modified by Human Action*; repr. 1965, ed. David Lowenthal (Cambridge, Mass.: Harvard University Press).

Martinez, V. (1987), 'Hacia la creación del Sistema Interamericano para la Conservación de la Naturaleza', in *Ambiente y Recursos Naturales*, 4/2.

Mowlana, H. and Wilson, L. (1990), *The Passing of Modernity: Communication and the Transformation of Society* (White Plains, NY: Longman).

Murphy, R. (1951), 'The Decline of North Africa since the Roman Occupation: Climatic or Human?', *Annals of the Association of American Geographers*, 41.

New Road: The Bulletin of the WWF Network on Conservation and Religion (1986/7), 1; and subsequent issues of this bulletin.

Pavlovsky, E. (1966), *Natural Nidality of Transmissible Disease: With Special Reference to the Landscape Epidemiology of Zooanthroponoses*, trans. F. K. Plous Jr. (Urbana, Ill.: University of Illinois Press).

Pollio, M. (1914), *The Ten Books on Architectures*, trans. Morris Hicky Morgan (Cambridge, Mass.: Harvard University Press).

Proceedings of a seminar co-sponsored by FEANI and UNESCO held at Stockholm, Sweden (1976), *Engineering and Education for Environment* (Stockholm: Sveriges Civilingenjorsforbund, CF-STF).

Shabecoff, P. (1986), 'World Lenders Facing Pressure from Ecologists', *New York Times*, 30 Oct.

Skjelsback, K. (1971), 'The Growth of International Non-governmental Organisation in the Twentieth Century', in R. O. Keohane and J. S. Nye (eds.), *Transnational Relations and World Politics* (Cambridge, Mass.: Harvard University Press).

Thomas, W., Jr. (1965), *Man's Role in Changing the Face of the Earth* (Chicago: University of Chicago Press).

Toth, F., Hizsnyik, E., and Clark, W. (eds.) (1989), *Scenarios of Socioeconomic Development for Studies of Global Environmental Change: A Critical Review* (Luxembourg, Austria: International Institute for Applied Systems Analysis).

Trigg, G. (1987), *The Antarctic Treaty Regime* (Cambridge: Cambridge University Press).

US Office of Technology Assessment (OTA) (1982), *Global Models, World Futures and Public Policy: A Critique* (Washington, DC: OTA–T–165).

Weiss, E. (1989), *In Fairness to Future Generations: International Law, Common Patrimony and Intergenerational Equity* (Dobbs Ferry, NY: Transnational Publishers).

White, L., Jr. (1967), 'The Historical Roots of our Ecological Crisis', *Science*, 155.

Wittfogel, K. (1957), *Oriental Despotism: A Comparative Study of Total Power* (New Haven, Conn.: Yale University Press).

World Bank (1974), *Environmental Health and Human Ecological Considerations in Economic Development Projects* (Washington DC: World Bank).

Wirth, D. (1986), 'The World Bank and the Environment', *Environment*, 28 Dec.

World Commission on Environment and Development (1987), *Our Common Future* (Oxford: Oxford University Press).

12

Cultural Beliefs as a Common Resource in an Integrating World

Avner Greif

INTRODUCTION

Recent developments in transportation, communication, and information technologies have strengthened the economic and cultural interactions between different societies throughout the world. Inter-society interaction is increasingly characterized by a deliberate borrowing of institutions and cultural attributes from one society by another, a process that has recently gained momentum from the events in Eastern Europe. Accordingly, social scientists have expanded their study of culture as a common resource that affects economic performance and the outcome of the interaction among individuals from different societies.[1]

Culture is defined by sociologists as consisting of cultural beliefs, values, and symbols. Cultural beliefs are the ideas and thoughts common to several individuals which differ from knowledge in that they cannot be proved empirically. Values specify 'the good, the true, and the beautiful'—the criteria individuals use to determine their attitudes towards the world around them, and to select goals of behaviour. Symbols and signs are used to facilitate communication, and in particular, the expression and the transmission of values.[2]

Economists have emphasized the importance of values and symbols in their study of the interrelations between culture and economic performance. Arrow (1974:23) has proposed that values such as trust, loyalty, and truth are

I wish to thank Partha Dasgupta for encouraging me to undertake this project, and Julie Anderson for insightful discussions concerning the role of cultural and social factors in the economic sphere. Raquel Fernandez, George J. Mailath, Douglass C. North, Ugo Pagano, Hilton L. Root, Jeroen Swinkels, Peter Temin, Barry Weingast, and Gavin Wright provided me with most helpful comments. Ben Wright rendered beneficial research assistance. This study was supported by a grant from the National Science Foundation. The usual caveat applies.

[1] For a definition and analysis of common resources in general, see Dasgupta (1982). On culture and institutions as public goods, see David (1990); Binger and Hoffman (1989).

[2] See, for example, Shapira (1983), 23–5; Davis (1949), esp. 52 ff. Hofstede (1980), 19, defines values as 'a broad tendency to prefer certain states of affairs over others'. An anthropological definition is 'culture consists of patterned ways of thinking, feeling and reacting, acquired and transmitted mainly by symbols, constituting the distinctive achievements of human groups, including their embodiments in artifacts; the essential core of culture consists of traditional (i.e. historically derived and selected) ideas and especially their attached values.' Kluckhohn (1951) cited by Hofstede (1980), 25.

'commodities . . . [which] increase the efficiency of the [economic] system'. Similarly, North (1981; 1990) has emphasized the roles of 'ideology' and 'informal constraints' in reducing transaction costs and directing economic behaviour.[3] Social scientists have also emphasized the importance of symbols and signs such as the language, and other means of co-ordination such as conventions, in achieving the co-ordination required to increase efficiency.[4]

This chapter points to the importance of cultural beliefs as a common resource that affects the social and organizational development of societies and hence economic performance. More specifically, it emphasizes the importance of a specific subset of cultural beliefs that will be referred to as *behavioural beliefs*. Behavioural beliefs are cultural beliefs concerning actions that will be taken by individuals in situations that will never occur. More precisely, behavioural beliefs are the expectations that members of the society have with respect to actions that will be taken off the path of play, and these expectations, as a cultural element, are common knowledge. Game theorists have long pointed to the possible importance of the off-the-path-of-play portion of the equilibrium strategy combinations in affecting the outcome of a given game. This paper points to the importance of behavioural beliefs that were crystallized with respect to a game on the social and organizational structures of society, and the equilibrium selection process when the game itself is changing exogenously and endogenously.

To demonstrate the importance of behavioural beliefs, this paper provides theoretical and historical studies. The theoretical study demonstrates the possibility of a relationship between behavioural beliefs and the emergence of divergent trajectories of social systems and economic organizations. The model is constructed in a way that enables comparison of its results with available historical evidence from the Muslim and Latin societies of the late Medieval period. The combined theoretical and historical analysis indicates the possible importance of behavioural beliefs as a common resource that actually contributed to diverse developments in these two societies.

---

[3] Values, in these works, are viewed as an end for their own sake, i.e., values shape utility functions. For an application of this view in economics, see Akerlof (1986) and Stewart (1990). In these works values function as a 'first-party enforcer'. On the role of 'revenge' as a tie-breaker, see Nalebuff and Shubik (1988). For experimental results concerning the importance of values, see Dawes and Thaler (1988); Hoffman and Spitzer (1985); Hoffman, McCabe, and Smith (1991). See also Hirshleifer (1985) and Opp (1985). It should be noted that some economists hold a different approach to values, influenced by works of behavioural biologists such as Wilson (1975) and Dawkins (1976). According to this approach, values are a means to achieve material rewards rather than an end in themselves: see, for example, Frank (1987). It should also be noted that I make a distinction between the interrelated, but distinct notions in sociology of cultural and social structures. Some of the works cited above touch on both issues at the same time. For works by economists in this vein, see Kandori (1989); Schotter (1981); Ullmann-Margalit (1977). On the evolution of social norms see Ellickson (1989) and Elster (1988; 1989).

[4] On culture as a co-ordinator, see Kreps (1990b); on conventions, see Lewis (1969); Sugden (1986, 1989).

In particular, the paper indicates the probable impacts and origins of specific behavioural beliefs on the development of individualism and unique institutional frameworks in Medieval Europe, a development that social psychologists and economic historians have pointed to. Social psychologists, in their study of cultural systems, have pointed out that the world's societies are divided into two main cultural groups; the individualist group and the collectivist group. In societies characterized by collectivism, a person's loyalty to a group, such as a family or tribe, overrides personal goals. Further, collectivist societies are relatively 'segregated' in the sense that many economic transactions are conducted within groups, including the supply of public goods and social services, such as insurance and health care. At the same time, collectivist societies are characterized by competitiveness and non-cooperation among members of different groups. Within each group, however, contract enforcement tends to be achieved through 'informal' institutions. In contrast, in societies characterized by individualism, personal goals take priority over a person's allegiance to groups and these societies are more 'integrated' in the sense that many transactions occur among individuals from different groups and individuals shift from one group to another frequently while public goods are supplied by impersonal institutions. Contract enforcement in these societies tends to be achieved through institutions that specialize in enforcement, from the court to the credit bureau.[5]

Studies conducted by social psychologists have indicated that the more affluent societies tend to be more individualist. Indeed, the Western world which had 'grown rich' relatively early was found to be the main individualist contemporary society.[6] While social psychologists have taken the economic growth of the Western world as exogenous, economic historians attempt to account for its rise. Some have advanced the view that the West's unique institutions, particularly during the period prior to the Industrial Revolution of the eighteenth century, accounted for much of this growth. A sequential development of increasingly sophisticated organizations enabled specialization, exchange, and reduction in transaction costs that led to economic growth and prosperity.[7]

These two complementary lines of research in social psychology and economic history suggest that the unique Western organizational structure played a key role in leading to its affluence, which in turn gave rise to the

[5] Triandis (1990), 47 defines collectivism to be 'subordination of individual goals to group goals, achievement aimed at improving the position of the ingroup'; while individualism is defined to be 'primacy of individual goals; achievement benefits primarily the individual'. See also Triandis, McCusker, and Hui (1990); Bellah, *et al.* (1985). Clearly, any society has some element of individualism and some element of collectivism. Thus, the distinction between collectivist and individualist societies is a matter of the relative importance of these factors: see, for example, Bellah, *et al.* (1985); Reynolds and Norman (1988); Triandis (1990).

[6] See the discussion in Triandis, McCusker, and Hui (1990); Triandis (1990).

[7] North and Thomas (1973); North (1981; 1987; 1991); Rosenberg and Birdzell (1986). For a formal investigation of the relationships between growth and incentive constraints, see Marimon (1988).

individualist character of its culture and institutions. Indeed, with the exception of Macfarlane (1978), who attributed the unique economic growth of England to an early rise of individualism, acceptance of this line of causation has implicitly or explicitly prevailed in the studies of social psychologists, economic historians, and historians who viewed Medieval Europe as a 'traditional' society.[8] This account, however, fails to address some interesting questions. If institutions are all that is required to reach economic prosperity, why did only the Western societies grow rich? Was Western individualism a result of affluence or was individualism a factor that led to unique economic organizations and affluence? If individualism was a cause rather than a consequence of affluence, what are the origins of Western individualism? How does individualism direct the evolution of economic institutions? Can we infer from the observed pattern of developing countries anything about the historical pattern of the West? This paper is aimed at demonstrating the importance of behavioural beliefs by addressing the above questions. The theoretical model, while general in nature, facilitates conducting a specific historical study that relates behavioural beliefs to the observed dichotomy in social structures and organizations in Europe and in the Muslim world, and traces the origins of the distinct behavioural beliefs in the diverse processes of city amalgamation and commercial expansion.

BEHAVIOURAL BELIEFS AND THE ONE-SIDED PRISONERS' DILEMMA GAME

Behavioural Beliefs

Culture provides individuals with a view of the world that affects their behaviour. Cultural beliefs, as a part of this view, have a direct bearing on the study of the economic and social organization of a society. Weber (1958), for example, advanced the hypothesis that it was a specific change in religious beliefs that led to the rise of capitalism in the Western world. Changing religious attitudes in certain protestant groups altered their perceptions concerning the meaning of material success in terms of reward in the next world. This change motivated members of these groups to adopt the patterns of behaviour that led to the rise of capitalism. Hence, cultural beliefs concerning outcomes in a situation that are never actually observed, namely after one's death, had a profound impact on the development of the economy and society over time. Cultural beliefs concerning the relationship between God and

---

[8] See discussion in Triandis (1990); Macfarlane (1978). More generally, economic historians and economic anthropologists have accepted as their working hypothesis that the Western historical experience can instruct us as to the development process that awaits the less developed economies, while the experience of less developed societies is instructive in understanding the historical experience of Europe. This approach is not surprising remembering the strong influence of Darwinism on economics. See, for example, Dalton (1971); Polanyi (1957); Polanyi, Arensberg, and Pearson (1957).

individuals, however, are not the only sub-set of cultural beliefs that affect behaviour, and this paper examines the implications of another sub-set of cultural beliefs.

Within a society, in particular in the economic sphere, individuals are constantly interacting with each other and the outcomes and nature of these interactions are affected by the expectations that each individual has with respect to actions that will be taken by others in different contingencies. These expectations are a sub-set of cultural beliefs that will be referred to in this paper as 'behavioural beliefs'. Behavioural beliefs affect behaviour directly and indirectly. They affect behaviour directly when members of a society interact with others from their own society or from other societies who hold the same or different behavioural beliefs. Behavioural beliefs impact on behaviour indirectly, as they provide the foundation for social structures and institutions that constrain and channel behaviour in economic and social interactions. The particular structure and functioning of these institutions and social structures feed back the particular behavioural beliefs that led to their development.[9]

Individuals embody the behavioural beliefs of their society; they hold them, they expect others to hold them, and they expect others to expect them to hold them, and so forth. In other words, within a society, behavioural beliefs are common knowledge. Behavioural beliefs become common knowledge through the same process of socialization by which individuals absorb all aspects of their society's culture.[10] Through this socialization process individuals develop expectations not only concerning behaviour in situations that they will encounter during their lifetime, but also with respect to behaviour in situations that will never occur.

The importance of behavioural beliefs—of the expectations that individuals hold with respect to actions that will be taken by others—in directing economic behaviour and trajectories of organizational and social structures is intuitive. Yet formal elaboration of the relationships between behavioural beliefs, economic organizations, and social structures is subtle. How can one examine the nature and the implications of behavioural beliefs with respect to situations that never transpire? What are the sources of behavioural beliefs? After all, by arbitrarily defining behavioural beliefs one can generate a variety of phenomena. Should behavioural beliefs be considered as rational? How do behavioural beliefs change? What exactly are the relationships between behavioural beliefs and organizational and social structures?

To facilitate formal examination of behavioural beliefs, their origins and implications, this paper restricts its attention to specific behavioural beliefs.

---

[9] For a general discussion concerning the relations between culture and institutions, see, for example, Hofstede (1980), 26; Triandis, et al. (1990). See also Stewart (1989), who elaborated on the relationships between institutions and values in the context of the market for human blood.

[10] See Cavalli-Sforza and Feldman (1981); Bandura (1977); Witt (1986), 254; Shapira (1983), 63 ff.; Davis (1949), 195 ff.

It focuses on behavioural beliefs that one has with respect to actions that will be taken by others in situations that never actually occur. More precisely, the origin of behavioural beliefs is expectations concerning the off-the-path-of-play portion of the strategy combination that generates the observed path of play in specific recurrent strategic interactions. Hence, the behavioural beliefs of an individual which are associated with a particular path of play make up a probability distribution over all the strategy combinations that generate that same path of play.[11]

Restricting attention to this set of cultural beliefs emphasizes their essence as ideas and thoughts common to several individuals that cannot be proven empirically. Further, this specification enables capture of the implications of diverse behavioural beliefs as opposed to the implications of diverse behaviours.[12] While associating behavioural beliefs with a particular path of play enables analytical examination, it still maintains the notion of behavioural beliefs as embodied in individuals, not games. The behavioural beliefs that were formed within a society at some point in time as a reflection of an equilibrium in a specific game become a cultural trait whose implications are far beyond that of affecting the original game. Focusing on this set of behavioural beliefs enables their rigorous and consistent analysis by requiring that behavioural beliefs and the path of play constitute an equilibrium. Furthermore, this specification enables the examination of the processes that led to the embodiment of specific behavioural beliefs, their implications, and the process through which behavioural beliefs change.

[11] To be certain that I have made clear the notion of behavioural beliefs that will be examined, it is restated below formally for the case of a finite perfect information repeated game in which only pure strategies are feasible. Denote by S the set of strategy combinations, by S_i the strategy set of player i, and by P a path of the play. Define $S(P)$ to be the set of all strategy combinations for which the path of play is P. Note that the difference between two elements in $S(P)$ is only in the off-the-path-of-play elements. Denote by $CB_i(P)$ a probability distribution of player i over $S(P)$. Since in each element of $S(P)$ the path of play is identical, the informative content of this probability distribution is about player i's expectation concerning the off-the-path-of-play portions of the strategy combinations.

The players' choices of strategies should be consistent with their behavioural beliefs. Thus,

$$s^*(P) \in S(P), \text{and } CB_i(P) \qquad \forall i$$

is an equilibrium, if and only if

$$U_i[s_i^*(P), CB_i(P)] \geq U_i[s_i, CB_i(P)] \qquad \forall i \text{ and } \forall s_i \in S_i,$$

where U_i is the appropriate utility function.

When all the players have the same behavioural beliefs and this fact is common knowledge, then if $s^*(P)$ is an equilibrium, the behavioural beliefs associated with it are all of the form

$$\text{Prob } [s^*(P)] = 1.$$

In such case, $s^*(P) \in S(P), CB(P)$ is an equilibrium, if and only if

$$U_i[s_i^*(P), CB(P)] \geq U_i[s_i, CB(P)] \qquad \forall i \text{ and } \forall s_i \in S_i.$$

[12] The implication of diverse previous behaviour on the process of equilibrium selection when individuals confront, over time, a sequence of games is examined in the literature about 'convention'. The seminal work in this area is that of Lewis (1969). See also Sugden (1986; 1989).

The conceptual distinction between behavioural beliefs and equilibrium strategies is important, since behavioural beliefs have qualities and implications that equilibrium strategies do not. Equilibrium strategies are defined with respect to a specific game, while behavioural beliefs are a quality of individuals, members of a particular society. Behavioural beliefs that were crystallized in a society at some point in time with respect to a specific game, constitute a cultural ingredient that co-ordinates expectations in games other than the original game and affects the endogenous development of organizational and social structures. Equilibrium strategy combination is a quality of a game which can be thought of as a reflection of the player's rational calculation in a specific strategic interaction. Behavioural beliefs form an individual quality which is developed in association with a specific game and then influence people's expectations concerning behaviour in other situations and impact the evolution of social structures and organizations. In other words, in game theory either each game is examined in isolation or the game is held fixed while the population, in terms of its strategy, changes. In the study of behavioural beliefs, the behavioural beliefs are held fixed while the game itself is changing exogenously and endogenously. The justification for holding behavioural beliefs fixed is based on sociology, while the justification for examining exogenous and endogenous changes in games is based on history.

Behavioural beliefs that were crystallized in a society at some point in time with respect to a specific game influence behaviour in other situations due to two interrelated factors. The first is the role of behavioural beliefs as a co-ordinator of expectations. That is, using the terminology of Schelling (1960), behavioural beliefs provide focal points. The second factor is the tendency of human beings to feel that culturally acquired patterns *ought* to be followed.[13] Thus, when members of a society encounter a new strategic interaction that 'resembles' in a culturally determined fashion a situation with respect to which they do have well-defined behavioural beliefs, they tend to feel that others ought to follow the specific course of action delineated by their behavioural beliefs (although the actions themselves are never taken). The behavioural beliefs that were crystallized in one situation are projected into another and influence behaviour in the new strategic situations.[14]

Encountering new strategic situations is, to a large extent, the essence of history, since the economic, social, and political opportunities available to members of societies constantly change. Changes in the rules of the game are a part of the historical process, and crucial turning-points in the cultural and institutional fabric of societies are, in many cases, a response to

[13] This observation is elaborated in Davis (1949), 52. See also Sugden (1989), 95, who also cites David Hume (1740), Bk. 3, pt. 2, sects. 1–3.

[14] Schelling (1960) has elaborated on the idea that culture is important in the process of equilibrium selection in multiple equilibrium games. Lewis (1969) in his study of 'conventions' pointed to the importance of past behaviour in providing a focal point.

them.[15] Some of these changes are exogenous to a given society, while others are endogenous, as members of the society attempt to improve their lot by establishing organizations which amount to changes in the rules of the game.

Conceptualizing behavioural beliefs as a probability distribution over the off-the-path-of-play portion of an equilibrium strategy combination enables the study of changes in behavioural beliefs. Projection from one game to another will not necessarily lead to an equilibrium. Motivated to act differently, individuals will, through time, change their behaviour. If this behavioural change is inconsistent with their behavioural beliefs, these will adjust accordingly. While behavioural beliefs provide individuals with initial expectations to be used to assess the behaviour of others in the new situation, the behaviour itself and the associated behavioural beliefs may change over time to generate a new equilibrium.[16] This interplay between culturally acquired expectations concerning behaviour and actual behaviour is captured in the words of the eminent sociologist Davis (1949). He argued that

in human society there is what may be called double reality—on the one hand a normative order embodying what *ought* to be, and on the other a factual order embodying what *is*. In the nature of the case these two orders cannot be completely identical, nor can they be completely disparate. The normative order acts, for example, as a determinant (though not the only determinant) of the factual order . . . . In turn, the factual order exercises an influence on the normative system, for the norms must always refer to events in the real world and take into account the factual situation. . . . The normative system, since it aims to achieve results in the factual world, is subject to constant modification by events in that world. (Davis, 1949: 52–3).

The specification of behavioural beliefs suggested in this paper provides a framework to analyse the impact of this sub-set of cultural beliefs on the evolution of behaviour, values, social structures, and organizations. Once a society faces a change in a specific game, or when members of one society encounter members of another society, their behavioural beliefs provide them with the initial mechanism for equilibrium selection. Behavioural beliefs, however, also affect the development of organizations in society, as organizations are endogenous modifications in the rules of the game. The specific behavioural beliefs associated with a game motivate the implementation of specific organizational changes, as well as the equilibrium selected in the modified game.

Behavioural beliefs also affect social structures within a society. Social structures, roughly speaking, contain norms (what to do), roles (with respect

15 A famous example of the relationships between exogenous change in the rules of the game and changes in the cultural and institutional fabric of a society, is the account given by Adam Smith on the decline of feudalism as a response to the exposure to long-distance trade.

16 This process need not converge to an equilibrium. See references to relevant 'dynamic stability' literature and results concerning supermodular games in Milgrom and Roberts (1990). The issue of dynamic stability is not important in the example elaborated below and hence will not be dealt with.

to whom) and statuses (who is who).[17] Behavioural beliefs associated with a specific game affect patterns of interactions among individuals and therefore give rise to norms, roles, and statuses not directly related to the original game. The sociologist Homans (1950) elaborated on the positive reinforcement between patterns of interactions and the emergence of social structures. He pointed out that the amount of (economic) activity carried out by individuals determines their level of social interaction, the intensity of the interactions, and the level of friendliness among them. In other words, when behavioural beliefs lead to a specific pattern of (economic) activity among individuals, this supports the creation of social structure. Clearly, a social structure that depends on specific behavioural beliefs may also change when the underlying behavioural beliefs change.[18] Behavioural beliefs provide social structures with their vitality.

Finally, by inducing particular patterns of behaviour, social and organizational structures, behavioural beliefs also impact on the development of a value-system. Diverse behavioural beliefs without any normative value induce different behaviours, each of which leads to the development of distinct value-systems as individuals attempt to find moral justification for their behaviour.[19] This conjecture concerning the line of causality—from behavioural beliefs, to behaviour, to value-system—finds support in the view of social psychologists that value-systems associated with collectivist and individualist societies develop as a response to the economic organization of the society. Simple hunting societies are (proto-)individualist; complex agricultural societies are collectivist; modern industrial and information societies are (neo-)individualist. This cycle reflects the development of the economic and political systems which lead to the transformation of values.[20]

Individualist and Collectivist Behavioural Beliefs in a One-Sided Prisoners' Dilemma Game

To demonstrate the importance of behavioural beliefs this paper examines the 'One-Sided Prisoners' Dilemma' game (OSPD). The main ingredients of

[17] More formally, norms are behavioural instructions. Status is the identification of an individual relative to norms. Roles are the expected behaviour of one status-bearer to another. Continuity in social structure requires that the individuals share subjective recognition of their belonging to the structure; they share solidarity feelings; in certain cases their behaviour towards each other differs from their behaviour towards non-members; they share some cultural heritage, like values, beliefs, common history, etc. See Shapira (1983), 75 ff.; Abercrombie and Hill (1984), 97–8.

[18] For a game-theoretical analysis of the relations between social norms and equilibrium in random matching games, see Kandori (1989); Okuno-Fujiwara and Postlewaite (1990). These papers aim to illustrate how a specific equilibrium can be sustained through social norms. The analysis in this chapter shows how a specific equilibrium leads to the emergence of a specific social structure.

[19] See, for example, Davis (1949), 52; Scott (1987), 16; Homans (1950). This view of culture as a 'legitimizing' mechanism is basic in the analyses of Marx and Durkheim.

[20] Triandis (1990), 72; Hofstede (1980), chs. 1, 5, and pp. 26–7, 359–61; Triandis, et al. (1990).

the OSPD game are the commitment problem and the ability of one set of players to initiate interaction with another set of players. The OSPD game captures the essence of the organizational problem associated with several economic transactions which are of importance in contemporary and past economies, such as labour relations and the supply of experience goods.[21] Thus, conclusions based on the analysis of this game are rather general in nature.

The OSPD game is a game played in an economy in which there are P principals and A agents, each of whom lives for an infinite number of periods. Further, we assume that $P > A$, and that agents have a time discount factor β. In each period a principal can hire an agent, and each agent can be hired by only one principal. Once a principal has hired a particular agent he can continue to employ him until the principal decides to terminate the relationship or until there is a forced separation between them, an event that can occur at the end of each period in probability σ. (The forced separation captures the limited ability of principals to commit themselves to rehire agents.) When such a forced separation occurs, or when a principal terminates his relationship with the agent he employed in the last period, he can hire an agent from the pool of unemployed agents. An unemployed agent receives a pay-off of ϕ_u (his reservation utility); a principal who chooses not to employ an agent receives a pay-off of 0. When hiring an agent, a principal offers him a wage $W \geq 0$, and the employed agent can then decide whether to be honest or to cheat.[22] If he is honest, the principal's pay-off is $\gamma - W$, and the agent's pay-off is W. If the agent cheats, however, his pay-off is α and the principal's pay-off is $-\delta$. It is assumed that $\alpha > \gamma > 0, -\delta + \alpha < \gamma, \phi_u < \gamma$, and that the history of the game is common knowledge.

In this game, it is socially optimal for each principal to employ an agent every period and for the agent to be honest.[23] However, when this game is played only once, the only Nash equilibrium (NE) is such that principals never hire agents and agents cheat. This is the only NE, since the best an employed agent can do is to cheat. Anticipating this behaviour, the best a principal can do is not to hire an agent. Members of this society cannot benefit from co-operation since agents do not have a way to commit themselves, *ex ante*, to be honest *ex post*. When the game is repeated infinitely, however, there are many Nash equilibria and Sub Game Perfect Equilibria (SGPE) in which co-operation can be sustained. The common element of these equilibria is that a principal makes future employment conditional on past conduct, and ensures that honesty is the best response of the agent by offering him a wage

---

[21] On relevant labour relations, see Shapiro and Stiglitz (1984), and Akerlof and Yellen (1986). On experience goods, see, for example, Klein and Leffler (1981); Rogerson (1983; 1987).

[22] The principal's offer, W, is credible, since the nature of the game is such that either the agent can determine the *ex post* allocation of the gains or the offer is legally enforceable.

[23] The analysis below holds also when cheating implies transfer and not efficiency loss. That is, when $-\delta + \alpha = \gamma$.

high enough so that the present value of the lifetime expected utility of an honest agent is higher than the present value of the lifetime expected utility of an agent who cheats and looks for alternative employment. Thus, to gain the benefits of future employment, an agent is honest in the present. In a sense, a future stream of income provides the bond required to enable the agent to commit himself, *ex ante*, to be honest, *ex post*. This mechanism to induce co-operation is usually referred to as the reputation mechanism.[24]

Within the equilibrium set of this repeated game, there is a sub-set in which agents do not base their actions on the history of the game. Proposition 1, below, illustrates how co-operation can be sustained through a reputation mechanism in these equilibria, and presents the factors that determine the magnitude of the wage, W, required to keep agents honest. Before turning to proposition 1, however, some additional notation is required. An unemployed agent who was honest in the last period he was employed will be referred to as an honest agent, while an agent who cheated in the last period he was employed will be referred to as a cheater. Unemployed cheaters and honest agents have some probability of being hired by a principal. We denote by h_h the probability that an unemployed honest agent will be hired, and by h_c the probability that an unemployed cheater will be hired.

The exact relations between the principals' strategies, h_h and h_c are analysed below. For the moment, however, it is assumed that each principal's strategy calls for not rehiring an agent who cheated him in the last period, and rehiring the same agent if he was honest (unless forced separation occurs). If cheating or forced separation does occur, the principal will choose (randomly) an agent from among the unemployed agents.[25] This specification facilitates the exposure of the differences between two equilibria that will be presented in proposition 2. Taking the parameters of the model and the principals' strategies as given, proposition 1 specifies the conditions under which a wage W^* can support co-operation:

Proposition 1

> For any α, σ, β, ϕ_u, h_c, h_h, there is W^*, which is the lowest wage for which it is an agent's best response to play honest if hired. Further, there is a function w, s.t. $W^* = w(\alpha, \sigma, \beta, \phi_u, h_h, h_c)$ and w is a decreasing function of h_h, and β, and an increasing function of h_c, σ, ϕ_u, and α.[26]

[24] On the concept of reputation in economic theory, see the discussion in Kreps (1990*a*).

[25] In other words, a principal fires an agent who cheated him and then regards him as any other agent who is in the 'pool' of unemployed agents. (This is analytically equivalent to the case in which the principal fires an agent who cheated him and never rehires him, but the number of principals who hire agents every period is large on the equilibrium path: see the discussion below.)

[26] It is assumed that $\beta \neq 0$, $h_c < 1$.

For ease of presentation it is assumed here and in the following proofs that $\phi_u = 0$. From the Optimality Principle of Dynamic Programming, to show that playing honest is optimal for the agent, it is sufficient to show that he cannot gain from playing cheat one period if offered W^*. Accordingly, let us denote by V_h the present value of lifetime expected utility of an employed agent who, whenever hired, plays honestly. Denote by V_h^u the present value of the lifetime expected utility of an unemployed honest agent. Denote by V_c^u the lifetime expected utility of an unemployed cheater (who will be playing honestly in the future if hired).

These lifetime expected utilities are:

$$V_h = W^* + \beta[(1 - \sigma)V_h + \sigma V_h^u]$$
$$V_h^u = h_h V_h + \beta(1 - h_h)V_h^u$$
$$V_c^u = h_c V_h + \beta(1 - h_c)V_c^u.$$

Rearrangement yields:

$$V_h = W^*/(\Sigma - \sigma\beta H_h), \qquad V_h^u = H_h V_h, V_c^u = H_c V_h$$

where

$$\Sigma = 1 - \beta(1 - \sigma),$$
$$H_i = h_i/[1 - \beta(1 - h_i)] \qquad i = h, c.$$

Based on these expressions the profitability of cheating can be examined. Consider an employed agent. Playing honestly forever yields V_h as the present value of lifetime expected utility. Cheating once, however, yields $\alpha + \beta V_c^u$ as the present value of his lifetime expected utility. (In the current period he receives α and the present value of the lifetime expected utility from the next period on is βV_c^u). Thus, an agent will not cheat if $V_h \geq \alpha + \beta V_c^u$. Substituting and rearranging yields that the agent will be honest for any

$$W \geq \alpha(\Sigma - \sigma\beta H_h)/(1 - \beta H_c) = W^*.$$

Thus, only when offered at least W^* is it an agent's best response to play honestly if hired. The above expression for W^* implicitly defines the function w whose properties can be easily derived.

The intuition behind proposition 1 is familiar to the student of repeated games and efficient wage theory. A principal motivates his agent to be honest by the carrot of a wage high enough and the stick of not rehiring him if he cheats. For a wage to be sufficiently high, the difference between the present value of the lifetime expected utility of an unemployed and employed agent is higher than what can be gained by one period-play of cheating. Thus, the best response of the agent is to be honest if hired. Proposition 1 specifies the minimum wage for which this difference is large enough to induce honesty. The intuition behind the relations between the parameters and W^* as captured by the function w is straightforward. For example, each element that increases the present value of the lifetime expected utility of a cheater (e.g. h_c) increases the wage that has to be paid to keep the agent honest.

Proposition 1 examines the minimum wage that can induce honesty without explicitly examining the principals' strategies which determine h_h and h_c. Two strategy combinations are of interest here, each of which incorporates the principals' behaviour assumed in proposition 1. The difference between these strategies captures an essential ingredient in the difference between collectivist and individualist societies. The individualist strategy combination specifies that the principal offers W^* to an unemployed agent, operates through that agent as long as he does not cheat him, and hires an agent from the pool of unemployed agents if his agent cheated him in the previous period, or a forced separation occurred.[27] (Each agent's strategy is to play honest if he is offered at least W^*, and to cheat otherwise.) This strategy is individualist, or 'anonymous', in the sense that a principal does not take into account whether the agent he is hiring has cheated any principal before. As proposition 2 clarifies, the principal does not take into account the agent's past behaviour, not because he necessarily does not know about it, but because he believes that other principals will ignore this fact and thus that the best he can do is to ignore it as well. Unemployed agents face the same hiring opportunities, independent of their past behaviour. The collectivist strategy combination differs from the individualist type precisely in this last respect. It specifies that a principal offers the appropriate W^*, but hires only agents who have never been cheaters before; the rest of the principal's strategy and the agents' strategy is identical to the individualist strategy. This strategy combination is collectivist in the sense that when a principal makes a hiring decision he takes into account the history of the agent with all previous principals. Proposition 2 establishes that each of these strategy combinations is a sub-game perfect equilibrium.

Proposition 2

> The individualist strategy and the collectivist strategy combinations are each a symmetric sub-game perfect equilibrium (SGPE) of the OSPD game.[28]

To prove this proposition it again suffices to show that neither a principal nor an agent can benefit from deviating once. Since under both strategy combinations a principal's strategy is in accordance with the strategy assumed in proposition 1, its result holds. Thus, given W^*, an agent does not gain from one period-play of cheating when he is supposed to play honestly. On the other hand, if offered less than W^* an agent's best response is to cheat. Thus, when offered W^*, agents cannot gain from deviating.

[27] The individualist strategy can be modified to call for a principal never to rehire an agent who cheated him without leading to changes in the results.

[28] It is assumed that under both strategy combinations $\gamma \geq W^*$, principals have non-negative gains from co-operation.

It is also clear that under both strategies it is optimal for a principal to offer W^*, since offering less induces cheating and offering more reduces his pay-off, $\gamma - W^*$. This is also the reason why a principal cannot punish an agent who cheated by lowering his wage, since this will ensure further cheating. Thus, each principal finds it optimal to fire a cheater.[29] To validate that the individualist and collectivist strategy combinations are equilibria, all that has to be verified is that it is optimal for a principal to follow the hiring procedure specified by his strategy.

Consider the individualist strategy first. Let us denote the probability that an unemployed cheater will be hired by h_c^i and the probability that an honest agent will be hired by h_h^i. These probabilities are determined by the principals' individualistic strategies, and thus are equal. Assuming that each unemployed agent has an equal probability of being hired, this probability equals along the equilibrium path the expected number of agents who will be hired in each period, divided by the expected total number of unemployed agents:

$$h_c^i = h_h^i = \sigma P / [A - (1 - \sigma)P].$$

Thus, the wage W^*, which is required to keep an unemployed agent, whether honest or a cheat, is identical. A principal is then indifferent to hiring an unemployed cheat or an unemployed honest agent.[30] Thus, the individualist strategy is optimal for the principal, and the individualist strategy combination is SGPE.

Consider now the collectivist strategy combination. We denote the probability that an unemployed cheater will be hired under this strategy by h_c^c and the probability that an honest agent will be hired by h_h^c. These probabilities are not identical under the collectivist strategy. In particular, h_c^c equals zero, since an agent who has ever been guilty of cheating will never be rehired, but h_h^c is equal along the equilibrium path $\sigma P / [A - (1 - \sigma)P] > 0$, since an agent who has always been honest will be hired in the future. These different probabilities generate a gap between the wage required to support co-operation with an honest agent and with a cheat.

[29] Since the model is a perfect information model, the principal does not increase his pay-off by hiring another agent, since the same wage is required to keep an agent honest. Accordingly, a principal's firing of an agent who has cheated him can be justified along the line proposed by Nalebuff and Shubik (1988), who proposed that when a player is 'indifferent' about his pay-off, 'revenge' may be used to break ties. When A is 'much' bigger than P, the analysis holds when a principal never hires an agent who has cheated him before. Alternatively, the agent's strategy can call for cheating in each period after which he cheated a principal and was not fired. The principal's best response is to fire an agent who has cheated him.

[30] While this indifference is sufficient to show that the individualist strategy combination is SGPE, it should be emphasized that the results of proposition 2 hold even if it is assumed that each principal, while hiring an unemployed agent, has some reason to prefer a particular agent over any other. That is, assuming that the co-operation between a particular principal and a particular agent yields $\gamma + \theta$. The principal then strictly prefers to hire the agent under individualist equilibrium even if the agent cheated in the past for any θ. Under collectivist equilibrium, however, there is always θ small enough so that the principal strictly prefers not to hire a cheater.

According to proposition 1, the wage required to support co-operation with a cheat is:

$$W^*_c = w(., h^c_h = 0, h^c_c = 0),$$

while the wage required to support co-operation with an honest agent is:

$$W^*_h = w(., h^c_h > 0, h^c_c = 0),$$

since the function w decreases in h_h, $W^*_c > W^*_h$. Hence a principal strictly prefers to hire an agent who has always been honest rather than an agent who has cheated. In other words, it is not profitable for the principal to deviate and to hire an agent who has cheated.[31]

Proposition 2 establishes that both individualist and collectivist strategy combinations are equilibria in which agents are hired and cheating never occurs. In these equilibria an employed agent is deterred from cheating by receiving a wage that makes the present value of the lifetime expected utility of an honest agent higher than that of a cheat. The fundamental difference between these equilibria is in the associated behavioural beliefs, that is, in what is expected to happen if an agent cheats. *Individualist behavioural beliefs*, the behavioural beliefs associated with an individualist equilibrium, imply that a principal would cease to operate through an agent who had cheated him, but that other principals will not cease to operate through him. Whatever transpired between a principal and an agent is not of interest to the principals' community at large. These behavioural beliefs are self-fulfilling in the sense that if each principal expects other principals to rehire a cheat he does not have any incentive not to rehire him, since the wage required to keep this agent honest is the same as that required to keep any other agent honest, assuming that the game is a perfect information game and the mere fact that an agent cheated in the past does not convey any information concerning future behaviour.

Collectivist behavioural beliefs, the behavioural beliefs associated with a collectivist equilibrium, differ from those associated with an individualist equilibrium. Under a collectivist equilibrium, it is believed that a principal would cease to operate through an agent who had cheated him, and from that period on none of the principals would rehire this agent. These behavioural beliefs are self-fulfilling in the sense that if a principal expects other principals not to rehire the agent, he would not hire the agent either, despite the fact that cheating in the past does not convey any relevant information about future behaviour. A principal will not hire an agent who has cheated in the past because he expects other principals not to rehire that agent, and

---

[31] Note that for this proof one does not have to assume that the history of the game is known. A weaker assumption, that members of the society can recognize the difference between agents who have never cheated and those who have, is sufficient. On the importance of 'social labels' of this sort in random matching games, see Kandori (1989); Okuno-Fujiwara and Postlewaite (1990).

consequently the wage required to keep this agent honest is higher than the wage required to keep an agent who did not cheat in the past honest. It is the relationship between the principal's gain from hiring an agent and the agent's expected future relations with other principals that makes the collectivist punishment self-enforceable. Principals follow the collectivist strategy despite the fact that the agent's strategy does not call for cheating any principal who violated the collective punishment, and despite the fact that principals do not 'punish' any principal who violated the collective punishment. It is the link between a principal's gain from employing a specific agent and the expected future relations between that agent and other principals that motivates principals to follow the collectivist strategy.[32]

Under collectivist and individualist equilibria, co-operation is achieved, and therefore the actions taken by the players are the same: principals randomly hire an unemployed agent, and employed agents never cheat. From the efficiency point of view, these two equilibria are the same, since each of them is Pareto-optimal. The fundamental difference between them is in the distinct behavioural beliefs on which they rest, or in the different behavioural beliefs to which they give rise. In each equilibrium cheating never occurs, yet, in each equilibrium principals and agents have different beliefs about what the reaction to cheating will be, although cheating never happens.

The discussion of collectivist and individualist equilibria illustrates the trivial result that equilibria with identical efficiency properties and identical actions may lead to different behavioural beliefs. In the next sections the implications of these different behavioural beliefs are analysed. Note that while the version of the OSPD analysed above is the simplest one that suffices for this illustration, individualist and collectivist behavioural beliefs can occur in other OSPD models that capture additional aspects of reality. This might happen, for example, in models in which cheating does occur along the equilibrium path, such as models in which an agent's time discount factor is subject to some one-period exogenous shock, in models with imperfect monitoring, in models with imperfect information about the wage paid to a specific agent by a specific principal, and so forth.[33]

However, it is possible to construct an OSPD game in which there are two types of agents, a bad type who always cheats and a good type who never cheats, and in which individualist equilibrium cannot be sustained. After all, it may be that an agent who cheated will never be rehired, since cheating reveals his type. Similarly, in the study of markets for experience goods two equivalent formulations are feasible. Technology may be such that a firm chooses the quality of its products once and for all, or it may be such that a firm can choose the quality of its products in every period. Clearly, each of

---

[32] Note that principals prefer the collectivist over the individualist equilibrium, since in the former the wage paid to an agent is lower than in the latter. The factors that may lead a community of principals to reach an individualist equilibrium are discussed below.

[33] This latter formulation is the one taken by Shapiro and Stiglitz (1984).

these formulations is appropriate in examining different aspects of the same issue.[34] In the study of agency relations it is also the case that each of these alternative formulations—the one-type model and the two-type model—is a priori feasible, and the choice between them should be based upon direct evidence or their ability to explain observed phenomena. In this paper attention is given to the one-type model, since it is capable of generating predictions that can consistently be examined in the light of historical evidence. In other words, without refuting the importance of the two-type model, the one-type model is examined here because it fits better the empirical observations discussed below.

BEHAVIOURAL BELIEFS, SOCIAL STRUCTURE, AND THE HISTORICAL EXPERIENCE OF THE MAGHRIBI AND GENOESE TRADERS

When members of one society share collectivist behavioural beliefs and members of another society share individualist behavioural beliefs the patterns of interactions, that is, the processes of hiring agents in these two societies, are identical as principals hire randomly from the pool of unemployed agents. These societies differ, however, in their behavioural beliefs—in particular, members of each society have different expectations about behaviour off the path of play. This section demonstrates, theoretically and historically, that diverse cultural beliefs have different implications with respect to the social structure of society. Diverse behavioural beliefs impact on the social structure of society at any given point in time. In particular, behavioural beliefs determine the internal structure of the society, whether its social structure is 'horizontal' or 'vertical'. Over time, diverse behavioural beliefs may give rise to one of the main differences between collectivist and individualist societies, a difference relating to the boundaries of a society, to the nature of relations across groups. Social psychologists have noted that collectivist societies tend to be 'segregated' in the sense that while there is a high level of co-operation among groups' members, the relations between individual members of different groups are characterized by competitiveness and non-co-operation. In contrast, individualist societies are more 'integrated' in the sense that there is a high level of co-operation among members of different groups. Accordingly, this section demonstrates that whether two economies, identical in all but their behavioural beliefs, become integrated or segregated is a function of their behavioural beliefs, which affects their response to a given change in the rules of the OSPD game. The specific change in the game that is considered is the ability of principals from one economy to hire agents from another economy. The examination of the implications of behavioural

[34] Compare, for example, Klein and Leffler (1981), and Rogerson (1983).

beliefs on the equilibrium selected after this change, while of importance for its own sake, illustrates the significance of behavioural beliefs and responses to exogenous changes in the rules of the game.

Integrated and Segregated Societies

When a game has a unique equilibrium, following the usual methodology in economics, one may assume that this equilibrium would be reached independent of previous behavioural beliefs. When a game has multiple equilibria, however, behavioural beliefs affect the selection of an equilibrium. The issue of equilibrium selection has attracted the attention of game theorists for a long time. The strength of the Nash equilibrium, the fundamental equilibrium concept in game theory, is that it indicates the strategy combinations that are not likely to be played. Thus, in games with multiple equilibria, any equilibrium, if it were expected by all players, could become a self-fulfilling prophecy by co-ordinating the actions taken by the players leading to the selection of that equilibrium.[35]

While there are mechanisms that can co-ordinate expectations that are not directly related to culture, it has been suggested that, in many important situations, culture plays an important role in surmounting this selection, or co-ordination problem. Schelling (1960) has suggested that in games with multiple equilibria 'focal-point effect' may direct the players to a specific equilibrium. Anything in their cultural heritage that focuses the players' attention on a certain equilibrium may make them expect it and hence play it. Game theorists have usually emphasized the role of values in generating a focal-point effect. Symmetry, status quo, seniority, boundaries, such intrinsic properties of the pay-off vector as equality, and simplicity or stationarity of the strategies are common examples of focal-point effects.[36]

In his study of conventions Lewis (1969), explicitly links previous actions, rather than values, to the endogenous evolution of focal points.[37] He proposes that in recurring co-ordination games with multiple equilibria, the players' experience of general conformity to an action in the past leads them by force of precedent to expect a similar conformity in the future.[38] Expectations of future conformity are a reason to go on conforming, since to conform is to achieve a co-ordination equilibrium and to satisfy one's own preferences. Once such a process gets started, it generates a meta-stable

---

[35] See Myerson (1989) for a general discussion of the Nash equilibrium as a solution concept, and the relationships between NE, focal point, and refinements that will be touched on briefly below.

[36] See, for example, Myerson (1989), Kreps (1990a), 415 specifies the following examples of 'focal principles': equity, uniqueness, geography, alphabetical order.

[37] The idea of 'focal point' is only implicit in his work.

[38] A co-ordination equilibrium in a pure co-ordination game is an equilibrium in which no one would have been better off had any one agent alone acted otherwise. A proper equilibrium is one that all the agents strictly prefer over every other co-ordination equilibrium.

self-perpetuating system of preferences, expectations, and actions capable of persisting indefinitely. This self-perpetuating system of preferences, expectations, and actions is defined by Lewis as a convention.[39]

While values and observed past behaviour are undoubtably influential in forming focal points, behavioural beliefs also impact the equilibrium selected in a game. To illustrate the possible impact of behavioural beliefs on equilibrium selection, a specific change in the OSPD is considered. Suppose that members of two identical economies within which either individualist or collectivist behavioural beliefs are part of their culture, become a joint economy, in the sense that, although players can identify members of their previous economy, principals now have the option of hiring agents from either economy. What will the patterns of hiring agents in the joint economy be? In the joint economy, both individualist and collectivist equilibria are possible for the very same reasons they were possible in each separate economy. Yet, behavioural beliefs may provide a link between the pre-change and the post-change equilibria.

While the existence of such links is intuitive, its exact nature is not easily defined. It is tempting to suppose that a player expects that the behavioural beliefs of the pre-change game will be carried over to the new game. But these behavioural beliefs are ill-defined in the new game, since the path of play of the new game is not specified, and behavioural beliefs are defined with respect to a path of play. Yet, when behavioural beliefs are projected into the new game, that is, when each player expects others to play as they were playing in the pre-interaction economies, the pre-change path of play and behavioural beliefs can then be viewed as initial conditions in some sequence of dynamic adjustment process that leads to a new equilibrium. Accordingly, once two economies become a joint economy, players expect others to retain their previous path of play and behavioural beliefs as crystallized in the separated economies. For example, if each of the separated economies reached a collectivist equilibrium, in the joint economy players believe that each principal would hire agents from his own economy and principals, members of the same economy will retaliate if an agent cheats one of them. Taking this 'initial condition' as given, an individual principal will play his best response.

This specification of 'initial' path of play and behavioural beliefs in the post-change game, however, is incomplete since it does not stipulate a complete strategy for principals. In the post-change game there are off-the-path-of-play situations that were not feasible in the pre-change game. For example, how will principals from one economy react to actions an agent took while employed by a principal from the other economy? The behavioural beliefs that crystallized in the pre-change game do not specify what actions will be taken by the principals in this situation since it was not feasible

---

[39] For an exact definition, see Lewis (1969), 41–3, 58. Sugden (1986, 1989) proposed identifying conventions with evolutionary stable equilibria.

in the pre-change game.[40]Thus, even when the pre-change paths of play constitute the post-change path of play, behavioural beliefs with respect to actions that can be taken after the change off the path of play but were not feasible in the pre-change game, can be any feasible beliefs.

In the OSPD game, however, there is an intuitive limitation on the post-change behavioural beliefs. The focus of the analysis here is whether a principal from one economy will hire an agent from the other economy given the pre-change behavioural beliefs and paths of play. Clearly, inter-economy agency relations will not be established unless the wage required to keep an agent from the other economy honest is not higher than that required to keep an agent from the principal's economy honest. Given the pre-change behavioural beliefs and paths of play, the wage in inter-economy relations is a function only of specific beliefs that were not crystallized in the pre-change game: namely, the beliefs regarding the responses of the principals from the agent's economy to his actions taken while he was employed by a principal from the other economy.[41]While the principals from the agent's economy can respond in many ways, there are two responses that are natural focal points. For any action taken by the agent while employed by a principal from the other economy, the principals from the agent's economy may regard him either as one who cheated one of them, or as one who did not cheat one of them. There is nothing in the pre-change equilibrium, however, that indicates which of these focal points will be selected. Accordingly, the best that can be done analytically is to assume that in the joint economy any belief which is some probability distribution over the two above responses is possible after any action taken by an agent while employed by a principal from the other economy.

To summarize, in the post-change game, each player takes as given the paths of play and the behavioural beliefs that were crystallized in the pre-change game. As for beliefs that relate to principals' responses while an agent is employed by a principal from the other economy, a situation that was not feasible in the pre-change game, players have some beliefs that can be any probability distribution over the responses of principals to actions taken by an agent while employed by a principal from his own economy.[42] Based upon these beliefs the players can derive the probability of future employment after inter-economy agency relations are established. These probabilities can be calculated as follows. Denote the two economies by K and J, and denote by P_s and A_s a principal and an agent from economy s respectively, where

[40] Clearly, the sociological notion of beliefs does not exclude the possibility that members of these economies will have common expectations about actions taken in non-feasible situations. The notion of pre-change behavioural beliefs, however, excludes such a possibility.

[41] Remember that throughout the analysis in this paper it is assumed that principals do not condition actions that may affect a principal's utility on the behaviour of the principal himself. Accordingly, a principal's decision whether to hire an agent from the other economy does not depend on the responses of the principals from that principal's economy.

[42] As noted above, behavioural beliefs are assumed in this paper to be common knowledge. Here it may be understood as common knowledge between the relevant agent and principal.

$s \in \{K, \mathcal{J}\}$. Denote by μ the probability that principals from economy t will consider an A_t last employed by P_s as cheat if he cheated when employed by P_s. Denote by η the probability that principals from economy t will consider an A_t last employed by P_s as a cheat if he played honestly when employed by P_s. For any $\mu \in [0, 1]$ and $\eta \in [0, 1]$, the implications of the corresponding beliefs with respect to future employment of A_t last employed by P_s are the following: $h_c^{s,t}(\mu) = \mu h_c^{t,t} + (1 - \mu)h_h^{t,t}$, is the probability that A_t will be hired if he is a cheat; $h_h^{s,t}(\eta) = \eta h_c^{t,t} + (1 - \eta)h_h^{t,t}$, is the probability that A_t will be hired if he was honest. In the post-change game, the pre-change paths of play and behavioural beliefs and the beliefs with respect to off-the-path-situations that were not feasible in the pre-change game, constitute the initial condition with respect to which players determine their best responses.[43] Under these assumptions, proposition 3 presents the nature of agency relations in a joint economy combined of two identical economies, as a function of the pre-change behavioural beliefs.

Proposition 3

Let us define the joint economy to be 'segregated' if, given the initial conditions, principals from each economy strictly prefer to hire agents from their own economy. Define an economy to be 'integrated' if, given the initial conditions, principals from each economy are indifferent about the original economy of their agent.

> If at least one pre-change economy is collectivist, the joint economy is segregated for any $\mu \in [0, 1)$ and $\eta \in (0, 1]$, and integrated only if $\mu = 1$ and $\eta = 0$. If the two pre-change economies are individualist, the joint economy is integrated for $\mu \in [0, 1]$ and $\eta \in [0, 1]$.[44]

Some additional notation is required for the proof. $W_{s,t}^*$ is the minimum wage that P_s has to provide agent A_t to keep him honest, $s \in \{K, \mathcal{J}\}, t \in \{K, \mathcal{J}\}$. (In what follows the first subscript (superscript) denotes the principal's economy and the second subscript (superscript) denotes the agent's economy). Suppose that an unemployed agent from economy s was last employed by a principal from economy t, and denote by $h_t^{t,s}$ the probability that this agent will be rehired if he took action i when he was last employed, where i is either h for honest or c for cheat.[45]

Assume that the two economies are collectivist (a similar proof can be constructed for the case in which only one economy is collectivist). Taking the

---

[43] Note that the pre-change paths of play and behavioural beliefs, and the probability distributions discussed above *do not* constitute a strategy combination. Accordingly, these probability distributions and the pre-change behavioural beliefs do not constitute post-change behavioural beliefs, yet, they are sufficient for deriving the results of proposition 3.

[44] I will not consider here the case in which one economy is collectivist and the other individualist.

[45] The first subscript or superscript denotes the principal and the second the agent.

pre-change paths of play and behavioural beliefs as given, will a principal hire an agent from the other economy? Clearly, P_s will not hire A_t if $W^*_{s,t} > W^*_{s,s}$, that is, if P_s has to pay to A_t more than he has to pay to A_s to keep him honest. Given the behavioural beliefs, the symmetry of the two economies, and the collective strategy held in each of them, it follows that

$$\eta h_c^{t,t} + (1-\eta)h_h^{t,t} = h_h^{s,t} < h_h^{s,s} \qquad \forall \mu \in (0,1] \qquad (1)$$

and

$$\mu h_c^{t,t} + (1-\mu)h_h^{t,t} = h_c^{s,t} > h_c^{s,s} \qquad \forall \eta \in [0,1). \qquad (2)$$

Inequality (2) simply states that if A_t may not be punished by the principals from economy t for cheating P_s then the perceived probability that he be hired after cheating P_s is higher than that of an agent from economy s. Simply stated, A_t, after cheating P_s has an employment option not available to A_s, namely, to be hired by the principals from his own economy.

Proposition 2 established that the function w increases in h_c, and decreases in h_h. Thus, for $s = K$ and $t = \mathcal{J}$:

$$W^*_{s,t} = w(h_h^{s,t}, h_c^{s,t}) > w(h_h^{s,s}, h_c^{s,s}) = W^*_{s,s} \qquad \forall \mu \in [0,1), \eta \in (0,1].$$

By symmetry the same result holds for $s = \mathcal{J}$ and $t = K$. The best response of a principal from one economy is never to hire an agent from the other economy unless $\mu = 1$, and $\eta = 0$. If this condition does not hold, the joint economy is a segregated one in which principals from one economy hire only agents from their own economy and play the collectivist strategy with respect to them.

Assume now that two individualist economies interact. Following the above line of argument and using the fact that $h_h^{s,s} = h_c^{s,s}$ in individualist economies, it is easy to demonstrate that within each economy a principal is indifferent about whether he hires an agent from his own economy or from the other, since the minimum wage (W^*) required to keep an agent honest is identical.[46] If all the principals are indifferent (and hence may as well hire randomly from both economies), the joint economy is an integrated one in which an individualistic strategy is played.

Proposition 3 states that if at least one pre-change economy is collectivist, the joint economy will be segregated unless beliefs are such that the players expect, with probability one, that an agent who cheated while employed by a principal from the other economy will be regarded as a cheat by principals from his own economy, and players expect, with probability zero, that an agent who was honest while employed by a principal from the other economy will be regarded as a cheat by the principals from his own economy. On the other hand, when the two pre-change economies are individualist, the joint economy will be integrated no matter what these expectations are. The

---

[46] Assume that the number of P and A in each economy is large enough so that one additional principal does not affect h_c and h_h.

intuition is, roughly speaking, that when inter-economy agency relations became possible in two collectivist economies, behavioural beliefs still specify collective punishment in intra-economy agency relations. Thus, if there is some uncertainty about whether a collective punishment will also be implemented in inter-economy agency relations, the wage required to keep an agent honest in inter-economy agency relations is higher than the wage required in intra-economy agency relations.[47] The wage in inter-economy agency relations is higher, since the uncertainty about the responses reduces the probability that an agent who cheated will not be hired (h_c) and this, as established with proposition 1, increases the wage required to keep an agent honest. This wage dispersion leads to segregation. When inter-economy agency relations become possible in two individualistic economies, even if similar uncertainty exists, the wage required to keep an agent honest in inter-economy agency relations is the same as that required in intra-economy agency relations. The behavioural beliefs are such that the uncertainty does not affect the wage required to keep an agent honest.

A collectivist equilibrium is always as efficient as an individualist equilibrium but not the other way around. Whether a segregated or an integrated economy is more efficient depends upon the parameters of the model. For example, if $\sigma = 1$, co-operation is possible only under a collectivist equilibrium and in segregated economies.[48] If, however, cross-economic-agency relations increase efficiency, that is, if γ is higher in inter-economy agency relation than in intra-economy agency relations, an integrated economy may be more efficient than a segregated economy, since in the latter principals will not establish inter-economy agency relations if the difference between the wage required in intra-economy agency relations and the wage required in inter-economy agency relations is larger than the increase in the total pay-off. Fundamentally, behavioural beliefs lead to inefficiencies due to their nature as a public good. However, while a public good usually leads to inefficiency because of the inability to exclude individuals from using it, behavioural beliefs lead to inefficiency due to their inability to include individuals in the realm of the behavioural beliefs.

Horizontal and Vertical Social Structures

When the OSPD game is played among individuals, collectivist behavioural beliefs are likely to generate a horizontal social structure, while individualist behavioural beliefs are likely to generate a vertical social structure. A horizontal social structure means that within a group of interacting individuals there is a symmetry of norms, roles, and statuses. That is, the group's

[47] Clearly, in reality such uncertainty may be a reflection of the mechanism for information-transmission; this is discussed further below.

[48] See the discussion in Greif (1989), and Kandori (1989), who provide a thorough examination of the advantages of collective punishment.

members have the same status and thus the behaviour of each member toward other members is expected to be identical to their expected behaviour towards him. A vertical social structure means that within a group of interacting individuals there is asymmetry of norms, roles, and statuses. That is, some sub-sets of members have different statuses from others, and distinct norms and roles are associated with each status.

To examine the relationships between behavioural beliefs and the endogenous emergence of different social structures, let us suppose that principals have a linear utility function, the same discount factor as agents, and in each period a principal can hire either an agent or a principal to serve as his agent.[49] A principal who functions as an agent will be referred to as 'principal-agent', and an agent who functions only as an agent will be referred to as an 'agent-agent'. The individualist behavioural beliefs in this modified OSPD game are as before. That is, players do not expect others to cease operating through an agent-agent or a principal-agent who cheated in the past. To retain the intuitive meaning of collectivist behavioural beliefs, however, a modification is required. Players also believe that an agent who cheats a principal who had cheated someone in the past would not be considered as a cheat. That is, players are expected to keep on hiring an agent who has cheated a principal-agent who had cheated in the past.

In the modified OSPD game, different social structures can emerge. When only (or mainly) agent-agents are hired, the economy is characterized by a vertical social structure. The group of individuals who interact through the OSPD game is heterogeneous and an individual functions as either a principal or an agent but not both. On the other hand, when only (or mainly) principal-agents are hired, the economy is characterized by horizontal social structure. The group of individuals who interact through the OSPD game is homogeneous and individuals function as agents while interacting with some individuals and as principals while interacting with the same or other individuals.

In the modified OSPD game, equilibria that generate either horizontal or vertical social structures are possible. However, collectivist behavioural beliefs are more likely to give rise to a horizontal social structure while individualist behavioural beliefs are more likely to give rise to a vertical social structure. The reasons for this dichotomy can be analysed using proposition 4.

Proposition 4

A principal-agent will be honest if

$$[V_h^a(\phi_u) - \beta V_c^{u,a}(\phi_u)] + (V_h^p - R_c - \beta V_c^p) \geq \alpha.$$

The honesty condition can also be written as

[49] As before, it is assumed that principals cannot commit themselves to future wage payments and hence principals still pay the lowest stationary wage that keeps the agents honest.

$$V_h^a(\phi_u) \geq \alpha + \beta V_c^{u,a}(\phi_u) + (R_c + \beta V_c^p - V_h^p),$$

in which an increase in the wage paid to a principal-agent increases the left-hand side by more than the right-hand side, while an increase in the principal's reservation utility increases the right-hand side by more than the left-hand side.

The notations used are the following: $V_h^a(\phi_u)$ is the present value of the lifetime expected utility of a principal from operating as an agent (who receives the reservation utility ϕ_u whenever he is unemployed as an agent). $V_c^{u,a}(\phi_u)$ is the lifetime expected utility from being an agent of a principal who cheated while being employed as an agent. R_c is the one-period return from employing an agent to a principal who cheated in the past while employed as an agent. $R_c + \beta V_c^p$ is the present value of the lifetime expected utility from being a principal of a principal who cheated in the past while employed as an agent. V_h^p is the present value of the lifetime expected utility from being a principal of a principal who never cheated in the past while employed as an agent. α is the one-period gain from cheating.

To derive proposition 4 some additional notation is required. Denote by R_h the one-period return to an honest principal from hiring an agent, and hence $V_h^p = R_h + \beta V_h^p$. Denote by V_c^p the present value of the lifetime expected utility of a principal who cheated from employing agents. That is, $V_c^p = R_c + \beta V_c^p$. Recall that

$$Vha(\phi u) = W + \beta[(1 - \sigma)V_h^a(\phi_u) + V_h^{u,a}(\phi_u)]$$

where $V_h^{u,a}(\phi_u)$ is the lifetime expected utility of an unemployed agent. Define $V_c^a(\phi_u)$ equivalently. Denote by $V_h^{p,a}(\phi_u)$ the present value of the lifetime expected utility of an honest principal who is being employed as an agent. That is, $V_h^{p,a}(\phi_u) = V_h^p + V_h^a(\phi_u)$. Denote by $V_h^{u,p,a}(\phi_u)$ the present value of the lifetime expected utility of an honest principal who is currently not employed as an agent. That is,

$$V_h^{u,p,a}(\phi_u) = V_h^p + \beta V_h^{u,a}(\phi_u).$$

Denote by $V_c^{u,p,a}(\phi_u)$ the present value of the lifetime expected utility of an unemployed principal who cheated as an agent. That is, $V_c^{u,p,a}(\phi_u) = V_c^p + \beta V_c^{u,a}(\phi_u)$.

Following the same line of reasoning that was used to derive the honesty condition for an agent in proposition 1, a principal will be honest when employed as an agent if

$$V_h^{p,a}(\phi_u) \geq \alpha + R_c + \beta V_c^{u,p,a}(\phi_u)$$

That is, the lifetime expected utility from being an honest principal and principal-agent is higher than that received during the period of cheating ($\alpha + R_c$), plus the present value of the lifetime expected utility of a principal who cheated in the past. Rearranging the above definitions yields the result that a principal will be honest while employed as an agent if

$$V_h^a(\phi_u) \geq \alpha + \beta V_c^{u,a}(\phi_u) + (R_c + \beta V_c^p - V_h^p).$$

The reasons for the relative increases in the right-and left-hand sides are clear from proposition 1.

Proposition 4 indicates that a principal-agent will be honest if the wage paid to him is such that the cost of cheating, that is,

$$[V_h^a(\phi_u) - \beta V_c^{u,a}(\phi_u)] - (R_c + \beta V_c^p - V_h^p)$$

is larger than the gain from cheating, α. The cost of cheating includes the reduction in his future utility as a principal and as a principal-agent due to cheating. The reduction in the present value of his lifetime expected utility from being a principal-agent equals $V_h^a(\phi_u) - \beta V_c^{u,a}(\phi_u)$, that is, the difference between the present value of the lifetime expected utility of an honest agent and a cheat. The reduction in the present value of his lifetime expected utility from being a principal equals $V_h^p - R_c - \beta V_c^p$, that is, the difference between the present value of the lifetime expected utility of an honest principal and a principal who cheated while employed as an agent. Further, it indicates that an increase in the wage paid to a principal-agent decreases the net gains from cheating, but an increase in his reservation utility increases the net gains from cheating.

Proposition 4 provides the honesty condition for a principal-agent for a given set of parameters and this condition can be directly compared with the honesty condition for an agent-agent. The honesty condition for a principal-agent is

$$V_h^a(\phi_u) \geq \alpha + \beta V_c^{u,a}(\phi_u) + (R_c + \beta V_c^p - V_h^p),$$

while the honesty condition for an agent-agent is

$$V_h^a(\phi_u) \geq \alpha + \beta V_c^{u,a}(\phi_u).^{[50]}$$

The comparison of these two honesty conditions indicates the factors that relate behavioural beliefs and social structures. Suppose that the probabilities that an unemployed principal-agent and an agent-agent will be hired are the same. Under individualist behavioural beliefs the lifetime expected utility of a principal from hiring agents is independent of his past behaviour as a principal-agent. (That is, $R_c + \beta V_c^p = V_h^p$). Hence, if agent-agents and principal-agents have the same reservation utilities, the honesty conditions for agent-agents and principal-agents are the same, and principals are indifferent regarding whom to hire. If, as is often the case, the reservation utility is positively correlated with being a principal, the wage required to keep a principal-agent honest increases. Thus, principals will hire agents rather than

---

[50] This condition was derived in the proof of proposition 1.

principal-agents.[51] While higher principals' reservation utilities also discourage their employment under collectivist behavioural beliefs, collectivist behavioural beliefs also encourage principals to hire principal-agents (other things being equal). Under collectivist behavioural beliefs, a principal's lifetime expected utility from being a principal decreases if he cheats when employed as a principal-agent. (That is, $R_c + \beta V_c^p < V_h^p$.) If a principal-agent cheats, he has to pay a higher wage to his future agents, since they will not be punished by other principals if they cheat him.[52] (That is, their h_c increases.)

This intuitive discussion indicates the forces that relate behavioural beliefs and social structures. Under collectivist and individualist behavioural beliefs, higher principals' reservation utilities discourage their employment as principal-agents, since they increase their wages. Under collectivist behavioural beliefs, however, the additional punishment imposed on principal-agents through the reduction in their future income as principals encourages their employment as principal-agents. Hence, holding reservation utilities fixed, a society reaches a horizontal social structure for a larger set of initial conditions under collectivist behavioural beliefs than under individualist behavioural beliefs. Furthermore, a society reaches a vertical social structure under individualist behavioural beliefs for a larger set of initial conditions than under collectivist behavioural beliefs. Hence, individualist behavioural beliefs are likely to lead to a horizontal social structure in which agent-agents are hired, while collectivist behavioural beliefs are likely to lead to a horizontal social structure in which principal-agents are hired.

The Maghribi and the Genoese Merchants

Were diverse behavioural beliefs important in determining social structures in the late Medieval world? Can the differences between collectivist and individualist societies, as predicted by the theory, be traced in the history of the Islamic world and Europe? Historical information concerning social structures and behavioural beliefs is not easy to come by. Fortunately, the OSPD game captures the essence of the organizational problem that characterized the relationship between Medieval merchants and their overseas agents, while the historical records are relatively rich in reflecting these relationships. In pre-modern trade, goods were sold abroad only after being shipped to their destination.[53] Since a merchant could decrease costs substantially by

[51] Clearly, under individualist behavioural beliefs the tendency of the principals to hire more agents will increase the probability that an unemployed agent-agent will be rehired. If the change in this probability is high enough, it may lead to equality in the wage required to employ an agent-agent and a principal-agent. In any case, there is no equilibrium in which an agent-agent has a lower probability of being employed than a principal-agent. Hence, mainly agents are employed.

[52] Under collectivist behavioural beliefs the fact that honest principals are more likely to be hired feeds positively into the reduction of the wage required to keep a principal-agent honest.

[53] de Roover (1965), 44; Gras (1939); Porter and Livesay (1971).

sending goods to an overseas agent rather than having to travel himself with his goods, a large efficiency gain could be achieved by employing overseas agents.[54] Contractual problems, however, characterized the merchant–agent relations, and the nature of these problems is captured by the OSPD game. While a merchant could hire an agent to work for him, the hired agent could embezzle some of the merchant's capital in his possession. Due to the high level of information asymmetry between the parties and the court, and the high cost of overseas litigation, legal systems were of little help in surmounting this organizational problem.[55] Henceforth the term 'merchant' denotes a principal, that is, the individual who initiates the OSPD relations, and the term 'trader' refers to both agents and merchants.

The historical records that reflect agency relations among the Maghribi traders of the eleventh century and the Genoese traders of the twelfth century indicate that their social structures differed in a manner consistent with the theoretical insights. The Maghribi traders were Jewish merchants active in Muslim Mediterranean commerce during the eleventh century. A rich picture of their commercial activities is reflected in an historical source known as the Geniza documents. This historical source contains about a thousand commercial documents of different natures—from commercial correspondence between business associates to legal contracts and records of court hearings. This historical source is unique in portraying the activities of traders who operated in the Muslim world. Although the Muslim world is known for its rich literature from the Medieval period, this literature does not contain even a single trader's biography or piece of correspondence that reflects the operations of a trader.[56] Although the Geniza documents reveal the operation of Jewish traders, the commercial practices reflected in them are believed to present an accurate picture of the commercial practices of the eleventh-century Muslim Mediterranean.[57] The operation of the twelfth-century Genoese traders is reflected in the cartularies of Genoese notaries. These cartularies are the largest primary source of historical information concerning overseas trade available from late Medieval Europe. The cartularies contain commercial contracts between merchants and their overseas agents.[58]

---

[54] The superiority of trading systems that employ agents over those that do not has been shown by many scholars. See, for example, de Roover (1965), 13, 45 ff., 70 ff., Postan (1973), 66 ff.; Lopez and Raymond (1955), 174.

[55] Clearly, the merchant–agent relationships were also characterized by a high level of information asymmetry between the parties involved. The merchant could not directly observe the trade realizations the agent faced. This information asymmetry can be incorporated into the analysis without changing its results. For a discussion of this contractual problem, as well as the contractual problems associated with inability to specify comprehensive contracts, see Greif (1989; 1990a).

[56] For an introduction to the Geniza documents, see Goitein (1967); Gil (1983b). For an examination of agency relations among the Maghribi traders see Greif (1989; 1990a).

[57] See the discussion in Goitein (1955; 1967).

[58] Byrne (1917; 1920); Krueger (1962); Greif (1990b).

Throughout their history, the Maghribi and the Italian traders faced a particular change in the nature of their trade. The Maghribi traders emigrated during the tenth century from around Baghdad to North Africa. This area prospered at the time under the control of the new caliphate, the Fatimid caliphate.[59] Once the Maghribi traders had emigrated to North Africa, however, they found that the scope of their trade was constantly increasing due to the expansion of the Fatimid caliphate and the decline in the naval power of the Fatimid's opponents. Indeed, the Maghribi traders expanded their trade from Spain to Constantinople. Similarly, during the twelfth century, the Italian traders found themselves capable of becoming active in long-distance trade on a scale and scope much larger than they had experienced in previous centuries. Political and military changes around the Mediterranean and within Europe, in which the Italians had little influence, allowed them contact with centres of trade that had previously been closed to them.

This particular change in the rules of the game is exactly the one that was examined theoretically. If the Maghribi traders did indeed hold collectivist behavioural beliefs before or throughout the process of the expansion of the scope of trade, segregation in agency relations should be observed. If the Genoese traders did actually hold individualist behavioural beliefs before, or throughout, the process of the expansion of the scope of trade, integration should be observed. The historical records provide confirmation of these two theoretical predictions.

As noted by several historians, agency relations among the Maghribi traders were established only internally. Agency relations between Maghribi and non-Maghribi traders (Jewish or Muslim) were rare. When a need to trade abroad arose, members of the Maghribi traders' group emigrated abroad and served as agents to their peers. During the eleventh century one finds Maghribi traders who emigrated from Tunisia mainly to Spain, Sicily, Egypt, and Palestine.[60] The Maghribi traders who lived in these colonies served as agents for other Maghribi traders, and generations after a Maghribi trader emigrated from the Maghrib, his descendants continued to operate in long-distance trade with the descendants of other Maghribi traders. This observation is consistent with the claim that agency relations among the Maghribi traders were governed by collectivist behavioural beliefs which led to segregation.[61]

While the segregation observed among the Maghribi traders is consistent with the theoretical results, emigration and segregation can also result from factors other than wage differentials. It should be noted that since Maghribi traders adopted the customs and language of the Muslim world, emigration within this world was probably culturally and materially easy and there were advantages to operating through an agent with whom a merchant was

---

[59] Gil (1974), 299–328.   [60] Goitein (1967), 156–9, 186–92; Gil (1983b), i. 200 ff.
[61] See the further discussion in Greif (1989).

familiar.[62] Thus, it is instructive to examine the response of the Maghribi traders to commercial opportunities opened to them in trade centres outside the Muslim world to which they did not emigrate. At least with respect to Italy, the Maghribi traders had an alternative to emigration—employing as agents Jewish traders who were active in Italy and with whom the communities within which the Maghribi traders lived held communal ties. To the best of our knowledge, there were no political restrictions that could have hindered such co-operation, while the historical records indicate that the Maghribi traders perceived trade with the Christian world to be a most profitable trade.[63] Yet, in spite of the opportunity and the economic incentive to co-operate, the Maghribi traders are never mentioned as having established agency relations with Jewish traders from the Christian world.[64] Why was this the case? The relationship between agency cost, behavioural beliefs, and segregation offers a plausible explanation. Employing Italian Jews as agents was 'too expensive' relative to hiring agents from among the Maghribi traders within the Muslim world.

If the Genoese traders did indeed hold individualist behavioural beliefs, they were likely to respond in a different manner to the possibility of establishing agency relations abroad. Genoese merchants were likely to establish agency relation with non-Genoese merchants abroad. While the process of establishing Italian commercial colonies abroad during the late Medieval period is well known, the focus of the study here is not to examine the dynamics of establishing commercial colonies, but to delineate the nature of the relationship between merchants and their overseas agents. Even though the Italian trade of the twelfth century was still conducted to a large extent through travelling traders, several studies indicate that Genoese merchants employed non-Genoese agents on a permanent basis.[65] For example, the two 'caravan' merchants, Manuelus Castellus and his brother Benedictus, employed two Piacenzans as procurators in the fair of Provins.[66] A contract recorded in Genoa on 28 March 1210 reflects the agency services provided

[62] The value of this familiarity rested on, but was not exclusive to, the sharing of the same Merchants' Law, an informal set of rules that governed agency relations. See the discussion below and Greif (1990a).

[63] The profitability of this trade is reflected in many documents. For example, in around 1055 a Maghribi trader reported that he sold brazil-wood (a wood grown in India from which red dye was produced) in a Palestinian port to Rum (Christians, most likely from the Latin world) for a 150% profit. About twenty years earlier a merchant from Palermo (Sicily) complained that even (!) the Rums were not ready to buy the inferior black ginger that had, therefore, to be sent to another European country in the hope that it would be sold there. Bodl. MS Heb. c. 28, fo. 11, ll. 171–213; Dropsie 389, b, ll. 6 ff.; Goitein (1973), 45.

[64] For a discussion of communal relationships and economic motives, see Goitein (1973), 44, 211. For an additional reference, see Greif (1989). A Maghribi trader who sailed to Amalfi does not mention any commercial co-operation with local Jews: see TS 8 Ja I, fo. 5, Goitein (1973), 44–5.

[65] See the general discussion in de Roover (1965). For information about inter-region agency relations, see Face (1958); Greif (1990b).

[66] Face (1958), 433.

by the Genoese Rubeus de Campo to Vivianus Jordanus de Lucca in London.[67] In another contract, dated 13 November 1191, a merchant from northern Europe, Manfredus Gorja, and a Roman, Laurentius Romani Anastasii, hired a certain Genoese Nicola Petri Hugozonis, to collect a debt of one hundred marks of silver owed to them by Walcerus, bishop-elect of Cambrai. The sum collected was to be used *causa negociandi*, that is, 'to do business'.[68]

The Maghribi traders' group and the Genoese traders' group differ not only in their external social structure. The historical evidence concerning the internal structure of these traders' groups is consistent with the theoretical results of proposition 4 and the conjecture that the Maghribi traders held collectivist behavioural beliefs and the Genoese traders held individualist behavioural beliefs. The Maghribi traders were largely middle class and although some of them invested in merchandise worth at least several thousands dinars—a considerable sum for a period in which middle-class household expenditures per month averaged less than three dinars—most were involved in business ventures worth no more than a few hundred dinars.[69] The traders in this group were principal-agents, and usually each of them served as an agent for several merchants while receiving agency services from them or other traders.[70] Sedentary traders served as agents for those who travelled, and vice versa. Wealthy merchants served as agents for poorer ones, and vice versa. Furthermore, the wealthiest Jewish traders who immigrated to the Fatimid caliphate did not become a part of the Maghribi traders group. For example, the Tustaris brothers, who were rich enough to be mentioned in Muslim sources and to present the Caliph Almustansr in 1044 with a silver model of a ship that weighted 400 kg. and was worth over 2,400 dinars, employed Maghribi traders as their agents, but did not serve others as agents.[71]

Among the Italian merchants of the late Medieval period the situation was rather different. More often than not, agency relations were established between wealthy merchants and ambitious young travelling traders.[72] Among the Genoese traders of the twelfth century, the major bulk of trade was conducted during this period by well-to-do merchants who rarely functioned as agents. The cartulary of John the Scribe, the earliest Genoese cartulary in existence, reflects agency relations during the period from 1154 to 1164. The number of merchants mentioned in the cartulary is about 180, twelve of

---

[67] Lanfranco (1202–26), i, no. 524, p. 234.
[68] Guglielmo Cassinese (1190–2), ii, no. 1325, pp. 83–4.
[69] Goitein (1967), 214 ff.; Gil (1983b), i. 200 ff. Goitein argues that middle-class family monthly expenditures were 2 dinars (p. 46), while Gil argues they were about 3 dinars (1983a), 91.
[70] See, for example, Stillman (1970).
[71] About the Tustaris, see Gil (1981).
[72] De Roover (1965), pp. 51 ff.; Lopez and Raymond (1955), 174, 185–6; Lane (1944), 178 ff.; and Sombart (1953), 31 ff.

whom invested some 40 per cent of the total (known) Genoese investment in trade. The number of agents mentioned in the cartulary is about 300. Only 36 individuals functioned as both agents and merchants. Generally speaking, their investments in trade were not heavy and amounted only to 11 per cent of the total.[73] The cartularies from the late twelfth century indicate that agents, by and large, were individuals from the lower ranks of society without substantial wealth. Byrne (1917) concluded that 'as a rule' the Genoese agents during the period were 'not men of great wealth or of high position in Genoa'. (159).[74]

The external and internal social structure of the Maghribi and Genoese traders groups is consistent with the theory of behavioural beliefs and the conjecture that the Maghribi traders held collectivist behavioural beliefs and the Genoese traders held individualist behavioural beliefs. The collectivist behavioural beliefs of the Maghribi led to the emergence of a segregated social structure as a response to new opportunities to trade abroad. The individualist behavioural beliefs of the Genoese traders led to the emergence of an integrated social structure as a response to the new opportunities to trade abroad, and Genoese merchants hired Genoese and non-Genoese agents alike. The collectivist behavioural beliefs of the Maghribi traders led to the emergence of a horizontal social structure of middle-class merchant-agents. The individualist behavioural beliefs of the Genoese traders led to the emergence of a vertical social structure in which well-to-do merchant-agents hired relatively poor agents with low reservation utilities.

BEHAVIOURAL BELIEFS, BUSINESS ASSOCIATIONS, AND ORGANIZATIONAL DEVELOPMENT

This section elaborates on the relationships between behavioural beliefs, the choice over alternative forms of business association, and organizational development. Proposition 4 is used to examine the relationships between behavioural beliefs and the choice over alternative forms of business association. The theoretical results are then compared with the information available concerning the forms of business association employed by the Maghribi and Genoese traders. Then the section provides three historical examples illustrating the relationship between behavioural beliefs and organizational changes. The first example touches on the development of the firm, the second touches on the use of a bill of lading, and the third on the organization that governed the relations between alien traders and rulers. An interesting feature of these examples is that the same behavioural beliefs characterize the equilibrium before and after the organizational innovation. Thus, they

[73] Krueger (1962).
[74] This description is appropriate for the period after 1187. See also Krueger (1962); Byrne (1920), 210–11; Byrne (1928), 160–1.

demonstrate that behavioural beliefs are one of the underlying factors that make organizations viable within a society.

Forms of Business Association

As discussed above, behavioural beliefs affect the internal social structure of a traders' group. Collectivist behavioural beliefs lead to a horizontal social structure while individualist behavioural beliefs lead to a vertical social structure. Under collectivist behavioural beliefs, principals prefer to hire merchant-agents, while under individualist behavioural beliefs merchants prefer to hire agent-agents. This preference is likely to be reflected not only in the social structure but also in the choice over forms of business association through which agency relations are established. To clarify the difference between an agent and a business associate, consider the case of a partnership. Usually partners operated in different trade centres, and each of them sold the goods that were sent to him, bought some merchandise, and shipped it to the other partner. Whenever a partner utilized the partnership's capital, he acted as an agent for the partnership. Since collectivist behavioural beliefs lead to the establishment of agency relations among merchants, the traders are likely to use forms of business associations in which both parties invest capital. On the other hand, since individualist behavioural beliefs lead to the establishment of agency relations among merchants and agents, the traders are likely to use forms of business associations in which only the merchants invest capital.

The Maghribi traders were familiar with five forms of business association: the sea loan, *commenda*, partnership, formal friendship, and factor relations. The Genoese traders were familiar with sea loans, *commenda*, *societas*, and factor relations.[75] A sea loan was a loan for fixed interest. Its repayment was contingent on the safe arrival of a ship or successful completion of a voyage. *Commenda* was usually established between two parties, one providing the capital, and the other providing the work in travel and transaction overseas. The parties allocated the profit and loss according to a sharing rule specified at the time the *commenda* was established. *Societas* was identical to the *commenda*, except that both parties invested capital. A partnership brought together two or more parties who invested capital and labour, though not necessarily in equal shares. The partners became joint owners of the capital and shared profit and loss in proportion to their share of the capital. Usually only one of them at a time (or a third party) handled the capital, or each of them handled part of the capital simultaneously.

---

[75] By 'familiar' I mean that either they actually used these forms of business associations or that these forms were authorized as legal. For an elaboration on these forms of business associations, and the differences between the Jewish and the Genoese ones, see Greif (1989; 1990a); de Roover (1965); Goitein (1967).

The essence of a formal friendship was that two traders operated in different trade centres, providing each other with services in their respective trade centres. Neither received pecuniary compensation. This exchange of services was not based on emotional ties, nor was it a reciprocal exchange; rather it was purely a business matter. The relationship was initiated by an agreement and could be terminated by either party at any time. As long as the relationship was in force, however, each party was bound to provide his friend with trade services. A 'factor' provided trade-related services to an absentee trader, probably for a commission. Some factors were authorized to represent a trader in court; some also held official or semi-official posts. Factors operated either for a single merchant or for several merchants at the same time. The most important factor was the merchants' representative, generally a relatively wealthy trader who had emigrated to the trade centre where he held his post.

As several scholars have observed, agency relations among the Maghribi traders mainly took the forms of partnerships, friendships, and factor relations.[76] In literally every business letter, friendships, partnerships, and factor relations are mentioned, while mentions of *commenda* relations and sea loans are hard to find. An examination of the Genoese cartularies of the late twelfth century indicates a very different situation among the Genoese traders. They used mainly *commenda* contracts, and progressively so. Krueger (1962) noticed that in 1200, 13 per cent of the Genoese overseas commercial contracts were *societas*, 72 per cent were *commenda*, and 15 per cent were sea loans. In 1216, out of 299 commercial contracts only two were of the *societas* form, and in 1220 out of 46 commercial contracts there was only one of this form. Thereafter up to 1230, in 205 contracts not a single *societas* was made for overseas trade.[77]

The environment in which the Maghribi traders and the Genoese traders operated was similar. Both groups of traders operated mainly in the western basin of the Mediterranean, and their merchandise largely consisted of textiles and luxury goods. Further, the two groups were familiar with similar forms of business association. Yet, despite these similarities the two groups differed in their choice of business associations. The nature of the difference is consistent with the conjecture that it was generated by diverse behavioural beliefs. The common denominator in the forms of business association utilized by the Maghribi traders—friendships, partnerships, and factor relations among merchants—is that both parties, the merchant and the agent, invested in trade. In contrast, the essence of the *commenda* contract is that only one party, the merchant, invested in trade.

---

[76] Goitein (1973), 11 ff.; Gil (1983b), i. 216 ff.

[77] Krueger (1962), 42. It should be noticed that the *societas* was widely used in agrarian and industrial endeavours throughout this period. On the generality of this phenomenon in Italy, see de Roover (1965).

Organizations

The discussion so far has assumed that individuals do not strive to improve their lot by changing the rules of the game. In reality, however, individuals tend to respond to incentives associated with a path of play, behavioural beliefs, or outcome by establishing organizations which are, in the context of this paper, the factors that determine the rules of the game.[78] Accordingly, establishing an organization amounts to changing the rules by introducing a new player (the organization itself), by changing the information available to players, by changing pay-offs associated with certain actions, and so on.[79] It seems that Hobbes (1588–1679) had in mind this type of organization when he viewed the state as a Pareto-improving device.[80]

The introduction of new organizations reflects a response to changing exogenous conditions or organizational refinements. The latter result from an increase in the stock of knowledge, an increase that is the outcome of an intentional pursuit of organizational improvement or the outcome of unintentional experimentation.[81] It has been recognized in the study of technological change that, in the short run, individuals take technology as given, while, in the long run, they may strive to improve available technology. Similarly, in the study of organizational change one has to recognize that, in the short run, individuals take the rules of the game as given, while, in the long run, changes in the organizational structure of the game are likely to be introduced.

While the ability to introduce new organizations in a specific game depends on the organizational structure of the society within which the game is embedded, organizational changes will not be introduced if the individuals capable of initiating the change do not gain from doing so. Whether a specific player will lose or gain from a specific organizational change depends on the pre-change and the post-change equilibria. Consequently, distinct equilibria reached in a multiple-equilibrium game lead to the development of distinct organizations that affect future equilibria. These different equilibria provide distinct incentives for the creation of new organizations, and so on.

---

[78] The merchant–agent game, for example, implicitly assumes the existence of an organization through which an agent and a merchant communicated, through which information about past behaviour was dispensed, and so forth. Note that the players' strategies are not a part of the organizational structure of the game. They are a part of the institution that governed the relationships among the players. For different definitions of organizations in economics, economic history, and sociology see Arrow (1974); North (1981; 1990; 1991); Williamson (1985); Scott (1987), 20 ff.

[79] For examples of historical and theoretical studies of these types of organizations, see Greif (1989); Milgrom, North, and Weingast (1990); Greif, Milgrom, and Weingast (1991).

[80] About a thousand years earlier, in *Ethics of the Fathers* the same idea appears: 'pray for the welfare of the government, without whose authority, men would swallow each other.' (III. 2.)

[81] Note then, that the increase in the stock of knowledge does not necessarily imply that individuals fully comprehend the functioning of the new organization.

A distinct trajectory of organizational development evolves through this path-dependence process.[82] Accordingly, behavioural beliefs that crystallized within a society at one point in time function as a common resource that directs future organizational development.

The Family Firm

The Italians are deservedly credited for their many trade-related organizational innovations during the late Medieval period, among which are the famous 'family firms'. The essence of the family firm as developed in Italy was that family members made up a permanent partnership with unlimited and joint liability that was not dissolved after one partner's death. The family firm first emerged in the early thirteenth century in Piacenza, Lucca, and Siena, and then diffused to other Italian cities, including Genoa.[83]

There is nothing, however, in the Genoese cartularies from the middle of the twelfth century that indicates the emergence of the family firm. Further, it is impossible to detect any significant difference between the Genoese and the Maghribi traders in agglomeration of family capital. Among the Maghribi traders, sons usually became active in long-distance commerce, but the intergenerational relations among the Maghribi traders were not aimed at preserving the family wealth under one roof. A trader's son started to operate as an independent trader during his father's lifetime. The father would typically help the son until he was able to operate independently. After the father's death, his estate was divided among his heirs and his business dissolved.[84]

The situation among the Genoese traders in the middle of the twelfth century was similar. The cartulary of John the Scribe (1155–64), the only Genoese source reflecting contractual relations from that period, contains many contracts in which the father provided his son with the capital required to become an agent for a non-family-member merchant. For example, in 1157 Ugo Mallonus provided his son, Rubaldus Mallonus, with the sum of 66.66 lire that Rubaldus invested in a partnership with Rolandus Cintracus, who invested 133.3 lire. Rubaldus carried the capital to the Levant and was entitled to half of the net profit.[85] Similarly, when brothers invested in trade, they usually invested in trade separately, each of them investing his own

---

[82] To fully comprehend this path-dependence view of organizational development an explicit analysis of the process of organizational innovations is required. On the theory of path dependence (mainly in technology) see David (1988a; 1988b); Arthur (1988; 1989). North (1990) has called attention to two forces that contribute to institutional path dependence in institutions: increasing returns and imperfect markets.

[83] See, for example, the discussion in Sombart (1953); de Roover (1965), 70 ff.; Rosenberg and Birdzell (1986), 123–4.

[84] Goitein (1967), 180 ff.; Gil (1983b), i. 215 ff.

[85] John the Scribe, No. CCXXXVI. See also document No. DLXXV.

capital.[86] Finally, the cartulary contains wills of several merchants which specify the allocation of the estate to the deceased's relatives and friends.[87]

Neither the Maghribi traders of the eleventh century nor the Genoese traders of the twelfth century attempted to preserve the family capital under one roof on a constant basis. But this similarity did not last long, as the Italian traders, including the Genoese, introduced the family firm during the thirteenth century. Why did the Italians, after a relatively short period of involvement in international trade, introduce the family firm? Why did the Maghribi traders not introduce a similar organization? After all, the Maghribi traders were active in long-distance commerce for several centuries, at least from the ninth to the twelfth century. Why did they not introduce their version of the 'family firm'? Were they just not innovative enough?

It is a widely held view among economic historians, following the work of Lane (1944) on the family firm in Venice, that the family firm was established to surmount agency problems. Lacking alternative institutions, the merchant–agent relations were organized within the family, in which solidarity guaranteed honesty. This assertion certainly captures some aspects of reality, but it falls short of providing a complete explanation and of addressing the right question. Why was a permanent partnership established? Why did family members not simply establish agency relations with each other? Furthermore, even a superficial examination of the internal structure of the important family firms reveals that agency relations were not necessarily established between family members. For example, the Peruzzi company, probably the largest Italian company during the late Medieval period, had, in 1335, fifteen overseas 'branch managers', only three of whom were members of the Peruzzi family. In 1402 none of the overseas employees of the Medici company was a Medici.[88]

An examination of the relationship between behavioural beliefs and incentives for creating organizations provides a rational explanation for the

[86] The best example is of two brothers, each of whom was a prominent trader during the period from 1154 to 1164: Ingo de Volta, who invested in trade 25 times, and his brother, William Burone, who invested in trade 13 times (see John the Scribe). They always invested separately. There are contracts in which an individual invests sums that belong to other members of his family. For example, on 27 August 1160, Ribaldus de Saraphia mentioned that he had invested 60 lire, 20 of which belonged to his nephews, Ribaldino and Fredencione (John the Scribe, No. DCCLI). It is instructive to note, however, that these sums are explicitly referred to as owned by the nephews and not as having belonged to all the family members jointly. Furthermore, since the two nephews never appear in the 15 contracts that Ribaldus had entered into, it is reasonable to suppose that they were minors. As this example illustrates and as the details of the relevant contract reveal, it is very likely that most of the contracts in which an individual invests sums that belong to other members of his family reflect special situations rather than a regular commercial practice.

[87] See, for example, the will of Ogerio Vento, in John the Scribe No. MXLVII. For his investment in trade, see, for example, Nos. DCCCXCII; CMIV.

[88] de Roover (1963), p. 44, table 7, p. 80, table 19. See also the discussion by de Roover (1948; 1965, 78–9); Herlihy (1985). For possible marriage relationships between members of different families, see Padgett and Ansell (1988).

questions posed above. It explains the nature of the family firm and the reason why it was not likely to be established among the Maghribi traders. The explanation rests on the finding, presented formally in proposition 1, that the lower the probability of forced separation, σ, the lower the wage required to keep an agent honest. Intuitively, the less likely it is that there will be a future to the relations between a specific agent and merchant, the more the merchant has to pay in each period to keep the agent honest. The gain from changing σ, however, is not independent either from the probability that a cheat will be rehired, or from the probability that an honest agent will be rehired. The lower the probability that a cheat will be rehired, and the higher the probability that an honest agent will be rehired, the lower is the gain from changing the probability of forced separation, σ. Furthermore, when an unemployed honest agent is rehired with probability 1, the gain from changing the probability of forced separation is zero.[89]

Among the Maghribi traders collectivist behavioural beliefs increased and might have brought to one the probability that an honest agent would be rehired and to zero the probability that a cheat would be rehired. Thus, among them the incentive to reduce the probability of forced separation was marginal, if not absent altogether. The Italian merchants, sharing individualist behavioural beliefs, were motivated to establish an organization that reduced the likelihood of forced separation. The family firm was a manifestation of this motivation, agglomerating the capital of several traders in an organization with an infinite life-span that replaced each individual merchant in his relations with agents who were not family members.[90]

The introduction of the family firm, that is, of an organization that replaced individual merchants in their relations with agents, was an 'organizational macro-invention' that led to modifying and refining 'micro-inventions'.[91] Family firms began to sell units, or shares, to non-members. For example, the capital of the Bardi company was made up of 58 shares: six members of the family were in possession of the majority of the shares while five outsiders owned the rest. In 1312 the capital of the Peruzzi company was distributed among eight members of the family and nine outsiders. In 1331 the Peruzzi family lost control of the company when more than half the capital belonged to outsiders.[92] Once shares became tradable, a need for a

[89] To be more precise, $d^2w(.)/d\sigma dh_c > 0$ (for $\beta > h_c$), and $d^2w(.)/d\sigma dh_h < 0$. This implies that the higher (lower) is h_c (h_h), the bigger (smaller) is the reduction in wage due to a given change in σ. Finally, $dw/d\sigma = 0$ when $h_h = 1$.

[90] More theoretical and historical work is required to establish the exact factors which enabled the family firm to achieve a level of commitment above that of each of its individual members. It seems that the ability to bind the investors legally was a key. It is instructive to note in this context some facts about the internal organization of the Medici company. There was a permanent, unlimited liability partnership between the individuals who provided the firm's capital, but only a limited liability partnership between the Medici company and each of its overseas branch managers. See the discussion in de Roover (1963).

[91] Mokyr (1990) introduced this terminology with respect to technological change.

[92] de Roover (1963), 77–8. See additional examples in de Roover (1965).

suitable market arose and stock-markets were developed. Furthermore, a separation between ownership and control was introduced, which required not only appropriate institutions to surmount the related contractual problems, but also improvement in information-transmission techniques and accounting procedures.[93]

The above hypothesis about the nature of the Italian family firm and the distinct incentives that led to its introduction in the West, but not the East, has its own theoretical and historical limitations. It specifies why the Italian merchants were motivated to establish an organization and the Maghribi traders were not. Recognizing the necessary conditions, however, differs from recognizing the sufficient conditions, and the previous discussion does not specify how this organization actually came about. Furthermore, additional historical examination of various aspects of the family firm is required to substantiate the hypothesis. The aim of this paper, however, is not to delineate the history and theory of the family firm. It is to demonstrate how distinct behavioural beliefs are likely to provide—and probably have actually provided—distinct incentives for the establishment of organizations. Furthermore, it exemplifies that the ability of organizations to change outcomes might be dependent on the society's behavioural beliefs, and an organization that changes outcomes within one society will not necessarily have the same impact on the same game played in another society.

Internal and External Enforcement—The Bill of Lading and the Merchant Guild

Different incentives generated by distinct behavioural beliefs governing agency relations are also likely to manifest themselves in the development of organizations not directly related to agency relations. In a segregated economy, membership in a group is a valuable asset to each individual, since there are severe limitations on co-operation outside one's group. This provides the group as a whole with leverage for ensuring compliance with behaviour that the group considers appropriate. Thus, when a collectivist behavioural belief governs relationships, it is likely that informal rules regulating behaviour will evolve and will be enforced through the same mechanism that supports agency relations. Under individualist behavioural beliefs, however, an informal enforcement mechanism based on collective punishment is not effective, since belonging to the group has no value. This asymmetry in the ability of the group as a collective to ensure compliance is likely to affect organizational development.

Consider, for example, the development of the modern bill of lading. This bill combines an earlier version of the bill of lading with the so-called bill of

---

[93] See, for example, the elaborate contractual relationships between the Medici and their managers described in de Roover (1963). For a general discussion of the European trade organization during this period see Gras (1939); de Roover (1965); Lopez (1976); Postan (1973).

advice. The former was the ship's scribe's (notary) receipt for the goods the merchant deposited on the ship. This receipt was sent by the merchant to his overseas agent, who then claimed the goods based on the scribe's own signature. The letter of advice was sent after the ship arrived at its destination by the ship's scribe to the consignee who did not come to claim the goods. The bill of lading and the letter of advice are organizations that come to surmount the organizational problem related to the shipping of goods abroad.

The historical records indicate that the Genoese and the Maghribi traders confronted this organizational problem differently. While the earliest known European bill of lading and letter of advice date from the 1390s and related to the trade of Genoa, the Maghribi traders hardly seem to have used bills of lading, even though their existence was known to them.[94] Why did the Genoese traders advance the use of the bill, while the Maghribi traders abandoned it? It is possible that the Maghribi traders did not use the bill of lading since they solved the related organizational problem by using their collective punishment, or, more precisely, based on their collectivist behavioural beliefs. Thus, a Maghribi trader could entrust his goods to other Maghribi traders travelling on board the ship that carried his goods. The use of this alternative is illustrated in a letter sent early in the eleventh century by Ephraim, son of Isma'il from Alexandria, to Ibn 'Awkal, a prominent merchant who lived in Fustat (old Cairo).

I wrote to M. Abu Sa'id son of Ya'qub—may God keep him—a letter in four copies, sending each copy . . . with different boats: namely, one with Salama Ibn Abu Khalil on the boat of alba'shushi; another on the boat of alandalusi, with Sahlan, may God keep him; a third copy, on the boat of Ibn alqaddar—may God keep him—I gave to the owner of the boat . . . .; the fourth, I gave to Salar, the 'boy' of Ibn alsahila. I instruct all [of them] . . . to watch carefully the seventy bales and one barqalu [containing the goods] until they will deliver them safely into the hands of Khalaf son of Ya'qub, the Andalusian.[95]

Instead of solving the organizational problem between the merchant and the ship's operator, the Maghribi traders circumvented it. This fact is forcefully illustrated in a letter sent from Sicily in 1057. It described what happened to loads of merchandise, the covers of which were torn during a voyage. The ship arrived in port, and the owner (operator?) of the ship started to steal merchandise. The writer of the letter remarked that 'unless my brother had been there to collect [the goods], nothing that belonged to our friends [i.e. the Maghribi traders] would have been collected.'[96] The fact that the ship's owner did not consider himself, and was not considered by the traders, responsible for protecting the goods is made clear in this letter. Similarly, if goods of unknown ownership were unloaded from the ship, or if

[94] For information on Genoa, see Bensa (1925). For the use of the bill of lading by the Maghribi traders and possible bias in the historical records, see Goitein (1973), 305 ff..
[95] TS 13 J 17, fo. 3. Goitein (1973), 313.
[96] Bodl. MS Heb. c. 28, fo. 61, a, ll. 12–14; Gil (1983a), 126–33.

the ship did not reach its destination, it was not the Captain but the Maghribi traders who took care of the goods.[97] The Genoese traders, among whom agency relations were governed by individualist behavioural beliefs, could not rely on fellow traders to protect their goods, and had to use other means of solving the organizational problem associated with shipping goods. The bill of lading, the letter of advice, and the legal responsibility they entail provided this means.

The ability to ensure compliance with collective decisions among traders who had held collectivist behavioural beliefs might also be fundamental to the development in Europe, but not in the Muslim world, of organizations that governed the relations between a ruler and alien traders who frequented their territory. These relations were characterized during the late Medieval period by a commitment problem. In his own town, the Medieval ruler had the ability to abuse the property rights of alien traders by using his coercive power. In the age before the emergence of the European state, alien traders could expect little military or political aid from their countrymen. Without any institutional arrangements that enabled a ruler to commit himself, *ex ante*, not to abuse alien traders' rights, *ex post*, the traders were not likely to frequent that ruler's town—an outcome that may have been costly for the traders and the ruler alike.

Greif, Milgrom, and Weingast (1991) have suggested that in late Medieval Europe, a specific institution, the merchant guild, functioned as a nexus of contracts that overcame the commitment problem associated with the ruler–trader relations by supplementing the operation of a bilateral reputation mechanism, that is, a reputation mechanism between the ruler and each individual trader. This organization co-ordinated alien traders' responses to transgressions by the ruler. These responses were in the form of trade embargoes, since the traders lacked military ability. Once an embargo was imposed, however, individual traders could benefit from free-riding by breaking the embargo and selling their goods in the city at a time of shortage.[98] To prevent the breaking of embargoes, the guild took advantage of its ability to regulate traders' activities outside the domain of the ruler. Thus, the European merchant guilds used their military, political, and commercial power within their territorial base to prevent embargo-breaking and to ensure the solidarity of incentives among traders necessary to surmount the ruler–trader commitment problem.

For example, in 1284 a German trading ship was attacked and pillaged by the Norwegians. The German towns responded by imposing an embargo on Norway. The export to Norway of grain, flour, vegetables, and beer was prohibited. According to the chronicler Detmar, 'there broke out a famine so great that [the Norwegians] were forced to make atonement'. The temptation

---

[97] e.g. Bodl. MS Heb., c. 28, fo. 61, a, ll. 9–17; Gil (1983a), 126–33) (unknown owners).
[98] For theoretical exposition, see Grief, Milgrom, and Weingast (1991).

for an individual German trader to smuggle food to Norway in this situation is clear. To prevent smuggling and sustain the embargo, the German towns had to post ships in the Danish Straits.[99] Similar attention to the need to guarantee solidarity among traders is also reflected in Flemish regulations, written in 1240, for trade at the English fairs.

If any man of Ypres or Daouai shall go against those decisions [made by the guild] . . . for the common good, regarding fines or anything else, that man shall be excluded from selling, lodging, eating, or depositing his wool or cloth in ships with the rest of the merchants . . . And if anyone violates this ostracism, he shall be fined 5s. . . .[100]

In Europe, a formal organization that specialized in enforcement was required to ensure solidarity of incentives, because the community without formal regulatory power could not induce individual members to follow its policy. Within the Muslim world, merchant guilds that fulfilled this function were not established.[101] While many factors are likely to have contributed to this difference in organizational development between the Muslim and the European worlds, it is still instructive to note that among traders organized like the Maghribi, there is no need for a formal organization to serve as an internal enforcer. The self-enforceable collective punishment may be sufficient to ensure solidarity of incentives. Indeed, when the Maghribi traders announced an embargo on Sicily in 1050, it was organized informally and without the support of any formal organization. 'Hold the hands of our friends [i.e. Maghribi traders] not to send to Sicily even one dirham [a low value coin]' wrote Maymun ben Khalpha from Palermo (Sicily) to Naharay ben Nissim in Fustat (old Cairo).[102]

Clearly, Europe was not uniform; some communities, in different times and places, were characterized by more or less individualism. Genoa, for example, was known during the late Medieval period for its individualism, in particular with respect to its great rival, Venice. Franco Sacchetti, a Florentine merchant-novelist, who in 1381 aimed to demonstrate that the Genoese were more individualistic than the Venetians, attributed this homily to a Genoese, who told his countrymen:

You are like donkeys. The nature of the donkey is this: when many are together, and one of them is thrashed with a stick, all scatter, fleeing hither and thither, so great is

---

[99] Dollinger (1970), 49. See also the description of the embargo on Novgorod, p. 48. Anyone who broke the embargo was to suffer the death penalty and the confiscation of his goods.

[100] Moore (1985), 298.

[101] Craft guilds known as *sinf, hirfa*, and by other names prospered in the Islamic world from the ninth to the twelfth century under the inspiration of the political, social, and religious movement of the *Karmatians*. Guilds that regulated trade were established by the Ottomans to ensure provisions to their large cities. Both cases, however, have nothing to do with the ruler–traders commitment problem. See the discussion in Lapidus (1988), 330–1; and in the *Encyclopedia of Islam*, the articles *Sinf, Karmati*.

[102] David Kaufmann Collection, Hungarian Academy of Science, Budapest, doc. no. 22, a, ll. 29–31, b, ll. 3 5; Gil (1983a, 97–106); Taylor–Schechter collection, University Library, Cambridge, England, doc. 10 J 12, fo. 26, a, ll. 18–20; Michael (1965), ii. 85.

their vileness; and this is exactly your nature. The Venetians are similar to pigs and are called Venetian pigs, and truly they have a pig's nature, for when a multitude of pigs is confined together and one of them is hit or beaten with a stick, all draw close and run unto him who hits it; and this is truly their nature.[103]

It is interesting to note, however, that this difference seems to support the hypothesis concerning the relations between individualism and the nature of European organizational development, since the Genoese, as a rule, introduced organizational innovations before the Venetians. Kedar (1976) has noted that

Venice lagged behind Genoa in developing and adopting new trade practices. The earliest marine chart that bears a date was drawn in 1311 by Petrus Vesconte, a Genoese; the oldest Venetian marine chart extant, that of Francesco Pizzigano, dates from 1367. The earliest insurance contract extant was drawn up in Genoa in 1342; in Venice insurance is unequivocally documented only from 1393 onward. (p. 11).

This section suggests that the difference between collectivist and individualist behavioural beliefs is apt to lead to different trajectories of organizational development both directly and indirectly. Different behavioural beliefs generate diverse incentives that lead to the use of different forms of business associations and that facilitate different organizations. Collectivist behavioural beliefs are likely to lead to segregation and thus provide communities with the ability to achieve internal enforcement and to ensure solidarity of incentives without employing organizations that specialize in enforcement. On the other hand, individualist behavioural beliefs do not provide the community as a whole with such an enforcement mechanism, thus leading to the development of institutions that specialize in enforcement. The historical evidence presented in this section supports the assertion that different behavioural beliefs did indeed affect the trajectories of trade-related organizational development in the Muslim and the Latin worlds. While additional historical research is required to demonstrate more forcefully that distinct equilibria have indeed led to distinct trajectories of organizational development, the historical evidence considered calls attention to the importance of behavioural beliefs in affecting the unique organizational development of Europe.

DID DIVERSE BEHAVIOURAL BELIEFS CHARACTERIZE THE LATE MEDIEVAL EUROPEAN AND MUSLIM SOCIETIES? ON THE ORIGINS OF BEHAVIOURAL BELIEFS AND THE UNIQUE EUROPEAN ECONOMIC DEVELOPMENT

The historical discussion so far has been based mainly on two case-studies— the histories of the Maghribi and the Genoese traders. Clearly, one cannot

---

[103] Cited in Kedar (1976), 7; see the general discussion there.

generalize from these two case-studies and argue that they are sufficient to support a claim about the general importance of diverse behavioural beliefs leading to different trajectories of social structures and organizations related to long-distance commerce in late Medieval Europe and the Muslim world. To substantiate the generality of this conjecture one has either to examine additional case-studies or the origins of diverse behavioural beliefs. That is, one has to examine what the factors are that led to the emergence of collect-ivist behavioural beliefs on the one hand, and individualist behavioural be-liefs on the other. Support for the general importance of behavioural beliefs can be gained if the factors that lead to individualist behavioural beliefs pre-vailed in the Latin commercial cities, while the factors that lead to collectivist behavioural beliefs prevailed in the Muslim commercial cities. Accordingly, this section examines the factors that are theoretically likely to lead to indi-vidualist or collectivist behavioural beliefs; the factors that led historically to the emergence of diverse behavioural beliefs among the Maghribi and the Genoese traders; the importance of these factors in the general history of the Latin and Muslim cities; and the factors that determine the possibility of changing from one set of behavioural beliefs to another.

The theoretical analysis indicates that a necessary condition for the emerg-ence and persistence of a collectivist equilibrium is the existence of a network of information transmission. Without some network of information trans-mission through which merchants can commit themselves to learn about agents who have been cheating (despite the fact that cheating does not occur on the equilibrium path), collective punishment cannot be supported. On the other hand, a sufficient condition for individualist equilibrium is the ab-sence of such an information-transmission mechanism.[104]

There is asymmetry in the relationship between changes in an economy's information-transmission mechanism and shifts from one equilibrium to another. If a collectivist equilibrium has been reached, once the information-transmission mechanism that supports it ceases to function, a shift to an indi-vidualist equilibrium will occur, since, without the ability to inform the group's members about cheats, the threat of collective punishment is not credible. If an individualist equilibrium has been reached, and later an information-transmission mechanism capable of supporting a collectivist equilibrium has emerged, a shift to a collectivist equilibrium will not occur. This shift will not occur, since, once individualistic behavioural beliefs have become a part of the cultural heritage of that society, any merchant, believ-ing that other merchants will follow the individualist strategy, will follow it as well, even if he finds out about cheating.[105] The individualist equi-librium has a 'lock-in' effect. Once it is reached, even if an information-transmission mechanism capable of supporting collective punishment

---

[104] Under the assumption that either collectivist or individualist equilibria are achieved.
[105] See proposition 2.

emerges at a later point in time, the economy will not reach a collectivist equilibrium.[106]

The historical records indicate that the nature of the information-transmission mechanism available to the Maghribi traders at the point in their history in which their behavioural beliefs were probably crystallized, was such that it enabled them to reach a collectivist equilibrium. In contrast, the nature of the information-transmission mechanism available to the Genoese traders at a parallel point in their history, was such that they could not reach a collectivist equilibrium.

The Maghribi traders operated in the Abbasid caliphate (centred in Baghdad) until the first half of the tenth century, when they migrated to Tunisia and elsewhere in North Africa. The social ties among these immigrants provided them with a mechanism for information transmission which, in turn, enabled them to reach a collectivist equilibrium. At the same time, the fact that Maghribi traders established agency relations only among themselves, gave their separate social identity a function and preserved the social network for information transmission. A social network for information transmission enabled the Maghribi traders to reach a collectivist equilibrium, while the patterns of behaviour generated by this equilibrium led to increasing social associations among Maghribi traders, thus reinforcing the social network for information transmission.[107]

The process through which the Genoese traders had been introduced to trade was rather different. For political reasons the number of Genoese active in trade rose dramatically after 1179. Instead of a few dozen or fewer traders active in commerce with a specific trade centre, hundreds and thousands of people became involved in trade. Furthermore, Genoa experienced a high level of immigration, and a high mortality rate among the well-established families, which probably led to the destruction of its social network of information transmission and to the emergence of an individualist equilibrium.[108] The difference in initial social networks for information transmission between the Maghribi and the Genoese traders at the moment in history in which trade expanded may have been the reason for the appearance of distinct equilibria.

The theoretical analysis and the history of the Maghribi and Genoese traders suggests that when cities and trade expansions are such that traders do not share a pre-expansion social network for information-transmission, an individualist equilibrium is likely to result. Furthermore, even if at a later period an information-transmission mechanism that can support a collectivist equilibrium does exist, a shift to collectivist equilibrium is not likely to

[106] On the 'lock-in' effect and its importance in the theory of path dependence (mainly in technology) see David (1988a; 1988b); Arthur (1988; 1989).

[107] Goitein (1967), 156–9, 186–92; Gil (1983b), i. 200 ff.; Gil (1974), 299–328; Greif (1989).

[108] Byrne (1920); Krueger (1962); and see the discussion in Greif (1990b).

occur. On the other hand, when cities and trade expansions are based upon existing traders' groups, each of which has a social network for information transmission, a collectivist equilibrium is likely to result. Interestingly, the former process was the one that occurred in the Latin world, while the latter was the one that occurred in the Muslim world.

The commercial expansion of the Latin cities in the late Medieval period was relatively sudden. The reduction in internal warfare and external threats during this period led to an environment favourable to long-distance trade. A process of rapid trade expansion followed, and previously closed small economies became interrelated through a commercial network of trading cities. This inter-city development led to social, economic, political, and demographic changes in those cities. In particular, they experienced a rapid rise in population, fuelled by the new economic opportunities and privileges given to cities and their residents by feudal rulers. The cities themselves encouraged immigration, which was necessary to reap the economic and political benefits the new situation offered. The mere fact that the residents of large areas of Europe, particularly Southern Europe, shared the Latin language and heritage as well as the Christian religion facilitated commercial interactions and the process of city amalgamation.[109]

The amalgamation process of cities and commercial expansion in the Muslim world followed a different route. When the Muslims established their supremacy during the seventh and eighth centuries in the land stretching from India to Spain, they facilitated commercial interactions between residents of previously different political units, such as the Byzantine Empire, the Sasanian Empire, and the kingdom of Spain. Furthermore, areas that had never been a part of the Middle Eastern empire, such as Transoxania, were brought under their control. The victory of the Muslims demolished political and legal barriers to trade in the short run, and, to a large extent, demolished linguistic and religious barriers to trade in the long run.

Long-distance commerce prospered in the early Muslim world, contributing to the expansion of existing towns through migration and the creation of new cities.[110] This process, however, differed substantially from that experienced by the Europeans, since it built on the existing urban communities whose inhabitants had for centuries been active in long-distance trade within and between the pre-Islamic political units. Furthermore, the inhabitants of these cities were divided along regional, religious, linguistic, cultural, and ethnic lines, and the expansion of Muslim urban communities was marked by these differences. Historical studies have suggested that each group of immigrants preserved its social structure and thus its original social network

[109] See, for example, Lopez (1976); Pirenne (1952); Postan (1973), 92 ff.; Cipolla (1980), 142 ff. This is not to say, however, that the patterns of settlement in the cities were independent of the patterns of previous settlement. In Genoa, for example, it is clear that immigrants from certain villages concentrated in particular neighbourhoods. See the discussion in Hughes (1977).

[110] See, for example, Lapidus (1988), in particular, 45 ff.

of information transmission. The later invasions of different ethnic elements into the Muslim world, and the conflicts between Arabs, Persians, Turks, Berbers, Mongols, and Slavs reinforced this process of immigration and the associated social networks for information transmission and left a diversity of immigrant groups in the cities. Muslim cities in the late Medieval period were an agglomeration of small quarters, each with its own homogeneous group of residents who formed, to a large extent, segregated economic and political units.[111]

In a relatively short period of time, the Latin world experienced the emergence of commercial cities that became centres of long-distance commerce. In a similar time-frame the Muslim world came to encompass well-established cities and trading communities. The historical contexts in which trade and city expansion occurred in the Muslim and Latin worlds were different. One likely manifestation of this difference was the dissimilar social information-transmission mechanisms. In the fast-growing cities and the newly established trade centres of the Latin world, the social network for information transmission had functioned less successfully than in the well-established merchants' communities of the Muslim world. A difference in information-transmission mechanisms led to the selection of different equilibria and diverse behavioural beliefs, which affected the evolution of distinct trajectories of social and organizational developments related to trade in each of these societies. As the theoretical discussion has established, even if, as was most likely the case, the cities in the Latin world had eventually established social networks for information transmission, the individualist behavioural beliefs that crystallized in the earlier stage were not reversed.

The examination of the processes of the amalgamation of cities and commercial expansion in the Latin and the Muslim worlds lends support to the conjecture that the differences between the Maghribi and the Genoese traders does not reflect some peculiarity of history. Rather, it implies that the process which led to the emergence of individualist behavioural beliefs among the Genoese traders was experienced, by and large, by Italian traders, while the process that led to the emergence of collectivist behavioural beliefs among the Maghribi traders was experienced, on the whole, by Muslim traders. Hence, this examination lends support to the conjecture that diverse behavioural beliefs that crystallized in each of these worlds contributed to the emergence of distinct developments of social structures, business practices and organizations, and organizations that specialized in enforcement. These differences, in turn, led to different patterns of commercial expansion.

In particular, the end of the first millennium of the Christian calendar was characterized by the re-emergence of stable and prosperous economies both in Europe and in the Far East. This ascending economic trend lasted until the upheavals brought about by the aftermath of the Mongol invasion, and the

---

[111] The main study of the internal organization of the Muslim cities in the late Medieval period was made by Lapidus (1984). See also Hodgson (1974), 105 ff.

Black Death put an end to it. It was the European traders, however, who seem to have benefited from the increase in the volume of trade between the Far East and Europe much more than the traders from the Muslim world, which was geographically placed as an intermediary. Even in the period prior to the emergence of Italian naval supremacy in the Mediterranean, that is, during the eleventh century, Italian traders frequented the Muslim ports rather than the other way around.

The difference between societies based on collectivist and individualist behavioural beliefs provides an explanation for this phenomenon. The commercial expansion necessarily meant expanding the number of merchants and agents. Western society, in which institutions and social structures were based on individualism, was capable of increasing the number of traders much more rapidly than a society based on segregation and collectivism. Under individualist behavioural beliefs, agency relations were basically of a bilateral nature and hence establishing agency relations among strangers was not an obstacle. Under collectivist behavioural beliefs, agency relations were of a multilateral nature and hence establishing agency relations among strangers was problematic, since entry to a group was restricted due to the need for co-ordination, while the motivation to establish efficient agency relations outside the group was reduced by the possibility of achieving profitable agency relations within the group.

The importance of Western individualism to the West's unique process of commercial development is also reflected in a study that examines the diverse patterns of commercial evolution in pre-modern Europe and China. The sociologist Gary H. Hamilton (1991) concluded that

in the West, commercial organizations in the private sphere rested upon legal institutions and upon individualism, neither of which had central importance in China. . . . Kinship and collegiality in China play roles analogous to those played by law and individuality in the West, but with very different developmental trajectories and outcomes. (pp. 1–2).

While the conjecture concerning the centrality of individualist behavioural beliefs in the commercial history of Europe still awaits additional support based on detailed historical case-studies, the history of the Latin and Muslim worlds gives rise to a broader conjecture; namely, that collectivist and individualist equilibria reached in Medieval cities affected the trajectories of social and organizational development in these worlds far beyond their direct impact on developments related to trade organization and traders' groups. The factors that lend support to this conjecture are the importance of cities in economic and social evolution during the late Medieval period, and the centrality of merchant–agent relations and other economic transactions characterized by the OSPD game in these cities.

Throughout history, and in particular in the Medieval world, cities were the frontiers of cultural, social, and political change, largely because city inhabitants engaged in long-distance commerce.[112] The large cities were commercial centres both in Europe and in the Muslim world. Many of the residents who were not administrators or soldiers were traders, constantly engaged in merchant–agent relations which, therefore, were a fundamental element of the economic and social fabric of the city. In addition, Italian and Muslim trade expansion was based on the capital provided by many investors, small and large, to travelling agents who traded abroad. Individuals from all segments of society, not only a limited class of professional traders, were active in trade, and the manner in which merchant–agent relations were organized affected them all. While this fact is well known with respect to the Italian cities, it was also one of the facts of life in the Medieval Muslim city. Cahen (1990) noted that in the Muslim cities 'all men of substance, from the caliph or sultan downwards, invested part of the income that they drew from their landed properties in trade' (525).[113]

Furthermore, the same differences between cities in the Muslim and the Latin worlds that led to the development of diverse behavioural beliefs in the relations between merchants and agents may also have led to the development of diverse behavioural beliefs in other OSPD games. As mentioned above, the OSPD game captures the essence of the organizational problem associated with economic transactions other than merchant–agent relations. For example, an OSPD game characterizes many labour relations as well as the relations between consumers and suppliers of experience goods. The same factors that contributed to the emergence of diverse behavioural beliefs in the cities of Europe and the Western world may have led to the selection of different equilibria in these OSPD games as well.

A theoretical and historical examination of the factors that led to diverse behavioural beliefs among the Maghribi and the Genoese traders indicates that they reflect different processes of the amalgamation of cities and trade expansion in the Latin and the Muslim worlds. This finding supports the conjecture that the historical evidence concerning diverse behavioural beliefs and their impact on the social and organizational structures of the Maghribi and Genoese traders' groups are general in nature. It strengthens the conjecture that during the late Medieval period collectivist behavioural beliefs in the Muslim world fostered segregation, a horizontal social structure, a particular set of business practices and organizations, and organizations based upon the ability of the community to achieve enforcement and ensure solidarity of incentives among its members. On the other hand, during the late Medieval period individualist behavioural beliefs in the Latin

[112] With respect to the European cities, this assertion is a part of the famous Pirenne thesis. As for the Islamic world, Cahen (1990) noted that 'in the Muslim world as in the ancient world ... the whole civilization was found in the town; it was only there that administration, law, religion and culture existed.' (521). See also Lapidus (1988).

[113] For information on the importance of trade in the Italian cities, see Reynolds (1945); Cipolla (1980), and in particular p. 198. For information on the importance of trade in the Muslim cities, see Cahen (1990).

world fostered social integration, vertical social structures, a particular set of business practices and organizations, and the development of organizations that specialized in enforcement. The differences in these trajectories of development directly and indirectly through their impact on future developments have been fundamental in leading to distinct patterns of economic growth.[114]

CONCLUSIONS

This chapter has attempted to illustrate the importance of behavioural beliefs in affecting the development of social structures and organizations. Behavioural beliefs beliefs serve as a co-ordinator—a common view of the world that indicates what individuals would do in different situations. At a given point in time, behavioural beliefs affect the social structures, business practices, and economic organizations of a society. Furthermore, behavioural beliefs that were crystallized in one period of time affect the equilibrium selected once the rules of the game are changed due to exogenous or endogenous reasons. The same changes in societies otherwise identical in behaviour and organizations but differing in their behavioural beliefs, may lead each economy to develop differently. Thus, economies that are identical in all but behavioural beliefs may develop along different trajectories.

To illustrate the possible implications of behavioural beliefs, a simple OSPD game suitable for the theoretical and historical study of collectivist and individualist societies was examined. The analysis indicated that for a given game, different behavioural beliefs lead to different social structures and organizations. Furthermore, once the rules of the game are changed, different behavioural beliefs, each of which supported the same regularity of behaviour *ex post*, are sufficient to generate, *ex ante*, different patterns of behaviour, social structures, and incentives for organizational modification. Thus, behavioural beliefs alone are sufficient to lead to the evolution of diverse social and organizational systems. Behavioural beliefs are an integral part of the functioning of institutions, and, thus, the ability of organizations

---

[114] Since this is not the place to elaborate on the exact mechanisms through which these difference in social and organizational structures actually led to diverse pattern of growth, I will only refer the reader to North (1990; 1991), who called attention to the relationship between mechanisms through which enforcement is achieved in directing economic growth. For related historical studies, see Rosenthal (1990); North and Weingast (1989). Clearly, the Latin and the Muslim worlds differed in many other aspects besides behavioural beliefs. For example, they differed in their religions and legal institutions. While elaboration on the interrelations between these factors and behavioural beliefs is beyond the scope of this paper, it should be noted that these factors are not independent from different incentives generated by diverse behavioural beliefs. Throughout history, even religiously based legal systems changed and adjusted according to the needs of the time. Thus, the mere fact that a particular legal systems developed along a specific path is likely to reflect some combination of incentives and of the particularities of that legal system.

to alter outcomes, and the incentives to establish organizations, depend upon them.

To show that behavioural beliefs may actually have been important in shaping different trajectories of development, a preliminary comparative historical study was conducted. Historical evidence, mainly concerning the Maghribi traders of the eleventh century and the Genoese traders of the twelfth century, suggests that different behavioural beliefs shaped the social and organizational development of each of these traders' groups. The postulate that members of each of these groups held different behavioural beliefs is supported by its ability to generate predictions that can be examined empirically. A rational and consistent explanation was advanced based on this postulate regarding diverse phenomena such as the choice of business associations, the social structure of the traders' group, inter-group relations, emigration, and organizational innovation.

It is plausible that the differences in behavioural beliefs, as reflected in the history of the Maghribi and the Genoese traders, existed among other European and Muslim traders' groups, and more generally, among the residents of cities in these two worlds. While additional historical research is required to substantiate this hypothesis, it seems that the difference in behavioural beliefs resulted largely from differences in the social networks for information transmission that existed at the moment of history in which trade and cities expanded. Thus, it is plausible that diverse behavioural beliefs contributed to the development of individualism in the Western world and collectivism in the Muslim world. Furthermore, it is plausible that the distinctive behavioural beliefs of the Western world account for its unique organizational development. Thus, different behavioural beliefs led to a simultaneous evolution of individualism and the trajectory of organizational development in the Western world. This unique trajectory of organizational development contributed to the affluence of the Western world, which further advanced its individualist nature.

The theoretical and historical study of the interaction between different economies in an earlier period leads to some insights into the current process of inter-economy integration. To understand the short-term economic implications and the long-run social, cultural, organizational, and economic consequences of inter-economy interaction, the behavioural beliefs in each economy have to be examined. Within each society, behavioural beliefs constitute a common resource that affects equilibrium selection in a constantly changing environment. World economic integration leads to changes in the rules of the games played within and across economies, and the pre-change behavioural beliefs may be fundamental in the selection of the new equilibrium. The nature of this equilibrium shapes the future development of cultural, social, and organizational systems within each society. From the economic point of view, as the example of late Medieval world integration illustrates, this development is not necessarily optimal, due to the path-dependent nature of organizational and cultural changes, and due to the fact that in each economy behavioural beliefs constitute a common resource that cannot necessarily be shared with individuals from other societies. Additional theoretical and empirical studies of the relationship between behavioural beliefs that crystallized in a pre-change game and the equilibrium selected in the post-change game are required to promote the optimality of this development.

Apart from exogenous changes in the rules of the game, the current world economic integration process is characterized by deliberate changes in those rules. For example, agricultural co-operatives like those established in continental Europe were introduced in Ireland, Asia, and Africa. Russia is in the process of adopting Western economic organizations. Glade (1969) has noted that the Latin American countries 'inspired by the example of the Thirteen Colonies in North America, . . . erect[ed] a mimetic system of government patterned after the norms of political liberalism'. (185–6). The deliberate adoption of these organizations followed their success, yet the results of implementing them in other than their original societies were, in many cases, disappointing.[115] Litwack (1990) has suggested that the failure of market reforms in centrally planned economies is, to a large extent, a reflection of the planners' inability to commit themselves to the organizational change.

This chapter has called attention to the role of behavioural beliefs as a source of the failure of organizational adoption. Behavioural beliefs crystallized within a society before a new organization was introduced, affected the equilibrium selected after the introduction of that new organization. Thus, the same organization, when advanced within a society that has a different common resource—different behavioural beliefs—may yield different results.

REFERENCES

Abreu, D., Pearce, D., and Stacchetti, E. (1986), 'Optimal Cartel Equilibria with Imperfect Monitoring', *Journal of Economic Theory*, 39: 251–69.

Abercrombie, N. S. and Hill, B. S. (1984), *The Penguin Dictionary of Sociology* (London: Penguin).

Akerlof, G. A. (1986), 'A Theory of Social Custom', in *An Economic Theorist's Book of Tales* (Cambridge: Cambridge University Press).

—— and Yellen, L. (1986), *Efficiency Wage Models of the Labour Market* (Cambridge: Cambridge University Press).

Arrow, J. K. (1974), *The Limits of Organization* (New York: Norton).

---

[115] About agricultural co-operatives, see the discussion in Guinnane (1991); Braverman, Guasch, and Huppi (1990). About Latin America, see Glade (1969), in particular pp. 185 ff.

Arthur, B. W. (1988), 'Self-Reinforcing Mechanisms in Economics', in P. W. Anderson, K. J. Arrow, and D. Pines (eds.), *The Economy as an Evolving Complex System* (Redwood City, Calif.: Addison-Wesley).

—— (1989), 'Competing Technologies, Increasing Returns, and Lock-in by Historical Events', *The Economic Journal*, 99: 116–31.

Bandura, A. (1977), *Social Learning Theory* (Englewood Cliffs, NJ: Prentice-Hall).

Bellah, R. N., Madsen, R., Sullivan, W. M., Swidler, A., and Tipton, S. M. (1985), *Habits of the Heart: Individualism and Commitment in American Life* (Berkeley, Calif.: University of California Press).

Bensa, E. (1925), *The Early History of Bills of Lading* (Genoa: Stabilimento d'Arti Grafiche).

Binger, B. R. and Hoffman, E. (1989), 'Institutional Persistence and Change: The Question of Efficiency', *Journal of Institutional and Theoretical Economics*, 145: 67–84.

Birnbaum, N. (1953), 'Conflicting Interpretations of the Rise of Capitalism: Marx and Weber', *British Journal of Sociology*, 4: 125–41.

Braverman, A., Guasch, J. L., and Huppi, M. (1990), 'Promoting Rural Co-operatives in Developing Countries: The Case of Subsaharan Africa', discussion paper 90–36 (San Diego, Calif.: University of California).

Byrne, E. H. (1917), 'Commercial Contracts of the Genoese in the Syrian Trade of the Twelfth Century', *Quarterly Journal of Economics*, 31: 128–70.

—— (1920), 'Genoese Trade with Syria in the Twelfth Century', *American Historical Review*, 25: 191–219.

—— (1928), 'The Genoese Colonies in Syria', in L. J. Paetow (ed.), *The Crusade and other Historical Essays* (New York: F. S. Crofts).

Cahen, C. (1990) 'Economy, Society, Institutions', in P. M. Holt, A. K. S. Lambton, and B. Lewis (eds.), *The Cambridge History of Islam* (Cambridge: Cambridge University Press).

Cassinese, G. (1190–2), *Notai Liguri del Sec. XII*, ed. M. W. Hall, H. C. Krueger, and R. L. Reynolds (Turin: Editrice Libraria Italiana, 1938).

Cavalli-Sforza, L. L. and Feldman, M. W. (1981), *Cultural Transmission and Solution: A Quantitative Approach* (Princeton, NJ: Princeton University Press).

Cipolla, C. M. (1980), *Before the Industrial Revolution* (New York: Norton).

Dalton, G. (ed.) (1971), *Primitive, Archaic and Modern Economics: Essays of Karl Polanyi* (Boston, Mass.: Beacon Press).

Dasgupta, P. (1982), *The Control of Resources* (Cambridge, Mass.: Harvard University Press).

David, A. P. (1988a), 'The Future of Path-dependent Equilibrium Economics', Center for Economic Policy Research, working paper no. 155 (Stanford, Calif.: Stanford University).

—— (1988b), 'Path-dependence: Putting the Past into the Future of Economics', technical report no. 533, IMSSS (Stanford, Calif.: Stanford University).

—— (1990), 'Information Technology Standards, Social Communication Norms, and the State: A Public Goods Conundrum', Center for Economic Policy Research (Stanford, Calif.: Stanford University).

Davis, K. (1949), *Human Society* (New York: Macmillan).

Dawes, R. M., and Thaler, R. H. (1988), 'Anomalies: Co-operation', *Journal of Economic Perspective*, 2: 187–97.

Dawkins, R. (1976), *The Selfish Gene* (New York: Oxford University Press).

Dollinger, P. (1970), *The German Hansa* (Stanford, Calif.: Stanford University Press).

Ellickson, R. C. (1987), 'A Critique of Economic and Sociological Theories of Social Control', *Journal of Legal Studies*, 16: 67–99.

—— (1989), 'A Hypothesis of Wealth-maximizing Norms: Evidence from the Whaling Industry', *Journal of Law, Economics and Organization*, 5: 83–97.

Elster, J. (1988), 'Economic Order and Social Norms', *Journal of Institutional and Theoretical Economics*, 144: 357–66.

—— (1989), 'Social Norms and Economic Theory', *Journal of Economic Perspective*, 34: 99–117.

Etzioni, A. (1988), *The Moral Dimension* (New York: Free Press).

Face, R. D. (1958), 'Techniques of Business in the Trade between the Fairs of Champagne and the South of Europe in the Twelfth and Thirteenth Centuries', *Economic History Review*, 10.

Festinger, L. (1950), 'Informal Social Communication', *Psychological Review*, 57: 271–82.

Frank, R. H. (1987), 'If Homo Economicus Could Choose His Own Utility Function, Would He Want One with a Conscience?', *American Economic Review*, 77/4: 593–604.

Gil, M. (1974), 'The Radhanite Merchants and the Land of the Radahan', *Journal of the Economic and Social History of the Orient*, 17: 299–328.

—— (1981), *The Tustaris, Family and Sect* (Tel-Aviv: Diaspora Research Institute; in Hebrew).

—— (1983a), 'The Jews in Sicily under the Muslim Rule in the Light of the *Geniza* Documents', MS (Tel Aviv University). repr. (in Italian) in *Italia Judaica* (Rome: Instituto Poligrafico e Zecca dello Stato).

—— (1983b), *Palestine During the First Muslim Period (634–1099)*, i–iii (in Hebrew and Arabic) (Tel Aviv: Ministry of Defence Press and Tel Aviv University Press).

Glade, W. P. (1969), *The Latin American Economies* (New York: American Book).

Goitein, S. D. (1955), 'The Cairo *Geniza* as a Source for the History of the Muslim Civilization', *Studia Islamica*, 2: 75–91.

—— (1967), *Economic Foundations: A Mediterranean Society*, i (Los Angeles: University of California Press).

—— (1973), *Letters of Medieval Jewish Traders* (Princeton, NJ: Princeton University Press).

Gras, S. B. (1939), *Business and Capitalism: An Introduction to Business History* (New York: F. S. Crofts).

Green E. and Porter, R. (1984), 'Non-cooperative Collusion under Imperfect Price Information', *Econometrica*, 52: 87 100.

Greif, A. (1989), 'Reputation and Coalitions in Medieval Trade: Evidence on the Maghribi Traders', *Journal of Economic History*, 49: 857–82.

—— (1990a), 'Contract Enforceability and Economic Institutions in Early Trade: The Maghribi Traders' Coalition' (mimeo; Stanford University).

—— (1990b), 'Reputation and Coalitions in Medieval Trade: Evidence on the Genoese Traders' (mimeo; Stanford University).

—— Milgrom, P. and Weingast, B. (1991), 'The Merchant Gild as a Nexus of Contracts' (mimeo; Stanford University).

Guinnane, T. (1991), 'Co-operative Agricultural Credit in Germany and Ireland, 1870–1914' (mimeo; Department of Economics, Princeton University).

Hamilton, G. G. (1991), 'The Organizational Foundations of Western and Chinese Commerce: A Historical and Comparative Analysis' (mimeo; Department of Sociology, University of California at Davis).

Herlihy, D. (1985), *Medieval Households* (Cambridge, Mass.: Harvard University Press).

—— Lopez, R. S., Slessarev, V. (eds.) (1969), *Economy, Society, and Government in Medieval Italy: Essays in Memory of Robert L. Reynolds* (Kent, Ohio: Kent State University Press).

Hirshleifer, J. (1985), 'The Expanding Domain of Economics', *American Economic Review*, Dec.: 53–68.

—— (1987), 'On the Emotions as Guarantors of Threats and Promises', in J. Dupre (ed.), *The Latest on the Best* (Cambridge: Cambridge University Press).

Hodgson, M. G. S. (1974), *The Venture of Islam*, ii (Chicago: Chicago University Press).

Hoffman, E. and Spitzer, M. L. (1985), 'Entitlement, Rights, and Fairness: An Experimental Examination of Subjects' Concepts of Distributive Justice', *Journal of Legal Studies*, June: 259–97.

—— McCabe, K. and Smith, V. (1991), 'Fairness, Property Rights, and Bargaining: Some Preliminary Experimental Results' (mimeo; University of Arizona, Tucson).

Hofstede, G. (1980), *Culture's Consequences* (Beverly Hills, Calif.: Sage).

Homans, G. C. (1941), *English Villagers of the Thirteenth Century* (Cambridge, Mass.: Harvard University Press).

—— (1950), *The Human Group* (New York: Harcourt).

Huges, D. O. (1977), 'Kinsmen and Neighbors in Medieval Genoa', in H. A. Miskimin, D. Herlihy, and A. L. Udovitch (eds.), *The Medieval City* (New Haven, Conn.: Yale University Press).

—— (1978), 'Urban Growth and Family Structure in Medieval Genoa', in P. Abrams and E. A. Wrigley (eds.), *Towns in Societies* (Cambridge: Cambridge University Press).

Hume, D. (1740), *A Treatise of Human Nature*, 2nd edn., ed. L. A. Selby-Bigge (Oxford: Clarendon Press, 1978).

John the Scribe (Cartolare di Giovanni Scriba) (1154–64), ed. M. Chiaudano and M. Moresco (Turin: S. Lattes & C. Editori, 1935).

Jones, E. L. (1981), *The European Miracle*, 2nd edn. (Cambridge: Cambridge University Press).

Kandori, M. (1989), 'Social Norms and Community Enforcement', CARESS working paper no. 89–14 (Philadelphia: University of Pennsylvania).

Kedar, B. Z. (1976), *Merchants in Crisis* (New Haven, Conn.: Yale University Press).

Klein, B. and Leffler, K. (1981), 'The Role of Market Forces in Assuring Contractual Performance', *Journal of Political Economy*, 89: 615–41.

Kreps, D. M. (1990a), *A Course in Microeconomic Theory* (Princeton, NJ: Princeton University Press).

—— (1990b), 'Corporate Culture and Economic Theory', in J. E. Alt and K. A. Shepsle (eds.), *Perspective in Positive Political Economy* (Cambridge: Cambridge University Press).

Krueger, H. C. (1962), 'Genoese Merchants, Their Associations and Investments

1155 to 1230', in D. A. Graffre (ed.), *Studi in Onore di Amintore Fanfani* (Milan: Multa Paucis).

—— and Reynolds, R. L. (eds.), (1954), *Lanfranco, 1202–1226* (Genoa: Notari Liguri del Secolo XII e del XIII, I–III).

Kurz, M. (1977), 'Altruistic Equilibrium', in B. Balassa and R. Helson (eds.), *Economic Progress, Private Values and Public Policy* (Amsterdam: North Holland).

Lane, F. C. (1944), 'Family Partnerships and Joint Ventures in the Venetian Republic', *Journal of Economic History*, 4: 178–96.

Lanfranco (1202–26), *Notari Liguri del Sec. XII e del XIII*, ed. H. C. Krueger and R. L. Reynolds (Genoa: Società Ligure de Storia Patria).

Lapidus, I. M. (1984), *Muslim Cities in the Later Middle Ages* (Cambridge: Cambridge University Press).

—— (1988), *A History of Islamic Societies* (Cambridge: Cambridge University Press).

Lewis, D. (1969), *Convention: A Philosophical Study* (Cambridge, Mass.: Harvard University Press).

Lieber, A. E. (1968), 'Eastern Business Practices and Medieval European Commerce', *Economic History Review*, 21: 230–43.

Lindenberg, S. (1985), 'Rational Choice and Sociology Theory: New Pressure on Economics as a Social Science', *Journal of Institutional and Theoretical Economics*, 141: 244–55.

Litwack, J. M. (1990), 'Co-ordination Failure and Repressed Inflation in a Planned Economy' (mimeo; Department of Economics, Stanford University).

—— (1991), 'Legality and Market Reform in Soviet-type Economies' (mimeo; Stanford University).

Lopez, R. S. (1976), *The Commercial Revolution of the Middle Ages, 950–1350* (New York: Cambridge University Press).

—— and Raymond, I. W. (1955), *Medieval Trade in the Mediterranean World* (New York: Columbia University Press).

Macfarlane, A. (1978), *The Origins of English Individualism* (Oxford: Basil Blackwell).

Margolis, H. (1982), *Selfishness, Altruism and Rationality* (Cambridge: Cambridge University Press).

Marimon, R. (1988), 'Wealth Accumulation with Moral Hazard' (mimeo; Hoover Institution and University of Minnesota).

Marsh, R. M. (1967), *Comparative Sociology* (New York: Harcourt, Brace & World).

Michael, M. (1965), *The Archives of Naharay ben Nissim, Businessman and Public Figure in Eleventh Century Egypt* (in Hebrew and Arabic). Ph.D. diss. (Hebrew University, Jerusalem).

Milgrom, P. R. and Roberts, J. (1990), 'Rationalizability, Learning, and Equilibrium in Games with Strategic Complementarities', *Econometrica*, 6: 1255–77.

—— North, D. C. and Weingast, B. R. (1990), 'The Role of Institutions in the Revival of Trade: The Law Merchant, Private Judges, and the Champagne Fairs', *Economics and Politics* 2/1: 1–23.

Mokyr, J. (1990), *The Lever of Riches* (Oxford: Oxford University Press).

Moore, E. W. (1985), *The Fairs of Medieval England* (Toronto: Pontifical Institute of Mediaeval Studies).

Myerson, R. B. (1989), 'Game Theory: Analysis of Conflict', (MS; Northwestern University, Evanston, Ill.).

Nalebuff, B. and Shubik, M. (1988), 'Revenge and Rational Play', discussion paper in Economics no. 138 (Woodrow Wilson School of Public and International Affairs, Princeton University).

Naroll, R. (1983), *The Moral Order* (Beverly Hills, Calif.: Sage Publications).

North, D. C. (1981), *Structure and Change in Economic History* (New York: Norton).

—— (1984), 'Transaction Costs, Institutions, and Economic History', *Journal of Institutional and Theoretical Economics*, 140: 7–17.

—— (1987), 'Institutions, Transaction Costs, and the Rise of Merchant Empires' (mimeo; Washington University, St. Louis).

—— (1990), *Institutions, Institutional Change and Economic Performance* (Cambridge: Cambridge University Press).

—— (1991), 'Institutions', *Journal of Economic Perspectives*, 5/1: 97–112.

—— and Thomas, R. P. (1973), *The Rise of the Western World* (Cambridge: Cambridge University Press).

—— and Weingast, B. R. (1989), 'Constitutions and Commitment: The Evolution of Institutions Governing Public Choice in Seventeenth-Century England', *Journal of Economic History*, 49: 803–32.

Okuno-Fujiwara, M. and Postlewaite, A. (1990), 'Social Norms and Random Matching Games', CARESS working paper no. 90–18 (Philadelphia: University of Pennsylvania).

Opp, K. D. (1985), 'Sociology and Economic Man', *Journal of Institutional and Theoretical Economics*, 141: 231–43.

Padgett, J. F. and Ansell, C. K. (1988), 'From Faction to Party in Renaissance Florence: The Emergence of the Medici Patronage Party', paper presented to the SSHA meeting in Chicago.

Parker, W. N. (1984), *Europe, America, and the Wider World*, i (Cambridge: Cambridge University Press).

Parsons, T. and Smelser, N. J. (1956), *Economy and Society* (London: Routledge and Kegan Paul).

Pirenne, H. (1952), *Medieval Cities* (Princeton, NJ: Princeton University Press).

Polanyi, K. (1957), *The Great Transformation* (Boston, Mass.: Beacon Hill).

—— (1966), *Dahomey and the Slave Trade* (Seattle: University of Washington Press).

—— Arensberg, and Pearson, H. (1957), *Trade and Markets in Early Empires* (New York: Free Press).

Porter, G. and Livesay, H. C. (1971), *Merchants and Manufacturers* (Baltimore, Md.: Johns Hopkins University Press).

Postan, M. M. (1957), 'Partnership in English Medieval Commerce', in *Studi in Onore di Armendo Sapori*, i (Milan: Instituto Editoriale Cisalpino).

—— (1973), *Medieval Trade and Finance* (Cambridge: Cambridge University Press).

Reynolds, C. H. and Norman, R. V. (eds.) (1988), *Community in America* (Berkeley: University of California Press).

Reynolds, R. L. (1929), 'The Market for Northern Textiles in Genoa, 1179–1200', *Revue Belge de Philologie et d'Histoire*, 8: 831–51.

—— (1931), 'Genoese Trade in the Late Twelfth Century, Particularly in Cloth from the Fairs of Champagne', *Journal of Economics and Business History*, 3/3: 362–81.

—— (1945), 'In Search of a Business Class in Thirteenth-Century Genoa', *Journal of Economic History*, 5: 1–19.

Rogerson, W. P. (1983), 'Reputation and Product Quality', *Bell Journal of Economics*, 14: 508–616.

Rogerson, W. P. (1987), 'The Dissipation of Profits by Brand Name Investment and Entry when Price Guarantees Product Quality', *Journal of Political Economy*, 95: 797–809.

de Roover, R. (1948), *The Medici Bank: Its Organization, Management, Operation, and Decline* (New York: New York University Press).

—— (1963), *The Rise and Decline of the Medici Bank, 1397–1494* (Cambridge, Mass.: Harvard University Press).

—— (1965) *The Organization of Trade, iii. The Cambridge Economic History of Europe*, (eds.) M. M. Postan, E. E. Rick, and M. Miltey (Cambridge: Cambridge University Press).

Rosenberg, N. and Birdzell, L. E., Jr. (1986), *How the West Grew Rich* (New York: Basic Books).

Rosenthal, J.-L. (1990), 'The Development of Irrigation in Provence, 1700–1860: The French Revolution and Economic Growth', *Journal of Economic History*, 50: 615–38.

Schelling, T. (1960), *The Strategy of Conflict* (Cambridge, Mass.: Harvard University Press).

Schotter, A. (1981), *The Economic Theory of Social Institutions* (Cambridge: Cambridge University Press).

Scott, W. R. (1987), *Organizations: Rational, Natural, and Open Systems* (Englewood Cliffs, NJ: Prentice-Hall).

Shapira, J. (1983), *The Basis of Sociology* (Tel Aviv: Am-Oved).

Shapiro, C. and Stiglitz, J. E. (1984), 'Equilibrium Unemployment as a Worker Discipline Device', *American Economic Review*, 74: 433–44.

Sombart, W. (1953), 'Medieval and Modern Commercial Enterprise', in F. C. Lane and J. C. Riemersma (eds.), *Enterprise and Secular Change* (Homewood, Ill.: Richard D. Irwin).

Stewart, H. (1989), 'Taking Goals Seriously: A Reconsideration of Rationality in Economics', Ph.D. Diss. (Harvard).

—— (1990), 'Rationality and the Market for Human Blood' (mimeo, Department of Economics, Harvard University).

Stillman, N. A. (1970), 'East–West Relations in the Islamic Mediterranean in the Early Eleventh Century', Ph.D. Diss. (Pennsylvania).

Sugden, R. (1986), *The Economics of Rights, Co-operation and Welfare* (Oxford: Basil Blackwell).

—— (1989), 'Spontaneous Order', *Journal of Economic Perspective*, 3/4: 85–97.

Triandis, H. C. (1990), 'Cross-Cultural Studies of Individualism and Collectivism', in J. Berman (ed.), *Nebraska Symposium on Motivation, 1989* (Lincoln: University of Nebraska Press), 41–133.

—— McCusker, C. and Hui, C. H. (1990), 'Multimethod Probes of Individualism and Collectivism', *Journal of Personality and Social Psychology*, 59: 1006–20

Udovitch, A. L. (1962), 'At the Origins of Western *Commenda*: Islam, Israel, Byzantium', *Speculum*, 37: 198–207.

—— (1970), *Partnership and Profit in Medieval Islam* (Princeton, NJ: Princeton University Press).

Ullmann-Margalit, E. (1977), *The Emergence of Norms* (Oxford: Clarendon Press).

Weber, M. (1958), *The Protestant Ethic and the Spirit of Capitalism* (New York: Charles Scribner).

Williamson, O. (1985), *The Economic Institutions of Capitalism* (New York: The Free Press).

Wilson, E. O. (1975), *Sociobiology* (Cambridge: Harvard University Press).

Witt, U. (1986), 'Evolution and Stability of Co-operation without Enforceable Contracts', *Kyklos*, 39: 245–66.

13

Cultural Diversity in the Global Ecumene

Ulf Hannerz

TWO ASPECTS OF GLOBALIZATION

The globalization which has proceeded with increasing intensity over the most recent centuries has two constantly interrelated but none the less analytically distinguishable aspects. On the one hand, populations and social structures which have previously been rather more separate now increasingly impinge physically and materially on one another's living conditions. This is the basis of most problems of 'transnational commons'. On the other hand, there is also a growing, more direct flow of culture, of meanings and modes of expression, between territories and populations. And for both reasons, we have to reconsider received notions about boundaries and conceptions of boundedness which we may long have taken for granted. Where anthropologists have previously tended to see an ethnographic mosaic there is now ever more noticeably a global ecumene of persistent interaction and exchange.[1] In this chapter I want to sketch a point of view on cultural diversity within this global ecumene. What can be the prognosis for its future? What arguments can be put forward for and against cultural diversity, and on what assumptions do such arguments rest? In what ways may arguments concerning cultural diversity parallel those concerned with biological diversity, and how would they differ? This is the conceptual terrain I will attempt to map.

I believe it can reasonably be argued that the balance between the two aspects of globalization I began by identifying has been somewhat altered over time. In the nineteenth and early twentieth centuries, as large parts of the world came under the increasingly comprehensive control of the metropoles, west–east and north–south influences were, in large part, in the nature of material and physical impingements. It was a matter of controlling environments and their resources, and for that purpose one would intrude into the life spaces of other peoples, or turn these peoples into labour forces. But broadly speaking, the interest of the centre in the peoples of the periphery was, in this earlier period, rather more with their bodies than with their souls.

In the twentieth century, there has certainly been no decrease in this material aspect of globalization; it, too, has surely continued. But the aspect of transnational cultural flow would seem to have increased more dramatically.

---

[1] For uses of the 'ecumene' concept by anthropologists, see Kroeber (1945) and Kopytoff (1987).

Major structures of administration and business have become in large measure standardized, with few principal variations compared to what has existed
earlier in world history. As these structures come to penetrate societies, in
what we have for some time called the Third World as well as elsewhere, their
members are drawn into modes of participation requiring much the same
competences, promoted by educational systems which, in the view of some
researchers at least, are becoming remarkably similar throughout the world.[2]
And as they are thus more similarly shaped as cultural beings in their local
settings, people also become more receptive to those long-distance cultural
currents which come with the increased mobility of people and goods, and
with the expansion of the media.

We may see this aspect of the ongoing integration of the global ecumene
as a matter of changing access to the world's inventory of meanings and
meaningful forms; perhaps of the access of cultures to people, as well as of
people to cultures. How is this access used, and will the use of it lead to the
depletion of the inventory itself?

One well-known scenario portrays only a very lopsided and temporary
access to the wider cultural inventory. It suggests a process of global homogenization, a large-scale transfer of culture from centre to periphery, resulting eventually in a uniform world culture.[3] It is a scenario which has several
things going for it. Perhaps it seems like a mere continuation of present
trends, and draws a certain plausibility from this. It also has the advantage of
simplicity: no nuances, no qualifications. And it is dramatic: there is a sense
of fatefulness, a prediction that large parts of the combined heritage of
humanity will soon be lost forever. As much of the diversity of its repertoire
of ideas and modes of behaviour is wiped out, *Homo sapiens* becomes more
like other species—in large part making its own environment, in contrast to
them, but at the same time adapting to it in a single, however complex way.

Facing such a prospect—if, for a moment anyway, we accept its credibility—we may ask whether we should try to put up some resistance. The value
of cultural diversity may have become so entrenched in contemporary
rhetoric that we rarely take time out to reflect on it. Yet let us try to look at it
as a matter of global cultural policy, as it were. What, in reasonably un-
ambiguous and down-to-earth terms, are the advantages or disadvantages of
cultural diversity?

In one way at least, there might in fact be something rather practical about
getting rid of diversity. We must not lose sight of the fact that culture is the
medium by which human beings interact. They make themselves more or less
well understood to one another through culture, and the more culture they
share, the more effective is, at least in some ways, their co-ordination in interaction. They become more transparent to each other, as it were, and often

[2] On the global spread of a system of mass education see for example Boli, Ramirez, and
Meyer (1986).
[3] For further comments on the scenario of global homogenization see Hannerz (1989*a*).

render themselves understandable to others even by way of quite minimal overt signals because so much can be left implicit, to be taken for granted. The organizational formula, ideally, is that 'I know, and I know that you know, and I know that you know that I know'. We are so thoroughly habituated to this culturally based effortlessness of interaction that we hardly notice it except in its breach—but such breaches seem to become increasingly frequent. Notions such as 'culture shock' or 'cultural collisions' seem to have become part of a twentieth-century vocabulary, rough labels for experiences which are certainly not new but which have become more common, and have led to more conscious reflection, as globalization has accelerated.

We need hardly be further concerned with this nuisance value of cultural diversity here, although we may at least remind ourselves when we listen to more high-minded praise of cultural diversity that it often conveniently disregards the minor and major irritants which come with not sharing a culture.

All the same, I will devote more attention to some arguments for cultural diversity. Whether mostly in passing or in some detail, I will identify seven types of arguments, and also try to indicate their respective limitations. They are certainly not entirely independent of one another, and at times they may be contradictory.

One of them entails advocating cultural diversity for its own sake, as it were, as a sort of monument to the creativity of humankind. Another argument would be based on principles of equity and self-determination. Yet another way of looking at the matter is to suggest that cultural diversity is beneficial in the adaptation of humanity to the limited environmental resources of the world. Fourthly, it may be argued that cultural diversity counteracts relations of political and economic dependency. One may alternatively, and fifthly, take a largely aesthetic stance towards the pleasures of cultural diversity, or, sixthly, view it as a useful provocation to the intellect. My seventh and final argument is that cultural diversity may be drawn on as from a fund of tested knowledge about ways of going about things.

THE RIGHT TO ONE'S CULTURE

Let us begin with the notion that people have a right to their own culture. Here terms like 'cultural heritage' and 'cultural identity' often enter the discussion. Humanity is no *tabula rasa*, cultural diversity is already there, and this fact can hardly be neglected in any debate over it. The basic assumption is that people are attached to their own culture, but since this in fact means that they are attached to different cultures, we have to 'agree to disagree', live and let live. This, then, in its pure form is not really an argument for the superior value of any experience of diversity as such; nor an argument for wider cultural access. Rather, it takes us back to the metaphor of the global cultural mosaic, of separate bounded units. Each individual should have the right to live his or her life encapsulated in a smaller world of the like-minded.

The persistence of diversity is merely a logical consequence of the central principle.

It is hardly an unreasonable idea that given in some sense a cultural choice, people will choose the culture they already have. To a considerable degree, anthropologists would tend to argue, people not only possess a culture, but are possessed by it; they have been constructed out of its materials of meaning and expression. The choice, if this premise is accepted, is not quite a real choice. Yet the argument can be pushed too far. It should not be taken as self-evident that an overall agreement pertains within a group or society on the intrinsic worth of that collective structure of meanings which we describe as its culture, since it may be merely a working arrangement reflecting the more or less contestable balance of power among the members. Slaves, lower castes, or oppressed women or youths might actually want to raise their voices, or vote with their feet, but are quite possibly not in a position to do so. It may be that a particular working arrangement is simply the best a group could put together with the resources at hand.

Presented with a choice, then, people may under some circumstances not opt for what may have seemed to be 'their' culture. They were perhaps never wholeheartedly for it in the first place. Moreover, human beings also have some capacity for remaking themselves, and their cultural repertoires may have some openings to new potentialities. In other words, presented with alternatives to the culture they have lived by, they might at times prefer to pursue these, whether they understand them in detail and in their implications or not.

Here, then, is a profound difference between the cultures of *Homo sapiens* and the biograms of other species. One kind of animal cannot choose to become another kind of animal; its right of survival as an individual and as a population can only be safeguarded by allowing it to be what it already is. In contrast, cultures may die while the people live on; and 'dying' here only means that a complex of ideas and the practices based on it pass into disuse. Watching out for people's right to choose must not be confused, then, with safeguarding a specific cultural heritage, or cultural diversity generally, for its own sake—the 'monument to human creativity' idea. Such safeguarding may be based on a judgement of mostly aesthetic and antiquarian nature, and is often based on vicarious pleasure, as it seems often to be outsiders who reach such a conclusion, and grieve for the cultures others leave behind. To make sure that existing varieties of cultures are preserved as living entities, obviously, one would have to transform 'the right to one's own culture' into a duty to that culture. And that would no doubt be a great deal more controversial.

CULTURE AND ECOLOGY

Cultural diversity could also be seen to have an ecological dimension. In so far as cultures entail different orientations to the limited environmental resources of the world, and not least different sets of knowledge about them, it could be advantageous to our long-term survival if the diversity of cultures would lead populations to place themselves in different niches. If the planet Earth is the home we share, it might yet be good not to have to share rooms. Anthropologists' studies of the relationship between culture and ecology have often shown how a people has achieved an enduring balance with its habitat—whether it is a rainforest, a steppe, or an Arctic sea—by way of keen observations of nature, a set of social and ritual practices the beneficial environmental implications of which may not be wholly understood, and a modest technology. And these studies have frequently also pointed to the way different groups coexist more or less successfully by drawing on different environmental resources.[4]

Whatever cultural diversity may contribute to the husbanding of the resources of our planet, however, we must by now certainly be aware that cultural differences do not necessarily lead away from ecological competition. As things stand, we are more likely to argue the other way around, that the access of particular populations to their habitats needs to be safeguarded because it is only in this way that they can be guaranteed the right to their own culture; the latter being intimately connected to a particular ecological adaptation, or actually consisting in large part of it. And this way of arguing, from principles of cultural equity to their ecological consequences, is necessary because the more immediately material aspect of globalization I referred to before tends to change human habitats in large parts of the world so radically. Western industrial culture has a propensity for expanding into new niches, whether these are already occupied or not. Where mines, power-plants, and forest companies enter, the hunters and gatherers and the horticulturalists are very often forced out, or marginalized. And this is obviously frequently not a matter of their choice, their attraction to new ideas or opportunities; not a way to upgrade their ecological know-how, but rather a way to render it useless. At present we discern such environmental change in particular as a threat to what we term the 'Fourth World', aboriginal peoples whose adaptations to their habitats are so specific that major intrusions may lead to cultural loss rather than to mere cultural change, and where furthermore the intrusions are sometimes so violent as to amount to genocide; a situation about as analogous to a threat to a biological species as one gets in the universe of cultural diversity.[5]

Whichever way we argue about ecology and cultural diversity along the lines suggested, it is once more a matter of seeing cultures as essentially separate. Our reasoning does not in these terms involve a view of access to

[4] See for example Barth's (1956) pioneering study of ecology and group relations in northern Pakistan, or Rappaport's (1984) interpretation of the ecological significance of ritual life among a New Guinea people.

[5] Organizations such as the International Work Group on Indigenous Affairs (IWGIA) and Cultural Survival are among those which strive to mobilize public opinion on such matters.

variations in meaning systems as either beneficial or disadvantageous, while it is a matter of how populations of different cultures may relate to one another in varied manners by way of their culturally constructed ecologies. In the next instance the argument for cultural diversity, as it is often implied or explicitly put forth, is more directly opposed to a certain kind of widened cultural access.

DIFFERENCE AS RESISTANCE

The flow of culture within the global ecumene is in large part asymmetrical, involving a stronger flow from centre to periphery than vice versa; in cultural terms, this is what defines centre and periphery. Yet centre and periphery may not be defined only in terms of cultural flow, to the extent that the latter is correlated with economic and political power.[6] To what extent, then, does the flow of meaning and meaningful form contribute to political and economic dependence and subjugation? It is a well-known argument that it does, that it is an important part of a hegemonic process. The culturally mediated access of centre to periphery is understood to constitute a sort of brainwashing, a way of tying the periphery even more closely, and on the face of it voluntarily, to the interests of the centre. Culture here is ideology.[7]

Cultural diversity, then, may be cultural resistance. The point of view is familiar for example from the world system theory of Immanuel Wallerstein (e.g. 1974; 1984), which has mostly paid scant attention to culture but which, when it has done so, has emphasized the ideological facet. As Wallerstein has also noted, it is a resistance often put up, not to say manipulated, by those élites of the periphery who thereby both draw the line *vis-à-vis* the centre and try to win a following among those masses of the periphery who presumably remain more habitually committed to local tradition. It is such élites, for example, who tend to launch political campaigns of 'authenticity'. What they aim at is a counter-hegemony, opposed to something anchored in some distant centre. It is likewise such élites who tend to regard as unreliable, and as possible adversaries, those of their compatriots who allow themselves to be 'accessed' by alien cultural flows, and who even draw pleasure and stimulation from these; one of those kinds of people to whom the label 'cosmopolitan' is frequently attached.

Yet resistance to imported culture as a manner of resisting political and economic domination is not always a matter of élite strategy; it can be more widely based. It should also be clear that this could be an argument for the maintenance of bounded cultures which can readily and fairly unobtrusively be combined in rhetoric with the claim of a right to one's own culture.

[6] I have commented briefly elsewhere on the relationship between culture and other dimensions in centre–periphery relationships (Hannerz 1989*b*).

[7] Things become a bit more complicated when it turns out that the periphery also imports the cultural auto-critique of the centre.

ENJOYING DIVERSITY

I turn now to arguments for cultural diversity which are of that other kind, emphasizing the value of access to diversity, and of the experience of diversity; arguments which see the global ecumene as a promise rather more than as a threat. Here I wish to distinguish between three somewhat different views of the benefits involved.

The first of these I see as principally an aesthetic attitude. 'Other cultures' are valued as experiences in their own right, that is, regardless of any readily identifiable concrete use-value. They become the materials for what I would regard as a major form, perhaps the truest form, of cosmopolitanism.[8] A person rooted in one culture enters another with its meanings and practices, or perhaps many of them serially, but usually temporarily. The aesthetic attitude entails being positively oriented towards such experiences, but also striving towards achieving some degree of competence in handling other cultures as ongoing arrangements of life. One masters them to a degree, and at the same time surrenders to them, trying for the moment to abide by their rules. And at the same time, this kind of competence entails a particular kind of mastery of one's own culture, as one shows that while one possesses it, one is not necessarily possessed by it; one can establish a distance from it. This is the attitude of a connoisseur, an aficionado. One might say about it that it tends to be based on cultural boundaries remaining largely in place. Although some (preferably not too many) individuals cross them, these individuals keep their experiences on each side mostly apart. The aesthetic attitude does not involve using those cultural experiences from somewhere else to effect change, except at some private level. From this perspective one may well mourn the passing of other cultures even as these are quite voluntarily deserted by their erstwhile creators and bearers. The attitude may appear somewhat self-indulgent.

CREATIVE CONFRONTATIONS

It may be only a rather short step, however, from it to the second kind of experience of diversity I have in mind; one where the coming together of distinct flows of meaning result in a generative cultural process. There have been differing opinions of the value of such confluences. Claude Lévi-Strauss (1985:24), one of the most eminent figures of anthropology, has argued that

all true creation implies a certain deafness to the appeal of other values, even going so far as to reject them if not denying them altogether. For one cannot fully enjoy the other, identify with him, and yet at the same time remain different. When integral communication with the other is achieved completely, it sooner or later spells doom

---

[8] See an elaboration on this theme in Hannerz (1990).

for both his and my creativity. The great creative eras were those in which communication had become adequate for mutual stimulation by remote partners, yet was not so frequent or so rapid as to endanger the indispensable obstacles between individuals and groups or to reduce them to the point where overly facile exchanges might equalize and nullify their diversity.

Yet at the same time it has often been pointed out that many of the most creative individuals in the history of human consciousness have been 'marginal men', people who have acutely experienced a contrast between ongoing cultural traditions and who have thereby been provoked into new understandings—bridging the cultures, synthesizing them, or scrutinizing them. Lévi-Strauss himself has been offered as an instance of this; Marx and Freud are likewise mentioned as examples.[9]

This may be a matter of the more precise circumstances under which people have to manage the encounter between cultural currents. The late Alvin Gouldner (1985: 204 ff.), a sociologist who took some special interest in the heterogeneous intellectual bases of Marx's theoretical achievements, argued that the most advantageous situation is one where one has access to more than one line of thought and can thus escape the control of any one of them; where one can move between them in a way which deviates from any conventional division of labour between them; and where one yet orders them hierarchically, thus presumably avoiding confusion and retaining a sense of direction. We should certainly be aware here that Marx, Freud, and Lévi-Strauss are all from an ethnic subculture which is not set very far apart from the surrounding mainstream. The question also arises, then, whether all kinds and degrees of contrast or affinity in the combinations of cultural difference can be expected to be equally productive. In response to Gouldner's formulation, too, one may wonder to what extent the intellectual fertility of an encounter between cultures necessarily entails drawing more directly on the resources of both cultures (or whatever number is involved). At times it might also be that the mere heightening of awareness stimulated by such a confrontation leads to a creative management of the resources available within one's own culture.

DRAWING ON OTHER CULTURES

Arguments about the aesthetic appreciation of cultural diversity and about the experience of cultural diversity as a source of creativity tend both, I believe, to be couched in terms of a micro-level, in terms of individual experience. What happens if such experiences are aggregated in a population is mostly left as an open or even unidentified question. The third kind of use of

[9] See, for instance, the rather controversial interpretation by Cuddihy (1974) along such lines.

an access to cultural diversity, in contrast, seems more often to involve actual or potential macro-level changes; of course, here as so often the contrast is relative and imprecise. What I have in mind here is the notion that cultural diversity within the global ecumene can be used as a kind of reserve of improvements and alternatives to what is at any one time immediately available in one's own culture, and of solutions to its problems.[10] One curious thing about the economics of culture, of course, is that this reserve, this particular kind of transnational common, does not risk becoming depleted merely because people borrow heavily from it, as people can keep giving their meanings and expressions away to others without losing them for themselves.

The economist Stephen Marglin (1990: 15–17), in his discussion of 'cultural diversity as a global asset', emphasizes this perspective (although he also refers to the right to one's own culture):

Cultural diversity may be the key to the survival of the human species. Just as biologists defend exotic species like the snail darter in order to maintain the diversity of the genetic pool . . . so should we defend exotic cultures in order to maintain the diversity of forms of understanding, creating and coping that the human species has managed to generate.

As one extreme variation on this theme there is the premonition that humanity will need its remaining hunters and gatherers to show the way when catastrophes, self-inflicted or otherwise, have destroyed more complicated forms of life. Marglin touches on this possibility. Alternatively, and certainly as a fairly common ingredient in recent cultural history, we may cast ideologically motivated glances across boundaries to find our Utopias most nearly approximated somewhere else. As the twentieth century has passed, we have seen several such imagined laboratories for humanity, mostly on the left: for example, the young Soviet Union, China, Cuba, Tanzania. But rather more continuously, the United States has also served in a similar way as a source of alternatives and materialized ideas of the future for people elsewhere, perhaps in this case moving with time from left to right. These sources, then, may be reasonably familiar (whether realistically understood or not) and popular with a great many people, or they may have their distant enthusiasts, sometime pilgrims perhaps, who act as middlemen advocates in arguing for large-scale change in accordance with the models thus identified.[11]

The argument for cultural diversity here, to repeat, is that it keeps alternatives alive; and not only in their existing state, it may be added, but also in their potential for further development. This is an appealing idea, but not without possible weaknesses. One of them is that it tends to assume that if the

---

[10] Salzman (1981) has a related argument about the way a rather less than fully integrated culture can maintain its cultural alternatives within itself.

[11] Caute (1973) and Hollander (1981) discuss the phenomenon of political pilgrims at some length.

alternatives are not continuously kept going, they will be lost forever. Perhaps one takes an unnecessarily bleak view of human inventiveness here; would people not be able to construct the alternatives as they need them, without seeing them continuously modelled? One might also ask what kind of documentation, as it were, is needed to maintain access to this cultural reserve. What difference does it make whether cultures are really kept fully alive, with fully employed participants, so to speak, or are merely preserved in the archives, through texts, recordings, or whatever? Archives, it is true, can also be destroyed, as can the skills required to use them. But unless we all become non-literate hunters and gatherers again, and out-of-practice hunters and gatherers at that, it seems that it will be through the antiquarian efforts of specialists that access to much of the accumulated cultural diversity of the world can most likely be guaranteed.

Yet another problem with the idea of global cultural diversity as a shared reserve to draw upon is the difficulty of transporting items of culture from one context to another, to be readily redeployed there. Certainly, cultural diffusion has taken place on a large scale in human history, but much of the analytical effort of anthropologists, for three-quarters of a century or so, has really gone into showing how cultures hang together, how particular beliefs and practices make sense only as parts of cultural wholes. Lately the discipline has perhaps seemed a little less committed to the idea of a culture as a tightly integrated entity, a 'seamless web', but it remains rather difficult to accept the idea that whatever seems to work in one culture can be predicted to be equally successful in some quite different context. (If that were the case, moreover, it might be that in the end, as all the good ideas had been identified and brought together, all the bad ones could be consigned to the dustbin of history, and diversity would thus have finished its job.)

CONCLUSION: THE FUTURE OF DIVERSITY

I have sketched very summarily some different arguments in favour of cultural diversity. As I suggested before, not a single one of them may be entirely without hitches. On the other hand none of them may have been proved entirely false either. It might yet be sound policy for the global ecumene to attach some value to cultural diversity. We may also well ask, however, to what extent it needs to be actively defended; to what extent that scenario of global homogenization to which I referred before is realistic.

I find it questionable. The prognosis for cultural diversity is not that bad. True, some cultural forms vanish, and the spectrum of what is alive and well may become narrower. As another prominent contemporary anthropologist, Clifford Geertz (1986: 253), has noted, 'we may be faced with a world in which there simply aren't any more headhunters, matrilinealists, or people who predict the weather from the entrails of a pig'. But at the same time, as some of the human cultural record remains available only through archives, museums, and monographs, there is a continuous reconstruction of cultural diversity within the global ecumene. In this, cultural diversity differs from biological diversity. Zoological and botanical species now become extinct much more rapidly than new species can develop; the development of new culture, in contrast, is not necessarily such a slow process.

This generative process draws partly on the contradictory implications of globalization itself.[12] If there is one tendency for culture to homogenize through diffusion, it is simultaneously true that globalization in its more material aspects places people in different situations, forces them into different life-spaces, makes them develop different perspectives towards the world; thus fostering diversity in another way (which is not always to be celebrated). But furthermore, increased cultural access also generates new variations. People can draw resources from the global cultural inventory as from a bank, but they can use these resources inventively, reintegrating them with what they already have, creating new and often locally anchored syntheses whose partly alien origins may at first seem disturbing rather than charming, but which are often fairly soon forgotten. And if we look at the cultures around us now, I think we can discern that much of their diversity is not merely old diversity in decline, but the new diversity that the global ecumene has bred.

REFERENCES

Appadurai, A. (1990), 'Disjuncture and Difference in the Global Cultural Economy', *Theory, Culture and Society*, 7/2–3: 295–310.
Barth, F. (1956), 'Ecologic Relationships of Ethnic Groups in Swat, North Pakistan', *American Anthropologist*, 58: 1079–89.
Boli, J., Ramirez, F. O., and Meyer, J. W. (1986), 'Explaining the Origins and Expansion of Mass Education', in P. G. Altbach and G. P. Kelly (eds.), *New Approaches to Comparative Education* (Chicago: University of Chicago Press).
Caute, D. (1973), *The Fellow-Travellers* (New York: Macmillan).
Cuddihy, J. M. (1974), *The Ordeal of Civility* (New York: Basic Books).
Geertz, C. (1986), 'The Uses of Diversity', in S. M. McMurrin (ed.), *The Tanner Lectures on Human Values*, vii (Cambridge: Cambridge University Press).
Gouldner, A. W. (1985), *Against Fragmentation* (New York: Oxford University Press).
Hannerz, U. (1989*a*), 'Culture between Centre and Periphery: Toward a Macroanthropology', *Ethnos*, 54: 200–16.
—— (1989*b*), 'Notes on the Global Ecumene', *Public Culture*, 1/2: 66–75.
—— (1990), 'Cosmopolitans and Locals in World Culture', *Theory, Culture and Society*, 7/2–3: 237–51.

---

[12] For one perspective towards these contradictions and their generative cultural implications see Appadurai (1990).

Hollander, P. (1981), *Political Pilgrims* (New York: Oxford University Press).

Kopytoff, I. (1987), 'The Internal African Frontier: The Making of African Political Culture', in I. Kopytoff, (ed.), *The African Frontier* (Bloomington: Indiana University Press).

Kroeber, A. L. (1945), 'The Ancient Oikoumene as an Historic Culture Aggregate', *Journal of the Royal Anthropological Institute*, 75: 9–20.

Lévi-Strauss, C. (1985), *The View from Afar* (New York: Basic Books).

Marglin, S. A. (1990), 'Towards the Decolonization of the Mind', in F. A. Marglin and S. A. Marglin (eds.), *Dominating Knowledge* (Oxford: Clarendon Press).

Rappaport, R. A. (1984), *Pigs for the Ancestors*, 2nd edn. (New Haven, Conn.: Yale University Press).

Salzman, P. C. (1981), 'Culture as Enhabilmentis', in L. Holy and M. Stuchlik (eds.), *The Structure of Folk Models* (London: Academic Press).

Wallerstein, I. (1974), *The Modern World-System* (New York: Academic Press).

—— (1984), *The Politics of the World-Economy* (Cambridge: Cambridge University Press).

Index